PRIVATE EDUCATION

YALE STUDIES ON NONPROFIT ORGANIZATIONS

Program on Non-Profit Organizations
Institution for Social and Policy Studies
Yale University

JOHN G. SIMON, CHAIRMAN
PAUL DIMAGGIO, DIRECTOR

Private Education

Studies in Choice and Public Policy

edited by

DANIEL C. LEVY

SUNY-Albany

New York · Oxford
OXFORD UNIVERSITY PRESS
1986

Oxford University Press

Oxford   New York   Toronto
Delhi   Bombay   Calcutta   Madras   Karachi
Petaling Jaya   Singapore   Hong Kong   Tokyo
Nairobi   Dar es Salaam   Cape Town
Melbourne   Auckland

and associated companies in
Beirut   Berlin   Ibadan   Nicosia

Published by Oxford University Press, Inc.,
200 Madison Avenue, New York, New York 10016

Oxford is a registered trademark of Oxford University Press

Library of Congress Cataloging-in-Publication Data
Levy, Daniel C.
   Private education & public policy.
   Includes index.
   1. Federal aid to private schools—United States
addresses, essay, lectures.   2. State aid to private
schools—United States—Addresses, essays, lectures.
3. School, Choice of—United States—Addresses,
essays, lectures.   4. Private schools—United States—
Finance—Addresses, essays, lectures.   5. Universities
and colleges—United States—Finance—Addresses, essays,
lectures.   I. Title.   II. Title: Private education
and public policy.
LB2827.4.L48   1986   379.3′2′0973   85-15568
ISBN 0-19-503710-3

Printing (last digit): 9 8 7 6 5 4 3 2 1

Printed in the United States of America
on acid-free paper

To
Morris Eli, Aaron Jacob,
and all other future students

Series Foreword

This volume and its siblings, comprising the Yale Studies on Nonprofit Organizations, were produced by an interdisciplinary research enterprise, the Program on Non-Profit Organizations, located within Yale University's Institution for Social and Policy Studies.[1] The Program had its origins in a series of discussions initiated by the present author in the mid-1970s while serving as president of Yale. These discussions began with a number of Yale colleagues, especially Professor Charles E. Lindblom, Director of the Institution, and Professor John G. Simon of the Law School faculty. We later enlisted a number of other helpful counselors in and out of academic life.

These conversations reflected widespread agreement that there was a serious and somewhat surprising gap in American scholarship. The United States relies more heavily than any other country on the voluntary nonprofit sector to conduct the nation's social, cultural, and economic business—to bring us into the world, to educate and entertain us, even to bury us. Indeed, the United States can be distinguished from all other societies by virtue of the work load it assigns to its "third sector," as compared to business firms or government agencies. Yet this nonprofit universe had been the least well studied, the least well understood aspect of our national life. And the nonprofit institutions themselves were lacking any connective theory of their governance and function. As just one result, public and private bodies were forced to make policy and management decisions, large and small, affecting the nonprofit sector from a position of relative ignorance.

To redress this startling imbalance, and with the initial assistance of the late John D. Rockefeller III (soon joined by a few foundation donors), the Program on Non-Profit Organizations was launched in 1977. It seeks to achieve three principal goals:

---

[1] The sharp-eyed editors at Oxford University Press requested that we explain the presence of an intrusive hyphen in the word "Non-Profit" in the Program's title, and suggested that the explanation might be of interest to this volume's readers. The explanation is simple: At the Program's inception, it adopted the convention, in wider currency than it is today but even at that time incorrect, of hyphenating "non-profit." Since then the Program has mended its ways whereever the term "nonprofit" is not used as part of the Program's title. But in the Program's title, for reasons both sentimental and pragmatic, the hyphen remains, as a kind of trademark.

1. to build a substantial body of information, analysis, and theory relating to non-profit organizations;
2. to enlist the energies and enthusiasms of the scholarly community in research and teaching related to the world of nonprofit organizations; and
3. to assist decision makers, in and out of the voluntary sector, to address major policy and management dilemmas confronting the sector.

Toward the first and second of these goals the Program has employed a range of strategies: research grants to senior and junior scholars at Yale and at forty-one other institutions; provision of space and amenities to visiting scholars pursuing their research in the Program's offices; supervision of graduate and professional students working on topics germane to the Program's mission; and a summer graduate fellowship program for students from universities around the country.

The Program's participants represent a wide spectrum of academic disciplines—the social sciences, the humanities, law, medicine, and management. Moreover, they have used a variety of research strategies, ranging from theoretical economic modeling to field studies in African villages. These efforts, supported by fifty foundation, corporate, government, and individual donors to the Program, have gradually generated a mountain of research on virtually every nonprofit species—for example, day-care centers and private foundations, symphony orchestras and wildlife advocacy groups—and on voluntary institutions in twenty other countries. At this writing the Program has published 100 working papers and has sponsored, in whole or in part, research resulting in no fewer than 175 journal articles and book chapters. Thirty-two books have been either published or accepted for publication. Moreover, as the work has progressed and as Program-affiliated scholars (of whom, by now, there have been approximately 150) establish links to one another and to students of the nonprofit sector not associated with the Program, previously isolated researchers are forging themselves into an impressive and lively international network.

The Program has approached the third goal, that of assisting those who confront policy and management dilemmas, in many ways. Researchers have tried to design their projects in a way that would bring these dilemmas to the fore. Program participants have met with literally hundreds of nonprofit organizations, either individually or at conferences, to present and discuss the implications of research being conducted by the Program. Data and analyses have been presented to federal, state, and local legislative and executive branch officials and to journalists from print and electronic media throughout the United States, to assist them in their efforts to learn more about the third sector and the problems it faces.

Crucial to the accomplishment of all three goals is the wide sharing of the Program's intellectual output not only with academicians but also with nonprofit practitioners and policy makers. This dissemination task has been an increasing preoccupation of the Program in recent years. More vigorous promotion of its working paper series, cooperation with a variety of non-academic organizations, the forthcoming publication of a handbook of research on nonprofit organizations, and the establishment of a newsletter (published with increasing regularity for a broad and predominantly non-academic list of subscribers) have all helped to disseminate the Program's research results.

These efforts, however, needed supplementation. Thus, the Program's working papers, although circulated relatively widely, have been for the most part drafts rather than finished papers, produced in a humble format that renders them unsuitable for the relative immortality of library shelves. Moreover, many of the publications resulting from the Program's work have never found their way into working paper form. Indeed, the multidisciplinary products of Program-sponsored research have displayed a disconcerting tendency upon publication to fly off to separate disciplinary corners of the scholarly globe, unlikely to be reassembled by any but the most dogged, diligent denizens of the most comprehensive of university libraries.

Sensitive to these problems, the Lilly Endowment made a generous grant to the Program to enable it to overcome this tendency toward centrifugality. The Yale Studies on Nonprofit Organizations represent a particularly important part of this endeavor. Each book features the work of scholars from several disciplines. Each contains a variety of papers, many unpublished, others available only in small-circulation specialized periodicals, on a theme of general interest to readers in many regions of the nonprofit universe. Most of these papers are products of Program-sponsored research, although each volume contains a few other contributions selected in the interest of thematic consistency and breadth.

The present volume, edited by Daniel C. Levy, Associate Professor of Educational Administration and Policy Studies and of Latin American Studies at the State University of New York at Albany and a long-time participant in the work of the Program on Non-Profit Organizations, deals with the finance, role, performance, and control of private nonprofit educational institutions, in comparison with public institutions, at both the college and university and the elementary and secondary school levels.

As the reader will already have observed, I do not write this foreword as a stranger. I am very much a member of the family, someone who was present at the creation of the Program of Non-Profit Organizations and continues to chair its Advisory Committee, and who also serves Oxford as Master of University College. What this extended family is doing to advance knowledge about the third sector is a source of considerable satisfaction. From its birth at a luncheon chat more than a decade ago, the Program on Non-Profit Organizations has occupied an increasingly important role as the leading academic center for research on voluntary institutions both in America and abroad. And now the publication by Oxford University Press of this volume and the other Yale Studies on Nonprofit Organizations enlarges the reach of the Yale Program by making its research more widely available within the scholarly community and to the larger world beyond.

London   Kingman Brewster
October 1985

Preface

Concern over the performance of public education has heightened interest in private educational alternatives. Unfortunately, private-public comparisons have been inadequately informed by research findings, partly because the literature on private education has been severely limited.

This volume attempts to contribute to our understanding of private education and to private-public comparisons related especially to private choice and public policy. In contrast to much of the private-public debate on education, the chapters that follow are neither proprivate nor propublic polemics. But they do point to ways in which one sector or the other may be preferable for certain groups or purposes. They consider a host of policy options for government, and also for students, parents, teachers, administrators, and donors. In doing so, the chapters move beyond the question of whether private schools outperform public schools in terms of student achievement scores, a question which has led to bitter debate but which does not appear to mark one of the crucial private-public differences. Instead, such differences are identified in matters such as finance, regulations, socioeconomic constituencies, client satisfaction, and contrasting missions.

The volume's approaches to the study of private education are broad and multi-faceted, fostered by several comparative foci. While it explores some of the enormous diversity within the private educational sector, it also focuses significantly on comparisons to the public sector. Unusually, the volume brings together work on elementary and high schools with work on higher education. Also unusual is the inclusion of international material in several of the chapters. Both the interlevel and international comparisons provide perspectives for viewing in context the particular settings the reader may know best. The comparisons should even provide some relevant information for policymaking. For example, the debate over public funding for U.S. schools can be usefully informed by analysis of U.S. financing and regulation in higher education and by the experiences at the grade-school level in countries like Canada and the Netherlands.

In focusing on private education, the volume deals with one of the largest fields of private nonprofit activity in the United States. It therefore considers matters of general concern in the study of nonprofit organizations.

These include, for example, the impact of public funding on institutional autonomy, private choice, and client satisfaction. These also include questions about the kinds of choices and accountability that can be associated with nonprofit organizations.

Additionally, the volume's approaches are interdisciplinary. The contributing authors study private education from perspectives found in history, political science, social psychology, economics, public policy, and law. But they have not written here principally for specialists in any one discipline. Instead, the volume is intended for anyone interested in private education and critically related questions of private choice and public policy. The currency of these questions is highlighted by developments (including restrictions on the use of federal funds to offer compensatory education in private schools and including the proposed conversion of some compensatory education funds into vouchers) that are unfolding even as the volume goes to press. The volume should provide contexts for evaluating such continually evolving controversies.

Like the entire Oxford series on the nonprofit world, this volume has drawn both initial inspiration and subsequent support from the Program on Non-Profit Organizations at Yale University. The editor is fortunate to have been associated with the program since 1980, first full-time, then part-time. During the entire period, the program's two directors—John G. Simon and Paul DiMaggio—have been extremely helpful, most recently as critics of this volume's introduction. Their consistent good cheer has helped with the sometimes frustrating tasks that editors face. Yale's Institution for Social and Policy Studies, into which the nonprofit program is integrated, also deserves grateful mention here, as does the Lilly Endowment, Inc., for its generous financial support.

While contributing authors have acknowledged colleagues for help with individual chapters, we are collectively indebted to Bruce S. Cooper for his time and advice concerning certain general features of the volume. Finally, Ella Sandor, Barbara Ruber, and Barbara Grubalski provided fine administrative and secretarial assistance.

Albany, N.Y.   D.C.L.
November 1985

Contents

III. Private Choice and Financial Policy in Higher Education

Contributors

Donald A. Erickson is considered by many the scholar most extensively acquainted with private schools. He has written widely on the subject and on broader issues of school organization and administration. Previously on the faculty at the University of Chicago, Erickson is now at UCLA's Graduate School of Education. He is the editor of the *Private School Monitor*. Professor Erickson received his Ph.D. in Educational Administration from the University of Chicago.

Roger L. Geiger, historian and higher education specialist, is currently a research associate at the Program on Non-Profit Organizations, Yale University. His two recent studies, a comparative analysis of private higher education in eight countries and a history of U.S. research universities from 1900 to 1940, will both be published in 1986. Geiger is presently engaged in a study of U.S. research universities in the contemporary period. He received his Ph.D. in history from the University of Michigan.

Mary-Michelle Upson Hirschoff is an associate with the New Haven law firm of Brenner, Saltzman, Wallman and Goldman. Previously, Hirschoff was on the faculty of the Indiana University School of Law and then was a research associate at the Program on Non-Profit Organizations, Yale University. Her publications and present research focus on parental rights in public schools and on regulation and other broad policy issues concerning private schools. Hirschoff received a J.D. from the Yale Law School.

Estelle James is Professor of Economics and Chair of the Economics Department, SUNY-Stony Brook. She is the author of *Hoffa and the Teamsters: A Study of Union Power* and numerous articles on the economics of education, nonprofit organizations and applied welfare economics. James is now engaged in extensive research on private education and has published in journals such as the *Journal of Human Resources*, the *Journal of Policy Analysis and Management*, and *Public Choice*. James received a Ph.D. in economics from M.I.T.

Mark A. Kutner is currently a Research Analyst with Pelavin Associates, Inc. in Washington, D.C. He was responsible for the School Finance Project's work on federal education programs. Kutner is completing a doctorate in public policy at the George Washington University.

Daniel C. Levy is an Associate Professor with the Departments of Educational Administration & Policy Studies and Latin American Studies at SUNY-Albany. He was previously at Yale University with the Higher Education Research Group and the Program on Non-Profit Organizations. Levy is author or co-author of three books, the latest comparing Latin America's private and public universities. He received his Ph.D. in political science from the University of North Carolina–Chapel Hill.

Richard J. Murnane, formerly on the faculty of Yale University's economics department, is now an Associate Professor at the Graduate School of Education, Harvard University. His research interests include teacher labor markets, the determinants of school effectiveness, and the regulation of public and private schools. Murnane's recent publications are found in journals such as the *Review of Economics and Statistics* and the *Journal of Business and Economic Statistics*. Murnane received his Ph.D. in economics from Yale University.

Joel D. Sherman is currently a Senior Research Analyst with Pelavin Associates, Inc. in Washington, D.C. He was Director of the School Finance Project and has written on Australian as well as U.S. private schools. Sherman received his Ph.D. in political economy from Columbia University.

Mary F. Williams, is co-editor of the *Condition of Education* at the National Center for Education Statistics, U.S. Department of Education. At the School Finance Project, Williams was responsible for the tuition tax credit survey and the work on intergovernmental finance. Williams received a Ph.D. in political science from Columbia University.

PRIVATE EDUCATION

Private Choice and Public Policy in Nonprofit Education

DANIEL C. LEVY

THE NONPROFIT CONTEXT

As several other volumes in this series on nonprofit organizations help us appreciate the importance of the private nonprofit sector in U.S. society, economics, and politics, we surely must recognize the weight of education within that sector. Quantitative profiles of the nonprofit sector are still sketchy, but the best figures show that education is one of the big four arenas of nonprofit activity, along with health, social services, and religious organizations, and perhaps (with health) even one of the big two. Data on salaried employees are illustrative. Private education's total of more than one million puts it second behind health within a nonprofit sector that accounts for 8% (and growing) of these employees.[1] And yet, even such figures give very conservative estimates of the significance of the nonprofit sector generally, and education in particular. For one thing, institutions such as private schools often rely heavily on voluntary work. More important, these institutions obviously serve many millions more than they employ.

Turning to education alone, enrollment figures give an idea of the private nonprofit sector's size. (By "schools" we will mean primary and secondary schools; see note 11.) As Erickson's chapter reports, private schools hold at least 10% of total school enrollments, their more than five million students spread out over roughly 18% of the total system's schools. And Geiger's chapter reports that the private share is even more impressive at the higher-education level. There, the more than two million private students account for roughly 22% of total enrollments, distributed over roughly half the system's institutions. Yet most observers of private education, including the two just cited, would argue that such numbers understate its significance. This significance derives from offering something different from the public sector, something often thought superior and influential, but something at least desired and supported by a substantial number of actors. In any case, behind such figures lies an intricate maze of private choices, made by students, their families, and others, as well as an intricate maze of public policies, at once responding to and shaping those private choices. Both these choices and these policies have been at the heart of increasingly strident private-public debates that themselves have been critical to national concerns over educational performance. Both the choices and the policies are dealt with in each chapter of this volume.

Thematic Concerns

Indeed, each chapter deals with several questions that have been central to a growing research endeavor on the nature of private nonprofit organizations, some of it conducted at Yale University's Program on Non-Profit Organizations. Issues include, for example, why, how, how much, and by whom nonprofit organizations are used, how they are financed, governed, and oriented, how major public policy alternatives would affect nonprofit organizations, and how these organizations themselves affect or should affect public organizations. Here, for illustrative purposes, we point to two major concerns, or clusters of concerns, in the study of nonprofits generally and in this volume's analysis of private education specifically.

The first is *finance*. Most chapters consider the basic issue of how nonprofit educational organizations are funded or, even more simply, who funds them. In fact, the issue is central to several of the chapters. Hirschoff analyzes present (and alternative) public policies for aiding private schools, as Kutner-Sherman-Williams do almost exclusively for federal policies. Both pieces provide a backdrop against which James points to striking differences in how the Dutch publicly fund their schools, as they characteristically rely on the publicly funded private production of services. At the higher-education level, Levy's last chapter explores private and public financing of private and public sectors internationally, while Geiger more intensively probes the quilted financing of U.S. private higher education. Several of these pieces take up the related matter of the circumstances in which nonprofits function without government aid. On the other hand, more consideration is given to the impact of government funding on the functioning of nonprofit organizations. Hirschoff analyzes the relationship between government funding and the regulation of schools, and Kutner, Sherman, and Williams confirm that the relationship is strong at the federal level. This relationship is followed to much greater extremes by James in the Dutch case. But even in chapters dealing less centrally with who funds the nonprofits, the effects of government financing are investigated. Erickson produces data on British Columbia showing that the advent of such financing was quickly followed by a frightful decline in client satisfaction. The introduction to Murnane's first chapter raises one of his major concerns: What might be the effect on private (and public) school achievement of expanded government aid to private schools, accompanied by changed regulatory procedures?

The impact of government funding appears to be less penetrating in higher education. James argues, in her second chapter, that universities (whether private or public) are left with considerable autonomy to allocate the funds they receive, a finding supported in Geiger's chapter. Both of Levy's chapters show that, internationally, heavy reliance on government funds often leaves substantial autonomy intact. Expectedly, however, there is also ample evidence that funds, government and private, often do limit university autonomy. But other evidence suggests that the potential regulation that accompanies government financing even of schools is by no means necessarily implemented. Furthermore, correlation does not substitute for causation. Despite the varied contributions of the chapters here, we still have a good deal to learn about the impact of funding on the governance and other functioning of nonprofit educational organizations.

A second concern, or cluster of concerns, that illustrates how questions about nonprofit educational organizations fit into broader questions about the nonprofit world involves *intersectoral comparisons*. While Erickson and Geiger intensively dissect the private sector, they also contrast the private to the public sector; most other authors devote their attention more equally to the two sectors, though the actual balance and the extent of the intersectoral comparisons vary by chapter. A thematic question is repeatedly addressed: What difference do intersectoral distinctions make or, stated more conservatively, represent? At least four broad dimensions by which sectors are often compared are explored in this volume: finance, governance, mission, and effectiveness. For example, James identifies the missions that distinguish the Neatherlands' private schools from its public ones, and both of Murnane's chapters reassess whether U.S. private high schools really outperform their public counterparts.

The evidence does not always show the private-public distinction to be decisive. Consider the debate over school achievement scores, a debate that has focused heavily on private-public questions, particularly since the Coleman-Hoffer-Kilgore report argued that private schools have an edge.[2] Murnane's second chapter highlights several of the report's findings that have not received adequate attention amid all the tumult. One is that schools really matter and that learning is not simply based on SES (socioeconomic status) and family environment; another, however, is that there are greater differences in achievement within sectors than between the two sectors' means. By the same token, James's second chapter repeatedly finds that the university-college distinction proves more important than the private-public one for the higher-education policies she considers.

This volume's authors do not treat private and public sectors as fully private or public (though they typically, if implicitly, identify "private" and "public" institutions according to legal nomenclature). We have already seen that many chapters deal with public financing and regulation of legally private organizations; Levy's chapter on finance also deals with private financing of public organizations and his preceding chapter tries to sort through and then go a bit beyond some of the confusing private-public blurs found in each sector with respect to finance, governance, and mission. In short, this volume takes the exploration of intersectoral differences as one important pathway to help us understand private education and public policy, but not the only one. The degree and relative importance of private-public distinctions naturally vary according to educational issue, level, nation, and epoch.

Relationship of For-Profit Education

In considering such issues as finance and intersectoral comparisons, the following chapters almost always deal with nonprofit as opposed to *for-profit* private education; in other words, *private* is to be read as shorthand for *nonprofit private* except where specifically stated otherwise. By paying comparatively little attention to for-profit organizations, this volume focuses on two of three sectors and on only one (nonprofit private versus public) of three possible intersectoral comparisons. In general, data are notoriously imprecise for the for-profit educational sector, even more than they are for the nonprofit educational sector. Nonetheless, a few words on for-profits in this introduction should be helpful in viewing the other sectors, particularly the nonprofit sector.

The for-profit sector has been much more important at the higher-education than the school level. Much depends on how rigorously one defines higher education. If commercially oriented institutions are liberally included, then there are perhaps better than 11,000 postsecondary U.S. institutions, more than 8000 of which are proprietary. By contrast, Hirschoff reports that only one in ten private schools is for-profit; for-profits probably account for fewer than 2% of all schools. As for-profit educational organizations tend to be smaller than their nonprofit and especially public counterparts, the for-profit school enrollment share would be significantly lower than 2%.[3]

Whatever the present figures may be, however, there are interesting suggestions of potential changes. One kind involves the continued transformation of for-profits into nonprofits, which has already been undertaken by organizations seeking legitimacy, security, and government aid and exemptions. But others involve for-profit growth. For example, some evidence suggests that for-profit two-year colleges may be expanding, especially in the South. However, interest—and concern—now also focuses on the school level, where there is a much weaker tradition of nonprofits sharing the private scene with for-profits. Major corporations, including ITT and Bell and Howell are considering the creation of for-profit schools. The impetus comes from the perception of serious disenchantment with public schools among groups capable of purchasing an alternative. The model comes largely from postsecondary education. Bell and Howell is already active at that level, its DeVry network claiming 30,000 students, while ITT has twenty-five postsecondary proprietary institutions. Interestingly, reaction from leaders of nonprofit schools is split between opposition to an undesirable corporate role, one that might weaken corporate aid for non-profit and public schools, and support (coupled with skepticism that corporations could realize profits where nonprofits already charge substantial tuitions and still struggle).[4] To speculate, a push in the for-profit sector could lead private nonprofit schools to emphasize their *nonprofit* nature much more than they have done, leading in turn to analyses of private schools that would concentrate more explicitly on nonprofit characteristics. Under past and present circumstances, it has been more sensible for both actors and scholars (including contributors to this volume) to stress the *private* aspect of private nonprofit schools.

Beyond these intersectoral factors, there are for-profit roles to be seen *within* the other two sectors; again sectors prove to be other than neatly defined and delineated. For one thing, for-profit enterprises have aided nonprofit and public educational institutions. As Geiger's chapter shows, this is particularly important in U.S. *higher* education, especially private but also public, whereas Levy's chapter on finance points out that outside the United States such involvement is unusual, and extremely rare for public sectors. But substantial attention has recently been focused on the U.S. educational sector normally considered least likely to see corporate involvement—the public school sector. Obviously, businesses sell materials to public (and nonprofit) schools; beyond that, in the 1960s, some tried to make profits by providing public schools with personnel and programs and receiving fees tied to improved student performance.[5] Then, in the early 1970s, particularly after California's Proposition 13 threatened the tax base on which local districts heavily rely to sustain their public schools, some districts established nonprofit foundations to secure funds from corporations (as well as parents). The trend soon spread to the state level, as in Kentucky and West Virginia. Supporters see for-profit enterprises acting on a solid American notion of enlightened self-interest through philanthropy while still avoiding the more problematic area of direct for-profit provision of services. Opponents fear corporate interference in nonprofit and public schools alike, commercialism, and a weakening of government responsibility for its own schools; better to protect sectoral boundaries than to allow such blurring. Critics also charge that private aid is found mostly in wealthy districts, thereby exacerbating inequities, even perhaps providing a "privatist" escape from legal decisions demanding increased equality in expenditures across public-school districts. Predictably, the long record of foundation support for higher education provides ammunition for both proponents and opponents of extending the foundation role to the school level.

Another kind of for-profit presence involves components of nonprofit and public educational organizations. There is a long history here and, again, it has mostly involved higher education. Economists have been aware of internal cross-subsidization, and James's second chapter shows how universities can operate their undergraduate programs as for-profit concerns, using the gains to absorb the losses sustained in graduate education and research. Similarly, we know that profits from some courses and fields of study financially sustain others, just as large freshman classes sustain senior seminars. At least, however, such examples involve a balancing among educational functions. Different concerns about sectoral blurring arise when educational organizations run for-profit *non*educational activities to sustain their educational activities, with debate over what is properly shielded by the special tax status of nonprofit and public organizations. A related concern arises when educational organizations run nonprofit activities in noneducational areas, and thereby compete "unfairly" with neighboring for-profit enterprises; for example, a university cafeteria that stays open for dinner can seriously undercut the business attracted by local restaurants, however surprising that may seem to many patrons of university cafeterias. Finally, intersectoral blurring occurs where educational organizations that maintain nonprofit legal status pervert educational missions by in fact making profits that they surreptitiously distribute or conspicuously consume on luxuries.

Whatever the for-profit roles, however, public policy generally strives to make important distinctions between for-profit and other educational organizations. This we see most pointedly in Hirschoff's chapter, as for-profits are excluded from most of the aid attracted by nonprofits—and are consequently freer from government regulation. Moreover, empirical research does suggest certain tendencies that distinguish for-profits from other educational organizations, at least by matters of degree. For-profits tend to be smaller, more tuition dependent, less government dependent in finance and governance, more hierarchically administered, narrower in their curriculum offerings and other missions, heavily job oriented, and lower in their academic prestige and perhaps in the average SES of their student bodies.[6] Still, there is room for more research on the for-profit role in education.

FURTHER ORIENTATIONS

Obviously, the nonprofit context, and the ways in which it is often analyzed, helps orient this volume. Fuller orientations involve (1) going beyond the finance and achievement issues addressed in other studies of private education and (2) "interlevel," international, and interdisciplinary perspectives, as well as intersectoral ones.

Beyond Finance and Achievement

Overall, research on private education still lags far behind research on public education (even allowing for the quantitatively greater importance of the public sector). As a prominent textbook on educational administration laments: "Not as much is known about [private] schools because the collection of data . . . has been sporadic, poorly coordinated, and even ignored."[7] Much of what has been written is unhelpfully polarized or scattered in various memoirs and unpublished reports. Moreover, few works on private education have effectively provided intersectoral comparisons. Nevertheless, significant strides have been made. Among the best of the recent volumes, for example, one could point to James and Levin on schools and Breneman and Finn on higher education.[8] But concerns such as public policy for private education are clearly broad and important enough to warrant much more work. Additionally, as the James and Levin and Breneman and Finn volumes illustrate, much of the work on private education and public policy has focused overwhelmingly on finance. As already pointed out, finance is prominently analyzed in this volume as well, but more than half of the chapters deal either primarily with nonfinancial issues or almost equally with finance and other issues.

If there has been a nonfinancial focus to the recent literature on private education, it has concerned the achievement, or "quality," issue.[9] (In fact, much of the discussion of financial policies has turned on this issue.) Here, of course, the pro-private findings of the Coleman-Hoffer-Kilgore report—and the numerous supportive and critical responses it has evoked—have been central. (The reader is directed especially to Murnane's two chapters.) But, *even* if one accepts the pro-private findings, this volume's information on choice, clientele, finance, regulation, and other matters strongly suggests that quality does not usually mark the most significant differences between sectors (except for those who would attribute other differences to quality). Beyond objective quality, a very difficult concept to define and measure, contributors such as Erickson, Kutner-Sherman-Williams, and James (on the Netherlands) discuss client satisfaction, particularly high in the private sector. The main point here, however, is that they and others also analyze, beyond objective or subjective quality, such matters as the contrasting reasons that families choose private or public institutions and the frequently decisive private-public differences in regulation and mission. In sum, this volume looks at many aspects of private education and of private-public comparisons.

"Interlevel" Perspectives

In so doing, the volume draws not only intersectoral comparisons but other kinds of comparisons as well.[10] One involves schools and higher education. This comparison is admittedly more implicit than explicit, with certain exceptions; nonetheless, it is most unusual for the two levels to be treated together in a given volume. Also, beyond the explicit comparisons that are drawn, the reader is encouraged to draw others by the fact that so many common themes are dealt with across the educational levels.[11] Choice is one such theme. Great variation is found within the private sectors at both levels (as Erickson and Geiger show for schools and higher education, respectively.) At the school level, however, the prime choosers are parents, while at the higher education level they are students. At the

school level there is greater concern for equal access and standardized socialization, which can limit choice, yet the actual degrees of intersectoral
distinctiveness tend to be greater than at the higher-education level, at least
in the United States. For another example, consider finance. We have already seen how for-profit roles long common in higher education have attracted considerable interest at the school level. Similarly, the Kutner-Sherman-Williams chapter discusses the rationale for "Baby-BEOGs," emulating
the policy rationale used for Basic Equal Opportunity Grants in higher education since the 1960s, to help nonprivileged groups enjoy a choice of
sector as well as guaranteed access to the public sector. To shift from proposals to present policy, one sees broad parallels in the practice of public
funding of private education at the school and higher-education levels in
the Netherlands (according to James's first and Levy's last chapters). And
perhaps a greater awareness of how cross-subsidization works in higher
education can spur consideration of how it may work at the school level,
perhaps within given private schools or, interinstitutionally, across a public system.

International Perspectives

Another kind of comparison worth highlighting here, and also useful for
both scholarly and policy considerations, involves international dimensions. These dimensions are found prominently in each of the volume's three
parts. By contrast, other books, whether edited or single authored, have
rarely included pieces on private education elsewhere. This is largely un-
derstandable in terms of the relative lack of relevant research, especially on
higher education. But cross-national perspectives are desirable for several
reasons. They help us see our own policies in a broader context. This helps
us to achieve better, deeper understandings and to avoid a parochialism
with which we are often justifiably charged. For example, some observers
wrongly view private higher education as a uniquely U.S. phenomenon.[12]
For another example, to return to school–higher-education comparisons,
the U.S. experience can be very atypical with regard to the relative acceptance of distinctively private sectors at the two levels. As Hirschoff points
out, U.S. private schooling was not secure until 1925, whereas the robust
support of U.S. private higher education described by Geiger has strong
roots preceding national independence; indeed, by most definitions, U.S.
private higher education established itself at the same time as, or even before, U.S. public higher education. But many other nations, notably in Europe and Latin America, have long allowed vibrant private schooling while
insisting on public monopolies or near monopolies in higher education. To
take a related example, explanations for the fact that in the United States
private-public distinctiveness is greater for schools than for higher education might consider the fact that elsewhere private-public distinctiveness is
often greater at the higher-education level than at the school level.

It is even possible that cross-national comparisons can not only inform but influence our consideration of policy alternatives. Realistically, direct replication is unlikely (properly so), but international policies can help raise ideas, debunk myths of either inevitable or impossible ramifications, and provide some clues as to what to do—and what to avoid. Moreover, those interested in nonprofit organizations should be aware that education probably comprises a larger share of nonprofit activity outside than within the United States, as many nations that lack a wide network of nonprofit activities do have formidable private education sectors.[13]

Two chapters in this volume, James's on the Netherlands and Levy's on finance, deal basically with education outside the United States, though they both try to provide a context for the consideration of U.S. policy and alternatives. For example, in showing how government policy sustaining a large private sector can control some of the stratifying selectivity issues that concern Murnane and others, James distinguishes between policies that could be emulated and those that could not be. Two other chapters (Geiger's and Levy's "Analysis"), while dealing most with the United States, use international examples to help provide context and comparisons.[14] Another (Erickson's) devotes roughly equal space to the U.S. and Canadian cases.

Interdisciplinary Perspectives

To this point we have discussed orientations that cut across sectors, educational levels, and nations. Additionally, the volume cuts across disciplines. This reflects the Program on Non-Profit Organization's interdisciplinary commitment (indeed, the commitment of Yale's Institution for Social and Policy Studies within which the program has functioned). The attempt is to stimulate dialogue not only across disciplines but between professional scholars and policymakers; to achieve such ends, writings must not be too discipline bound. (All but two chapters in this volume, the Erickson and the Kutner-Sherman-Williams, were written by scholars who have spent several years in some substantial involvement with the program, either in full-time residence or in some affiliated relationship.) The "home" disciplines from which the authors depart range rather widely from economics (James, Murnane), to political economy (Sherman), to political science (Williams, Levy), to public policy (Kutner), to social psychology (Erickson), to history (Geiger), to law (Hirschoff). In some cases these backgrounds are manifest, as when Hirschoff considers the relationship of federal and state constitutions to nonprofit agencies (private schools) as opposed to government agencies (public schools). Even the language is sometimes an identifying mark, as when Hirschoff discusses the Establishment Clause, state action doctrine, statutory authority, and constitutional amendments, or when Murnane (in his first chapter) discusses competitive markets, incentives, delivery systems, and market models. But *even* the lawyer's and economists' chapters are accessible to the nonspecialist; if this editor can follow the economists' chapters (give or take an equation or two), surely the reader can.

CHOICE AND PUBLIC POLICY: CHAPTER SUMMARIES

Nonetheless, despite the diversity of foci found here—in terms of disciplines, geography, educational levels, and sectors—and despite the fact that this volume does not emerge from a single conference built around inter-related papers, several crucial concerns cut across the chapters. Some of these concerns have already been discussed. They include intersectoral comparisons and the relationship of education to major questions of general interest to the nonprofit world. This section highlights the common concerns of *choice* and *public policy,* as it offers a brief overview of the individual chapters.[15] In fact, each author deals at least partly with both issues. Several emphasize intersectoral choice—for example, why families choose private or public schools—while Erickson, Geiger, and James (on higher education) also focus on choices within the private sector. Regarding public policy, there is a range between authors who deal primarily with it (e.g., Kutner-Sherman-Williams) and those who deal with it more in terms of the ramifications of empirical findings (e.g., Erickson).

Part I

Part I opens with our broadest landscape of private choice and public policy concerning U.S. schooling. Reviewing present policies, posing basic arguments, and emphasizing that practical policy decisions involve different private-public mixes, Hirschoff concentrates on one major basis for decisions: parental choice.[16] Controversies about the legal rights of private schools and about the government role in them turn on favorable and unfavorable assessments of the degree and kind of choice that the private sector distinctively offers. Interestingly, quality is but one choice criterion, not the key one, in determining the extent of the private schools' rights under the law. Using legal perspectives, Hirschoff considers different reasons for parental choice of private schools as well as policy alternatives. Crucial court cases are discussed. Overall, then, Hirschoff establishes important legal parameters within which choice and policy debates occur.

Pursuing several of Hirschoff's themes, the Kutner-Sherman-Williams chapter concentrates on federal policy. In fact, this chapter is rooted in federally sponsored research. Congress, in its educational legislation of 1978, mandated a study of private schooling and the actual and alternative federal roles associated with it. The Kutner-Sherman-Williams chapter represents a revised portion of a much longer report written, under Sherman's direction, by the National Institute of Education's School Finance Project. The chapter traces the growing federal role since landmark legislation in 1965, exploring the rationales for federal support of private choice to date and considering rationales for potentially expanded support. To help understand choice, the project conducted a survey of the different reasons that families choose private and public schools. Additionally, the project tried to probe potential choices by asking whether different levels of tuition tax credits would spur inter- and intrasectoral shifts.

Whatever the limits of such a survey, and other surveys are now being conducted, it provides some data to help answer a basic question posed by several authors, none more substantially than Erickson. This is why families choose what they do. Corroborating the preceding chapters, Erickson finds considerable support for the notion that parents choose private schools with knowledge and care and because free public schools do not offer what they want. He searches for the most precise explanations for private sector growth and decline and for choices of particular kinds of private schools.[17] In so doing, Erickson walks us through some of the enormous variation within the private sector and therefore in the reasons for which parents choose private schools. He draws his findings from a selective literature review and from original findings on British Columbia. His findings have substantial relevance to theoretical attempts to explain the existence and growth of nonprofits in terms of public or government "failure" models, though Erickson properly expresses reservations about facile applications of the "public school dissatisfaction" hypothesis.[18]

Part II

Following in the direction pointed to by the Kutner-Sherman-Williams survey and the Erickson case study of British Columbia, the school chapters in Part II bring empirical research to bear on specific issues within the broad concerns raised in Part I. They turn especially close attention to the intersectoral dynamics and consequences of different policies. The Dutch case gives James a long time span over which to evaluate such dynamics and consequences, as public funding of private schools has gone so far (whereas Erickson chose a case where public funding was only recently introduced, and is less extensive). James finds that Dutch private schools historically arose to expand choice, especially for religious groups and minorities, beyond just the "bundle of public goods." This expansion of choice was partly limited by religion's major role, putting together a church "package," but secularization has helped untie it; in this we might find comparisons to trends documented by Erickson for the U.S. private sector. A striking feature of the Dutch system, however, has been the centerpiece government role in promoting choice through the private sector. Too often, perhaps, Americans associate government with limits on choice. Further counter to some American intuitions, James shows that choice can be restricted by the nonprofit sector. But the most powerful findings do sustain widespread expectations about links between government's financial involvement and restrictions on choice, autonomy, and innovation for private schools. With heavy government regulation, compared to which the U.S. regulations previously described by Hirschoff and Kutner-Sherman-Williams pale, Dutch families enjoy comparatively little intersectoral choice in terms of finance, school policies, or quality. Alongside Erickson's findings on the immediately deleterious effects accompanying public funding of private schools, at least some readers will conclude that there is cross-national evidence to oppose certain policy alternatives for the United States.

Working with domestic data, Murnane then argues that there is further reason to be concerned about the growing U.S. interest in providing social services through government-aided nonprofits. As suggested above, his chapters focus heavily on the relationship between achievement scores and private choice and on the need to consider such matters intersectorally. When the Coleman-Hoffer-Kilgore report concluded that private high schools are outperforming public ones, it provided an empirical base for notions that many parents and policymakers already had. According to Murnane, however, the conclusions are more justified for parents than policymakers. What the parent needs to know to make a rational private choice is that the average quality is higher in a given private school than in a public school. Parents gauge this in several ways, often using high SES as an indicator. In fact, SES is correlated with performance, and individual students are likely to do better if placed in with high- rather than low-achieving peers. But policymakers should know much more. They should know not only which sector is providing more "value added" but also whether even value added is the result of factors that public policy can maximize. Chief among such factors is choice, not just family choice but school choice. How much is private success dependent on not just the SES but the motivation and self-selection of clients along with intersectorally different regulations concerning admission and dismissal? The contours of choice differ significantly between the two sectors. At the same time, Murnane calls for more research on choice within the public as well as the private sector. For now, he fears that policies such as tuition tax credits might well undermine, rather than promote, desired private choice. Herein lie some of the formidable difficulties, discussed below, of proceeding from empirical findings to policy ramifications.

The intricacy of intersectoral analysis becomes thematic in the ensuing chapter by Levy. Picking up on several of the dimensions frequently used in analyzing educational and other arenas of nonprofit activity, he tries to help sort out what *private* and *public* mean. Although it obviously does not provide an introductory schema guiding the usage found across the chapters, the analysis may encourage some readers to think about that usage as well as alternatives. Even as the chapter's emphasis and examples mostly concern higher education, the definitional issues are treated as relevant to the school level as well. While *private* and *public* still generally have clearer meaning in U.S. schools than in higher education, that is not the case in many other nations, and even U.S. distinctions are inconsistent and often inexplicit; furthermore, as several preceding chapters suggest, the growth of government financing and regulation concerning private schools has contributed to increased private-public blurring, a trend that prominent policy alternatives such as tuition tax credits would surely forward. Thus, the chapter identifies the principal ways in which we presently define *private* and *public* in higher education, argues that no way consistently accords with legal or popular nomenclature, and then proceeds to propose alternative ways in which we might try to pursue greater definitional consistency and improved analysis. Even with some modest modifications in usage, however, scholarly analysis, private choice, and public policy, at all educational levels, will remain confusingly complicated by the complexity of private-public realities.

Part III

Part III continues to analyze higher education but turns toward both a financial and empirical focus. Levy's contribution identifies five principal financial policy patterns, internationally, based on the proportional size of each sector and the balance of private and public income each receives. As public policies and contours of private choice vary greatly across the five patterns, the chief rationales and proposed alternatives to each are discussed. In contrast to U.S. practices, many nations avoid intersectoral differences in finance, and others minimize these differences while still others maximize intersectoral differences through private sectors that rely fully on private finance and public sectors that rely fully on public finance. Overall, the role of U.S. private finance appears impressive when contrasted to the absence of private sectors in many nations, the public funding of private sectors in some others, and the lack of parallels to the U.S. degree of private funding of public higher education.

Yet the domestic payoffs of comparative analysis are most fruitfully realized when we combine such analysis with direct and discriminating analyses of U.S. finances, such as that provided by Geiger. Not only is the United States itself a comparative laboratory with its fifty state systems, but there is enormous diversity within each sector. While diversity within the public sector is striking in cross-national perspective, so is the diversity within the private sector. Indeed, the latter, which Geiger concentrates on, is much greater than the former. Just as Erickson dissected the private school sector, Geiger dissects private higher education. He links differences in finance to different functions among which students and donors (including government) can choose. When seen intersectorally, these functions include providing something more, different, or better than found in the public sector. However, what is provided, as well as how it is provided, varies greatly within the private sector. This incredible intrasectoral diversity, along with intersectoral contrasts, offers unparalleled choice to a variety of actors—and a perhaps baffling array of differences on which to base public policies. Still, no matter how much the private sector is sustained by voluntary support, it also depends greatly on those public policies.

Finally, James's analysis of cross-subsidization continues the exploration of how finance relates to choice and public policy. Choice is explored partly in terms of how different types of institutions emphasize undergraduate teaching, graduate studies, and research. Finance is explored as we see how different types of institutions fund each of these missions. Although this piece is not as centrally concerned as the others with private education per se and although it establishes other distinctions as more decisive than the private-public distinctions, it sees some of the latter as significant. And we could reasonably go further by seeing the former in a private-public context, as community colleges are overwhelmingly public and four-year liberal arts colleges without graduate programs or much research are overwhelmingly private (and research universities are found prominently in both sectors). A striking finding is that both private choice and public policy can be perverted at research universities. In recent decades, an increased share of resources has been devoted to costly graduate studies and research, both activities heavily subsidized by undergraduate education. Consequently, the private sector's undergraduate students, and the alumni from the days when missions were different, may choose to support an institution without realizing what their money buys. Similarly, the public policymakers who fix levels of financial support for public universities, and also the heavily subsidized private ones, may choose on the basis of misleading impressions.

No chapter fully answers the major questions it tackles. Therefore, without even identifying issues not analyzed here, a formidable research agenda could be developed just by carrying forward the questions and explorations found herein.[19]

THE STAKES: PUBLIC POLICY AND INTERSECTORAL COMPETITION

Along with the importance of the private nonprofit sector and fundamental matters concerning its behavior come crucial policy issues. Although an exhaustive treatment clearly lies beyond this volume's scope, each chapter deals with some aspects of policy, as just described. This final introductory section may provide a small backdrop for the fuller policy discussions that ensue by sketching some general aspects of intersectoral competition, juxtaposing schools and higher education. This competition both shapes and is shaped by our public policies for private and public education.

We have already seen that such competition is trisectoral, but that the for-profit sector is mostly left aside in this volume. Without doubt, however, the major private-public policy issues affecting education have overwhelmingly involved the nonprofit and public sectors. At the same time, intrasectoral competition merits more attention than it receives in this introduction. That is particularly true in the United States, where the public sector is often more decentralized than it is elsewhere. More strikingly, in the United States especially, intrasectoral competition tends to be greater in higher than school-level education, and certainly tends to be much greater in private than in public sectors. All that said, the prominence of intersectoral competition is manifest. Moreover, it has been intensifying in many nations, notably so in the United States.

Shifting Balances?

Listening to debates over private and public schools, one might guess that the private sector is thrashing the public sector. Widespread perceptions of public failure have been reinforced by reports deploring the sorry state of our public schools. Most politically significant was the government-sponsored 1983 report *A Nation at Risk,* warning of a rising tide of mediocrity.[20] Whatever the facts about school quality intersectorally, the perception of significant private enrollment gains amid public losses has been fostered not only by many private boosters and much of the media but probably also by such public defenders as union leader Albert Shanker.[21] Yet enrollment data do not sustain notions of a big shift in private-public shares, at least not yet. Instead, as Erickson's chapter shows, the private share and total actually *dipped* from the mid-1960s to the mid-1970s, with only some recovery since then; more generally, percentages have been remarkably steady for many decades, varying by not more than 6%. A major change in intersectoral competition stems instead from a considerable reshaping within the private sector, as public schools come to compete increasingly, over a widened geographical span, including rural areas, with non-Catholic private schools, whether affiliated with other religious groups, fundamentalist or independent. In any case, the relative stability of public enrollment shares makes sense in terms of survey results, such as those reported by Kutner-Sherman-Williams, showing much less public disapproval of public schools than is often supposed.[22]

It is not at the school but at the higher-education level that the private-public numerical balance has changed dramatically. Here the great concern, continually demonstrated in reports of the Carnegie Council on Policy Studies in Higher Education (created in 1973), has been over *public* sector gains at *private* sector expense. And here the concern has an enrollment basis. In the third quarter of this century, the private share dropped from one-half to under one-fourth. But even here, as Geiger's chapter notes, intersectoral shifts are easily exaggerated. For one thing, the new private percentage has been holding fairly steady; in the late 1970s, the private sector actually outpaced the public sector in adding new enrollments. For another, even the "decline" resulted from unprecedented public growth, particularly in the community college arena (in which the private sector hardly competes), while private enrollments also increased. Additionally, private colleges that closed or slipped into life-or-death situations were generally among the weakest, while other private institutions were created and most found themselves facing difficult but manageable challenges.[23] Nevertheless, there is reason for concern over the special difficulties that the private sector faces in times of systemwide "retrenchment." Even a steady, or moderately declining, share of a shrinking pie could constitute a more serious threat than the greatly diminished share of the rapidly expanding pie of earlier years; for one thing, the impact on given institutions could be more destabilizing. By the same token, public schools still face the danger of proportional losses to private schools amid systemic constraints.[24]

Intensified Competition

With so much at stake, it is not surprising that each sector has turned increasingly to vigorous advertising. Much of this, especially for the public sector, involves boosting its accomplishments before government officials. Toward this end, educational interest groups have increasingly split along private-public lines, as with the creation in the 1970s of the National Association of Independent Colleges and Universities, "aggressively private" in its approach.[25] On the other hand, a good deal of the competition involves marketplace efforts. There is, to be sure, more legitimizing tradition for this in higher education than on the school level and in private as compared to public institutions. Many private colleges and universities have taken to increasingly direct invidious comparisons with competitors (private and public), while even public counterparts sell themselves through media and other campaigns in ways once thought unbecoming. The same can now be said of many private schools as they launch major media efforts, often drawing on seminars run by for-profit concerns. Defenders say such advertising is a fair way to capitalize on dissatisfaction with public schools and to inform potential clients of what they offer. Detractors say that these private schools are behaving increasingly like for-profit enterprises and are contributing to negatively invidious comparisons and ill will.[26]

In short, intersectoral debate has become more combative. Allowing for exceptions and variations, it seems that partisans of both sectors have broadcast basic pro-private and pro-public arguments more loudly and explicitly than before. Private partisans claim special virtues in autonomy from government control; direct accountability to concerned parties; client choice; diversity; religious, cultural, and political pluralism; adaptability; experimentation; innovation; and excellence and efficiency through competition. Partisans of public education claim special virtues in public accountability; democratic or popular control; coordination; equity; cultural cohesiveness; national unity; respect for heterogeneity as fostered by diversity within institutions; and attention to difficult, diverse, and progressive social responsibilities that private institutions can bypass.

Crucial to private-public debates at both the school and higher-education levels in the United States, however, is the widespread acceptance by both sides of a dual-sector system. Thus policy choices turn largely on the juxtaposition of the two sectors.[27] To some extent, the acceptance of dual sectors limits the stakes involved in U.S. private-public debates. By contrast, many nations have been bitterly divided over the creation of private sectors. Historically, in much of Europe and Latin America, this issue was one of the politically most volatile, often overlapping with broad church-state controversies. As discussed above, the United States did not resolve the issue of private school legality until 1925. But for some nations, historical passions remain contemporary ones. In France, in 1984, a government shake-up was needed after a bill to increase official control over private schools met heavy opposition not only from church and other private groups concerned about autonomy but also from the political left (including members of the government's own Socialist party), hostile to any private schooling and committed since the Revolution to a unified public school system. Soon thereafter a similarly explosive mass confrontation erupted in Spain. Nonetheless, the rule in most non-Communist nations is that some form of private schooling is accepted.[28] The issue of whether to have a private sector remains much more divisive at the higher-education level. Some Western European nations have not been prepared to allow any private universities, while others have allowed only marginal ones. Most Latin American nations refused to allow private higher education until the 1950s and 1960s, and the controversy that surrounded its creation remains more than an echo. Just since the 1970s, nations such as Costa Rica, England, Italy, New Zealand, and West Germany have created private universities amid great opposition, while nations such as Greece and Nigeria have considered it. By contrast, U.S. private higher education celebrates a long and prestigious tradition.

Nevertheless, to point out that the U.S. debate (as in so many policy fields) occurs within a more limited ideological range than seen in other nations is not to minimize what is at stake in U.S. private-public debates. One need only consult the brief list, just presented, of claims commonly made by partisans of each sector. The range of possible intersectoral balances is significant, the potential variations in private-public contours multiple. Furthermore, recent U.S. history strongly shows what seems logical: When change means decline rather than expansion, private-public competition can become especially embittered.

The embittered U.S. competition is found most strikingly in higher education where, indeed, the intersectoral balance has changed as both sectors deal unhappily with lean times. Consider New York, admittedly an extreme case, the state with the largest private higher education sector in absolute terms and the third largest in proportional terms. In 1983, the annual meeting of its Association of Colleges and Universities was bypassed by eighty private institutions, a show of anger specifically against both the city and state university expansion plans and generally against a public sector policy agenda deemed antagonistic to the private sector. The mutuality of hostility was reflected in the inability to form the traditional united higher-education front before the state legislature. While leaders of both sectors publicly lamented the estrangement, the president of the Independent Colleges Commission pointed to its roots: "Competition in a contracting marketplace . . . is vicious."[29]

Perhaps it is helpful, at least in reading through this volume, to distinguish two kinds of intersectoral competition, though real-world situations usually find mixes. One kind involves competition through separateness. For example, as illustrated by Geiger's discussion of "ecology" and institutional specialization, private institutions can find niches where they shape themselves differently from public institutions and try to attract actors that would not feel comfortable there. A second kind of competition, however, occurs on shared "turf." Here institutions in both sectors compete for those who desire similar things by convincing them that they do it better (or at least comparably). Both the shift of private schooling toward the secular and the expansion of public institutions into fields where previously only private institutions operated may represent significant movements toward increased competition on similar turf. Several of the chapters in this volume, by reporting on the different and overlapping missions of private and public institutions, provide information on how much competition has been taking place on substantially shared turf. Several also show that competition can be pushed onto common ground by public policies that aid, and regulate, private education—making it more like public education; James's piece on the Netherlands provides the extreme case, still well beyond U.S. practice. (In passing, note that we have already seen how competition can be moved onto similar turf when public institutions seek private aid, as public schools show some signs of doing and as public universities are increasingly doing with regard to corporations.)

Policy Alternatives Concerning the Private-Public Balance

Even a glance over ensuing chapters suggests how much public policy affects private-public competition and the numerical balance between the sectors. For the sake of brevity, we here consider only certain kinds of policies, pertinent at once to the school and higher-education levels, those aimed at expanding (or restricting) the size of the private sector.

At least in this volume, the most prominent kind of public policy alternative to promote the private sector involves financial aid to students and their families. At both educational levels, such aid goes much more to the private sector than aid to institutions does. Until now, higher education has been the main arena, as student aid often allows the recipient to choose his or her institution; this helps explain the anxiety of private colleges and universities over President Reagan's efforts to cut student aid, although public counterparts were also concerned. But both vouchers and tuition tax credits, if implemented, would affect the school level as well. Basically, vouchers give families the right to choose any institution within the participating system, with costs covered by government, though particular proposals vary so much that, for example, advocates of one plan consider that other plans could constitute "the most serious setback for the education of disadvantaged children in the history of the United States."[30] James shows how far vouchers have gone in the Netherlands while nations such as Britain and Italy and states such as Colorado have been considering vouchers.

Not vouchers, however, but tuition tax credits have drawn the most policy attention for U.S. schools. Whether one looks at proposals by President Reagan or by Senators Packwood and Moynihan, the basic idea is to allow families a certain break on taxes if their children attend private institutions. Some proposals would include higher education. Naturally, policies that help defray tuition costs especially benefit the only sector that charges tuition (or, in higher education, the sector that charges higher tuition). To lessen the intersectoral hostility engendered and the constitutional questions raised by such proposals, Minnesota has allowed tax benefits to parents of students in both sectors, and states such as New York have held hearings on the subject.[31]

Like aid to individuals, aid to institutions is considered in several subsequent chapters, so that here we merely note the relationship to intersectoral competition. Policies by which government gives money directly to private institutions have become increasingly common at both educational levels, but public institutions remain easily the prime beneficiaries. They therefore tend to favor this over aid to individuals. Heated intersectoral debate concerning subsidies to institutions has mostly involved higher education, not only because that is where most government subsidies of private institutions are found but also because that is where the degree of subsidization of public institutions is bitterly contested. Of course, there can be a school debate also, where the public sector feels that policies aiding the private sector rob it of funds or good students; but in higher education the tuition issue is added. The public sector often considers it unfair that it must raise tuition while private institutions, beneficiaries of their own support system, often privileged, receive subsidies that help them reduce the intersectoral "tuition gap." On the other side, the private sector often argues that liberal subsidization of public colleges and universities constitutes unfair competition.

Beyond finance, other public policies seriously affect the intersectoral numerical balance. For example, in higher education, policies to establish new public institutions, or new courses or fields of study within existing ones, can provoke the ire of private institutions previously operating in a less competitive enclave. This is one of the major reasons for the intersectoral strife noted above in New York as, illustratively, the private Rensselaer Polytechnic Institute faces competition from expanding engineering programs on SUNY campuses, even where private pressure is sufficient to keep engineering off SUNY-Albany, the potentially most proximate competitor.[32] More generally, at both educational levels, the degree and shape of regulation is a major issue. Concern focuses mostly on government regulations over private institutions, often placing burdensome costs through compliance itself and through the personnel and procedures necessary to prove compliance. There is also the complaint that government regulation handicaps intersectoral competition by limiting the distinctive ways in which the private sector can make its appeal. At the same time, however, the public sector often argues that government regulation cripples its capacity to compete effectively. Whatever the increased controls over private institutions at both levels, controls over public institutions have also increased, remaining much more extensive and restrictive. This can make it more difficult for public than private institutions to build or to maintain the environment (whether laudable or not) that many parents and students want. At the school level, examples include policies on integration, dismissals, prayer, sex education, and so forth. Although the private sector is frequently seen to have an edge in innovation, it may also have a competitive edge in its ability to resist change.

To push further, we see that public policies affect not just the numerical balance but also the character of the two sectors. Indeed, at least three factors suggest that policymakers should be at least as sensitive to intersectoral issues involving private*ness* and public*ness* as to issues involving numbers. One is that intersectoral enrollment shares have not been varying wildly.[33] Another is that the privateness of the private sector at both educational levels is threatened by government finance and regulation. The third is that many policy proposals to improve the public sector involve emulating policies (as in school dismissals or college tuition) associated with the private sector.[34] However, as seen especially in Part II, to consider questions of privateness and publicness is to consider complex dilemmas, as, for example, policies to expand the private sector may "dilute" its special essence. So it is that private institutions are frequently divided on whether to lobby for or even accept public money. Complications have been greater at the higher than school level in the United States, as intersectoral blurring has gone further in higher education, but they are found increasingly at both levels.

To illustrate, we can briefly consider a general policy rationale concerned more with the privateness than the size of private sectors. Assumptions such as the following could be zealously embraced. Private expansion, contrary to the viewpoint of those who see it as representing increased importance and therefore meriting more government attention,[35] is a sign of private health arguing *against* such attention. On the other hand, a contracting private sector does not necessarily warrant help, especially if such help dulls its adaptive senses. Institutional death is consistent with sectoral vitality. A more general assumption might be that the private sector is less a whole than a loose aggregation of vastly different institutions and subsectors.[36] Thus even while Catholic schools were suffering greatly in the mid-1960s to mid-1970s, other private subsectors were booming as never before. Similarly, Geiger finds that the folding of weaker private colleges has tended to steer attention away from the "robust health of many others." Under our assumptions, a great problem with public policy for private sectors is that these sectors are so internally diverse that policies seemingly appropriate for some subsectors are inappropriate for others, possibly fostering an undesirable homogenization; alternatively, policies would have to be incredibly differentiated and detailed, probably destructively if not hopelessly so. Flowing from these and other concerns about privateness could emerge two related assumptions that would further guide public policy. One is that government would interfere with private education only for reasons deemed compelling, not merely desirable.[37] The complement to this restraint would be that private institutions would seek government help only for compelling reasons, would not be expected to rally automatically to the support of suffering sister institutions, and would not claim that public subsidization of public institutions constitutes unfair competition.[38]

Policy Alternatives and Research

Of course, policy deliberations on private-public matters should be informed by considerations that go beyond such assumptions about the privateness of the private sector, even when coupled with concern over private-public numerical balance. Nonetheless, once we get beyond preoccupations with numerical balance to issues involving privateness and publicness, it is especially clear that policymaking concerned with intersectoral issues can be extraordinarily complex. Also, policy-making would involve formidable complexities even if we were to expand greatly our understanding of intersectoral dynamics. For a basic problem now familiar to students of the policy process manifests itself here: how to move from empirical research to improved policy-making.[39]

This problem has become more and more salient as public policies for private institutions have widened, as both the quantity and quality of social science research has improved, and as government actors such as the courts try to use this research to guide the policies. Among the difficulties, political feasibility ranks high. As Charles E. Lindblom has pointed out, good policy analysis influences policy-making only if it is successfully joined to a political strategy; it does not substitute for it. Illustratively, Denis Doyle writes that vouchers still are an "idea in search of a constituency."[40] Another major difficulty, tied to the complexity of the realities in question, intra- and intersectorally, is that empirical findings are more likely to lead to further conflict rather than consensus, more questions than answers. Furthermore, this applies to both shoddy and methodologically sophisticated and ably conceived research. Are we nearer or further from clear empirical lessons for policy-making when, for example, James concludes that cross-subsidization in higher education produces equity ramifications different from those suggested by previous economic studies?

To focus here on one crucial private-public issue, consider Murnane's chapters. Probably more than any others in this volume, they highlight the difficulty in moving from empirical findings to policy recommendations. Put aside all the intense debates about the methodologies used in the Coleman-Hoffer-Kilgore study, debates to which Murnane contributes and which have produced anything but consensus among fine researchers; put aside even normative questions about private school performance, such as those involving social restrictiveness. We would still be left with the issue posed in Murnane's second chapter regarding the extension of desired characteristics: "How do we get there from here?" Murnane argues, in effect, that while policies like tuition tax credits would alter the intersectoral numerical balance, they would also alter the nature of each sector. Not only would those "left behind" find themselves in a weakened public sector, but the expanded private sector would lose some of what public policy was trying to maximize in the first place.[41] Further examples of possible alterations in characteristics associated with the private sector, when that sector enlarges, are found in Erickson's case study of British Columbia, James's chapter on Dutch schools, and Levy's discussion of international financial patterns.

Clearly, then, there is ample reason for humility when tackling the subject of private education and public policy. Even if we knew much more about the former than we do, ramifications for the latter would not flow unambiguously. Private education and public policy are subjects not for mastery but for serious and continued attention.

NOTES

1. These are 1982 figures. Gabriel Rudney and Murray Weitzman, "Significance of Employment and Earnings in the Philanthropic Sector, 1972–1982," PONPO working paper no. 77, Yale University, New Haven, Conn., November 1983, pp. 3, 11. Private education accounts for 16% of the nonprofit wages and salaries, mostly because of higher education. In fact, private higher education, without private schools, ranks among the major four arenas of nonprofit employment in terms of numbers of workers, and its position is even stronger in terms of earnings, probably because it tends to surpass private schools in average salaries while having lower proportions of female to male teachers, voluntary to salaried labor, and students to instructors. For purposes of these figures and our general discussion, *nonprofit* refers to privately controlled tax-exempt organizations. The bulk of the nonprofit sector is "philanthropic"; as opposed to nonprofits (e.g., social clubs, labor unions) that confer mutual benefits on its members, philanthropic organizations can receive tax-deductible contributions. There is a major twist in education, however. This is that even *public* higher education can receive tax-deductible contributions; nevertheless, it is excluded from these figures and from our general category of nonprofits because it is publicly controlled. This last criterion can be fuzzy, as Levy's "Analysis" chapter argues, and some observers have considered public higher education as nonprofit. Nonetheless, in this volume, only James's chapter on higher education defines any public institution as nonprofit, and even then private-public distinctions are drawn. For more on both data and definitions, see Gabriel Rudney, "A Quantitative Profile of the Nonprofit Sector," PONPO working paper no. 40, Yale University, New Haven, Conn., November 1981, p. 2 and passim. A revised and updated substitute for the two working papers cited in this note can be found in Gabriel Rudney, "The Scope of the Nonprofit Sector," in Walter W. Powell, ed., *Between the Public and the Private: The Nonprofit Sector* (New Haven: Yale University Press, 1986).

2. James S. Coleman, Thomas Hoffer, Sally Kilgore, *High School Achievement: Public, Catholic and Private Schools Compared* (New York: Basic Books, 1982). Their report sparked a controversy that preceded publication of their book. See especially the special issues of the *Harvard Educational Review* 51, 4 (1981), and the *Sociology of Education* 55, 2–3 (1982). The fact that the analyses of both Coleman and his critics show that neither sector has a decisive edge in raising student achievement allows attention to turn not only toward examining achievement differences across schools on other than a sectoral basis but also toward comparing private and public on bases other than student achievement. Such bases can deal with finance, governance, mission, and effectiveness not defined by standard achievement tests. For elaboration, see Daniel C. Levy, "A Comparison of Private and Public Educational Organizations," in Powell. The article, complementing our volume, concludes that intersectoral differences are substantial despite important exceptions, and that many of these differences

relate to a lesser scope and greater "specialism" in private as opposed to public educational institutions.

3. For the postsecondary figure, see David A. Trivett, *Proprietary Schools and Postsecondary Education* (Washington, D.C.: ERIC Clearinghouse on Higher Education Research Report no. 2, 1974), p. 9. On the school percentage, see Cindy Currence, "Corporations Considering Creation of For-Profit Schools," *Education Week,* April 11, 1984. Rudney, "A Quantitative," p. 16, reports estimates that 95% of private education's salaried employees are in the nonprofit sector. However, this figure is shaped, on the one hand, by inclusion of "correspondence and vocational schools," where nonprofits make up only 26% of the workforce and, on the other hand, by considering private elementary schools, secondary schools, colleges, and universities as fully nonprofit; for our purposes, the last data-simplifying assumption cripples the figures, but it reflects a belief that for-profit activity is minimal.

4. Currence, "Corporations." Recent research suggests a huge and growing corporate role in retaining and educating its own employees. Perhaps 8 million employees and a cost of over $40 billion per year are involved. Carnegie Foundation for the Advancement of Teaching, *Corporate Classrooms: The Learning Business* (Princeton, N.J.: 1984).

5. The role of nonprofits as major purchasers of for-profit goods and, to a lesser extent, as sellers to for-profits, is too often overlooked. See Rudney and Weitzman, "Significance," p. 3.

6. See Levy, "A Comparison"; private-public differences appear to increase significantly if for-profit institutions are included.

7. Roald F. Campbell, Luvern L. Cunningham, Raphael O. Nystrand, Michael D. Usdan, *The Organization and Control of American Schools,* 4th ed. (Columbus, Ohio: Charles E. Merrill Publishing Company, 1980), p. 424.

8. Thomas James and Henry M. Levin, eds., *Public Dollars for Private Schools: The Case of Tuition Tax Credits* (Philadelphia: Temple University Press, 1983). (It should be noted that the James and Levin volume appeared after drafts for this volume had been prepared and, unfortunately, would have proven too difficult to incorporate beyond this introduction.) David W. Breneman and Chester E. Finn, Jr., eds., *Public Policy and Private Higher Education* (Washington, D.C.: The Brookings Institution, 1978). Major forthcoming additions to the literature will include: Thomas James and Henry M. Levin, eds. *Comparing Public and Private Schools* (Falmer Press, in press) and a large study in progress on state policy and private higher education by William Zumeta and Carol Mock.

9. See note 2, above. An additional focus is found where the literature directs itself to special issues in religious education, mostly Catholic. To cite just one work on schools and one on higher education, see Andrew M. Greeley, *Catholic High Schools and Minority Students* (New Brunswick, N.J.: Transaction Books, 1982); and Neil G. McCluskey, ed., *The Catholic University: A Modern Appraisal* (Notre Dame: University of Notre Dame Press, 1970). Although none of the authors in the present volume deals primarily with religious education per se, there are numerous references to such education, and its weight within private education generally is acknowledged. Erickson analyzes how the Catholic school share of U.S. private school enrollments declined from nearly nine in ten in the mid-1960s to six in ten at the beginning of the 1980s. James points out that religion is a major reason for choosing private schools in the Netherlands, where nearly 90% of private enrollments are in religiously identified schools. Murnane points out that his analyses, following as they do on Coleman-Hoffer-Kilgore's, deal basically with Catholic (and public) high schools. Hirschoff discusses some of the policy issues concerning the separation of church and state and how it affects government funding and regulation of religious schools. Part III deals less with the religious subsector, reflecting the lesser weight and less marked orientation of religion at the higher-education level.

10. We are grateful to Bruce S. Cooper for helping to identify as salient the several types of comparisons found throughout this volume.

11. All the school chapters deal with elementary *and* secondary schools. The only partial exception would be Murnane's; but while his data are on high schools, most of his arguments and concepts deal with school levels inclusively. Future research, and perhaps policy, could

consider disaggregating the elementary and secondary levels more than is generally done in the United States; international perspectives suggest that, for some purposes, it may be fruitful to link secondary a little more with higher education than we in the United States have tended to do. For many views of explicit secondary-higher links, see Burton R. Clark, ed. *The School and the University: An International Perspective* (Berkeley: University of California Press, forthcoming).

12. See, for example, Howard Howe II, "What Future for the Private College?" *Change* 2, 4 (1979), p. 28.

13. See Estelle James, "Non-Profit Organizations in Developing Countries," in Powell. For figures on higher education, see Levy's chapter on finance in this volume. Private shares of school enrollments vary from minimal to well over 50% in Western Europe, with similarly great variation in Asia and Africa; in Latin America, the primary figure (average 13%) generally varies between a few and 20%, while the secondary figure (average 29%) more generally varies between 15% and 50%. For a fuller summary of such data, see Levy, "A Comparison."

14. Most chapters in this volume have been authored (or coauthored) by scholars working on major projects concerning private education outside the United States. The Kutner-Sherman-Williams piece is revised from a School Finance Project report that included comparative work on Australia, British Columbia, and the Netherlands. The work on Australia was done by Sherman; see his "Government Finance of Private Education in Australia," *Comparative Education Review* 26, 3 (1982), pp. 391–405. The section on British Columbia was based on Erickson's earlier work (since then greatly updated and elaborated as partly reported in his contribution here). The section on the Netherlands was based on James's work, obviously elaborated here but also part of a multination study under way. At the higher-education level, Geiger has written probably the first major multiregional study of private institutions, *Private Sectors in Higher Education: Structure, Function and Change in Eight Countries* (Ann Arbor: The University of Michigan Press, 1986). Also see Daniel C. Levy, *Higher Education and the State in Latin America: Private Challenges to Public Dominance* (Chicago: The University of Chicago Press, 1986).

15. The focus on choice is particularly appropriate, as it relates to broad concerns in the study of nonprofit organizations. We ask, for example, how these organizations expand the range of choice or, though it generally receives less attention, restrict the range of choice for some, but in any case shape the overall contours of choice. With concerns such as choice crosscutting the chapters, delineation of the chapters into three major parts is somewhat arbitrary, especially as regards those bridging chapters ending Parts I and II and those opening Parts II and III. Different delineations could be as reasonable. For example, while the higher-education chapters need not have been grouped, the most intensely cross-national chapters could have been. In any case, the plan here was to make some division between schools and higher education, and then to divide within the first group partly according to the level of generality. Thus, the three chapters in Part I are overviews, though they present some new findings on very specific concerns; and though the subsequent chapters on schools provide some general material, there is a discernable shift away from overviews to more intensively focused analyses. The changed focus in Part II is also marked by increasingly explicit attention to intersectoral comparisons. In this connection, Levy's "Analysis" is a swing chapter, leaning toward Part III because of its higher-education focus but tied to Part II because of its intersectoral focus. Part III is thereby left to revolve around higher-education finance, while its opening chapter retains an intersectoral focus. Similarly, James's first chapter might have marked the end of Part I as an overview, with data (on the effects of government funding on private schools) which parallel data in the latter half of Erickson's paper, but it fits into Part II because of its greater attention to intersectoral comparisons (and because it provides an overview of the Dutch, not the U.S., system).

16. Hirschoff's wider work will more fully contrast the value of parental choice to the needs of "social unity." For an interesting discussion, see Henry M. Levin, "Educational Choice and the Pains of Democracy," in James and Levin, pp. 17–38.

17. For a relevant historical view of why our dual-sector structure evolved, and of chang-

ing notions of *private* and *public*, see Thomas James "Questions About Educational Choice: An Argument from History," in James and Levin, pp. 55–70.

18. Erickson points out that "public failure" may occur alongside differential rates of growth and decline in various kinds of private schools. Personally, I would interpret this less as limiting the validity of "public failure" than as compelling a carefully discriminating use of the hypothesis. On the broad relevance of the "public failure" hypothesis, see James Douglas, "Political Theories of Nonprofit Organization," in Powell.

19. For example, Hirschoff continually identifies points where legal judgments about alternative public policies could be informed by expanded knowledge, Kutner-Sherman-Williams call for better assessments of how tuition tax credits would affect family choice, Erickson regards his foray into the complexities of private sector heterogeneity as tentative, and so forth. Drawing from this introduction alone, some (among many) targeted areas for future research would include for-profit institutions, the casual relationship between funding and control, the politics of private education, and comparisons across sectors, levels, systems, and disciplines. To push further, still without at all approaching a comprehensive agenda, might be to hope for more work on specific cases, decentralized public alternatives, public "success stories," particular institutional characteristics (within either sector) that seem to promote success, the governance of private institutions, "home schools," publicly aided private schools serving the handicapped, and achievement at the elementary level and in non-Catholic private schools (indeed, on many aspects of the proliferating non-Catholic institutions). In fact, most of this article's notes could suggest further research lines, as some (e.g., 2, 5, 6, 11, 27, 34, 38, 40, 41) already do.

20. National Commission on Excellence in Education, *A Nation at Risk: The Imperative for Educational Reform* (Washington, D.C.: Government Printing Office, 1983). Among other major studies on profound problems were Ernest L. Boyer, *High School: A Report on Secondary Education in America* (New York: Harper & Row, 1983); Theodore R. Sizer, *Horace's Compromise: The Dilemma of the American High School* (Boston: Houghton Mifflin Co., 1984); John I. Goodlad, *A Place Called School: Prospects for the Future* (New York: McGraw-Hill, 1983).

21. See, for example, Albert Shanker, "What's the Attraction of Private Schools," advertising column in the *New York Times*, June 8, 1980; also see *Newsweek*'s "Private School Boom," August 13, 1979. On the other hand, Senator Daniel Patrick Moynihan, "Tax Credits and Private Schools," *National Review* 31, 31 (1979), p. 462, wrote that we "face a great contraction in the non-government sector in education. I feel this will be a loss to pluralism, and yet another instance of the conquest of the private sector by the public sector about which Schumpeter wrote a quarter-century ago."

22. According to results reported to William Schneider, "The Public Schools: A Consumer Report," *American Educator* (Spring 1984), pp. 13–17, the public does see a decline in public schools but commensurate with, and explained by, declines in other public institutions and the family. The National Center for Educational Statistics estimates that the nation's 5,686,000 private school enrollments (1983) break down into 56% in Catholic schools, 24% in other religiously affiliated ones, and 20% in nonaffiliated ones. "Estimated Changes in Private Elementary/Secondary Statistics," mimeo, Washington, D.C., September 28, 1984.

23. Carnegie Council on Policy Studies in Higher Education, *The States and Private Higher Education* (San Francisco: Jossey-Bass, 1979, p. 137 and passim; and William W. Jellama, *From Red to Black?* (San Francisco: Jossey-Bass, 1973), pp. 8–9. An interesting parallel to the school level is found in the fast growth of evangelical colleges. Clark Kerr calls them possibly "the most successful individual segment of American higher education." He also notes the high morale in new Hispanic institutions, alongside declining morale in more established private and public institutions. "Impressions 1984: Higher Education Once Again in Transition," Earl V. Pullias Lecture in Higher Education, University of Southern California, 1984.

24. On potentially significant increases in private school percentages, possibly to 15% by 1990, see Bruce S. Cooper, Donald H. McLaughlin, Bruce V. Manno, "The Latest Word on Private School Growth," *Teachers College Record* 85, 1 (1983) pp. 88–98; but not all observers predict such private gains. In any case, there is evidence of a big private explosion,

since the mid-1970s, in *pre*-school enrollments, as baby-boom parents seek advantages for their children in highly selective (!) institutions. See Cindy Currence, "Private Lower Schools Face Deluge of Determined Applicants," *Education Week,* March 21, 1984.

25. Edward S. Gruson, "The National Politics of Higher Education," report of the Sloan Commission on Government and Higher Education, November 1977, mimeo, p. 17.

26. Currence, "Private Lower." Especially at the school level, however, there are also important examples of increased private-public cooperation, some actively promoted by the Department of Education.

27. Broadly speaking, some of the issues may be viewed in relation to "politics and markets"—the degree to which market replaces government or vice versa. See Charles E. Lindblom, *Politics and Markets* (New York: Basic Books, 1977). For Third World nations they may be viewed in relation to alternative development models. A related perspective could focus on prevalent models linking state and society. "Pluralist" models might sustain the existence of spontaneously created, nonsanctioned, independent, competitive, and decentralized institutions, while "corporatist" models might sustain the planned creation of officially sanctioned, functionally and explicitly coordinated, noncompetitive institutions within a single system which monopolizes the policy field. Private or private-public systems *generally* approximate the pluralist type more than public systems do. While such a contrast of ideal types might represent the extremes within which policy choices can be made, the proliferating literature on corporatism emphasizes the degree to which private and public often blur in reality. Here we simply observe that private-public may be viewed within a large political-economic framework, while Levy's first higher-education chapter picks up the point that there can be publicness in nominally private institutions and privateness in nominally public ones. See Philippe Schmitter, "Still the Century of Corporatism?" in Frederick Pike and Thomas Stritch, eds., *The New Corporatism* (Notre Dame: University of Notre Dame Press, 1974), pp. 93–96.

28. See note 13, above, and, for example, Peter Mason, *Private Education in the EEC* (London: National Independent Schools Information Service, 1983). In addition to the volatile French and Spanish cases, even a nation such as Ireland, with an unusually large private sector, may face challenges to private legitimacy; see Guy Neave, "The Non State Sector in the Education Provision of Member States of the European Community," report to the Educational Services of the Commission of European Communities, Brussels, 1983. For reports on France and Spain, see, for example, the *New York Times* accounts: E. J. Dionne Jr., "850,000 Jam Paris in a Schools Protest," June 25, 1984; and Edward Schumaker, "Spaniards Assail Law Imposing State Rule on Schools," November 19, 1984.

29. Quoted in Samuel Weiss, "New York Colleges Aren't so Collegial," *New York Times,* October 30, 1983. For another relevant news feature, nationally oriented, see Gene I. Maeroff, "Public-Private College Rivalry Heats Up," *New York Times* (Education, summer survey), August 19, 1984.

30. Judith Areen and Christopher Jencks, "Education Vouchers: A Proposal for Diversity and Change," in George R. LaNoue, ed., *Educational Vouchers: Concepts and Controversies* (New York: Teachers College Press, 1972), p. 54. In higher education, too, there have been proposals to move beyond student aid toward full-fledged vouchers.

31. See Sherman, "Government Finance," for recent comparative insights on dual-sector political feasibility.

32. There have been several attempts to assess trade-offs. For example, on financial trade-offs, see Susan C. Nelson, "Financial Trends and Issues," in Breneman and Finn, p. 68; and on enrollment trade-offs, see Michael S. McPherson, "The Demand for Higher Education," in Breneman and Finn, especially the summary statement (p. 194) that competition is "quite close" between some types of private and public institutions.

33. Naturally, one must consider how much stable intersectoral enrollment shares have depended on public policy.

34. Interestingly, most policy discussions conerning intersectoral learning turn on the public sector learning from the private sector (though both often copy the other in part). This is the case, for example, with regard to determinants of achievement, dismissing unruly students, molding harmonious relationships between schools and their families, and so forth.

Why does less explicit attention focus on what private sectors should learn from public sectors? It cannot be that public sectors are better at nothing. It may be, in part, that we often assume that many private institutions cannot or will not agree to emulate public practices (e.g., in costly curriculum offerings). It may also be, depending on how we frame the issue, that private copying of public sector ways is not unusual, but is often imposed through regulation, as in insisting on certain credentials or on nondiscrimination.

35. For example, Cooper, McLaughlin, and Manno, p. 98, conclude that private enrollments will lead to increased support for some policies considered pro-private. Issues involved in public policies to save private educational institutions parallel, to some extent, those involved in public policies to save for-profit enterprises, such as Lockheed and Chrysler.

36. Michael T. Hannan and John Freeman make the supportive argument that organizational change occurs largely through the failure of existing institutions and the birth of new ones more than through the evolution of existing ones. "The Population Ecology of Organizations," *American Journal of Sociology*, 82, 5 (1977), pp. 929–964.

37. This first guideline harkens back to Donald A. Erickson's "Freedom's Two Educational Imperatives," in Erickson, ed., *Public Controls for Nonpublic Schools* (Chicago: The University of Chicago Press, 1969), pp. 159–175. His two imperatives are that good state regulations preserve and even encourage both (a) plural goals (b) and plural means, especially as public policymakers and professionals alike really have not provided public school policies and results that cry out for emulation. Obviously, this restrained orientation, while often undermined by public policy, has been repeatedly endorsed; for one recent example, see Diane Ravitch, "The Schools and Uncle Sam," *The New Republic*, December 3, 1984.

38. A related alternative could be to distinguish two categories of private institutions, those involved with government money and regulation and those much more independent of both. This, in fact, is the situation in some West European settings, as Neave (p. 1) refers respectively to "non state" and (more truly) "private" schools. Some U.S. distinction along these lines emerges between nonprofit and for-profit institutions, but the nonprofit sector itself comprises a wide range of mixes.

39. See, for example, Charles E. Lindblom, *The Policy-Making Process* 2nd ed. (Englewood Cliffs, N.J.: Prentice Hall, 1980), pp. 18–25 and passim; and, specifically on education, David K. Cohen and Janet A. Weiss, "Social Science and Social Policy: Schools and Race," in Carol H. Weiss, ed., *Using Social Research in Public Policy Making* (Lexington, Mass.: D. C. Heath, 1977), pp. 67–83.

40. Lindblom, *The Policy-Making*, especially pp. 1–37; Denis P. Doyle, "The Politics of Choice: A View from the Bridge," in James S. Coleman et al., *Parents, Teachers, & Children: Prospects for Choice in American Education* (San Francisco: Institute for Contemporary Studies, 1977), p. 235. There is a crying need for more research on the politics of private education, not just on the content and desirability of present and alternative public policies but on interest groups, federalism, the internal governance of private educational institutions, and so forth; in short, a wide range of concerns commonly stimulating political scientists should be applied to this arena. For one good example on higher education, see Robert O. Berdahl, "The Politics of State Aid," in Breneman and Finn, pp. 321–352.

41. Naturally, one can be impressed by such problems and still believe that empirical findings can help inform public policy. For example, even some critics of the Coleman-Hoffer-Kilgore study believe that the public sector should be allowed to emulate some private sector practices (e.g., in dismissing unruly pupils). More broadly, as with comparative analysis, empirical analysis generally can be looked to for guidance more than definitive answers, for orientations, perspectives, contexts, checkpoints, warnings about gross danger zones, and, of course, for political ammunition. Additionally, some research (such as the surveys discussed by Kutner-Sherman-Williams) can be directly geared toward probing alternatives.

I

Overviews of Private School Choice and Public Policy

1

Public Policy
Toward Private Schools:
A Focus on Parental Choice*

MARY-MICHELLE UPSON HIRSCHOFF

INTRODUCTION

Not since the 1920s has our society faced so much controversy about public policy toward private elementary and secondary schools. Then, the major issue was whether private schools should be allowed to exist as alternatives to public schools. That issue was resolved in *Pierce* v. *Society of
Sisters*,[1] in which the Supreme Court upheld the right of parents to choose
private schooling, and thus foreclosed a public monopoly. Today, our mixed
system of private and public elementary and secondary education confronts increasing pressures for both fiscal and regulatory change. Most
prominent in public debate are proposals for tuition tax credits and voucher
systems and challenges to government regulation of private school teacher
qualifications, curriculum, and admission practices (especially as the latter
affect racial segregation).

Two major public policy issues have replaced the issue of whether private schooling should exist at all: (1) To what extent should government
encourage or discourage the choice of private schooling, that is, what balance between public and private schooling should government try to achieve?
(2) What differences between private and public schooling should government promote or prohibit?

Despite this change in emphasis, todays debates echo those of the 1920s

*Much of the work for this chapter was supported by a grant from the Charles Stewart Mott
Foundation of Flint, Michigan, and by general funds of the Program on Non-Profit Organizations, Institution for Social and Policy Studies, Yale University, for which I am most grateful.
I also thank John Simon, Richard Murnane, Dan Levy, and Jon Hirschoff for their helpful comments. An earlier version of this chapter was Working Paper No. 91 of Yale's Program on
Non-Profit Organizations. The views expressed herein are those of the author and do not necessarily reflect the views of funding organizations.

in many respects. Just as the proponents of the 1920s laws restricting private schools feared that those schools would harm efforts to Americanize the children of immigrants, some argue today that private schools exacerbate social, economic, racial, religious, and ethnic divisions within the society and that aiding private schools will increase such undesirable effects. Now, as then, advocates of private schooling rest their arguments on the rights of parents to direct their children's education and on the benefits to society of diversity in schooling. Most dispute claims that private schools increase social stratification to any greater degree than do the public schools or that they are less effective in creating good citizens.

One of the major factors that distinguishes today's debates from those of the 1920s is the greater attention paid to the impact of private schools on the quality of education. Proponents of tuition tax credits and voucher systems often assert that private schools are more effective, efficient, and responsive than public schools, and that they serve as a competitive spur to improved public school quality. Some opponents claim that the existence of private schools reduces public school quality. Others (see, e.g., Murnane's contributions to this volume) argue that increasing the incidence of private schooling would not necessarily lead to improved educational quality. Proponents of greater state regulation of private schools, on the other hand, charge that many private schools provide an education that is below acceptable levels if the purposes of the compulsory school attendance laws are to met.[2]

Although some participants in these debates take strong pro-public or pro-private positions, the primary question is what kind of *mixed* system of public and private schooling we should try to achieve and how. Because individual participants usually focus on specific proposals for change and on only one or a few public policy goals, they fail to address basic questions that need to be asked in order to justify any proposal for change: What are the values that we want a mixed elementary and secondary school system to serve? How do we define them? How well or poorly is the current mixed system serving these goals? The debates also obscure the existence of a much greater range of options for fiscal and regulatory change than those most frequently discussed.

The debates do suggest four categories of goals that encompass possible objectives for our mixed educational system: parental choice, pluralism, social unity, and educational quality. They can be defined as follows: *Parental choice* is simply the ability of parents to choose the kind of schooling they want for their children. Such choice serves parental liberty, the right of parents to direct the education and upbringing of their children. *Pluralism* includes both diversity in schooling and diversity within the society as a whole. *Social unity* encompasses two goals. The first is to attempt to assure that all citizens share the values, attitudes, skills, and knowledge that are considered basic to the proper functioning of our society. The second goal is to assure equal educational opportunity, so that one's adult position in society depends on merit rather than accidents of birth, thus eliminating the potential for social division based on perceived unfairness in the competition for jobs and power. *Educational quality* includes both the goal that all schooling meet minimum standards and the goal that the system as a whole exhibit as high a degree of quality as possible. Quality includes not only instructional effectiveness (what is learned), but responsiveness (what is taught and to whom) and resource allocation and efficiency (the amount of resources devoted to schooling and how efficiently they are used).

This chapter focuses on parental choice. The ability of parents to choose private schooling is a fundamental characteristic of any mixed elementary and secondary school system, regardless of the basis on which the system is justified. Among justifications for public policies that favor private schools, parental choice has the longest history. Because Supreme Court decisions grant some constitutional protection to the choice of private schooling, fiscal and regulatory policies that are designed to further other objectives must be judged in part by their effects on parental choice. In addition, parental choice as an independent ground for maintaining or changing our present mixed system does not raise empirical questions as difficult to answer as those raised when the basis of justification is quality, social unity, or even pluralism. Parental choice may be, therefore, the most politically viable basis for justifying fiscal or regulatory change, if evidence indicates that change is necessary to facilitate the choice of private schooling.

Pursuit of parental choice as the primary goal of a mixed system would obviously affect other goals, just as their pursuit would affect parental choice. Actual decisions about maintaining or changing the existing regulatory and fiscal system should be based on judgments about those effects and on efforts to strike a balance among the values that support competing goals. This chapter does not, however, address the relationship of parental choice to pluralism, social unity, and quality. To achieve analytical clarity, the discussion of parental choice proceeds as though it is the only justification for public policy regarding private schools.

To provide necessary background, the first part of this chapter presents an overview of the existing legal structure of the mixed system. The second part analyzes the ways in which private schools may serve parental choice and explores arguments that may be made to support fiscal and regulatory policies toward private schools that facilitate parental choice. It is beyond the scope of this chapter thoroughly to survey or examine relevant empirical evidence. The reader will be referred, where appropriate, to other works in this volume that do undertake this task.

THE CURRENT LEGAL STRUCTURE

The Existing System

The purpose of this section is to provide an overview of the legal structure of our mixed elementary and secondary school system. Because of the federal structure of our government and the primary role of the states in education, it is not a uniform structure. Laws vary from state to state—in sometimes idiosyncratic ways—and general statements will therefore be less accurate for some state systems than for others.[3]

A central fact is that significant differences exist between public and private schools with regard to both financing and regulation. Public schools are financed through taxation, and are tuition free. Private schools depend primarily on tuition payments, donations, and volunteer or low-priced labor for fiscal support, despite some government assistance.[4] Historically, regulations of private schools have not been rigorously enforced or, if enforced, have been minimal in fact.[5] Private schools have enjoyed considerable freedom to differ from the more heavily regulated public schools.

About 11% of all elementary and secondary school children attend private schools. Approximately 89% of these schools are nonprofit.[6] As Erickson's contribution to this volume indicates, private schools follow a variety of different educational approaches and philosophies. Thus, public and private schools in the mixed system are close to the ideal public and private types posited by Levy in the last chapter of this volume, with respect to finance and control, and frequently even mission.

Financing

Government assists private schools by exempting them from taxation and by providing services or financial aid. Nonprofit private schools are exempt from state property and state and federal income taxes. Donations to private nonprofit schools may be deducted from the donor's taxable income. Such assistance is provided to a broad range of charitable organizations, including educational and religious organizations. It should be noted that scholars concerned with taxation disagree as to whether exemption from taxation and the deductibility of donations should technically be considered government aid. I use the term *assistance* for convenience and not to suggest any position on that debate.

Government services and financial aid technically go to private school *students* or their *parents*. Typically, such aid is only available to those who patronize *nonprofit* private schools. (Similar aid is provided to public school parents or students—presumably to counter claims that the aid constitutes an establishment of religion, to be discussed more fully below.) More than half the states provide one or more of the following kinds of aid: bus transportation, textbook loan programs, health services, aid for the handicapped, guidance and counseling, instructional materials loans, psychological testing, remedial instruction and testing.[7] Since 1955, Minnesota has allowed a tax deduction for nonprofit private school tuition, textbooks (interpreted to include a wide variety of instructional materials), and transportation.[8]

Federal aid to nonpublic school students is administered by state and local educational agencies unless state law prohibits their participation. The most important program of federal aid has been Title I of the Elementary and Secondary Education Act of 1965, now Chapter I of the Education

Consolidation and Improvement Act of 1981, which focuses on aiding educationally disadvantaged children. It was estimated that 3.8% of all private school students participated in this program in the 1979–80 school year, most of them attending Catholic schools. For a history of federal aid to private school students and a description of federal aid programs, see the Kutner-Sherman-Williams chapter in this volume.

Public schools receive about 8% of their financing from the federal government. States fund public schools from both state taxes and local property taxes. The latter have been historically the dominant source of funding for public schools, but with pressures for equalization of the resources available to local school districts, state financing has become increasingly important.[9] Depending on state law, public schools can charge fees for extracurricular activities and may charge tuition for students residing outside school district boundaries.

Regulation
The interests of the state in achieving the goals of compulsory education are the same regardless of whether the schooling is received in public or private institutions. Because government operates and funds public schools, however, regulations are imposed on public schools that are not imposed on private schools.

Public Schools   As government agencies, public schools must comply with limits on government action imposed by the federal Constitution. Supreme Court decisions of the last few decades have proscribed prayer and other religious exercises in public schools, protected student free speech, required segregated public school systems to desegregate and required that pupil suspensions and expulsions be imposed in accordance with standards of fairness under the due process clause (notice of the charges against the student and an opportunity to hear the evidence and to provide his or her side of the story).[10] Many of the laws now governing the operation of public schools are arguably required on constitutional grounds, for example, the requirement that public schools be open to all school-aged children within the applicable geographical area.[11] (Unless otherwise indicated, references to the Constitution are to the federal Constitution. State constitutions place limits on public schools and on government action toward private schools, but vary from state to state.)

What is taught in public schools, how it is taught, and how the schools are otherwise operated is determined both by state legislatures and state boards of education and by locally elected or appointed boards of education. It is the general public, through processes of democratic control, to whom the public schools are, at least theoretically, responsible. The current patrons of a particular public school—the parents of its students—may, indeed, prefer a type of schooling different from that being provided. Much of the federal regulation of public schools—even that which is directed toward assuring compliance with constitutional requirements, for example, desegregation—is tied to federal financial assistance to public schools.[12] State grant programs that are not automatically available to all public schools also typically impose additional regulations on those public schools that receive the grants.

Private Schools   Private schools—because they are *not* government agencies—need not comply with the constitutional requirements imposed on public schools. Constitutional law does affect private schools, however, to the extent that it prescribes limits on government regulation and financial assistance to such schools, to be discussed below.

Private schools are subject to the same general laws that apply to any private business, except to the extent that their educational functions lead to the imposition of additional regulations, and their nonprofit status, if adopted, entitles them to special treatment. Partly because private schools have been almost entirely funded by private funds, it appears to have been thought inappropriate to regulate them beyond what was considered necessary to fulfill the purposes of compulsory school attendance laws. Neither tax exemptions for private schools nor aid to private school parents and students commonly have led to greater regulation of private schools, other than the typical requirement that private schools be organized as nonprofit organizations in order to receive the benefits, and the more recently imposed prohibition against racial discrimination.[13] Proprietary schools may (and do) exist; they simply are ineligible for most government assistance.

State requirements imposed on private schools due to their educational function may be enforced directly, through mandatory state accreditation, approval or licensing requirements, and/or indirectly, by finding parents in violation of compulsory education or school attendance laws if they send their child to a noncomplying school. O'Malley's survey of state departments of education found that eighteen states have some form of mandatory accreditation, approval, or licensure. One of these states, Alabama, requires a license for proprietary but not for nonprofit schools. A few states exclude church-related schools from mandatory requirements. Voluntary accreditation, approval, or licensure is available to private schools in many states.[14] If such state sanction is important to attracting patrons, even voluntary programs may have significant regulatory impact.

Comparisons of Public and Private School Regulation   The most important differences in the federal and state regulation of public and private schools involve (1) school control, (2) teacher hiring and firing, (3) student selection and discipline, and (4) school curriculum.[15]

School control: State laws prescribe eligibility requirements for membership on the public school board, as well as whether the board must be elected or appointed, and whether parents, students or teachers must be involved in some decision-making processes.[16] Public school boards are subject to varying degrees of state administrative control. In most states, private schools may remain unincorporated or need only comply with applicable incorporation statutes. They need not organize as nonprofits. However organized, as long as they meet technical requirements, they are basically free to govern themselves as they wish, that is, they may select whomever they want to serve on the board, make it self-perpetuating or not, and proceed with or without teacher, parent, or student involvement in decisions.

Teacher hiring and firing: State laws prescribe education requirements for public school teachers (teacher certification) and establish rules and procedures governing teacher dismissal, tenure, and retirement. Under the Constitution, public school teachers are also entitled to certain free speech and due process rights. Most states now have collective bargaining laws that govern the subjects and process of negotiation with school employees, including teachers. Only thirteen states impose teacher certification requirements on private schools.[17] For the most part, private schools may hire whomever they wish. The terms and conditions of teacher employment are governed by private contract. Although collective bargaining in secular private schools is protected by the National Labor Relations Act, most eligible private school teachers have not unionized.[18]

Student selection and discipline: Public schools are required to educate any child of eligible age living within the geographical boundaries of the school district. They must adopt and enforce rules regarding discipline, suspensions, and expulsions following specified procedures. Some of these rules are constitutionally required; others are imposed by state statute. In many public school systems, however, students are tracked into specified instructional programs; some systems have specialized public schools with admission requirements other than geographical residence. Federal statutes prohibit discrimination on the basis of race, color, national origin, sex, or handicap by schools that receive federal funds.[19] (To the extent that private schools receive federal financial assistance, these laws apply to them as well.)

Private schools are free to teach only those students they wish to admit, although under a federal statute, 42 U.S.C. 1981, derived from the reconstruction-era Civil Rights Act of 1866, they cannot discriminate on the basis of race. Discipline, suspensions, and expulsions from private schools are a matter of contract between the school and its patrons.

Curriculum:[20] Regulation of the private school curriculum varies from state to state. Some states impose no curriculum requirements on private schools. Others simply delegate the power to prescribe curriculum to state education agencies (including local school administrators charged with enforcing compulsory education laws), often stating that instruction must be "equivalent" to or "substantially the same" as that provided in the public schools. Such standards leave administrators with wide discretion in determining how rigorously private school curriculum should be regulated, and there is considerable variation among states in administrative interpretation. Historically, most states have allowed private schools to operate without extensive oversight, possibly in part because traditional private schools were regarded as sufficiently similar to public schools. Especially recently, however, some state education agencies have rigorously enforced extensive administratively prescribed curriculum requirements on private schools.

A number of states, including some of those that delegate regulatory power over private schools to a state agency, require private schools by statute to teach specific subjects. Typical requirements include instruction in U.S. history, civics, government, the federal and state constitutions, reading, writing, spelling, and arithmetic. Other, less frequently imposed requirements include health and drug education, instruction in patriotism and good citizenship, and recognition of the accomplishments of women and minorities. Many states require that all instruction (usually excluding foreign languages and sometimes religion) be in English.

The curriculum of the public school is subject to far more extensive state regulation, although, again, variation exists from state to state. Textbooks must often be chosen from a state-approved list. Public schools are often required to teach subjects such as sex education, consumer education, and, for students wanting it, vocational education. By state and federal law, public schools are also required to provide "special education" to mentally and physically handicapped children. Federal law requires public schools that receive federal funds to remedy any language deficiency that prevents equal participation of non-English-speaking children in school programs. Some states specifically require bilingual and even bicultural schooling where appropriate.

PARENTAL CHOICE

With this overview in mind, we can now consider how one of the goals for the mixed system, parental choice, may justify maintaining the existing legal structure or adopting options for regulatory or fiscal change. As noted above, the following discussion considers parental choice as though it were the only goal to be served by public policy toward private schools. Such an approach tends to give the discussion a pro-private cast. It is therefore important to recall that actual decisions about maintaining or changing the existing mixed system will require a balancing of parental choice against other goals—pluralism, social unity, and quality—each of which will be similarly examined in later work.

In 1925, the Supreme Court held in *Pierce* v. *Society of Sisters*[21] that private schools have a constitutionally protected right to exist as alternatives to public schools. In doing so, the Court recognized parental liberty, the liberty to direct the education and upbringing of one's children. Neither *Pierce* nor other decisions pertaining to the choice of private schools protect complete freedom of parental choice. *Pierce* permits "reasonable" regulation of private schooling by government. It also does not require any governmental subsidization of the choice of private schooling.[22] Before considering justifications for regulatory and fiscal policies that facilitate the choice of private schooling, it will be helpful to set out a theoretical analysis of how parental liberty—viewed broadly rather than limited by constitutional interpretation—can be served by the ability to send one's children to private schools. The analysis is supported in part by surveys of private and public school parents reported elsewhere in this volume by Kutner-Sherman-Williams and by Erickson. The survey questions do not, however, exactly conform to the analytical categories used below—categories chosen because they make distinctions that are important in discussing support for parental choice in constitutional law.

How Private Schools Serve Parental Liberty

Parents may choose private schooling for their children because a conflict exists between the available public school and the parents' educational objectives for their children or because the private school offers something that cannot be obtained in the public school. Such choices could be necessary even if the public school system offers a wide range of schooling options. (When permitted by state law, instruction of children in the home by their parents or tutors also serves parental liberty. Full protection, however, must also include the ability to educate one's children in an organized private school with other children.) Although parents are likely to have more than one reason for choosing or wanting to choose private schooling,[23] different reasons support different justifications for maintaining or changing the existing system and therefore warrant separate consideration. Choices made because of conflict will be discussed first.

Conflict

The curriculum, methods of instruction, or even general atmosphere of the public school may conflict with parents' religious beliefs or with their secular values—political, moral, or cultural in nature.[24] As Erickson's chapter notes, the growth of Fundamentalist schools in recent years is largely explained by conflict between the religious beliefs of Fundamentalist parents and the atmosphere and curriculum of public schools. The private school serves as an escape from the public school, and in most cases it is not necessary that the private school do anything to affirmatively assist parents with their educational objectives for their children. It need only do nothing to hinder them.

Conflicts may also occur on pedagogical grounds—because the child's program of study or the instructional methods are opposed by the parents as inappropriate for their child. For example, a child may be put in a general or vocational track rather than college preparatory against the wishes of the parents, or a disciplinary method or approach to the teaching of reading may be used that the parents believe to be ineffective or even harmful to their child.

No Conflict

In the absence of conflict, parents may choose private schooling for substantive and nonsubstantive reasons. Substantive reasons include the ideas, values, skills, attitudes, and knowledge that a school seeks to impart to its students. Nonsubstantive reasons are concerned with all other characteristics of schooling.

Substantive Reasons   First, among substantive reasons, parents may choose a private school to assist them in inculcating their religious beliefs and political, moral, or cultural values in their children. Public schools can neither provide religious instruction nor allow school prayer. (Teaching about religions in the context of such courses as comparative religion, history, civics, and ethics is, however, permitted.) Even though public schools are not as restricted in teaching secular values as they are in teaching religious beliefs, most commentators believe that they must, at least as to controversial issues, maintain neutrality.[25] Such a neutrality would not be as helpful to parents seeking to inculcate specific values in their children as would a private school that could actively espouse those values.

As to both religious and secular value inculcation, parents might be able to supplement public schooling with after-school-hour instruction. Complete substitution of private for public schooling is not absolutely necessary in the absence of conflict with the public schooling. Nonetheless, parents may legitimately believe that truly effective inculcation of their religious or secular values requires that those values permeate most or all of the schooling experience.

Other substantive reasons include obtaining a particular course of instruction, for example, German or swimming, the use of a different educational method, or adherence to a particular educational philosophy. In the first case, supplementary instruction after public school hours might suffice. There is, however, a natural limit on the number of hours available for instruction after school, so that the more deficient the public school in terms of desired instruction, the more necessary the substitution of a private school would be.

Nonsubstantive Reasons   Each of the nonsubstantive reasons for choice of private school requires substitution of private for public schooling rather than supplementation of public schooling. The first of these reasons is perceived superior instructional quality. Factors that parents may consider indicative of that quality include the qualifications of the staff, better physical facilities, and better enforcement of disciplinary rules. There need be no difference between the public school curriculum, its methods of instruction or educational philosophy and that of the private school chosen. Second, choice may be based on the desire to have one's children attend school with certain kinds of other children. Such a reason for choice may stem from a belief that a particular mix of students is necessary in order not to contradict in practice the ideas or values that are being taught at home and in school, or that the mix of students will lead to more effective schooling for one's children. (See Murnane's first chapter in this book regarding the effect of student body composition on achievement.) Private schools can control student body characteristics and hence the school atmosphere through student selection and discipline.

Third, parents may want a different kind of organizational control over school policies and school administration than that of the public school, for example, more parent or student involvement in policy-making, more teacher autonomy. Fourth, school location may be the reason for the choice of a private school. In the case of boarding schools, parents may want their child to live away from home for their own convenience or because they think it important for the child's development. Day schools may be chosen because their location is closer to home or otherwise judged more convenient than the available public school. A fifth possible reason is a family tradition of sending children to private school.

Public Policy and Parental Choice

The discussion that follows explores arguments that may be made—to judges, legislators, or administrators, as appropriate—to support fiscal and regulatory policies toward private schools that serve parental choice. It should be noted, however, that parents may be hampered in sending their children to a private school that serves their educational objectives simply because there are not enough like-minded parents and teachers to form such a school. Neither regulatory nor fiscal policy changes could assist them. In addition, support for increased fiscal aid to private schools may depend on what regulations could be imposed on private schools—either as a condition for receipt of the aid or directly. Nonetheless, the discussion that follows considers fiscal and regulatory policies separately.

Parental Choice and Fiscal Policy
Although the Constitution does not require any government financial assistance to facilitate the choice of private schooling, Supreme Court decisions are a source of constitutional values that can be used to support arguments for maintaining the existing system of financial assistance or increasing that assistance. Supreme Court decisions also limit the nature and perhaps the degree of financial assistance that the government can give; these limitations will be considered at the end of the following discussion.

Justifications for Aiding Parental Choice The existence of conflict between public schooling and parents' religious, cultural, political, or moral values is probably the strongest justification for maintaining or increasing financial aid to those who choose private schooling. The *Pierce* opinion clearly expressed concern over the possibility of indoctrination when it stated that "[the] fundamental theory of liberty upon which all governments in this Union repose excludes any general power of the State to standardize its children by forcing them to accept instruction from public teachers only."[26] In *Wisconsin* v. *Yoder,*[27] the Court recognized that requiring Amish children to be instructed in a public school curriculum that conflicted with the tenets of the Amish religion unconstitutionally burdened the parents' free exercise of religion. As I have argued elsewhere, principles of neutrality toward religion and nonreligion on the part of government should lead to an equal concern with a public school curriculum that conflicts with parents' deeply held secular values. Since children in public school constitute a captive audience of the government, the ability to escape to a private school is an important protection against the possible indoctrination of children in values opposed by their parents. Such indoctrination conflicts with the protection of freedom of conscience that is implicit in First Amendment guarantees of freedom of speech and the free exercise of religion. It also conflicts with the First Amendment's implied protection of a marketplace of ideas.[28]

Pedagogical conflicts—objections to a course of instruction, educational philosophy, or method of instruction that parents consider harmful to their child's preparation for a future career and life-style—do not pose risks of indoctrination and thus do not raise concern about harm to First Amendment values. Nevertheless, choice of occupation and life-style are important liberties under our system of government[29] and the inability of parents to send their child to a private school in order to avoid having their child instructed in a way that may limit the child's choice of occupation and life-style is certainly a cause for concern.

All of the reasons for choice that do *not* stem from conflict with the available public schools may be regarded as bearing some relationship to freedom of association—the right of people to join together in groups to further shared ideas, values, beliefs and goals.[30] Each is related to the general parental liberty to direct the education and upbringing of one's children. Some reasons, however, are more closely tied to the central concerns of the First Amendment than others. In fact, *Runyon* v. *McCrary,* to be discussed later in connection with regulatory policies, suggests that the communication of ideas, values, and knowledge has a greater degree of constitutional protection than methods of instruction or other school characteristics.

Obviously, parents choosing a private school in order to help them inculcate their religious beliefs are engaging in the free exercise of religion. The choice of private schools to help instill secular values in one's children may be regarded as an exercise of freedom of speech, important to the protection of a free marketplace of ideas. When a private school is chosen in order to obtain courses, methods of instruction, or adherence to an educational philosophy not provided as an option by the available public school, that choice also may be regarded as an exercise of freedom of speech. Factors related to instructional quality, student body characteristics, and organizational control as reasons for the choice of private schooling arguably affect the success with which ideas, skills, and values are taught. In addition, both student body characteristics and organizational control may be critically interrelated with the provision of schooling that differs in content and method from that of the public school. Independent of their impact on school effectiveness, content, or method, however, none of these reasons bears a significant relationship to freedom of speech or the free exercise of religion, just as convenience of location and family tradition do not.

If all reasons for choice of private schooling are considered adequate justification for aiding the choice of private schooling, then the only empirical information needed to determine whether a change in fiscal policy is necessary is the extent of the financial burden on existing private school parents and the extent to which parents who would like to send their children to private school are precluded from doing so for financial reasons.[31] If, however, only some reasons are considered sufficient justifications for aiding the private school choice, then one must also ascertain which reasons for choice would be served by financial aid.

Deciding whether or not there is need for greater financial assistance also involves judgments about the extent of the fiscal burden that parents should bear in choosing private schools.[32] In addition, consideration should be given to whether fiscal support feasibly could be limited, in some cases, to supplementation of the public school program with after-school-hour private instruction. When the reason for choice stems from conflict with the available public school, the strength of parental objection undoubtedly varies from sharp disagreement to only mild disapproval. It is likely that the stronger the degree of felt conflict, the greater the efforts parents will have made to provide alternative schooling. It is possible then that virtually all parents whose choice of private schooling stems from significant (to them) conflict with the available public school already do send their children to private school (unless they are barred by insufficient financial resources or no private school alternative exists for them). If this is the case, fiscal change to lighten their burden could be justified, but there would be no need for aid that would significantly increase the numbers of students attending private schools.

Options for Fiscal Change   A wide range of fiscal options could be adopted by state legislatures and, in most cases, Congress, to serve parental choice. Public discussion has focused primarily on tuition tax credits, voucher systems, and, more recently, tax deductions for private and public school expenses, including private school tuition. Both tuition tax credit and tax deduction proposals have limits on the amount of credit or deduction from taxes that could be claimed. Under most voucher proposals, the voucher could be used to attend either a public or private school. The different voucher systems proposed vary in the amount of the voucher, whether schools accepting voucher students must accept it in full payment of tuition, whether the voucher varies according to family financial need (income and number of children), and the extent of regulation imposed on participating private schools. Some voucher proposals would extend only to "disadvantaged" students, to be used in public or private schools. For a more extensive discussion of voucher and tuition tax credit proposals, see the Kutner-Sherman-Williams chapter in this volume.

Other fiscal options for change include scholarships for use only in private schools by specified categories of students, for example, needy, talented, handicapped;[33] increasing the tax benefits of donations to private schools; increasing the number and amounts of grant programs to private school students; making more services available to private school students; and increasing the geographical boundaries in which free bus transportation to private schools is available.

In addition, the financing of *public* schools could be changed. Tuition could be charged at public schools in order to eliminate the competitive advantage of public schooling. (Presumably local property taxes would be significantly reduced, and subsidies could be given to those who could not pay tuition.) Short of this, public schools could charge fees for extracurricular activities and certain courses (especially those that are not directly linked to the purposes of compulsory school attendance laws).[34]

All of the options for fiscal change mentioned so far would tend to encourage the choice of private schooling. To discourage that choice the obvious options would be to reduce or eliminate existing forms of aid. If the choice of private schooling is discouraged by the current financing of public schools—free of tuition, wholly tax supported—this negative impact could be increased by more spending on public schools, supported by higher taxation.

Constitutional Restrictions on Government Aid to Private Schools   Assuming that fiscal aid is appropriate, any system of government financial assistance that facilitates the choice of private schooling must abide by another clause of the First Amendment, the prohibition against establishment of religion, which is applicable to both state and federal governments. Since its 1971 decision in *Lemon* v. *Kurtzman,* the Supreme Court has used a three-part test to determine whether statutes violate the establishment clause. To be upheld, a statute must meet the following criteria: "First, the statute must have a secular legislative purpose; second, its principal or primary effect must be one that neither advances nor inhibits religion . . . ; finally, the statute must not foster 'an excessive government entanglement with religion.' "[35]

Ironically, then, even though the First Amendment's protection of the free exercise of religion supports the choice of private schooling by parents who want religious instruction for their children or wish to avoid conflicts between public schooling and their religious beliefs, such a basis for legislative changes designed to facilitate that choice would be considered to violate the First Amendment's prohibition against an establishment of religion under the *Lemon* v. *Kurtzman* standard. It is, however, not difficult to frame legislation designed to facilitate choice of religious schools in terms of secular purpose, so long as the aid is available to those choosing nonreligious schools. The more difficult standards to meet are the primary effect and entanglement criteria. Their application to attempts to assist the choice of private schooling is discussed in the following paragraph.

When the aid under challenge has been in the form of materials, equipment, or services to private school students (or their parents), it has not been fatal to the constitutionality of the legislation that most of the recipients of the aid attend religious schools. In the words of Professor Laurence Tribe, the critical distinction has been between "permissibly separable aid . . . [and] aid impermissibly integrated into the parochial school."[36] Thus, salary supplements for parochial school teachers or aid that goes directly to the parochial schools themselves is prohibited, but secular textbook loan programs for individual student use and the provision of bus transportation to and from school similar to that provided public school students is acceptable. Parochial schools cannot control the content of the services provided at public expense, nor those who supply the services, and contact between the providers of the services and the children and school officials must be minimal. Some services must be provided off the parochial school premises.

All such aid may be regarded as reducing the burden on those already choosing private schooling to the extent that it has any impact on parental choice. Monetary aid in the form of tax credits or tax deductions would also reduce the burden on those choosing private schools, but might also serve to enable some parents to send their children to private schools who might otherwise not be able to do so. In dealing with this type of aid under the *Lemon* v. *Kurtzman* standard, the Court appeared to find it constitutionally fatal for the aid to go primarily to parents who choose religious schools for their children.[37] The Court's recent decision in *Mueller* v. *Minnesota*,[38] however, suggests that so long as aid is also given to public school students, the fact that private religious school students benefit disproportionately is of no concern.

In the *Mueller* case, the Court upheld a Minnesota tax deduction plan that allows both public and nonprofit private school parents to deduct from their gross income for state income taxes up to $500 for each dependent in grades kindergarten through 6 and $700 for each dependent in grades 7 to 12, for expenses on tuition, secular textbooks (interpreted to include a wide variety of instructional materials), and transportation. Those challenging the law had submitted uncontroverted statistical evidence that private school parents benefited much more than public school parents because of the former's greater expenditures on deductible items (i.e., tuition) and that 96% of private school children attended religiously affiliated schools. The Court held that this was in no way determinative of the constitutionality of what they termed a "facially neutral law." Although the Court also noted that this deduction was only one among many tax deductions and cited the traditional rule of deference to legislative classifications in tax statutes in justifying its decision upholding the Minnesota law, the opinion does suggest that other possible options for increasing financial assistance to facilitate the choice of private schooling might be upheld, even if they are not tied to tax statutes.

It appears to be critical that both public and private school students are equally entitled to participate, even though the actual choices of schooling show an increase in the number or percentage of students attending religious schools. It was important to the Court's decision that the choices were made by individual parents, thus removing the possibility of conferring the " 'imprimatur of State approval' . . . on any particular religion, or on religion generally." Despite the fact that the opinion eschews consideration of factual information about who benefits most from the statutory scheme, the Court also noted that any "unequal effect . . . can fairly be regarded as a rough return for the benefits [providing an educational alternative, wholesome competition with public schools, relieving the tax burden incident to the operation of public schools] . . . provided to the state and all taxpayers by parents sending their children to parochial schools."

Parental Choice and Regulatory Policy

There are three ways in which private school regulation could interfere with parental choice. First, it could prohibit private schools from providing educational choices that parents want. Second, private schools may be required to provide instruction, use methods, or staff the school in ways that conflict with parental educational objectives, values, and pedagogical preferences. Third, regulation may increase the cost of private schooling, making it more burdensome or impossible to pay tuition to send one's child to private school.

Possible changes that might aid parental choice include decreasing the number of subjects that must be taught, eliminating any regulations that prescribe methods of instruction, class size, or teacher certification requirements for private schools, and substituting testing of private school students for all direct regulation. At least one form of additional regulation might aid parental choice—requiring disclosure of information to prospective patrons. Government-imposed admission requirements and disciplinary standards could aid the choice of some (by making private schools accept or retain students they would otherwise exclude), but deny parental choice to those who prefer different requirements or standards.

Such regulatory changes could be adopted by legislative or administrative action or, in some cases, could result from judicial decisions.

Legislative and Administrative Change   From the standpoint of constitutional law, no regulation of private schools is required (unless government assistance triggers application of the state action doctrine, discussed below). Thus, legislators and, within their delegated authority, administrators are free to eliminate some or all regulation of private schools if they are successfully persuaded to do so by arguments that particular regulations impede parental choice. Such arguments would draw upon the previously discussed constitutional values that are served by parental choice and demonstrate how specific regulations interfere with particular reasons for choice.

Judicial Change   Courts can invalidate administrative regulations on the ground that they exceed the scope of authority delegated to the administrator by the legislative body or that the delegation of power is unconstitutional.[39] The discussion that follows focuses on the extent to which regulations (whether statutory or administrative) may be held unconstitutional on the ground that they violate constitutionally protected rights related to the choice of private schools. There are two categories of regulation—direct regulation and regulation that is tied to the receipt of government aid. Constitutional law regarding direct regulation will be considered first.

Direct regulation: It is clear that some regulation of private schools is permitted. Even though the *Pierce* case did not involve regulation, but the prohibition of private schooling, the Court specifically stated:

> No question is raised concerning the power of the State reasonably to regulate all schools, to inspect, supervise and examine them, their teachers and pupils; to require that all children of proper age attend some school, that teachers shall be of good moral character and patriotic disposition, that certain studies plainly essential to good citizenship must be taught, and that nothing be taught which is manifestly inimical to the public welfare.[40]

The same court's earlier decision in *Meyer* v. *Nebraska*,[41] decided in 1923, struck down a state law prohibiting the teaching of German in private schools prior to the eighth grade, saying it was an unreasonable interference with parental liberty and the rights of teachers to teach. In *Runyon* v. *McCrary*[42] the Court upheld a prohibition against racial discrimination by private schools. *Pierce* and other Supreme Court decisions suggest that private schools may be required to teach reading, writing, and arithmetic and to provide instruction in our system of government, as well as to assure that students learn English.[43] It is also clear that direct regulation that is so extensive as to leave virtually no freedom to private schools is unconstitutional.[44]

There are two different constitutional bases for challenging direct regulation. The first is a claim that the regulation is "unreasonable" within the meaning of the *Pierce* and *Meyer* cases, a claim that would rest for doctrinal support not only on those decisions but on First Amendment protection of freedom of speech, and the implied protection of freedom of association, the marketplace of ideas, and freedom of conscience. The second basis is a claim that technically concedes the reasonableness of the regulation in general, but maintains that the regulation burdens the free exercise of religion protected by the First Amendment.

In *Wisconsin* v. *Yoder*,[45] decided in 1972, Amish parents claimed that the last two years of compulsory school attendance in a secondary school conflicted with tenets of the Amish religion and threatened their ability to inculcate their religious values in their children and to preserve the Amish way of life. The Court recognized that such a conflict could destroy or severely hamper the continued existence of the Amish community and held that the state's interests in requiring two additional years of schooling in a regular secondary school did not meet the following standard: "only those [state] interests of the highest order and those not otherwise served can overbalance legitimate claims to the free exercise of religion." The Court found evidence that the conventional education already received by the Amish children and the informal vocational education they would pursue in the Amish community satisfied the state interests in preparing children for citizenship and assuring a "self-reliant and self-sufficient" populace. The case can be interpreted to entitle private religious schools to exemption from any private school regulation that burdens the free exercise of their religion under the First Amendment, unless the state interest is sufficiently compelling to override the burden.

Runyon v. *McCrary*,[46] decided in 1976, is the most recent Supreme Court decision to provide some guidance about constitutional limits on direct regulation of private schools when challenged on the ground that such regulation unreasonably deprives parents of their liberty to direct the education of their children. In that case, the Court upheld—against such a challenge—a federal statue interpreted to prohibit racial discrimination by private schools. The opinion repeatedly states that the regulation in question does not prevent the schools from inculcating the values and standards desired by parents, thus reaffirming *Meyer*'s restrictions on the prohibition of instruction. It does not, however, indicate what courses may be required and what may not. The opinion also repeatedly distinguishes between practices and value inculcation. The Court did not find any conflict between the prohibition of the practice of racial discrimination and the ability of parents to inculcate the value of racial segregation. This suggests that the Court would uphold all noncurriculum regulation of private schools, such as teacher certification, pupil-teacher ratios, admissions requirements, standards of discipline, and even methods of instruction. As I have argued elsewhere,[47] however, prior precedents and the possibility that some noncurricular characteristics of schools can affect what is taught, caution against such a broad reading of the opinion. In addition, the state's interest in eliminating racial discrimination is itself supported by constitutional guarantees. Other regulations are unlikely to be so supported, and thus the state's interest in them may not be sufficiently compelling to override evidence that the regulations unreasonably prevent parents from providing their children with the kind of education they want for them.[48]

Regulations tied to receipt of government benefits: There is even greater uncertainty about constitutional law as it pertains to government regulation of private schools because they receive government benefits. At one extreme, constitutional law might lead to judicial imposition of regulation on private schools under the state action doctrine, depending on the nature and extent of the aid and the accompanying regulations. If "state action" is found, the private school would be required to adhere to some of the same constitutional constraints applicable to public schools.[49] In addition, certain regulations attached to aid that goes to religious private schools might lead to invalidation of the aid altogether because of the "entanglement" between church and state their administration would require. The following discussion focuses on whether some conditions on aid would be considered unconstitutional, so that the regulations, but not the aid, would be invalidated.

In *Bob Jones University* v. *United States*,[50] the university and a private elementary and secondary school that engaged in racially discriminatory policies based on religious beliefs claimed that an Internal Revenue Service (IRS) policy that denies tax-exempt status and charitable deductions for contributions to schools that discriminate on the basis of race unconstitutionally burdened their free exercise of religion. The Court rejected that claim because, despite the substantial impact that denial of tax benefits would have on their operation, it would "not prevent those schools from observing their religious tenets," the governmental interest was clearly compelling, and "no less restrictive means" were available to accomplish it.[51]

Most of the Court's opinion concerns the question whether the IRS had the authority to impose the regulation under existing legislation. It found that the statute required tax-exempt institutions to "serve a public purpose and not be contrary to established public policy." That public policy, it later said, must be "fundamental," a finding it easily made for public policy against racial discrimination. The opinion suggests that private schools might be required, by the IRS, and certainly by Congress, to abide by other fundamental public policies in order to be eligible for tax-exempt status.

In *Grove City College* v. *Bell*,[52] the Court rejected a First Amendment challenge to a requirement that if students enrolled at the college received federal education grants, the college must comply with a federal regulation designed to prohibit discrimination on the basis of sex. (The case is best known for its holding that the statute in question prohibited discrimination only in the assisted program, not in college operations as a whole.) The Court said: "Congress is free to attach reasonable and unambiguous conditions to federal financial assistance that educational institutions are not obligated to accept." Although the brief consideration that the Court gave to Grove City's claim suggests that it would find almost any regulation reasonable that could be avoided simply by not accepting the aid, this statement does leave open the question of what is reasonable regulation. As finally interpreted, the regulation in this case required only that the financial aid office not discriminate on the basis of sex and that the college sign an Assurance of Compliance to that effect. Had the regulation prohibited the teaching of certain subjects, for example, a stronger claim that the regulation violated First Amendment rights could be made. In addition, prohibition of sex discrimination is arguably close to prohibition of racial discrimination in constitutional significance, so that even though the Court did not engage in any balancing of the government and private interests, the importance of the government interest might have influenced the decision. Thus, it might be possible to challenge successfully other government conditions on the receipt of aid in the future. Arguments would have to be made on the basis of general principles of constitutional law informed by constitutional protections of parental choice. The development of these arguments is, however, beyond the scope of this paper.

CONCLUSION

Both the differential regulatory treatment of public and private schools and fiscal policies toward private schools undoubtedly permit a significant number of parents to choose the kind of private schooling they want for their children. If fiscal or regulatory change is to be justified on grounds of parental choice, evidence must exist that regulations hamper parental educational choices that ought to be permitted or that financial burdens make such choices difficult or impossible.

Even if evidence indicates that more fiscal support to the choice of private schooling is needed in order to serve parental liberty, adoption of fiscal options to that end without careful consideration of the regulatory consequences could lead to less rather than more parental choice. Although Supreme Court decisions suggest that greater government financial assistance to the choice of private schooling may be constitutionally permissible, they also raise questions about how much protection the Constitution affords against regulations imposed on private schools directly or as conditions on receipt of aid, even if they significantly interfere with parental choice. Adoption of increased fiscal support would undoubtedly be a result of political compromises that recognized other objectives for the mixed system—quality, social unity, or even pluralism. Thus additional regulations of private schooling probably would be attached to receipt of the aid. The greater attention to private schools might also lead to the adoption of additional direct regulation. There is also always the possibility that aid would trigger judicial imposition of constitutional constraints on private schools under the state action doctrine.

Particularly with regard to fiscal change, then, one might conclude that the present legal structure of the mixed system—with perhaps minor adjustments—maximizes parental choice more than would the major changes on which public discussion usually focuses.

NOTES

Due to space limitations and the primarily nonlegal audience to which this book is addressed, the notation is less extensive than is common in law review articles.

1. 268 U.S. 510 (1925). *Pierce* held unconstitutional, as an unreasonable interference with the liberty of parents and guardians to direct the upbringing of their children, an Oregon law that required every parent, guardian, or other person having control of a child between the

ages of eight and sixteen years to send that child to a public school. For a history of the case, see David B. Tyack, "The Perils of Pluralism: The Background of the Pierce Case," *Amer. Hist. Rev.* 74 (October 1968), pp. 74–98.

2. This appears to be behind the impetus for more rigorous regulation of private schools and is mainly directed at Fundamentalist Christian schools.

3. Except as otherwise indicated, statements about the law are supported by the author's independent legal research and by Stephen R. Goldstein, *Law and Public Education* (Indianapolis: Bobbs-Merrill Co., 1974), and Mark G. Yudof, David L. Kirp, Tyll van Geel, and Betsy Levin, *Kipp & Yudof's Educational Policy and the Law*, 2nd ed. (Berkeley: McCutchan, 1982).

4. Otto F. Kraushaar, *American Nonpublic Schools: Patterns of Diversity* (Baltimore: Johns Hopkins University Press, 1972), p. 206, Table 5. A few schools also have endowment income, p. 208.

5. John Elson, "State Regulation of Nonpublic Schools: The Legal Framework," in Donald A. Erickson, ed., *Public Controls for Nonpublic Schools* (Chicago: Univeristy of Chicago Press, 1969), pp. 123–125 (1969); Michael J. Stolee, "Nonpublic Schools: What Must They Teach?" *Schools & Society* 92 (October 1964), pp. 274, 276.

6. This estimate was calculated using data from the United States Census of Other Service Industries, 1977, which counted 2237 proprietary (taxable) elementary and secondary schools among the nonsectarian schools that it surveyed, and data from the National Center for Education Statistics for 1976–77, which gave 20,084 as the total number of all private elementary and secondary schools. (Since some nonprofits are not tax-exempt because they practice racial discrimination, the percentage of nonprofits may be slightly higher. In addition, if the NCES total does not include the same number of proprietary schools as the census figure, the percentage would vary accordingly.) U.S. Department of Commerce, Bureau of the Census, *1977 Census of Service Industries, Other Service Industries,* Washington, D.C., Parts 1–4. Geographic Area Studies (SC77-A-53); U.S. Department of Health, Education and Welfare/Education Division, National Center for Education Statistics, Bulletin NCES 80-B01, *Selected Public and Private Elementary and Secondary Education Statistics, School Years 1976–66 through 1978–79,* Washington, D.C., Table 1.

7. Department of Education, School Finance Project, Vol. 2, *Private Elementary and Secondary Education* (Washington, D.C., 1983), p. 21.

8. Minn. Stat §290.09(22) (1982). *Education Week* 3, 24, pp. 1, 18, reported, on March 7, 1984, that thirteen states were considering similar laws.

9. In 1970, the national average for state contributions to public school district budgets was 40%. In 1981–82, the average state contribution was 49%, with local government providing an average of 42.9% and the federal government 8.1%. In that year, however, the growth in local revenues was greater than in state revenues. Caldwell, "State Aid to Education Wanes, Reversing Decade-Long Trend," *Education Week* 1, 37 (July 28, 1982), pp. 1, 12.

10. See, for example, *School District of Abington Township* v. *Schempp,* 374 U.S. 203 (1963); *Tinker* v. *Des Moines Independent Community School District,* 393 U.S. 503 (1969); *Brown* v. *Board of Education,* 347 U.S. 483 (1954); and *Goss* V. *Lopez,* 419 U.S. 565 (1975), respectively.

11. See *Plyler* v. *Doe,* 457 U.S. 202 (1982), holding unconstitutional the exclusion of children of illegal aliens from free public education in Texas.

12. See Title VI of the Civil Rights Act of 1964, 42 U.S.C. §2000d (1970), authorizing termination of federal financial assistance to recipients that discriminate on the basis of race, color or national origin.

13. Indeed, Minnesota, with possibly the most generous assistance to the choice of private schooling, is among those states that regulate private schools the least. Tyll van Geel, *Authority to Control the School Program* (Lexington, Mass.: Lexington Books, 1976), Figure 8-1, p. 155. Atypically, while a state commission was studying sex education in Florida, tax-exempt (nonprofit) schools were not permitted to teach human reproduction. Florida Sec. 233.02 (repealed).

When government becomes virtually the sole source of private school funding, however, extensive regulation appears to become the norm. In New York State, for example, where tuition at schools for the handicapped is fully funded by government, such private schools are now extensively regulated. See Michael A. Rebell, "Educational Voucher Reform: Empirical Insights from the Experience of New York's Schools for the Handicapped," *The Urban Lawyer* 14, 3 (Summer 1982), pp. 453–461. Arguably, however, such regulation may be justified on the ground that these private schools are being used by public schools to fulfill the public schools' responsibility to the students, a claim that could not be made when aid is given in order to facilitate parental choice.

14. Charles J. O'Malley, *Survey of State Regulation of Private Schools* (Florida State Department of Education, unpublished, 1981). However, van Geel, op. cit., pp. 153–154, cites statutory authority in support of his statement that twenty-seven states require registration and approval of private schools.

15. Private schools must, of course, comply with generally applicable laws such as building, zoning, fire and health codes, and with laws governing charitable solicitations and preventing consumer fraud, which are inapplicable to public schools. Public schools, unlike private schools, are usually required to provide free transportation to their students.

16. An Indiana statute requires an advisory committee made up predominantly of teachers and parents to make recommendations regarding the selection of textbooks to the superindent, who in turn makes recommendations to the school board. Ind. Code Ann. §20-10.1-9-21 (Burns Supp. 1984).

17. These range from requiring that the private school teacher have a bachelor's degree to mandating compliance with all requirements imposed on public school teachers, for example, education courses and practice teaching. Two of the states apparently do not enforce their requirements. O'Malley, *Survey.*

18. In *National Labor Relations Board* v. *The Catholic Bishop of Chicago*, 440 U.S. 490 (1979), the Supreme Court held that the NLRB did not have statutory authority over religious schools as employers of lay teachers, even though they also teach secular subjects. According to Robert L. Smith, executive director of the Council for American Private Education, there is virtually no unionization of teachers within the secular area of nonprofit private education. However, in about a dozen major Catholic diocesan school systems, there are teachers' unions.

19. Title VI of the Civil Rights Act of 1964, 42 U.S.C. §2000d (1970); Title IX of the 1972 Education Amendments, 20 U.S.C. §§1681–86; §504 of the Rehabilitation Act of 1973, 29 U.S.C. §794, respectively. Although Title IX explicitly permits single-sex elementary and secondary schools, single-sex public schools may violate the equal protection clause of the Fourteenth Amendment to the Constitution.

20. This summary of the regulation of private and public school curricula is based on the previously cited Elson article and the van Geel book (an extensive treatment of curriculum regulation in both public and private schools) and on research done by Mary Curran while she was a student at the Yale Law School.

21. 268 U.S. 510 (1925).

22. For an argument that First Amendment principles require a voucher system, see Stephen Arons, "The Separation of School and State: *Pierce* Reconsidered," *Harv. Educ. Rev.* 46, 1 (1976), pp. 76–104. In *Norwood* v. *Harrison*, 413 U.S. 455 (1973), however, the Court stated that *Pierce* "said nothing of any supposed right of private and parochial schools to share with public schools in state largesse. . . ." No government funding of abortions is required, even though (like the right to send one's children to private school) the right to have an abortion is constitutionally protected from unreasonable government interference. *Harris* v. *McRae*, 448 U.S. 297 (1980).

23. The full survey of reasons for choice reported in part by Kutner-Sherman-Williams show that when asked for very important reasons rather than the most important reasons for the choice of private schooling, parents cited the following: staff (87.7%), discipline (87.1%), academic standards (84%), civil moral values (75.1%), courses (62.4%), religious instruction (61.5%), convenience (25%), mix of student backgrounds (22.3%), and desegregation (12.9%).

A third (33.7%) cited child's desire, but there is no indication of the child's reason, and 16.7% cited finances. Department of Education, School Finance Project, Vol. 2, *Private Elementary* p. 54.

24. The parents could value neutrality as to all secular and religious beliefs and therefore be in conflict with a public school that was not sufficiently neutral.

25. See, for example, *West Virginia State Bd. of Education* v. *Barnette*, 319 U.S. 624, 637 (1943); Nahmod, "Controversy in the Classroom: The High School Teacher and Freedom of Expression, *Geo. Wash. Law Rev* 39 (July 1971), pp. 1032, 1042–1050. William Van Alstyne, "The Constitutional Rights of Teachers and Professors," *Duke Law Journal* 5 (October 1970), pp. 841, 856–57.

26. 268 U.S. at 535.

27. 406 U.S. 205 (1972).

28. For a complete discussion of this argument in a different context, see Mary-Michelle Upson Hirschoff, "Parents and the Public School Curriculum: Is there a Right to Have One's Child Excused from Objectionable Instruction?" *S. Cal L. Rev. 50*, 5 (1977), pp. 871, 897–941. A right to be excused from specific public school instruction is not as effective in avoiding indoctrination as attendance at a private school would be.

29. Selective Draft Law Cases, 245 U.S. 366, 378 (1918); Laurence H. Tribe, *American Constitutional Law*, §15-12,14,16 (1978).

30. Freedom of association is implied from First Amendment protections of freedoms of speech, press, petition and assembly. See Tribe, op. cit., §12-23.

31. The full School Finance Project survey showed that 23.5% of those parents who had transferred their children from a private to a public school did so because of cost (p. 55). Among public school parents who had considered transferring their child to a private school, 57.1% cited cost as a reason for not doing so (p. 56). Department of Education, School Finance Project, Vol. 2., *Private Elementary.*

32. When asked to describe the financial burden placed on them by private school costs, respondents to the School Finance Project survey reported as follows: none (21.2%), light (19.8%), moderate (37.6%), and heavy (21.4%) (p. 58).

33. Parents of handicapped children who now send their children to private schools at public expense must receive the approval of the public school board before enrolling, thus the funding is not a true voucher or scholarship.

34. E. G. West was an early advocate of user fees for public schools. See "An Economic Analysis of the Law and Politics of Nonpublic School Aid" in E. G. West, ed., *Nonpublic School Aid* (Lexington, Mass.: Lexington Books, 1975), pp. 23–26. Erickson suggests, in his contribution to this volume, that charging fees can help assure parental interest and involvement in schooling.

Faced with increased costs, declining enrollments, and taxpayer reluctance to raise local property taxes, a few public school systems have begun to charge fees for extracurricular activities and nonrequired courses. "Looking Ahead, Town Uses Student Fees, Not Taxes, to Cover School Frills," *N.Y. Times,* August 31, 1981, p. A-10; "Extracurricular Activities Get 'Extra Expensive,' " *N.Y. Times,* Jan. 10, 1982, Sec. 13, p. 49.

35. 403 U.S. 602, 612–613 (1971). Under these criteria, aid to religiously affiliated colleges and universities has been upheld that would not be upheld if given to parochial elementary and secondary schools. The former are assumed not to have religious indoctrination as a substantial purpose. *Tilton* v. *Richardson*, 403 U.S. 672 (1971). Some states have more restrictive limits on government financial aid to private, particularly religious, schools than apply to the federal government.

36. Tribe, op. cit., §14-9.

37. See *Committee for Public Education* v. *Nyquist,* 413 U.S. 756, 768 (1973).

38. 77 L. Ed. 2d 721 (1983).

39. For example, see *Bangor Baptist Church* v. *State of Maine,* 576 F. Supp. 1299 (1983), no power delegated to prevent unapproved school from operating; and *Packer Collegiate Institute* v. *University of the State of New York,* 298 N.Y. 184, 81 N.E. 2d 80 (1948), unconstitutional delegation of power.

40. 268 U.S. 510, 534 (1925).

41. 262 U.S. 390 (1923).

42. 427 U.S. 160 (1976).

43. *Wisconsin* v. *Yoder*, 406 U.S. 205,212 (1972), suggesting that basic education may be required, including reading, writing and arithmetic; *West Virginia State Bd. of Educ.* v. *Barnette* (1943), stating that it was legitimate for public schools to require instruction in American history, governmental organization, and the guaranties of civil liberty.

44. *Farrington* v. *Tokushige*, 273 U.S. 284 (1927); *State* v. *Whisner*, 47 Ohio St. 2d 181, 351 N.E. 2d 750 (1976).

45. 406 U.S. 205 (1972).

46. 427 U.S. 160 (1976).

47. Mary-Michelle Upson Hirschoff, "Runyon v. McCrary and Regulation of Private Schools," *Ind. Law Journal* 52, 4 (1977), pp. 747–60.

48. In a number of recent court decisions upholding state regulations, the challengers did not present evidence to show how compliance with specific regulations, such as curriculum requirements or teacher certification, would conflict with religious tenets or interfere with the teaching of religious beliefs. Instead, they asserted that the state had no authority to regulate their (Fundamentalist) church schools—that they were subject only to the authority of God, not the state. The state courts uniformly rejected the suggestion that the state's interests could be adequately served by testing the students rather than regulating the schools. See, for example, *State* v. *Rivinius*, 328 N.W. 2d 220 (N.D., 1982); *State* v. *Faith Baptist Church*, 301 N.W. 2d 571 (Neb., 1981).

In *Kentucky State Board* v. *Rudasill*, 589 S.W. 2d 877 (Ky., 1979), however, the Kentucky Supreme Court struck down teacher certification and other regulations governing private schools and held that testing of students was adequate to serve the state's interest in educating children. It relied on a state constitutional provision protecting freedom of conscience.

49. A finding of state action basically means that the government has involved itself with the action of a private party to such a degree that those actions may be regarded as governmental in nature. Supreme Court decisions do not, however, offer clear rules as to when state action will be found, relying instead on "sifting facts and weighing circumstances." *Burton* v. *Wilmington Parking Authority*, 365 U.S. 715, 722 (1961). In *Norwood* v. *Harrison*, 413 U.S. 455 (1973), the Court held it unconstitutional for a state to loan textbooks to racially discriminatory private schools. Private schools receiving similar types of government assistance would seem to be prohibited from discriminating on the basis of race as well. What remains unclear is whether such assistance would also require private schools to abide by other constitutional requirements such as following due process procedures in suspending and expelling students.

50. 76 L. Ed. 2d 157 (1983).

51. The opinion thus leaves open the possibility that the direct regulation prohibiting racial discrimination by private schools upheld in *Runyon* v. *McCrary* might be successfully challenged on free exercise grounds by such schools.

52. *Law Week* 52 (Feb. 28, 1984), p. 4283.

2

Federal Policies for Private Schools

MARK A. KUTNER

JOEL D. SHERMAN

MARY F. WILLIAMS

The appropriate governmental relationship with private education has been the subject of controversy for many years. Some argue that parents should be able to choose private or public schools for their children without financial sacrifice and that the limitations on public financial support for private schools should be eliminated. Others maintain that financial support for private education is an improper use of public funds, that aiding private schools is unconstitutional, and that aid to private schools could have undesirable social consequences. Even among those who endorse some private school support, there are major disagreements over what the limits should be, what forms of aid are desirable, and what should be expected of private schools that receive public support.

The policy debate concerning federal aid for private schools has shifted during recent years. Where once it focused on including requirements for program services to private school students in federal education legislation, most of the current debate centers around new types of aid arrangements which would enhance educational choice. The impetus behind this refocused policy debate is threefold. First, the federal government is funding limited services to children attending private schools. The major federal elementary and secondary education programs include provisions requiring the equitable provision of services to eligible students attending private schools. As a result, there is now an established relationship between the federal government and private schools. Second, over the past few years there has been a significant increase in concern about the quality of American public education and the effect that a virtual public monopoly over education has on educational achievement. Third, the concern that without federal assistance private schools would disappear has subsided. As shown in the Erickson contribution to this volume, the latest available fig-

57

ures indicate that enrollments in private schools as a percentage of total elementary and secondary school enrollments have stabilized.

This paper traces the evolution of the federal role in the area of private elementary and secondary education finance and examines critical issues that relate to the possible expansion of federal funding for private education. In the first section, the provisions of past and current federal programs are described and a brief review of the experience with private school participation in federal programs is presented. The second section examines policy proposals to expand the scope of federal aid for private education in order to enhance parental choice over school alternatives for their children. Finally, the third section provides survey research findings sbout parental choice and the possible impact of one federal policy alternative, tuition tax credits, on educational choice.[1]

FEDERAL AID PROVISIONS FOR PRIVATE SCHOOL STUDENTS

The federal government currently provides financial support for children in private schools within the framework of its elementary and secondary education programs. Miller and Noell have estimated that direct federal support for private school students through program expenditures distributed by either a grant or a formula was $606 million in fiscal year 1981.[2] Of this total, $279 million came from the U.S. Department of Education (ED) and the remainder from either education programs in other Cabinet-level departments or federal programs with other primary concerns, even though education is involved (e.g., Head Start in the Department of Health and Human Services).

Two factors relating to ED programs need to be understood before examining the provisions requiring private school student participation. First, the Department of Education provides relatively little funding for public schools (about 7% in the 1982–83 school year) in comparison with the contribution of state and local governments.[3] In addition, the federal government does not provide states and localities with general aid for elementary and secondary education. Rather, federal aid is typically targeted on specific groups of students (e.g., economically and educationally disadvantaged, handicapped, or limited-English-proficient students) or for specific educational purposes (e.g., vocational education). It is within this program framework that private school students are entitled to receive an equitable share of federally funded services.

Second, although the federal government provides funds, it does not provide services. States and localities are active participants in shaping the federally funded services provided in schools. Because federal programs must be administered through the intergovernmental system, the specific services ultimately provided in schools depend upon state and local interpretations of federal requirements.[4] Thus, the extent of private school student participation in federally funded education programs depends upon the willingness of state and local education agencies to provide the services.

The following paragraphs summarize the provisions in federal education programs pertaining to private school student participation since federal involvement in elementary and secondary education was expanded in 1965.

The Elementary and Secondary Education Act of 1965

The Elementary and Secondary Education Act (ESEA) of 1965 redefined the federal role in education and was the first federal program to contain provisions requiring federally funded services for private school students. Prior to passage of this legislation, the issue of federal aid to religious schools had been an obstacle to federal aid for education. The breakthrough which enabled congressional approval of ESEA came in the form of an agreement between interest groups representing both public schools and religious organizations over a child-benefit approach to federal aid. As embodied in ESEA Title I, the federal compensatory education program (now Chapter 1 of the Education Consolidation and Improvement Act of 1981), this program "was to focus on educationally disadvantaged children in both public and private schools; it was not to be considered aid to the school itself."[5] The result of this agreement was that local school districts were required to make available to eligible private school students educational services paid for by the federal government.

The ESEA statute also included a Title II, School Library Resources, Textbooks and Other Instructional Materials, which authorized federal grants to states for the purchase of materials for both public and private schools. Under this title, if state law prohibited involvement in programs for private schools, the U.S. commissioner of education was responsible for providing these program benefits directly.

The Evolution of Federal Aid Provisions

Since 1965 the provisions relating to private school student participation in Title I have become increasingly explicit, and private school students have been included in most federal education programs. A chronological review of the federal education provisions concerning services for students in private schools follows.

Vocational Education Act of 1968
Part G of the 1968 Amendments to the Vocational Education Act required all states participating in cooperative vocational education programs to make provisions in their state plans for participation by students in nonprofit, private schools. States were also required to ensure that nonprofit private school students, whose educational needs were of the type for which vocational education programs were designed, receive services on an equita-

ble basis with public school students [Sec. 173 (a)(6)]. This represented the
first statement of federal intent related to private school student participation in vocational education.[6]

Education Amendments of 1974

These amendments included legislative provisions to ensure that eligible
students in private schools received services under Title I and required that
private school students receive services on an equitable basis under the new
Title IV, which consolidated ESEA Titles II and III.

Title I   Local education agencies were specifically required to "make provision for including special education services and arrangements (such as
dual enrollment, educational radio and television, and mobile educational
services and equipment) in which such children can participate" to the extent consistent with the number of eligible pupils enrolled in private elementary and secondary schools [Sec. 141A(a)].

The commissioner of education was also authorized to provide educational services to private school students if (1) "a local education agency
(LEA) is prohibited by law from providing . . . special programs for educationally deprived children enrolled in private elementary and secondary
schools" or (2) "if the Commissioner determines that a local education
agency has substantially failed to provide for the participation on an equitable basis of educationally deprived children enrolled in private elementary and secondary schools" [Sec. 141A(b)(1)(2)]. This provision is known
as the "Title I bypass."

***Title IV, Libraries, Learning Resources, Educational Innovation and
Support***   Title IV of the 1974 amendments required that students in nonprofit private schools, after "consultation with the appropriate private school
officials," receive an equitable share of "secular, neutral and nonideologi-
cal services, materials, and equipment including the repair, minor remod-
eling, or construction of public school facilities as may be necessary for
their provision" [Sec. 406(a)]. Provisions were also included to allow the
federal government to provide services directly if state law prohibits participation by private school students or if such students are not receiving
an equitable share of the services [Sec. 406(2)(d)(e)].

Title VII, Bilingual Education   Grant applications submitted by LEAs were
required to include provisions for the equitable distribution of services to
nonprofit private school students whose educational needs are consistent
with the services to be provided [Sec. 721(b)(2)(c)(ii)].

Education for All Handicapped Children Act of 1975

This act, also known as P.L. 94-142, requires states to ensure "a goal of
providing full educational opportunity to all handicapped children" by
providing "a free appropriate public education for all handicapped chil-

dren between the ages of three and eighteen" [Sec. 612(2)(A)]. In addition, states must submit a plan to the federal government that shall "provide satisfactory assurance, that to the extent consistent with the number and location of handicapped children in the state who are enrolled in private elementary and secondary schools, provision will be made for participation of such children in programs assisted or carried out under this part" [Sec. 613(A)(2)].

Vocational Education Act of 1976

Federal intent regarding private school participation in vocational education, as required by the 1968 amendments to the Vocational Education Act, had largely been ignored. As a result, the 1976 amendments to the Vocational Education Act included a number of provisions explicitly designed to increase participation of nonprofit private school students in federal vocational education activities. Specifically, (1) basic grant funds could support services in private, profit-making vocational schools [Sec. 120 (a)(1)(n)]; (2) both state and national vocational education advisory councils were required to include individuals who represented and were familiar with nonprofit private schools [Sec. 105(a)(9)]; and (3) LEAs could only receive funds set aside for disadvantaged students if provisions were made for nonprofit private school students to participate [Sec. 140 (b)(2)].

The 1978 Education Amendments

This legislation tightened and further clarified provisions relating to participation by private school students in all federal programs authorized by the Elementary and Secondary Education Act of 1965 and subsequent amendments. Essentially, provisions requiring private school student participation and establishing complaint procedures were authorized for all federal education programs. Local education agencies were required to provide private school students with equitable services under Title I, compensatory education; Title II, basic skills; Title III, special projects; Title IV, educational improvement resources and support; and Title IX, gifted and talented education.

Procedures allowing the federal government to provide direct services if state law prohibits assistance were authorized for Title VII, bilingual education, and simplified for both Title I and Title IV. Formal procedures for hearing complaints concerning the participation of private school students were included in Title I and Title V, state leadership. Title V also authorized state education agencies to provide information and technical assistance to private schools wishing to participate in Title I and Title IV.

The Education Consolidation and Improvement Act of 1981

The objective of this legislation is to provide federal support to state and local education agencies, "but to do so in a manner which will eliminate burdensome, unnecessary, and unproductive paperwork and free the schools of unnecessary federal supervision, direction, and control" (Sec. 552). Several provisions relate to the participation of private school students. Although Chapter 1 modified several requirements of Title I, the provisions relating to private school student participation (including equitable provision of services and direct provision of services under certain conditions) remain unchanged (Sec. 557).

Chapter 2 consolidates twenty-nine of the smaller categorical programs into a block grant for educational improvement. Included were many of the programs that contained provisions for participation by private school students—ESEA Titles II, III, IV, V, and IX. This legislation did not include ESEA Title VII, bilingual education, which remains a separate program. The provisions relating to private school student participation are very similar to those in the antecedent programs. For example, state education agencies (SEAs) and local education agencies (LEAs) must ensure that private school students receive equitable services. Also, SEAs must provide services and materials to private school students even if the LEA in which the private school is located does not apply for Chapter 2 funds.

As with Chapter 1, Chapter 2 also contains "bypass" provisions authorizing the federal government to provide services for private school students if state law prohibits aid to private schools or if the secretary of education determines that either an SEA or LEA has failed or is unwilling to provide equitable services (Sec. 586).

Private School Student Participation in Federal Programs

As the previous sections indicate, the federal government has paid increasing attention to providing services to eligible students in private schools. Yet, despite these federal provisions, which require services for private school students, there is relatively little information about the operation and effects of federal aid programs for students in private schools. This is due largely to methodological problems related to defining the universe of private schools, and difficulties in obtaining a representative sample and securing access to all types of private schools.

Recent studies have only begun to examine the extent to which private school students participate in federal programs, and a great deal remains to be learned about structural arrangements that affect the equitable distribution of program benefits among public and private school students. In two studies which separately examined Title I and Title IV (programs which have since been consolidated by ECIA) some information pertaining to services for private school students was collected. A study examining vocational education services for private school students has also been completed. The most relevant findings from these three studies are now presented.

Title I
The Department of Education reports that during the 1979–80 school year private schools served 192,994 students in Title I programs, representing about 3.8% of total private enrollments. A study of Title I district prac-

tices reported that during the 1979–80 school year about 25% of the Title I LEAs provided services for students in private schools—a slight decline over a four-year period. The report states:

> From a national perspective, the overall participation level of nonpublic school students over the last four years has at best been at a steady state, although several indicators point to a relative marginal decline in nonpublic students' access to Title I services. For example, when reviewing changes in Title I non-public and public enrollment patterns between 1976 and 1980, the nonpublic participation rate in Title I increased by less than 6%, while the public partic-ipation rate in Title I increased by almost 18% during this time. Also the pro-portion of Title I districts serving private students residing in Title I attendance areas declined from 59% in 1978 to 56% in 1981.[7]

If there is a decline in the participation rate, it may well reflect a basic change in the composition of the private school universe. That is, a net decrease in participation might have been anticipated, with the schools that have been most active in Title I, the Catholic schools, enrolling a decreas-ing percentage of all private school students, and with the schools that have participated least in federal programs, the Christian-Fundamentalist schools, enrolling an increasing percentage.

Within-district comparisons of Title I services between public and pri-vate schools revealed that for private school students receiving Title I ser-vices: (1) classes were shorter; (2) classes were smaller; (3) the instructor-pupil ratio was lower; (4) instructors had the same number of years of ex-perience as those in public schools; and (5) Title I might be better coordi-nated with the regular classes.

Title IV

A 1980 study of ESEA Title IV (since consolidated under ECIA Chapter 2), showed that although the majority of private schools received services under Title IV-B, only between one-quarter and one-third of Title IV-C in-novative projects provided services to students in private schools.[8] The study also found that few of the sample private school principals and superinten-dents were consulted by public school officials in the planning and design of IV-C programs.

A number of reasons for nonparticipation of private schools in Title IV-C were identified. These included: (1) failure by SEAs to monitor LEA assurances that private schools were being equitably treated; (2) failure by SEAs and LEAs to provide technical assistance to private schools; (3) the competitive nature of IV-C; and (4) the unwillingness of private schools to actively pursue their fair share of funds. In addition, private school offi-cials were found to be generally uninformed about Title IV-C projects.

Vocational Education

Private schools generally do not offer vocational education programs. Ac-cording to a survey undertaken by NCES during the 1977–78 school year, less than 3% of the private schools offered their own vocational education programs. About 65% of the private schools that offered vocational education services were religiously affiliated.[9]

FEDERAL AID PROPOSALS FOR PRIVATE SCHOOL FAMILIES

As indicated in the previous section, federal education legislation currently includes requirements for the equitable participation of private school students. As a result, the debate concerning federal policies for private school students has shifted and there has been an increasing interest in establishing federal policies that would promote parental choice in elementary and secondary education. In this section three possible mechanisms for providing financial assistance to private school families will be reviewed: tuition tax credits, education vouchers, and compensatory education grants.

Tuition Tax Credits

In recent years, tuition tax credit proposals have been promoted at both the federal and state levels as a means of expanding school choice for parents and providing tax equity for private school parents. At the federal level, several tuition tax credit plans have been introduced in Congress over the last fifteen years. These proposals have differed on several dimensions, including the maximum credit amount, the portion of private school costs covered by the credit, and whether refundability provisions are included for families whose incomes are too low for them to pay income tax and thus benefit from a credit.

Tuition tax credit proposals have usually contained civil rights guarantees based on school eligibility requirements but they have differed in the ways those requirements would be enforced. Some proposals have applied to elementary through higher education, while others have excluded higher education. This chapter focuses only on the elementary and secondary levels; for more on the federal financing of higher education, see the relevant sections of Levy's two chapters in this volume.

Advocates argue that a system of tax credits would have advantages for the educational system. They are seen as a means of improving educational quality, promoting diversity, and increasing efficiency by encouraging competition among public and private schools. Specifically, tuition tax credits are viewed as a mechanism for promoting educational choice by reducing or ending the "double burden" of public school taxes and private school tuition.

Opponents of tuition tax credits for elementary and secondary education argue that such a policy would undermine public education and violate the constitutional principle of separation of church and state. They maintain that tax credits would flow disproportionately to higher-income groups and that without refundability provisions, low-income families would derive little benefit because they pay little or no income taxes. It is further argued that tax credits could result in increased racial and social class stratification, produce an uneven distribution of benefits across the country, and lead to increased tuition costs, which would mean that private schools could reap the benefits of aid intended for families.

Although there is relatively little experience with tax credits, Minnesota has provided tax deductions for educational expenses since 1955. Under the current Minnesota law, parents of both public and private school students are provided with a deduction against their state income tax of up to $500 for students in grades kindergarten to 6 and $700 for students in grades 7 to 12. Expenditures that qualify for the deduction include tuition, instructional materials, and transportation.

Starting in 1971, a $100 tuition tax credit was permitted. However, the credit was declared unconstitutional by the courts in 1974. During this period no noticeable shift emerged in public and private enrollment trends. Since 1974, the current deduction has, in effect, permitted tax savings of up to $85–$100 per pupil for families with taxable incomes of over $20,000. The state estimates that over half the students benefiting from this provision are attending public schools.

At the federal level, between 1967 and 1977, six tuition tax credit proposals passed the Senate, only to be omitted during the House-Senate conference committees at the insistence of the House. The most serious attempts to enact tuition tax credit legislation occurred in 1978, when a Senate bill providing tax credits for up to 50% of higher-education expenses, up to a maximum of $500 and with no refundability provisions, passed the Senate by a margin of 65 to 27. A House measure providing tax credits for up to 25% of educational expenses, with a maximum credit of $100 at the elementary and secondary levels, and a maximum credit of up to $300 at the higher-education level, also with no refundability provision, passed the House by a vote of 237 to 158. The two chambers, however, could not agree on the legislation and instead decided to support the Carter administration's Middle Income Student Assistance Act, which increased federal postsecondary education assistance to middle-class families.

Reagan administration tuition tax credit proposals have not passed either the Senate or the House of Representatives. In 1982, the Senate Finance Committee approved a phased-in tuition tax credit plan for up to 50% of tuition, with a maximum level of $100 in the first year and $300 in the third year. Families with incomes below $40,000 would have been eligible for the full credit, and benefits would gradually be reduced to zero at income levels above $50,000. A refundability provision was also included.

Legislation was sent to the Congress by the administration in February 1983 that was similar to the 1982 bill, except that it did not provide refundability and the income cap was set at $60,000. As with the earlier legislation, detailed measures were included to prevent claims for tuition paid at racially discriminatory schools. Although approved again by the Senate

Finance Committee, with a $50,000 income cap and refundability provisions, the full Senate defeated the measure.

Vouchers

Vouchers for educational expenditures are another policy instrument that has been proposed to enhance educational choice. While vouchers have yet to be used on a permanent basis as a policy instrument in elementary and secondary education, direct financial transfers from the federal government to individuals have been used extensively in other domestic policy areas (e.g., Pell Grants in higher education).

The voucher approach to education finance is basically intended to create a competitive market for schooling. It first received serious consideration during the late 1960s, and many of the arguments for vouchers are associated with the work of economist Milton Friedman, whose "pure voucher" scheme called for a government grant for each child in elementary and secondary school equal to the average of public school costs.[10] Under this specific proposal, the government's role would be limited to issuing vouchers to parents and establishing a minimum level of education that a school would have to provide in order to participate. However, Friedman's "unregulated model" would permit schools to charge whatever tuition the demand for schooling would support.

Voucher proposals incorporate such considerations as family financial need and limitation of tuition charges in excess of the voucher. Differences in voucher plans generally fall under three broad areas: finance, regulation, and the provision of information to consumers.[11]

Proponents of vouchers generally argue that government assistance for all types of education under a voucher system would encourage greater efficiency, diversity, and choice of schooling. Since schools would compete for students and receive income only to the extent that they succeeded in the competition for students, public—as well as private—schools would have to be responsive to consumer preferences and needs. Opponents of vouchers center their concerns around issues of separation of church and state, financial costs, and economic and racial segregation.[12] They contend that vouchers would undermine support for public schools, make the public schools a "dumping ground" for the poor, and increase racial and class segregation in society. They further argue that vouchers would create excessive government entanglement with religion and thus could not pass judicial scrutiny.

The experience to date with vouchers in the United States has been quite limited. In some sparsely populated New England communities, small jurisdictions have chosen to provide school-age children with entitlements to schooling rather than attempt to operate their own public schools. While some districts enter into contractual arrangements with neighboring schools to provide elementary or secondary education, other districts provide parents with the option of free schooling in a nearby town or a voucher that can be applied toward the cost of education at any public or nonsectarian private school, in state or out.

During the early 1970s, efforts to stimulate voucher experiments were made by the Office of Educational Opportunity (OEO) and the National Institute of Education (NIE). One voucher demonstration project began operation during the 1972–73 school year and lasted for five years. Although private school participation was planned in the "Alum Rock" demonstration, it was precluded at the outset by state law and never materialized even after state enabling legislation was passed. Parental choice of educational programs was therefore limited to those offered by the minischools in the participating public schools.

Nevertheless, evaluations of the Alum Rock experiment focused on a number of areas that seem particularly important in thinking about the consequences of a broader voucher system involving both public and private schools. At the height of the demonstration, over 20% of the participating students had enrolled in nonneighborhood schools. However, a battery of achievement tests administered over the course of the demonstration did not find any significant differences in performance between schools that extended a greater degree of choice to parents than those that did not provide greater choice.

The studies also found that parents varied widely in their awareness of schooling options and in the accuracy of their information about the rules governing choice, but that the differences tended to be reduced as parents gained more experience with the program. In addition, more-educated parents tended to have more sources of information and to rely more heavily on printed information from the school than those with less education.[13] This latter finding suggests that for a voucher system to provide effective options to less-educated and disadvantaged families, the schools would have to tailor their communications to fit this particular subpopulation.

Full education vouchers, however, are typically not seen as an appropriate financial instrument for the federal government. Because states and localities provide over 90% of the revenues for public elementary and secondary education, such vouchers are more appropriate policy instruments at the state level. However, limited voucher proposals, as described in the next section, are intended to provide low-income families with children enrolled in public schools and receiving federal compensatory education services, with a measure of influence over their children's education. Voucher proposals are designed to expand the range of public and private school options that parents of disadvantaged children can choose and therefore increase these parents' control over their children's education by allowing them to choose the school which best provides the education they desire.

Compensatory Education Grants

One of the major purposes of federal programs in elementary and secondary education has been the expansion of education opportunities for children with special educational needs. ECIA Chapter 1, for example, currently provides about $3 billion annually to school districts to provide supplementary educational services for educationally disadvantaged children from low-income families. An alternative approach to serving these children calls for federal scholarships or grants to low-income families to help them defray the costs of private education.

One proposal intended to expand parental choice of education for low-income families involves the conversion of Chapter 1, the federal compensatory education program, into a "minivoucher." In March 1983, President Reagan sent a plan to Congress which included an optional compensatory education voucher. Under this plan, states and local districts could give low-income parents vouchers to spend on their children's education at public schools outside their home district or at private schools. Districts opting for vouchers would have to continue providing compensatory education services for voucher recipients who remain in the districts' schools and for any Chapter 1 students who do not receive vouchers.

Another proposal is modeled on the Pell Grants (formerly BEOG) in higher education and has often been characterized as a "Baby-BEOG." Under the proposal introduced in Congress by Senator Moynihan (D.-N.Y.) in 1980, families sending their children to schools qualifying as nonprofit corporations under Section 501(c)(3) of the IRS code would be eligible to receive financial assistance. Grant allowances to families would be based on two major factors: family financial need and the costs of private schooling; families with less income would generally receive larger grant allowances.

Proponents of this type of plan say that federal need-based scholarships would increase the economic power of poor families in choosing public and private schools and would provide help to those who most need additional options in education—families of poor children who are not well served by the public schools. The Baby-BEOG plan would allow a child's family to exercise leverage on the public schools by giving parents the financial resources to send their children to private schools.

TUITION TAX CREDITS AND PARENTAL CHOICE

Of the new alternatives for providing federal aid to private schools discussed in the previous section, tuition tax credits have received the greatest attention in recent years. Vouchers are not considered an appropriate federal policy instrument since states and localities provide over 90% of the support for elementary and secondary education. Although Compensatory Education Grants are a more suitable federal policy option, the political support necessary for passage of a program of this type does not appear to be forthcoming.

Despite the interest in tuition tax credits, little is known about the possible consequences of implementing them. The Department of Education's School Finance Project generated additional information through an opinion survey on parental choice of schools and tuition tax credits. Parents in a national random sample of approximately 1200 households with school-age children were interviewed by telephone for fifteen minutes in June and July 1982. This section summarizes the most important results from the survey.[14]

The first portion of the survey dealt with the choice of school a child was currently attending. Parents were asked what kind of school that was and why it had been chosen. These questions were asked both because of interest in parental decision making in selecting a school and because of the implications for alternative federal policies for aid to private schools.

Current Choice

For the vast majority of public school children in the survey, there was little parental consideration of alternative schools. In general, parents are far more likely to think about schools when deciding where to live than when enrolling a child in a particular school. For example, the parents of approximately half the children said the public schools their children would attend influenced their choice of a place to live, and for 18% it was the most important factor in their choice of residence. However, once a choice of residence had been made, attending public school was typically a standing decision that the household did not question. For 80% of public school children, no school other than the one that the child was currently attending was considered. This pattern was evident in virtually all the demographic categories examined, and these findings are generally consistent with the limited evidence on this topic.[15]

Public and private school parents demonstrated systematic differences in their characteristics. Respondents with a child in private school tended to be better educated, to have higher family incomes, to be Catholic, to have attended private schools themselves, and to live in large or medium-size cities. The survey revealed that public school parents were more likely to live in nonmetropolitan settings and to have attended only public schools themselves.

Factors Associated with School Choice

All respondents were asked to specify the most important factor influencing the choice of school for their child. Three types of factors were mentioned most frequently and accounted for two-thirds of the responses: assignment of the child to a particular school (25%), transportation or convenience (22%), and academic considerations (20%). No other specific factor was mentioned by more than 10% of the parents.

The relative importance of the specific factors contributing to school choice varied a great deal between public and private school parents. The private school parents tended to mention three reasons: discipline (12%), values or religious instruction (30%), and academic quality (42%). Public school parents also emphasized three factors:—academic quality (17%), transportation (24%), and the fact that the student was assigned to a particular school (28%). However, public school parents who had considered other schools and private school parents did not differ as much. For both these groups the most frequently mentioned reason concerned academics. The areas of difference were factors of finances (mentioned by public school parents) and values/religion (mentioned by private school parents).

The survey also collected information on reasons that parents choose a specific type of private school. Parents chose different types of private schools for quite different reasons. Religious schools, in particular, were chosen because of their religious orientation (with less concern for academics), while nonreligious schools were selected primarily because of their academic characteristics. Catholic schools, however, were chosen for both reasons. Similar patterns are explored by Erickson in the next chapter.

Factors Associated with School Transfers

Some children in the sample had attended both private and public schools, and additional insights into the reasons for school choice were gained by looking at these children. Nearly one-half of private school students had once attended public schools, while 17% of public school students had once attended private schools. The moves from private to public schools were primarily attributable to two major factors: cost and availability. The cost of private schooling was the reason most often mentioned (24%) as the reason for the switch to public school.

Two other factors related to availability were also prominent: change of residence (21%) or the private school did not have higher grades (9%). Availability of public alternatives (17%) was also important in accounting for switches from private to public schools in cases where children were enrolled in private kindergartens because there was not a public kindergarten or where the child started in private school because she/he was too young to enter kindergarten or first grade in the public school that year. For these children, public schooling was not available initially, but when it became an option, the parents transferred the child to the public school.

Very different kinds of reasons were mentioned for switching from public to private schools. Academics were cited most frequently (27%), with discipline (25%), religious instruction or value orientation (25%), and teachers (12%) as other frequently mentioned factors. In general, parents appeared to transfer a child from a public to a private school because of dissatisfaction with the public school, while a move from private to public schools resulted not from dissatisfaction but from financial or logistical reasons. This may reflect the greater dissatisfaction with the current school on the part of public school parents (14.3% vs. 3.4% for private school parents).

The cost of a private school education had quite different consequences for public and private school parents. While cost was a major factor inhibiting the selection of a private school for public school parents, particularly less affluent ones, it was not a major factor influencing the choice of private school parents. Furthermore, many private school parents did not perceive what they were paying in private school costs to be a particular burden. The prominence of the cost factor suggests that public policies which reduce the costs of private schools might have a considerable impact on parental decision making concerning schools. Financial assistance to parents might decrease the proportion of parents who do not consider alternatives to neighborhood public schools and increase the proportion opting for private schools.

The factors identified in the survey as being associated with school choice and the transfer from one school to another were also consistent with the results of previous research. For example, parents tend to choose private schools because they are dissatisfied with or cannot find what they want in the public schools. However, neither public nor private school parents represented undifferentiated groups in terms of the nature of the choice process; as mentioned, public school parents who had considered options other than the present school more closely resembled private school parents in the factors they cited.

PARENTAL INTEREST IN TUITION TAX CREDITS

In the second part of the survey, parents were asked whether they would consider changing their child's school placement if there were a federal tuition tax credit at three different levels: $250, $500, and for all tuition costs. The questions on tuition tax credits asked respondents whether they would be "very likely," "somewhat likely," "somewhat unlikely," or "very unlikely" to change their child's school if a tax credit were available. Most of the following discussion is based on parents of public school children who said they would be "very likely" or "somewhat likely" to transfer their child to a private school if a $250 credit were available. Parents who said they would be "very likely" or "somewhat likely" to switch schools were asked what type of school (e.g., Catholic, other religiously affiliated, or independent) they would transfer their child to, and the most important factors they would consider in choosing the new school. First, the responses to the survey items are presented and then the reasons why these may overestimate the enrollment changes that would occur under a tuition tax credit are discussed.

Approximately 55% of survey respondents had heard of a tuition tax credit before, although private school parents were far more likely to be aware of the credit than public school parents. This pattern held across all racial, religious, educational, and income groups, and also across regions and place of residence. Among public school parents, whites, those living in the suburbs, and those with higher incomes and more education were more likely to have heard of tuition tax credits. There was, however, no significant relationship between prior knowledge of a tuition tax credit and region or religion. Awareness of tuition tax credits was also higher among public school parents who had greater contact with or knowledge about private schools or who had given some thought to the choice of their child's current school.

Parents were asked how likely they would be to change their child's school under a tax credit. Over half the parents (55%) indicated they probably would not switch their child out of public schools even if all tuition costs were covered. With a tuition tax credit of $250, 23.5% of the public school parents said they would be "very likely" or "somewhat likely" to transfer their child to private schools. At $500, 32% indicated they would move their children. Private school parents were less inclined, especially at higher credit levels, to change their choice of school in response to a credit—19% at $250, 22% at $500, and 28% with a credit covering full tuition. Perhaps this is the result of the greater satisfaction with their current school expressed by private school parents.

Public school parents who said they were inclined to switch to private schools under a $250 tax credit were disproportionately black or Hispanic, had less education and lower incomes, and were residents of large or medium-size cities (Table 2.1). These with Catholic or other religious affiliations were slightly more prone to express an inclination to switch to private schools than respondents who were Protestant or had no religious affiliation. There were no differences in the preferences about a $250 tax credit by region or between parents who had attended public or private schools themselves as children.

Table 2.1 shows that public school parents without prior knowledge of a tuition tax credit were more inclined to say they would switch to a private school under a $250 credit than those who had heard of a tax credit before—23.5% of the total public school sample were likely to switch, in contrast to 16.8% of public school parents who had heard of tuition tax credits. This suggests that, for at least a portion of the sample, the inclination to switch schools as a result of a tax credit may not have been based on a great deal of information.

Analysis of responses of a more informed subsample of public school parents, that is, those who had heard of a tuition tax credit, produced a decline in the proportion of possible transfers among all categories of parents. However, the pattern for the "informed" group resembled that found for the entire sample—blacks were more interested in switching than whites, as were parents with less education and lower incomes. There were no significant differences in the proclivity to transfer to private schools related to religion, region, or place of residence for the more informed parents.

Responses to higher levels of a tuition tax credit—$500 and all tuition costs—generally displayed similar patterns to those at $250. Groups with the highest propensity to switch at $250 were also those most inclined to switch at higher credit levels. However, the differences among groups in the propensity to switch were less pronounced at higher credit levels and in some cases were not statistically significant. Black, Hispanic, less-educated,

Table 2.1 Public School Parents Responding They Were "Very Likely" or "Somewhat Likely" to Switch Children to Private Schools with a Tax Credit of $250

	Total Public School Sample	Public School Parents Who Have Heard of a Tuition Tax Credit
All Respondents	23.5% (N = 1687)	16.8% (N = 852)
Race		
White	18.8% (N = 1272)	15.8% (N = 722)
Black	38.1 (N = 251)	22.7 (N = 93)
Hispanic	43.6 (N = 125)	a
Other	14.9 (N = 34)	a
Religion		
Protestant	21.1% (N = 980)	16.1% (N = 507)
Catholic	27.2 (N = 422)	16.8 (N = 212)
Other	27.4 (N = 174)	18.0 (N = 73)
None	23.6 (N = 89)	15.8 (N = 51)
Parent's Education		
Non–High School Graduate	31.7% (N = 308)	26.8% (N = 69)
High School Graduate	23.1 (N = 764)	17.9 (N = 329)
Some College	24.5 (N = 312)	18.5 (N = 207)
College Graduate	16.8 (N = 169)	13.4 (N = 138)
Postgraduate	11.3 (N = 119)	5.2 (N = 96)
Family Income		
Under $7,500	32.6% (N = 161)	27.1% (N = 42)
$7,500–$14,999	33.2 (N = 288)	29.2 (N = 97)
$15,000–$24,999	29.1 (N = 419)	22.0 (N = 202)
$25,000–$49,999	16.9 (N = 614)	13.4 (N = 397)
$50,000 and Over	10.6 (N = 109)	8.0 (N = 75)
Region		
Northeast	21.9% (N = 195)	14.2% (N = 106)
North Central	21.7 (N = 487)	17.1 (N = 254)
South	24.4 (N = 710)	17.3 (N = 359)
West	25.2 (N = 284)	17.6 (N = 128)
Place of Residence		
Large City	34.7% (N = 353)	20.3% (N = 113)
Suburb	18.8 (N = 256)	15.7 (N = 183)
Medium City	28.3 (N = 337)	17.0 (N = 166)
Small City or Town	19.4 (N = 504)	18.3 (N = 272)
Rural	14.0 (N = 232)	11.5 (N = 118)

[a] Fewer than thirty cases.

and lower-income parents constituted a smaller proportion of those who would switch at credit levels above $250. For whites and higher-status groups, a higher percentage of the switches would occur at credit levels above $250.

Parents satisfied with the current public school indicated that they were less likely to switch their child to a private school under a $250 tax credit than dissatisfied parents. Greater experience with private schools among public school parents was associated with an inclination to switch to private schools in response to a tuition tax credit. Parents who had given some thought to school alternatives in choosing their current public school were more than twice as likely (41% vs. 19%) to say they might switch to a private school with a tuition tax credit than those who had not. However, consideration of schools as a factor in choosing a place to live was not related to responses to a tuition tax credit.

Public school parents who had mentioned financial factors as an element in their current choice were far more likely (36% vs. 15%) to say they would be inclined to switch under a tax credit than those for whom cost was not a factor. Furthermore, public school parents whose prior decisions about an actual or possible school transfer had been influenced by financial considerations were more inclined to say they would take advantage of a tuition tax credit than others. These patterns are generally consistent with the findings for current choice of school. Financial costs are an important negative factor preventing some parents from sending their children to a private school.

Each type of private school could gain additional students under a $250 tax credit. A much higher proportion of the potential new private school students might be enrolled in non-Catholic private schools than is presently the case. This pattern was particularly evident for credit levels above $250 and for independent schools. It would appear that financial considerations have been a particular deterrent to the choice of an independent school, which is consistent with Erickson's finding that tuition is highest in such schools.

Reasons given for selecting a private school under a tax credit were quite similar to those given by current private school parents. Academic standards, policies, and courses were the reasons most frequently given for selecting a private school at all levels of tuition tax credits, and the quality of instructional staff was generally the second-most-important factor. Religion and discipline were also mentioned frequently as factors that would influence the new school choice.

A majority of the parents in the survey indicated they would be unlikely to change their child's school placement at any level of a tuition tax credit. Approximately half these parents identified two reasons for not changing schools: satisfaction with the current school or availability of programs or facilities in the present school they could not obtain elsewhere. Public and private school parents differed in the reasons given for not switching. Private school parents were more likely to cite satisfaction with their child's current placement. In particular, parents with children in church-related schools mentioned the availability of religious instruction. Public school parents were more apt to mention logistical reasons—transportation, no private school available, or no income tax liability—or the child's preference for the current school. Public school parents also gave philosophical reasons for not changing their current school choice—a belief in the public schools or opposition to a tuition tax credit.

The inclinations of survey respondents to take advantage of a tuition tax credit were affected by a variety of factors. These included the level of the credit, household characteristics, and attitudes related to school choice. Furthermore, some groups now underrepresented in private schools—low-income and minority groups—expressed the greatest interest in using tuition tax credits, although that tendency was not quite as strong at credit levels above $250 as it was at $250.

The attitudinal factors associated with the likelihood of transferring schools and with the selection of a new school under a tax credit have much in common with those for the choice of current schools. This is particularly true regarding the role of cost considerations and reasons given for choosing the private school to which a child would be transferred under a credit.

The level of interest in tax credits among survey respondents was quite similar to results obtained from other polls.[16] However, the household survey indicates much greater interest in switching schools in response to a credit than previous cross-sectional studies. Estimates by Gemello and Osman of income elasticity applied to the household survey data would produce an estimate of very few transfers (.01%) from public schools under a $250 tuition tax credit with no percentage limit.[17] Noell and Myers estimated that less than 2% of public school parents would switch in response to a $250 tax credit covering 50% of tuition.[18]

IMPLICATIONS OF THE SURVEY RESULTS

For several reasons, preferences about tuition tax credits expressed in the survey probably overestimate the extent to which children would actually change schools if a tax credit were implemented. The process of transferring a child from a public to a private school in response to a tuition tax credit would involve four steps: (1) interest in taking advantage of the credit; (2) application to one or more private schools; (3) admission to at least one private school; and (4) enrollment in a private school. The reasons why parents may drop out between steps 1 and 4 can be related to the demand for and supply of private schools under a tuition tax credit. (Murnane discusses some demand and supply considerations in his first chapter in this book.)

Demand for Private Schools Under a Tax Credit

Parents who had not heard of a credit before expressed an interest in moving their child to a different school far more frequently than those who had heard of a credit. This was true for both public and private school parents. For those who had not heard of a tuition tax credit before, once they learned more about the workings of such a tax credit, their enthusiasm might dim and their responses to a credit might resemble more closely those of parents who had previously heard of a tuition tax credit.

If all parents were to respond in the same way as those who had heard of a tuition tax credit before, the proportion of potential new private school applicants would decline from 23.5% to 16.8%. However, that may overstate the impact of wider knowledge. Those who had not heard of a tuition tax credit were disproportionately less affluent and nonwhite; and among those who had heard of credits before, such parents tended to be more responsive to a credit. Taking race or income into account yields estimates of the pool of potential new private school applicants of approximately 18–19% of public school students.

Another reason that the survey may overstate the demand for private schools under a credit is the wording of the questions about tuition tax credits. Most tuition tax credit proposals contain not only a dollar limit but also a percentage ceiling on the proportion of tution costs covered. This limits the benefit of the credit to families sending their children to low-tuition schools. Under a credit of the same dollar amount with such a percentage limitation, fewer families might transfer their children than under a credit of the same dollar limit without a percentage limit. For the sake of clarity and simplicity, however, only a dollar maximum was posed in the tuition tax credit questions in the survey. From the survey there is no nonarbitrary way of determining the extent to which the proportion of parents interested in taking advantage of a credit would be reduced by limiting the percentage of eligible tuition costs.

In addition, the responses of public school parents may be based on unrealistic assumptions about private schools, particularly about their costs. Fully one-third of the public school parents could not give even a rough estimate of tuition costs for any of the three types of private schools in their community. Once a credit was in operation, parents might decide that an acceptable private school was not convenient or affordable, even with the tuition tax credit.

Supply of Private School Places Under a Credit

People appeared to respond to the questions about tuition tax credits as if the supply of private schools were infinitely elastic, that is, that tuition costs would not rise at all as the result of the implementation of a credit, and that there would be enough seats in private schools in appropriate locations to accommodate all who would want to apply. Neither is a realistic assumption. If the supply of private school places is less than perfectly elastic, some of the demand stimulated by the tax credit would go unsatisfied and there would be less of an increase in private school enrollments. There might also be an increase in private school tuitions. The extreme case would be if the supply were totally inelastic, in which case private school enrollments would not rise at all. (However, the particular children in private schools could change. For example, if tuitions rose sharply and/or admission standards were tightened, some children currently in private schools might be replaced by children presently attending public schools.)

Several supply factors suggest the extent of switching that would actually take place, particularly in the short run, would be limited. These supply considerations include: (1) possible price responses on the part of private schools (which might be restrained by ceilings on the level or proportion of tuition covered by the credit) and (2) the availability of a place in an appropriate private school for the child in question. Even where a private school exists in an area, it could already be operating at capacity, the child might not qualify for admission, or it might not be the type of school desired by the parents. Private schools may not be able to absorb large numbers of new students in the short run. In the first year, private schools might be able to accommodate a modest increase in enrollments through small-scale expansion in existing schools. However, further expansion might come slowly and could require substantial capital investment, which might be difficult to finance.

Furthermore, private schools may not be interested in expanding sufficiently to accommodate all the potential increase in demand. Some schools may prize their relatively small size, seeing the resulting intimacy among parents, students, and staff as an advantage. In addition, by creating a waiting list or "pent-up demand," they might be able to raise admission standards, increase tuitions, or both.

Potential New Applicants to Private Schools

Estimates of the potential number of public school transfers can be derived from this survey. Separate accounting for certain demand conditions (knowledge of a tuition tax credit and intensity of preference) and supply conditions (availability of a private school) produces much lower proportions of public school parents who might move their children to private schools. Table 2.2 shows that with no modifying conditions 22.8% of the total sample is either "very or somewhat likely" to transfer their children to a private school. This figure declines to 9.7% to 16.2% under one modifying condition and 6.2% to 12.7% under two conditions. Taking intensity of preferences, knowledge of a tax credit, and availability of private schools into consideration simultaneously suggests that less than 5% of all public school children might be possible new applicants to the private school sector under a $250 tax credit. Furthermore, this is still apt to be an overestimate because it does not adequately capture the possible supply constraints or include the effect of a percentage limit on eligible tuition costs.

The three conditions also would have an effect on the characteristics of the pool of potential new students in the private school sector. Table 2.3 shows that when all three conditions are in effect, the group of potential public school transferees is skewed further in the direction of low-income children than is the case without the conditions. With no modifying con-

Table 2.2 Impact of Demand and Supply Conditions on Proportions of Children
Who Might Be Transferred under a $250 Tuition Tax Credit

	Total Sample		Public School[c]		Private School[c]	
Modifying Conditions[a]	Very Likely	Very or Somewhat Likely	Very Likely	Very or Somewhat Likely	Very Likely	Very or Somewhat Likely
1. None	9.7%	22.8%	9.2%	23.5%	12.8%	18.6%
		(N = 1947)		(N = 1687)		(N = 260)
2. Heard of a Tuition Tax Credit	6.2	16.2	5.6	16.8	8.6	14.0
		(N = 1060)		(N = 852)		(N = 207)
3. Private School Available[b]	6.5**	15.3	5.9†	15.4	10.1	14.9
		(N = 1921)		(N = 1661)		(N = 260)
4. Heard of Tax Credit and Private School Available†	5.2†	12.7	4.7†	12.8	7.6	12.2
		(N = 1056)		(N = 848)		(N = 207)

[a]The N's for the different sets of conditions vary for two reasons. The number of respondents providing usable answers differs across variables. Percentages for Conditions 2 and 4 are based on those respondents who replied they had heard of a tuition tax credit prior to the household survey.

[b]Under Conditions 3 and 4, public school respondents who said they were "very" or "somewhat likely" to switch but that no private school was available serving the appropriate grade were classified as being unlikely to move their child. The N's for the "very likely" category are slightly higher under conditions 3 and 4 (12 and 4, respectively) than listed in the table for public school parents and the total sample.

[c]For the purpose of this table, children were classified on the basis of the type of school the parent said the child would attend in the 1982–83 school year.

ditions, 38.4% of the sample households that were "very likely" or "some-what likely" to switch their children to a private school had incomes under $15,000. In contrast, under the three modifying conditions, 49.4% of those who were either "very likely" or "somewhat likely" to switch had incomes under 15,000.

That group which under the three modifying conditions is very or some-what likely to switch to private schools is considerably less affluent and more nonwhite than either public or private school students as a group. Based on the survey responses, it does not appear that one of the greatest fears of opponents of tax credits—the exodus of more privileged children from the public schools—would be realized. Instead, groups now under-represented in private schools, those from minority and lower-income fam-ilies, exhibit average to above average inclinations to respond to a tax credit.

The implications of a credit for households vary according to who would switch and the nature of the credit. The beneficiaries of a credit will consist of two groups: families of children currently in public schools but who would switch them to private schools under a credit, and families whose children are currently in private schools. The latter are disproportionately white and higher status, while the survey suggests the former might be more heavily black or Hispanic and have lower family incomes. Therefore, the distri-

Table 2.3 Comparison of Pool of Potential New Private School Applicants with Current Private and Public School Students

Characteristics	Potential New Applicants to Private Schools under a $250 Tuition Tax Credit		School Child Would Attend without a Tax Credit	
	No Modifying Conditions	All Three Modifying Conditions[a]	Public	Private
Race	(N=394)	(N=87)	(N=1715)	(N=268)
White	60.6%	59.6%	75.3%	80.5%
Nonwhite	39.4	40.4	24.7	19.5
Household Income	(N=385)	(N=95)	(N=1622)	(N=254)
Under $15,000	38.4%	49.4%	28.5%	14.5%
$15,000–24,999	31.7	32.2	26.4	24.6
$25,000 and over	29.9	18.5	45.0	60.9

[a]Calculated using the assumption that all parents will have the same preferences as those with similar characteristics who had heard of a tax credit prior to the household survey.

bution of benefits among racial and income categories would depend on the extent of switching to private schools that actually took place. The higher the number of children transferred to private schools as a result of a tuition tax credit, the higher the proportion of beneficiaries from groups now underrepresented in private schools might be. Higher credit levels are apt to provide a larger share of benefits to higher-income and white families (as would percentage limits on the amount of tuition covered).

Another possible consequence for individuals is the prospect that public school parents who would like to switch their children to private schools may be unable to do so. The potential for such unmet expectations may be greatest for less-affluent families. They would be least able to afford even the reduced private school costs and might not be able to meet the admission requirements.

CONCLUSION

The federal role in the financing of private schools has remained relatively minor, in keeping with the generally limited range of federal precollegiate activities. Provisions for participation by private school students in these activities have expanded greatly during the past fifteen years and they require full services to eligible students. At this time the need may be for more federal monitoring and enforcement of state and local administration of existing federal requirements, as well as technical assistance to these jurisdictions, rather than for additional legislation.

The federal policy for increasing support for private education that has received the most attention in recent years has been tuition tax credits. One of the goals such a policy may promote is the expansion of parental choice of schooling. The extent to which a tuition tax credit would expand choice and access to private schools would be a function of the demand for and supply of private schools and the characteristics of the credit. If no child changes schools in response to a credit, then choice would not be expanded. Such an extreme case is unlikely, but a relatively small shift is possible if supply considerations predominate (i.e., supply is rather inelastic and/or tuitions rise substantially). If relatively few families switch their children to private schools, the primary goal that will have been served is providing greater tax relief for families with children already enrolled in private schools.

The responses about tuition tax credits expressed in the survey probably overestimate the extent to which children would actually change schools if a tax credit were implemented. Nevertheless, the responses to the household survey suggest that access to private schools could be considerably enhanced for minority and less-affluent families who are now underrepresented among private school students and that supply constraints may determine how children will change sectors.

In designing a federal tuition tax credit, trade-offs between the level of the credit and the proportion of tuition to be covered are necessary if the cost is to be kept at a reasonable level, since increases in both raise the revenue losses to the federal government. The results of the School Finance Project survey suggest that, for any given level of federal funding, access and choice would be expanded most for low-income and minority families by increasing the proportion of tuition eligible at the expense of a lower level of credit.

NOTES

1. For more information see School Finance Project, *Private Elementary and Secondary Education* (Washington, D.C.: U.S. Department of Education, 1983).

2. Vic Miller and Jay Noell, *Estimating Federal Funds to Education: A New Approach Applied to Fiscal Year 1981*, Technical Analysis Paper, Planning and Evaluation Service, U.S. Department of Education.

3. National Education Association, *Estimates of School Statistics 1982–83* (Washington, D.C., 1983), p. 37.

4. School Finance Project, *Federal Education Policies and Programs: Intergovernmental Issues in their Design, Operation, and Effects* (Washington, D.C.: U.S. Department of Education, 1984).

5. Advisory Commission on Intergovernmental Relations, *The Federal Role in the Federal System: The Dynamics of Growth*, A-81 (Washington, D.C., 1981).

6. Raymond G. Wasdyke, George W. Elford, and Terry W. Hartle, *Providing Students in Nonprofit Private Schools with Access to Publicly Supported Vocational Education Programs* (Princeton, N.J.: Educational Testing Service, 1980).

7. Richard Jung, *Nonpublic School Students in Title I ESEA Programs: A Question of "Equal" Services* (McLean, Va.: Advanced Technology, 1982), pp. 36–37.

8. Lorraine M. McDonnell and Milbrey W. McLaughlin, *Program Consolidation and the State Role in ESEA Title IV* (Santa Monica, Cal: The Rand Corporation, 1980).

9. Wasdyke, Elford, and Hartle, *Providing Students.*

10. Milton Friedman, "The Role of Government in Education," in Robert Solo, *Economics and the Public Interest,* (New Brunswick, N.J.: Rutgers University Press, 1965).

11. Henry Levin, *Educational Vouchers and Social Policy* (Palo Alto, Cal: Standford University, Institute for Research on Educational Finance and Governance, 1979). Among other major works on vouchers, see John E. Coons and Stephen D. Sugarman, *Education by Choice: The Case for Family Control* (Berkeley: University of California Press, 1978).

12. Kent McGuire, *Choice in Elementary and Secondary Education,* Working Paper No. 34 (Denver, Col.: Education Commission of the States, 1981).

13. R. Gay Bridge and Julie Blackman, *A Study on Alternatives in American Education: Family Choice in Schooling* (Santa Monica, Cal: The Rand Corporation, 1978).

14. Mary F. Williams, Kimberly Small Hancher, and Amy Hutner, *Parents and School Choice: A Household Survey,* Working Paper (Washington, D.C.: School Finance Project, U.S. Department of Education, 1983).

15. See, for example Richard Nault and Susan Uchitell, "School Choice in the Public Sector: A Case Study of Parental Decision Making," in M. Manley and S. Casimir, eds, *Family Choice in Schooling: Issues and Dilemmas* (Lexington, Mass.: Lexington Books, 1982).

16. George Gallup, "The 14th Annual Gallup Poll of the Public's Attitudes toward Public Schools," *Phi Delta Kappan,* September 1982, pp. 37–50.

17. John M. Gemello and Jack Osman, *Analysis of the Choice of Public and Private Education,* paper prepared for the Tuition Tax Credit Seminar sponsored by Institute for Research on Educational Finance and Governance, Washington, D.C., October 1981.

18. Jay Noell and David Myers, *The Demand for Private Schooling: A Preliminary Analysis,* paper presented at the 1982 Annual Meeting of the American Education Finance Association, Philadelphia, Pa., 1982.

3

Choice and Private Schools: Dynamics of Supply and Demand

DONALD A. ERICKSON

In this chapter an attempt is made, in the light of evidence from the United States and Canada, to explain in general terms the ebb and flow of private school options.

Both public and private school growth and decline are affected by demography. Thus, a massive drop in Catholic school enrollment from 1966 to 1981 reflects, in part, a birthrate decline and a migration of Catholics from central cities, where many Catholic schools existed, to suburbs, where there were few Catholic schools. But unlike public school attendance, which rarely involves user fees and is considered normal if not laudatory in the United States and parts of Canada, private school attendance generally occurs when parents decide to depart from normal practice, incurring extra cost, extra effort (many private school patrons must drive their children considerable distances to school), disruption of their children's friendships (many private school students are not in the schools which most of their neighborhood friends attend), and sometimes social disapproval.[1]

To a far greater extent than public school enrollment, then, private school enrollment depends on patron motivations. To return to the Catholic example: Even if the Catholic birthrate were high and Catholic schools were universally accessible, those schools would soon collapse unless many Catholic parents considered them worth extra expense and effort.

Also, while public schools are everywhere available, parents often cannot find the private schools they prefer. Some schools exist primarily for certain religious and ethnic groups. Schools of some types are available only in a few major cities. Some schools are beyond the fiscal reach of most people.

It is no accident, in this regard, that religious options are more plentiful in private schools than curricular or pedagogical options. Most religiously oriented schools enjoy subsidies from religious groups. Many schools open in the facilities of churches and synagogues, thus avoiding major expense.

Sometimes churches and other denominational agencies directly sponsor schools. Even when they do not, they often assist by taking special collections, or their members provide free labor. Many Jewish day schools are subsidized through Jewish community funds. Churches and synagogues are good sources of people who, for religious reasons, will teach for meager salaries. For many decades, Catholic schools were underwritten massively through the contributed services of nuns, priests, and brothers. Denominational colleges recruit and prepare teachers with special knowledge, skill, and dedication. Many religiously oriented schools can escape the expense of small classes, state-of-the-art science laboratories, and fancy libraries, for their clients, attracted primarily by religious inducements, will accept some unavoidable academic risk. Sometimes—as in the case of Fundamentalist schools, discussed later—special systems of programmed instruction enable groups with little instructional and organizational expertise to start schools readily.

In contrast, when people create a Waldorf school, an American Summerhill, or simply an academically superior school, they are pretty much on their own. They must find or erect a building, hire skillful teachers, do all the other complicated things involved in starting a school, and finance the enterprise continuously. Not surprisingly, most nonreligious options in education are expensive—available mostly to the well-to-do.

AN OVERVIEW OF PRIVATE SCHOOL INCENTIVES

The explanation most commonly offered for private school growth is disenchantment with public schools. It is assumed that private schools grow when public schools are in disfavor, and decline when public schools are in good repute. That explanation has but limited validity. As we shall see, the private school share of total U.S. enrollment at elementary and secondary levels has remained remarkably constant for decades, despite the fluctuating fortunes of public schools, and at any given moment some private schools may be plummeting in popularity while others grow at a furious rate. Figure 3.1, which plots recent enrollment trends in Catholic, Hebrew, and Fundamentalist schools, demonstrates that these groups cannot be growing and declining in response to the same factors. Data from other private school groups would exhibit even further diversity.

An analogy may be helpful. If Ford automobiles were made available to all citizens at tax expense, most drivers would undoubtedly own some Ford product. It would never occur to some people to consider other automobiles. Some people would look elsewhere because of bad experiences with Ford, but many others would do so, without any conviction of Ford inferiority, because they strongly preferred other cars. If the Ford Government Service (FGS) dropped its sports cars, some patrons would defect to Corvette and Porsche. If FGS abandoned its compacts, other drivers would switch to Honda and Volkswagen. If FGS discontinued Lincoln Continen-

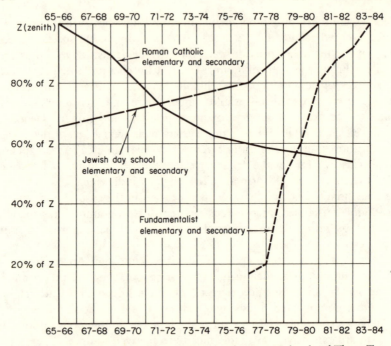

Figure 3.1: Differential Growth Trends of Private Schools of Three Types.

SOURCES: *a*Eduardo Rauch, "The Jewish Day School in America: A Critical History and Contemporary Dilemmas," in James C. Carper and Thomas C. Hunt, eds., *Religious Schooling in America* (Birmingham, Al.: Religious Education Press, 1984), pp. 130–165.

*b*Bruce S. Cooper, Donald H. McLaughlin, and Bruno V. Manno, "The Latest Word on Private-School Growth," *Teachers College Record* 85 (Fall 1983), pp. 88–98.

*c*Data provided to the author by telephone in February 1984 from the Association of Christian Schools International, La Habra, Ca.

tals, the market for Cadillacs and twelve-cylinder Jaguars would benefit. However, many Rolls Royce afficionados would probably never consider an FGS product, regardless of the diversity available under that label. In their minds, nothing rivals a Rolls. In the minds of some parents, nothing rivals the type of private school they patronize. Public education could never offer such special benefits.

If there really were a Santa Claus called FGS, the diversity of available automobiles might in fact diminish. Since FGS would capture most of the market, other carmakers might be forced to concentrate on a few special offerings, just as private schools are forced to concentrate mainly on religious options. FGS, protected from open competition and subject to political pressures, might neglect products purchased by "elitist" or other unpopular groups. Other options might be rendered impossible by legal limitations on the use of imported products and materials by public agencies. The judiciary might declare some options unconstitutional when offered at public expense, as U.S. courts have done repeatedly in public schools.

Tuition-free public schools have had an enormous impact on private school enrollment. (In a 1982 survey, 40% of public school parents in British Columbia said they would patronize private schools if public and private schools were on an equal financial footing.)[2] However, the ups and downs of different private schools are determined by additional complex factors. Much depends, as in the above-discussed FGS example, on the choices offered by the public agency. Most citizens seem content with public schools as long as their special interests are decently satisfied or protected. Important groups move from public to private schools, and vice versa, for different reasons and at different times, partly because of shifts in public school policy and practice.

Unfortunately, no comprehensive analysis of this topic can be based on firm evidence, for little relevant empirical work has been done. The discussion that follows is derived both from available findings and from less systematic information and impression gathered during more than two decades of inquiry on private schools. The focus is on a few clear tendencies, leaving a more exhaustive analysis to a later occasion.

MAGNITUDE AND DISTRIBUTION OF PRIVATE SCHOOL ENROLLMENT

To begin with a backdrop on private schools as a whole: According to the latest available data, 89% of U.S. households with children in elementary and secondary grades patronize public schools only, 9% patronize private schools only, and 2% patronize them both.[3] At the elementary and secondary levels, about 18% of all schools in the United States are private, enroll 10% or 11% of all U.S. students, and employ about 11% of all teachers.[4]

The best available estimates of total U.S. enrollment in private elementary and secondary schools are 6,299,717 in 1965–66, 5,186,329 in 1970–71, 4,497,653 in 1975–76, and 5,256,000 in 1980–81.[5] The first ten years in this period were marked by enrollment losses, but recent growth is evident. However, private schools have not regained their erstwhile 13.5% share of the schoolchild market.[6] Shifts in that share have been modest over a period of many decades, within a 6% range. Nationally, private schools are not threatening to overshadow public schools, though there may be scattered local instances of such a possibility. More dramatic national fluctuations might occur if government were not distorting the school market, or if parental preferences were to shift dramatically. One can imagine conditions that would reduce the market distortion. The Supreme Court could alter the constitutional interpretations that now prevent public aid to private schools. If public schools became sufficiently unpopular, their tax support could diminish so much that they would not take much money from private school patrons.

THE SHIFTING ENROLLMENT DISTRIBUTION

The composition of the private school sector is constantly changing. Between 1965–66 and 1980–81, U.S. Catholic school enrollment diminished to a little more than half its original size, dropping from 5,573,810 (5,574,354 by another estimate) to 3,106,000. At the same time non-Catholic private schools were growing, rising from 725,907 to 2,150,000.[7] The picture shifts from one private school group to another.

Table 3.1 provides an approximate[8] idea of the distribution of private school enrollment, a distribution changing notably between 1965–66 and 1982–83.

Three Divergent Patterns of Development

To illustrate the disparate dynamics of enrollment in different private schools, it may be useful to sketch the history of three groups.

The Catholic School Picture

The earliest major U.S. Catholic school growth was partly a response to militant Protestantism in public schools, though ethnic and social class considerations played a prominent role.[9] During the same period, many Protestant schools disappeared, partly because public schools, then so congenial to Protestants, were increasingly free of user fees and widely available.[10] (Many of the latter schools might have survived apart from government interference with the market.)

More recently, U.S. Catholic schools experienced the precipitous losses mentioned above. The reduction has been leveling off and could be near an end, though recent changes in Catholic schools, discussed later, make those schools vulnerable to a new set of enrollment determinants.[11] Since the complex dynamics of the Catholic school enrollment decline since 1966 have been discussed in detail elsewhere, a brief summary may be sufficient for present purposes.[12] As has been suggested, the early Catholic schools were popular partly because many Catholics felt their church, in predominantly Protestant America, was under siege, its young particularly subject to attack in the public schools. Never able to provide Catholic schools for the majority of its members, the Catholic church worked (with other groups) to reduce the pronounced Protestantism of many public schools. These efforts were so successful that public schools are now congenial to many Catholics. Developments revolving around the Catholic church's Second Vatican Council (ending in 1965) raised serious questions about the religious desirability of Catholic schools,[13] and in the minds of many people, apparently, about the attractiveness of religious communities of nuns, priests, and brothers. The religious orders withered. Many remaining nuns and brothers, given new freedom, in the wake of Second Vatican, to choose areas of service, left Catholic schools for other ministries, thus forcing the

Table 3.1[a]   The Demographic Diversity of U.S. Private Schools by Type: 1965–1983

	1965–66		1982–83		Percent Growth/Decline: 1965–83	
	Students	Schools	Students	Schools	Students	Schools
Roman Catholic	5,574,354	13,292	3,027,312	9,432	−46	−29
Lutheran Total:	(208,209)	(1,896)	(280,559)	(2,480)	+35	+31
Amer. Lutheran Church	8,795	147	31,284	376	+256	+155
Missouri Synod	171,966	1,364	198,061	1,603	+15	+18
Evangelical Lutheran			5,144	37		
Wisc. Evang. Lutheran	27,448	239	35,550	391	+30	+14
Jewish Total:	(73,112)	(345)	(100,202)	(572)	+37	+66
Orthodox Jewish	68,800	321	86,321	497	+25	+55
Conservative Jewish	3,489	19	12,341	68	+254	+258
Reform Jewish	823	5	1,540	7	+87	+40
Seventh Day Advntst.	64,252	884	81,507	1,324	+27	+49
Independent NAIS	199,329	697	336,797	873	+69	+25
Episcopal	59,437	347	78,214	527	+32	+52
Greek Orthodox	2,205	13	7,590	23	+24	+77
Friends (Quaker)	10,878	36	13,853	53	+27	+47
Mennonite	13,256	276				
Calvinist (CSI)[b]	51,240		74,541	382	+45	+78
Evangelical[c]	110,300		912,985	10,741	+627	+223
Assembly of God	3,110					
Special Education	NA		10,233	66		
Alternative	125		11,592	128		+0.4
Military	NA					

[a]From Bruce S. Cooper, "The Changing Demography of Private Schools: Trends and Implications," *Education and Urban Society* 16, 4 (August 1984), p. 432.

[b]Christian School International.

[c]Evangelical is a category of self-confessed, "born-again" Christian schools, such as Baptist or Methodist, that have indicated a Fundamentalist ideal.

schools to replace them with far more costly "lay" teachers. The "religious" who remained in the schools became more expensive, for their communities, with few young people joining, were supporting an increasing proportion of elderly persons. The loss of the "religious" not only affected finances, but made it difficult to maintain the traditional religious atmosphere. Partly for this reason perhaps, and partly because religious motivations seemed on the wane, many Catholic leaders sought to cater to academic motivations. Religious reasons for patronizing Catholic schools are now secondary, at least in some areas, and are considerably less pronounced in Catholic schools than in other church-related schools.[14] But where public schools have enviable reputations, it is difficult to see how Catholic schools, with their more limited budgets, can survive mainly on academic grounds. When operating well, public schools can maintain decent discipline, one of the traditional incentives for parents seeking aca-

demic quality in Catholic schools, and can usually afford facilities, equipment, and programs that are impossible in most Catholic schools. Under
these circumstances, when public school academic quality seems at least
equal to the quality provided in nearby Catholic schools, why should patrons pay extra (in Catholic schools) for what they can obtain free (in public schools)?

The new emphasis on academics was unimaginatively executed. Catholic
leaders reduced class size, increased teacher salaries, and, by diminishing
teacher turnover, ensured that more teachers would be paid at higher levels on salary schedules. Though very costly, these approaches have little
promise for improving student learning, especially in comparison with other
strategies.[15] The spiraling costs, compounded by decreasing economies of
scale produced by declining enrollment, soon forced many Catholic schools
to close. Partly because they were not yet properly aware of the effects of
the birthrate decline and the migration to the suburbs, and thus attributed
the enrollment losses mainly to patron disenchantment, and perhaps partly
because they themselves were losing faith in Catholic schools, most U.S.
bishops halted school building construction; now new schools could not
be created to serve Catholics in the suburbs. Some Catholic scholars insisted that there was an enormous pent-up demand in the suburbs.[16]
Nevertheless, many Catholics had lost interest in Catholic schools. There
may also be a large pent-up demand among low-income inner-city minorities (including many non-Catholics), who flooded inner-city Catholic schools
after most white middle-class Catholics left for the suburbs.[17] These inner-
city Catholic schools, unable to support themselves on fees from impov-
erished patrons, may not last long without new sources of revenue.

The Picture in Fundamentalist Schools

While Catholic schools were declining, Fundamentalist schools were bur-
geoning. By losing Protestant attributes and becoming acceptable to Catholics, public schools had become "Godless" in the minds of many Fundamentalists. While Catholics were shedding a siege mentality, Fundamentalists
were feeling a new need to shelter their young. In a Fundamentalist school
studied intensively by Peshkin, church and school worked together closely
and intensely to form a "total institution" designed to effect "the broadest
possible control" over students.[18] The school, no less integral to the church
than the Sunday morning service, extended its single-minded purview far
beyond the instructional hours, demanding deep involvement in church af-
fairs and abstention from many worldly pursuits. "We feel like we are
wasting time," the headmaster observed, "if we're teaching a kid six hours
a day, if all we're doing is having a student here and then he goes out and
leads his own life. If we're not touching his life, we don't care to have him."[19]
According to Peshkin's evidence, the school was remarkably successful in
an exceedingly difficult task—to make normal for its students what the society as a whole would regard as deviant. In the process, moreover, it did

not produce inhibited, oppressed adolescents. Many Americans, like Pesh-kin, would lament this school's religious views, but it may provide the best example in recent literature of how an institution may be organized to ef-fectuate "moral commitment."[20] Peshkin's study, involving only one school, needs replication. However, many of its findings are already echoed in less comprehensive work, and strongly corroborate this writer's impressions over many years.[21]

It is important, in this connection, to clarify the meaning of *Fundamen-talist school*. Almost every major religious group has a fundamentalist wing. However, most schools regarded as Fundamentalist are associated with the right wing of Protestant Fundamentalism—with independent Baptist or charismatic groups of "born-again" Christians. Within this movement, the American Association of Christian Schools caters primarily to independent Baptist groups. The Association of Christian Schools International (not to be confused with Christian Schools International, discussed later) serves a broader variety of groups, including charismatics (Pentecostals, Nazarenes, etc.). Calvinist schools, generally associated (though not formally affili-ated) with the Christian Reformed Church, also have mostly "born-again" patrons but are not generally considered part of the Fundamentalist school movement, for the Calvinist schools exhibit less of a siege mentality and separationist stance and have their origins mostly in an earlier era and dif-ferent incentives. Similarly, schools operated by Seventh-Day Adventists and by Lutherans of the Wisconsin and Missouri Synods (the two most con-servative Lutheran groups), though fundamentalist in some doctrinal re-spects, do not fall within the Fundamentalist school group, for Adventist and Lutheran schools, like Calvinist schools, were generally established earlier than Fundamentalist schools, and for different reasons.

The parameters and expansion of the Fundamentalist school movement, as defined above, are difficult to delineate with precision. Fundamentalist schools, like many other private schools, tend to be fiercely individualistic. Some, belonging to no associations, do not show up on association lists. Some belong to two or more associations, thus appearing twice or more in estimates. Though most states require all private schools to register and report their enrollment, enforcement is uneven. Many schools fail to reg-ister, sometimes on the ground that they are not really "schools" but an aspect of church ministry. Many schools, both inside and outside the Fun-damentalist camp, resist research, fearing the data will be misused. In the available figures, it is often difficult to determine how much enrollment ex-tends beyond kindergarten (many Fundamentalist schools begin at that level, adding grades as finances and demand permit).

Conducting a dissertation in Fundamentalist schools in 1961–62, this author had difficulty securing an adequate sample, for such schools prob-ably numbered no more than 250 or 300 nationally at the time and were generally very small, often limited to a kindergarten or the first one or two grades.[22] By 1984, in contrast, the Association of Christian Schools Inter-

national (in La Habra, California), the most broadly based association of
Fundamentalist schools, reported the following membership data to the
author by telephone:

School Year	Number of Schools	Total Enrollment
1976–77	500	63,131
1977–78	611	74,460
1978–79	1051	185,687
1979–80	1294	220,001
1980–81	1482	289,001
1981–82	1728	320,950
1982–83	1933	337,550
1983–84	2148	364,070

The totals for all Fundamentalist schools could be triple these figures,
which describe only one association. Explosive growth has occurred. Before the Supreme Court outlawed official prayer and Bible reading in public schools in the 1960s, most right-wing Fundamentalist churches were officially opposed to the "Christian day school movement," insisting that public
schools were sufficiently neutral to be patronized by Fundamentalists, that
children would grow up to be stronger Christians if not unduly sheltered,
and that Fundamentalists were obligated to "witness to their faith" within
public schools. The Court's decisions, symbolic to Fundamentalists of a
humanistic, antitheistic takeover in public schools, apparently did much to
reverse that posture. Additionally, "sex, drugs, rock and roll," and other
behavior repugnant to Fundamentalists appeared to flare up in many public schools. Then came sex education, publicity over controversial books in
school libraries, and the growing refusal of public educators to discuss cre-
ationism in science classes. If courts and public educators had conspired to
alienate these one-time public school supporters, they could hardly have
done a more thorough job. Most right-wing Fundamentalist church leaders
have reversed themselves on the school issue, now promoting Fundamentalist day schools.[23] Another profound impetus behind this movement is
the availability of "prepackaged schools" from several sources. The approach was pioneered by a firm known as Accelerated Christian Education
(ACE) in Lewiston, Texas. ACE offers programmed learning materials that
drastically reduce the instructional and administrative skill needed to start
a school, along with time-proven formulas for virtually every phase of school
functioning. For several reasons, including extensive reliance on student independence, the ACE system involves academic risk. However, many Fundamentalist parents seem sufficiently concerned about religious and moral
dangers in public schools to take a few chances academically. The gamble
is often temporary; many Fundamentalist schools move, after the initial pains
of getting under way, from the ACE system to more conventional instruction and administration. Evidence introduced in several court cases sug-

gests, moreover, that students in "ACE schools" generally master the central academic subjects rather well.[24] Their disadvantages may relate mostly to the development of discussion skills and certain higher-level mental capabilities. It must not be assumed, moreover, that all Fundamentalist schools use programmed materials of this type, for many do not, and many never did.

The Jewish Day School Picture

During the years after 1966 when Catholic schools were declining rapidly, U.S. Jewish day schools, like Fundamentalist schools, were growing. But whereas rapid growth was just beginning in the 1960s in Fundamentalist schools, it had started twenty years earlier in Jewish day schools (see Fig. 3.1). Among the many possible reasons for that growth in Jewish day schools are the following:[25] The upswing of religious sentiment during and after World War II in the United States, coupled with discontent with what could be accomplished in part-time agencies of religious instruction, prompted many Jewish leaders to take a new interest in Jewish day schools. Holocaust and other manifestations of Hitlerism made it apparent that the Jewish community could no longer rely on Europe as the fountainhead of Jewish scholarship and creative effort. The creation of the state of Israel in 1948 catalyzed a new sense of pride and identification with Jewish life. A birthrate decline and much intermarriage gave U.S. Jewish leaders reason to look for new mechanisms for the preservation of Jewish ethnic and religious distinctives. Many Jews, living in areas where public schools had deteriorated seriously, were looking for an alternative. Many Jewish leaders who were familiar with intensive forms of Jewish education in Europe had migrated to the United States, where they helped proliferate and modify Jewish schools. Many segments of American Jewry, previously unable to afford Jewish day schools, were experiencing new prosperity. Rauch suggests that the idea of accentuating Jewish distinctives was less threatening to many Jews once these differences were reduced from an all-encompassing scope to "more limited religious dimensions."[26]

According to Rauch:

> The year 1940 marks the beginning of the period of phenomenal growth for the Jewish day school movement. More than 360 schools, 95 percent of all existing day schools were established after this date. In 1940, at the beginning of this era, there were 35 schools with about 7,700 pupils. By 1958 there were 214 schools with 43,000 students, and by 1964 the number of schools had risen to 306 and the enrollment to 65,000. In 1976 there were 80,000 students enrolled and by 1980 the number surpassed 100,000.[27]

In the 1940s, at the beginning of this period of development, most Jewish leaders in the United States were adamant in opposition to the day school movement. (American Jews, whose forebears had often been excluded from state-provided educational opportunities in Europe, generally advanced very rapidly in U.S. public schools and became some of that institution's most avid proponents.) By the end of the period, Rauch says, most U.S. Jewish leaders had become at least reasonably supportive of the Jewish day school movement.[28] The most telling shift, apparently, was among orthodox Jewish leaders, for most Jewish schools are orthodox in basic orientation.

Other Evidence of Diversity

Patterns of growth and decline continue to differ as one more from one private school group to another. At the end of World War I, in the context of rampant antiforeign sentiment, many private schools dropped their ethnic trappings and promptly went out of business.[29] Amish schools arose at the end of World War II, when simple public schools in the countryside, where Amish children could be protected from the influences of mainstream culture, were replaced with bus rides and consolidated schools in nearby towns.[30]

In the shadow of the Vietnam War, military schools became singularly unpopular, but more recent interest in discipline has reversed that trend. Many private schools sprang up in the Progressive Education era, and "free schools" later, in the heyday of the 1960s emphasis on "doing your own thing."[31] Black Muslim schools appeared in the context of an emphasis on "Black Power."[32] Since private education's share of national enrollment has remained relatively constant, as has been noted, it is obvious that when new options emerge, some older ones tend to falter. Many changes occur within groups. Single-sex schools have often become coeducational. Seventh-Day Adventists have largely abandoned an old pattern in their secondary schools: At one time these schools were often supported financially by associated industries (including farms, furniture factories, and even institutions for the mentally ill) in which almost all students worked part-time.

Many of these options would be difficult or impossible to maintain in public schools. Government not only discourages them in private schools by putting private schools at a fiscal disadvantage, but often through arbitrary regulations. The Fundamentalist school studied by Peshkin had been resisted by public authorities through capricious application of health and safety codes.[33] In fact, opposition to Fundamentalist schools has been widespread in recent years.[34] Much earlier, state attempts in Nebraska, Oregon, and Hawaii to outlaw private schools or, in effect, to take them over by regulating them in great detail were halted only when the cases reached the Supreme Court.[35] Today there is much interest in developing new relationships between schooling and work, but the above-mentioned Seventh-Day Adventist efforts along that line, in an earlier time, met extensive state discouragement. In 1968, the author visited a Quaker school called Scattergood, near West Branch, Iowa. Located on a farm, the school was devoted to the education of head, heart, and hand, involving all students in an extensive round of experiences in cooking, housekeeping, crop management, animal husbandry, and numerous other aspects of life and learning on a farm. The superintendent of public instruction was threatening at the time to rescind the school's state approval because not enough formal courses were being offered in the "practical arts," though it was difficult to imagine how the school's actual instruction in that area (not offered in a course format, but as part of a required extra curriculum) could be surpassed. The Old Order Amish were harassed in many states until a Supreme Court decision in their favor. They were hauled into court repeatedly; their children were "kidnapped" by truancy officials; they were often jailed. At times, when they ran out of funds to pay their fines, their property was sold at public auction. Some Amish groups left for Central and South America in search of religious liberty.[36]

PRIVATE CHOICES IN BRITISH COLUMBIA

Further evidence of differences among private school groups is available from two recent surveys in British Columbia.[37] In one of these surveys, conducted in 1981, 264 public school parents and 268 private school parents, reached through random-digit dialing, were asked why they preferred the school or school type which they had identified as their preference. The question was open-ended and asked early in each interview (to minimize our influence on responses). Interviewers were instructed to probe for as many as five answers, to record them verbatim (as much as possible), and to ask each respondent which answer represented the most important reason for preferring the school or school type.

It became evident, from data in Table 3.2 and other data, not included here, that preferential differences among school types were more distinct when one focused on the top-priority reason given by each respondent. In private schools as a whole, the reasons most often identified as primary by parents had to do with religion or spirituality (mentioned as primary by 22.0% of private school respondents), academic quality (mentioned by 20.5%), discipline (mentioned by 16.8%), smallness or individual attention (5.6%), and "atmosphere" (5.6%). When one considered the first three reasons given, however, discipline was the motivation mentioned by the most people in private schools (48.5%), followed by academic quality (mentioned by 39.6%) and religion or spirituality (35.1%). The dominance of religious concerns was, of course, a function of the prevalence of religiously oriented schools and did not reflect the motivational structure of all private schools, as will be evident later.

The pattern of patron inducements was different in the public school sample. Considering only the top-priority reasons given for preferring public schools, those most often mentioned concerned low cost (mentioned as primary reason by 13.3%), proximity or convenience (mentioned by 12.5%), and academic quality (9.4%). The remarkably infrequent mention of discipline (mentioned as first reason by only 1.8%) did not necessarily reflect a lack of concern for discipline, for parents were explaining why they pre-

Table 3.2   Major Reasons Given by Private and Public School Parents in B.C. for Preferring Their School and School Type

| | Given as First Reason | | | | Given as One or More of Three Reasons | | | |
| | Private | | Public | | Private | | Public | |
Reason	%	(n)	%	(n)	%	(n)	%	(n)
No Reason Given	0.0	0	0.0	0		104		270
Academic Quality/Emphasis	20.5	55	9.4	25	39.6	106	15.5	41
Teacher Dedication	3.0	8	2.6	7	10.4	28	6.4	17
Accent on the Basics	1.5	4	0.37	1	3.7	10	1.1	3
Beyond the Basics	2.2	6	5.6	15	8.2	22	9.4	25
Smallness, Indiv. Attention	5.6	15	0.37	1	19.8	53	3.7	10
Discipline	16.8	45	1.8	5	48.5	130	4.9	13
Religion, Spirituality	22.0	59	0	0	35.1	94	0.75	2
Atmosphere	5.6	15	1.5	4	13.4	36	3.0	8
Relationship to Home								
Congruence with Home Values	1.9	5	0.0	0	7.8	21	1.9	5
Social Integration,								
Heterogeneity	0.7	2	3.0	8	1.5	4	4.1	11
Better Administration	0.4	1	2.6	7	3.0	8	3.7	10
Good Reputation	3.7	10	2.6	7	9.3	25	8.7	23
Family Solidarity	0.7	2	6.0	16	4.9	13	13.6	36
Child's Preference	1.5	4	1.8	5	3.4	9	4.1	11
Child's Friends, Siblings	1.1	3	1.8	5	4.1	11	7.9	21
Proximity, Convenience	2.6	7	12.5	33	11.2	30	29.9	79
Cheapness	0	0	13.25	35	0.4	1	19.3	51
Prefer this School Type	4.9	13	4.5	12	13.8	37	9.8	26
Other School Unavailable	0.4	1	4.5	12	4.5	12	6.8	18
Don't Know	0	0	13.63	36	0	0	17.0	45
Other	4.9	13	11.4	30	18.3	49		66
Totals	268		264		268		264	

SOURCE: See note 1, p. 107.

ferred public schools, and not necessarily what they considered most important. They may have implied in these responses that discipline was not good in their public schools and therefore did not represent a sensible reason for preferring schools of that type. When one considers the first three reasons given by each public school respondent, proximity/convenience was mentioned by the most people (by 29.9%), followed by low cost (19.3%), academic quality (15.5%), and such matters of family solidarity as patronizing a school or school type as a matter of family tradition or because a member of the family worked there (13.6%)

For present purposes, however, Table 3.3 is more interesting, for it indicates the reasons given by parents of three different social class levels for preferring private schools of three different types: Catholic schools, Calvinist schools (as defined earlier in this chapter), and schools with high tuitions. Two tendencies are very clear in Table 3.3. First, the preferential differences were much more pronounced among school types than among

Table 3.3 Number and Proportion of B.C. Parents Citing First Reasons for Preferring Schools in Each of 14 Categories, by Social Class (Hollingshead ISP), Three Major Private School Types

Reason Catgry	Catholic Schools			Calvinist Schools			High-Tuition Schools		
	Upr/Mdl N %	Lwr/Mdl N %	Wkg/Lwr N %	Upr/Mdl N %	Lwr/Mdl N %	Wkg/Lwr N %	Upr/Mdl N %	Lwr/Mdl N %	Wkg/Lwr N %
Acdmic Emph.	11 20.37	12 20.68	5 14.70	2 18.18	0 0.00	0 0.00	11 35.48	3 75.00	0 0.00
Other Acdmc[a]	7 12.96	10 17.24	4 11.76	2 18.18	0 0.00	0 0.00	3 9.67	0 0.00	1 100.00
Strict Dscpln	9 16.66	12 20.68	8 23.52	1 9.09	1 10.00	0 0.00	5 16.12	0 0.00	0 0.00
Rlgn/ Sprtlt	9 16.66	11 18.96	6 17.64	5 45.45	8 80.00	5 100.00	0 0.00	0 0.00	0 0.00
Like Home[b]	4 7.40	1 1.72	5 14.70	1 9.09	0 0.00	0 0.00	3 9.67	0 0.00	0 0.00
Good Name[c]	3 5.55	1 1.72	0 0.00	0 0.00	0 0.00	0 0.00	4 12.90	0 0.00	0 0.00
Family Sldrty	0 0.00	0 0.00	0 0.00	0 0.00	0 0.00	0 0.00	1 3.22	0 0.00	0 0.00
Happy Child[d]	3 5.55	1 1.72	0 0.00	0 0.00	0 0.00	0 0.00	1 3.22	0 0.00	0 0.00
Prxmty to Hme	1 1.85	2 3.44	3 8.82	0 0.00	0 0.00	0 0.00	0 0.00	0 0.00	0 0.00
Lw Cst or Nil	0 0.00	0 0.00	0 0.00	0 0.00	0 0.00	0 0.00	0 0.00	0 0.00	0 0.00
Prefer Type	3 5.55	4 6.89	1 2.94	0 0.00	0 0.00	0 0.00	2 6.45	1 25.00	0 0.00
School Unavl.	0 0.00	0 0.00	0 0.00	0 0.00	1 10.00	0 0.00	0 0.00	0 0.00	0 0.00
Other Rsons	3 5.55	4 6.89	2 5.88	0 0.00	0 0.00	0 0.00	1 3.22	0 0.00	0 0.00
Total	54 .00	58 100.00	34 100.00	11 100.00	10 100.00	5 100.00	31 100.00	4 100.00	1 100.00

[a]Composed of former categories: Teacher Dedication, Focus or Basics, Wide Range of Programs, Smallness/Individual Attention.

[b]Composed of former categories: Atmosphere, Congruence with Home.

[c]Composed of former categories: Good Administration, Good Reputation.

[d]Composed of former categories: Child's Preference, Child's Friends.

SOURCE: See note 1, p. 107.

social class strata. The data suggest that private school types, rather than being mere products of social stratification, attracted parents with different preferences, with little regard to social class. The schools were products, as it were, of different preference structures. Second, the differences among school types fit the pattern of logic suggested in earlier passages of the present chapter. High-tuition schools were the schools where the highest proportions of parents gave academic quality or emphasis as the top-priority reason for preferring a school or school type, and in these schools not a single parent in the sample gave religion/spirituality as the most important reason. (As was suggested much earlier, parents with religious preferences can usually find what they want in relatively inexpensive schools.) Academic inducements, which Catholic educators have been emphasizing increasingly in recent years, were more prominent in Catholic schools than in Calvinist schools, and, as the other side of the coin, religion/spirituality was a far more prevalent top-priority inducement in Calvinist schools than in Catholic schools. Discipline, one of the best-known traditional strengths of Catholic schools, apparently remained so in the eyes of many patrons, for discipline was more often given as the primary reason by Catholic school patrons than by patrons in Calvinist or high-tuition schools.

It would be safe to say that the preferences of private school patrons, as reflected in Table 3.2, were based on more impressive considerations than were the preferences of public school patrons. This is not surprising, since private school patronage represents a departure from conventional behavior and entails extra cost, trouble, and effort. Our British Columbia surveys provide much other evidence to indicate that people who made active educational choices were more sophisticated, thoughtful, and concerned about their children's learning than were the people who simply followed the normal pattern of public school patronage, giving the matter little thought. The active choosers were in general better educated, of higher occupational and social status. They had devoted more time to the choice and had consulted a variety of sources of information more consistently. The tendency was not entirely limited to private school patrons. One generally impressive group was composed of people who said they chose their areas of residence with the quality of the local public schools in mind. They, like private school patrons, had sought out schools that met their educational preferences.

In a second British Columbia survey, conducted in 1979, 983 parents who had been interviewed earlier by telephone were requested by mail, with their prior permission, to rate the schools they were patronizing as "excellent," "good," "fair," "poor," or "very poor" in each of seventeen areas of performance. Of the 983 parents, 712 (72.4%) responded with usable data. The results are summarized in Table 3.4.

If one ranks the categories, for public and private schools separately, from the one with the highest proportion of positive ("excellent," "good," "fair") ratings to the one with the lowest proportion of positive ratings (see Table 3.4), it appears that social climate considerations, or considerations relevant to character-building, were the ones on which private schools as a

Table 3.4 Ranking of Areas of Performance by Percentage of Positive and Negative Ratings by Parents in British Columbia

	Public Schools				Independent Schools		
Item	% Pos	% Neg	Ranking	Item	% Pos	% Neg	Ranking
16: Physically Safe	79.7	2.2	HIGH	11: Right from Wrong	96.9	.5	
4: Competent Principal	80.1	4.5		5: Courteous and Kind	95.9	.8	
9: Skillful Teachers	68.4	2.9		10: Dedicated Teachers	95.6	.8	
8: Discourages Prejudice	68.2	7.1	MODERATE	17: Morally Safe	94.8	.5	
7: Think for Themselves	67.3	6.6		13: Parental Respect	94.4	.3	
10: Dedicated Teachers	64.7	4.6		6: Motivates Students	93.6	.8	VERY
3: Response to Parents	63.0	7.0		8: Discourages Prejudice	93.9	1.3	HIGH
6: Motivates Students	63.9	10.5		4: Competent Principal	93.7	1.6	
1: Good Discipline	63.2	11.0		1: Good discipline	93.4	1.3	
14: School Spirit	61.4	10.3		7: Think for Themselves	92.0	1.1	
17: Morally Safe	58.2	7.9	LOW	12: Get Along with Others	92.0	1.3	
11: Right from Wrong	56.7	10.7		9: Skillful Teachers	91.0	1.3	
12: Get Along with Others	53.7	10.4		16: Physically Safe	90.2	1.3	
15: Student Self-confidence	53.4	10.7		3: Response to Parents	87.6	1.6	
2: Individual Attention	55.5	14.2		15: Student Self-confidence	87.5	1.6	HIGH
5: Courteous and Kind	54.8	14.5		2: Individual Attention	87.2	1.1	
13: Parental Respect	48.7	11.3	VERY LOW	14: School Spirit			

SOURCE: See note 1, p. 107.

whole excelled the most in the eyes of most parents. This is not surprising in a group of schools predominantly religiously affiliated. As a whole, in the minds of these patrons, private schools did best at helping students tell right from wrong, encouraging students to be courteous and kind, providing dedicated teachers (who set a good example, among other things), maintaining morally safe conditions, encouraging students to be respectful toward parents, motivating students to do their best, and discouraging prejudice against minorities. The areas of performance (within this set of seventeen) on which public schools enjoyed positive ratings from more than 80% of their patrons were quite different in nature, dealing with physically safe conditions and the competence of the principal. Even in these areas, private schools were given a higher proportion of positive ratings.

Further analyses, not elaborated here, showed that parents associated with schools of four types (public, Catholic, other church-related, and high-tuition) were remarkably consistent in describing the relative strengths and weaknesses of their schools. The ratings, like the preferences discussed earlier, differed significantly from one school type to another, but not by social class. For example, religiously affiliated schools were rated higher than any others in character-building respects. High-tuition schools were rated higher than any others in academic respects. In each type of private school, parents thought they were getting high performance in the areas they had identified when expressing preferences.

In summary, the data suggest that parents who actively seek out schools that fit their preferences are unusually well informed, sophisticated, thoughtful, and concerned about their children's schooling. In exercising their preferences, these parents sort themselves out into schools with different emphases and obtain much greater satisfaction than do the parents who do not actively choose. If the ratings by these people may be taken at all seriously, the quality of their children's schooling might have been inferior if the options in question had not existed.

CANADIAN GOVERNMENT ATTEMPTS TO FOSTER EDUCATIONAL DIVERSITY

In contrast to the United States, in a number of countries where different constitutional guidelines and political traditions prevail, a variety of secular and sectarian schools have been given tax support as a way of fostering choice and diversity. But is this a promising way to ensure that diverse schools will emerge and die, grow and decline, in response to the fluctuating preferences of citizens? Evidence to illuminate this question is available, fortunately, from research on two pertinent arrangements in Canada.

Evidence on a Traditional Canadian Approach

In comparison with the early U.S. colonies, the Canadian colonies were severely divided, both internally and externally, especially along the lines of

religion and language. The national tendency was not toward a single publicly supported nondenominational school system, as in the United States,
but toward government protection and support of denominational schooling. At the time of Confederation (1867), a pattern of publicly supported
denominational schools was firmly in place and given constitutional protection.

In Ontario, Saskatchewan, and Alberta, as one of the several Canadian
patterns of school finance, the schools of the majority of citizens in each
area were known as public schools. The minority in each of these areas,
whether Protestant or Catholic, could secure a system of "separate" schools,
financed and organized in substantially the same manner as the public
schools. Before 1978 in British Columbia, and in parts of Manitoba, denominational schools and other nongovernmental schools were denied significant tax support.

Beginning in 1975, under a grant from the Spencer Foundation, this author, in collaboration with Richard Nault, decided to capitalize on the fact
that, while Catholic schools in three western provinces (Alberta, Saskatchewan, and Ontario) were supported entirely by taxes (except for the top
two grades in Ontario), one could find Catholic schools in Manitoba and
British Columbia that were not.

In the first phase of these "Spencer Interviews,"[38] we consulted twelve
highly placed key informants in Catholic school systems in the above-
mentioned provinces. In the second phase, we interviewed twenty-four
teachers and eight parents. (Catholic school leaders in major cities in the
five western provinces—Vancouver, Calgary, Saskatoon, Regina, Winni-
peg, and Toronto—were asked to identify parents and teachers who had
recently moved to their schools from other provinces, and from this list
respondents were selected who had moved from publicly supported to privately supported Catholic schools, and vice versa.) In the third phase, after
we had analyzed the earlier data, we interviewed eleven key Catholic educators to learn their reactions to our earlier analysis and then interviewed
twenty additional teachers, systematically selected to ensure that the total
sample was equally representative of nuns and lay teachers, and of teachers who had moved in the two directions (from publicly supported to privately supported schools, and vice versa). After the respondent's experience with Catholic schools of both types was verified, each teacher and
parent was asked a single open-ended question: "Did you notice any important differences between the two schools?" As the respondents an-
swered, we probed for clarification, expansion, and explanation of the ideas
expressed.

Evidence from the Spencer Interviews convinced us that the lengthy period of total support had significantly "deprivatized" Catholic schools in
Alberta, Saskatchewan, and Ontario, attenuating or obliterating numerous
characteristics which elsewhere distinguished Catholic schools from public
schools. Since parents did not have to make special efforts to patronize
Catholic schools in those three provinces, and in fact were often required

by law to patronize them, the vast majority of nominal Catholics were Catholic school patrons, including many who were uncommmited and perhaps relatively irreligious. The point of highest agreement among respondents concerned the commitment of teachers, almost unanimously described as stronger in the privately supported Catholic schools. In the view of many respondents, low salaries in privately supported schools performed the useful function of screening out would-be teachers with little dedication to Catholic education. As another possible explanation, we reasoned that it would be harder to find large numbers of highly committed teachers (needed in the provinces where Catholic schools were publicly supported and extensively patronized) than it would be to find small numbers (in the provinces where the schools were privately supported and patronized by a small Catholic minority).

In the provinces with publicly supported Catholic schools, far smaller proportions of Catholic school teachers were nuns than in the other provinces. The need to recruit far larger numbers of teachers may be part of the explanation, again, but we were repeatedly informed that many nuns had left because they felt the tax-supported Catholic schools could easily afford to hire "lay" teachers to replace them, and sometimes because they felt resented by members of teacher unions.

Traditionally, in Catholic elementary schools, as was noted earlier, relationships between school and parish were extensive and strong. Teachers and administrators could invoke not merely their authority as educators, but the resources and authority of the church. The schools, in concert with the parish, were, in Peshkin's use of Goffman's phrase (see the earlier passage on Fundamentalist schools), "total" institutions. In Alberta, Saskatchewan, and Ontario, however, full legal authority over Catholic schools was held by elected school boards. Religious leadership in Catholic schools had been assumed largely by professional educators in the downtown office; priests and other "normal" religious leaders often felt excluded and ignored. Catholic school systems had generally organized their school attendance areas to coincide with the attendance areas of public schools, rather than to coincide with parish boundaries. Furthermore, when the vast majority of Catholics were patronizing Catholic schools, so many classrooms were required that it was no longer possible, without introducing a system of large schools, to maintain the traditional pattern of a single school adjoining each church.

In 1984, while concluding the British Columbia study described below, we interviewed eighty-six B.C. Catholic school people, including a diocesan leader, thirteen members of boards and educational committees, two priests, eight administrators, thirty-nine parents, and twenty-three teachers. Though many obviously had lived in other Canadian provinces, it had not occurred to us to ask about Catholic schools elsewhere. Nevertheless many respondents volunteered comments about publicly supported Catholic schools in Alberta, Saskatchewan, and Ontario, usually lamenting the loss of distinctive Catholic school qualities. For example:

Compared to other places in Canada, the British Columbia funding is really quite string-free, you know. . . . The schools can still determine their religion programs, they can determine their staffing. . . . The bishop and the parish priests still control the schools (Interview 2510, p. 8, school 030)

My brother has children in the system in Alberta, and he just says, "If you had full government control, you wouldn't like it." (Interview 1708, p. 7, school 022)

You see, if they [government officials] were totally funding us, I think it would be different. But they're not, so we've got a lot of leeway. . . . Cause I know, like on the Prairies, I think they really have their hand in there. (Interview 2602, p. 21, school 022)

[After mentioning Ontario] I feel that we're getting more for our [tuition] money here because the parents are having to sacrifice, therefore there's more commitment. (Interview 925, p. 11, school 030)

Evidence on British Columbia's Approach

In 1978, British Columbia introduced a far different approach to encouraging educational diversity. The legislation in question was in many respects a consequence of the educational ideas and political skill of a minister of education ("Pat" McGeer) who was a strong spokesman for the benefits of private enterprise, and who sent his own children to a private school.[39] B.C.'s leaders were determined not to rob private schools of their distinctive qualities. B.C.'s aid would be partial rather than total, at least initially. The attached regulations would be minimal, carefully drafted to protect the public interest without homogenizing schools. Private schools were offered two levels of partial support. The higher level, which virtually all participating schools selected, provided 30%, per pupil per year, of local public school per-pupil operating costs. By 1984, the average amount provided to private schools was $1,000 per pupil per year.

In April 1978, with the financial support of the British Columbia Ministry of Education, the (U.S.) National Institute of Education, and other U.S. sources, the writer began a six-and-one-half-year study of the consequences of British Columbia's aid program.[40] In the light of persuasive indications that the B.C. government was determined not to curtail educational diversity, the study seemed especially promising. If B.C.'s program, with all it had going for it, turned out to force private schools toward the typical public school modus operandi, one might logically doubt the promise of aid to private schools elsewhere.

The B.C. study was complex, involving the surveys discussed earlier and many other components. In the light of that complexity and the fact that the study will soon be reported comprehensively elsewhere (the results are available at present only in preliminary draft), it is feasible to consider only a few general findings here.

One set of findings emerged from two parallel "social climate" surveys, one conducted in the spring of 1978, before B.C.'s private schools had received their first dollar under the new aid program (in fact, before they had been informed of the amount of aid they could expect), and the second conducted in the spring of 1980, after the private schools had nearly two academic years of experience with the aid. Designed, in keeping with a prior conceptualization, to determine whether certain social climate characteristics would be affected negatively by the inflow of public money, the surveys provided data strongly suggesting that was the case. Some changes occurred both in schools receiving the aid and in schools not receiving it (including, in some cases, public schools), but the following changes, predicted by the conceptualization and occurring only in the tax-aided private schools, seemed logically attributable to the aid program.

In Catholic elementary schools, the data suggested a dramatic decline, between 1978 and 1980, in teacher commitment as perceived by parents and in parent commitment as perceived by teachers. In Catholic secondary schools, the schools where the data suggested the most pronounced negative consequences of the aid, there was a notable decline in the sense among parents that their schools needed their help, in the extent to which parents viewed their schools as responsive, in teacher commitment as perceived by both parents and students, in parent commitment as perceived by teachers, in student affection toward teachers and classes, and in the perception by students that their schools, rather than being just like public schools, were doing something special. In the non-Catholic schools participating in the aid program, there are notable declines between 1978 and 1980 in the extent to which parents thought their schools were responsive to them, in teacher commitment as perceived by parents, and in student commitment as perceived by the students themselves.

In 1984, we held 250 personal interviews with B.C. private school personnel (teachers, parents, board and committee members, pastors, association executives), partly to discern the meaning of the above-mentioned changes and partly to seek evidence of later stability and change in social climate. In 1984 interviews suggested that part of the above-mentioned deterioration in school social climate had occurred because of early difficulties and misunderstandings concerning the use of new money. In the main, these difficulties and misunderstandings arose because parents were not given the tuition relief they had been led to anticipate. In Catholic schools, where teacher salaries by all accounts had been scandalously inadequate, most of the money by far was used to increase those salaries. In other private schools the money was more broadly allocated, but parent's fees were not reduced. By 1984, when the heat of those misunderstandings had subsided, most respondents (though far from all) said they believed, in retrospect, that the money had been used fairly. It is possible, then, that some of the social climate damage had been rectified. In all independent school groups in 1984, however, some respondents complained in one way or another about the loss of old distinctiveness. These respondents perceived, for example, that improved salaries were attracting a new breed of teacher, less dedicated and more money oriented, or that the schools were becoming less communal and flexible and more formal and rule bound (in one school, for instance, a parent complained that no one could now manage to let children in out of the rain a little early, as before, when their parents dropped them off on the way to work), or that (in Catholic schools, as an echo of what we found in other Canadian provinces) pronounced centralization was occurring, along with the breakdown of relationships between school and parish; or that the schools were becoming more academic in orientation, losing their religious distinctives. Once again, the evidence of negative changes was found primarily, though not exclusively, in Catholic schools.

The negative 1984 comments came from a minority of respondents, as one would expect. Since the B.C. aid was only partial (30% of what public schools were spending) and had been in place for less than six years, and since independent school leaders were still vigilant to maintain their schools' distinctive qualities, the negative impact of the aid on school social climates was probably still in its mild, initial stages, not nearly so pronounced as the impact seen in Catholic schools elsewhere in Canada, after decades of total public support. If the impact was still mild, many people would not yet notice it, especially busy parents who had only minimal contact with their schools. Many 1984 respondents commented, in fact, that they were unacquainted with many aspects of life in the schools.

A second set of major findings from the British Columbia study concerns the regulations attached to the aid program. Despite its apparent determination not to stamp out distinctive qualities in private schools, the government could not simply leave the private schools alone at a time when it was coming down hard on public schools, for this would particularly rile the citizens who were already angry about the aid to private schools. When demanding that certain basic subjects be allocated specified minimum periods of time in all public schools, the government was forced politically to make similar demands in private schools. When legislating certain courses (e.g., consumer education) in areas where the citizenry seemed seriously deficient, government could not easily get away with exempting private schools. When imposing mandatory twelfth-grade tests to ensure that illiterates would not continue to graduate with high school diplomas, government was under pressure to be equally demanding of the two publicly supported sectors of schooling—public and private. The political realities would have been quite different if private schools were receiving no significant public support, as in previous years. Government leaders may have expected some of those demands, at least, to be welcome in private schools, for the provincewide testing, for example, would give private schools an excellent, well-publicized opportunity to demonstrate that their students were generally performing at higher levels than were public school students. Since some tendencies mentioned below might well have occurred to some extent in the absence of the aid program, one must draw conclusions with great care, considering many nuances that cannot be analyzed properly here. With that caveat recorded, it may nevertheless be useful to illustrate the tendencies: In several schools, including the most elite school in our sample, teachers said they had been forced to replace vastly superior courses with one that was ludicrous in their eyes—the government-prescribed consumer-education course. Many teachers in church-related schools complained that religious instruction was being minimized by government specification of the time to be allocated to many areas of the curriculum. Two Fundamentalist schools had totally dropped the above-described programmed-instruction methods when seeking public support. The mandatory government examinations, by the testimony of many teachers, were so content specific as to dictate curriculum in considerable detail, in a manner destructive of superior teaching. These effects, like others, could still be characterized as rather mild, though they had come close to inducing some private schools to withdraw from the aid program. More important, the principle had been established that government, which had almost totally ignored private schools when they received no public aid, would now regulate them; statutory demands now in the code books could be given a more onerous interpretation by a less benevolent government. It seemed unrealistic to assume that less sympathetic authorities would never come to power. In the eyes of most respondents by far, the private schools, with rare exceptions, were thoroughly "hooked" on the aid, unlikely to back out if their freedom were destroyed in small increments. In the words of one headmaster: "All men are whores. As long as we are prostituted slowly, extreme regulation will not be noticed."

A Comparison to the Netherlands

While a much fuller analysis of the Dutch case appears in the following chapter, a parallel to the British Columbian case can be tentatively suggested here. This is that government subsidization may lead to dissatisfaction among private school clients. On the one hand, such findings could qualify Estelle James's conclusions about private popularity (as reflected in the Dutch private sector's 70% enrollment share); on the other hand, however, discontent may be traced to the weighty regulations and bureaucratization that James identifies as accompanying subsidization.

In any event, much like aforementioned comments of B.C. respondents about publicly supported Catholic schools elsewhere in Canada, our 1984 interviewees expressed fervent feelings about publicly supported Catholic schools elsewhere in Canada, and our 1984 interviews produced numerous unanticipated comments about publicly supported Calvinist schools in the Netherlands. Many respondents in B.C. Calvinist schools, being of Dutch extraction, were aware, often through firsthand experience, of the apparent consequences of the long-standing policy in the Netherlands of providing equal tax support to "secular," Catholic, and Calvinist schools. Every B.C. respondent who mentioned the Netherlands had distinctly disparaging comments. One said he had lost his religious faith in a publicly supported "Christian" school in the Netherlands. Several reported that many

Calvinists in the Netherlands, disenchanted with tax-supported Calvinist schools, were planning to begin all over again, establishing their own threadbare, privately supported Calvinist schools, vowing never to accept the first contaminating pittance of public money. To cite two verbatim examples:

> [Teacher] In Holland, in 1920, we got government funding, and that was total, . . . 100 percent. Teachers were paid by the state, and at first we were left alone. . . . When I went to high school we had the double system—government exams and school exams, so we could write our school exams according to how we were taught. . . . Then, . . . the job market was this way, that the people looked about what the government exams said, and not any more about what the school exams said. . . . Right now, they don't bother about school exams any more, and it goes totally in the directions of, whatever the public schools do, we do too. . . . And right now an awful lot of Christian schools . . . have closed their doors. We can't do our own thing anyway, so what's the use? (Interview 2404, pp. 8–9, school 001)

> [Teacher] Just speaking about the way it went in Holland when the government totally funds the schools. . . . Well, it seemed like all the time, well, the government started to dictate a little more of how the schools were run, and the people here quite remember that yet, what happened in Holland. . . . They don't want the Christian school system in Canada, specifically here, to deteriorate like it did in Holland. (Interview 2305, p. 25, school 001)

CONCLUDING THOUGHTS

The history of private schools suggests that when government does not interfere, schools tend to appear and die, grow and decline, in response to variegated, constantly changing preferences of citizens. Citizens who actively choose the schools which their children attend, from among a variety of available options, seem far more satisfied with their schools than are parents who simply do the "normal" thing, with little thought. Moreover, the active choosers appear to be more concerned, informed, and sophisticated.

In the United States, particularly, the responsiveness of the schooling market to consumers seems considerably dampened by government interference of three types. First, government makes one type of school (the publicly administered type) available to all citizens at tax expense, thus placing a fiscal handicap on all other schools. Second, political and constitutional realities limit diversity in public schools. Third, government discourages diversity in private schools through arbitrary and capricious regulatory strategies.

In Canada, under two approaches extending tax support to a variety of schools, including denominational schools, government appears to avoid much of the fiscal handicap imposed on private schools in the United States, but at the expense of limiting diversity in those schools, both through regulation attached to the aid and as an unintended side effect of shifting drastically the relationship between school and client. In the writer's view, however, British Columbia's regulatory grip in the context of sizable public aid is far less strangulating than what states like Hawaii, Iowa, Kentucky, Maine, Michigan, Nebraska, North Carolina, Ohio, Oregon, South Dakota, and Wisconsin have attempted from time to time in the absence of significant public support. It is also the writer's impression that in education classes in Canadian universities, as compared with U.S. universities, one encounters dramatically less tendency for educators to assume that they, rather than parents, should make the major decisions about the goals and methods to be used in institutions serving for compulsory school attendance purposes.

Beyond illuminating the question to some extent through evidence presented earlier, the present chapter is not the place to analyze in detail the purported benefits of educational diversity and choice. If one assumes for the moment, for the sake of this discussion, that diversity and choice should not be subjected to the limits now evident in the United States, then a few implications appear to follow.

First, it is difficult to see how much can be done, at a fundamental level, about the political and constitutional factors that limit diversity in publicly administered schools, though the matter may warrant considerable analysis. Second, the persistent and widespread tendency for educational officials in the United States to act as if they, rather than parents, should be primarily in control of the goals and methods of child-rearing for all future citizens deserves careful inquiry. Third, the Canadian examples cited here do not lend much credence to efforts to encourage educational diversity by extending public funds to private schools.

In one important sense, what the British Columbia government is attempting is far from unusual. Faced with evidence of what they have done to bias the marketplace, governments have often attempted to rectify the situation by returning to citizens, for their unbiased use, some of the funds previously extracted from them through taxation. It soon turns out, unfortunately, that the money has been transformed by passing through the public pipeline. It cannot now be freely used. It has become a political instrument, laden with constraints produced by the anxieties, pressures, and concerns of public officials.

This is not to say that aid to private schools or their patrons will always have the same precise consequences, regardless of its form and regulatory framework. One suspects, for instance, that aid provided directly to parents, perhaps in the form of vouchers, would have encouraged less centralization and loss of parental influence than has occurred in Canadian Catholic schools; would have produced, in B.C., more financial relief for parents (rather than being absorbed almost entirely by the private schools); would have done less to destroy patron commitment in some schools; and would have produced less school addiction to the money. Tax credits or deductions might have still different effects.

Even so, it may be fundamentally difficult to provide tax-financed aid in any form, direct or indirect, without hampering diversity. Logic seems to suggest, then, that there be discussion and experimentation concerning a seldom-considered strategy: to leave educational monies in the hands of citizens so they may directly finance their own publicly administered and privately administered schools by means of fees at the schoolhouse door, free of the inefficiency and bias of public finance. Since schooling is no more essential to human well-being than food, clothing, shelter, and medical care, there seems to be no more logical basis for government financing of everyone's education than for government funding of everyone's physical nourishment, raiment, housing, and health care. In any scheme for the provision of life's essentials, the poor must be accommodated, but to demonstrate the need for food stamps or medical benefits or education vouchers for the poor is not to justify public provision of services to citizens who can afford their own, especially if the public generosity produces profound damage and inefficiency. If it seems desirable to foster educational diversity and choice by relieving private schools of the fiscal handicaps now visited heavily upon them, then surely, within the limits of human invention, the handicaps can be removed in a manner not counterproductive, without destroying the diversity and choice.

NOTES

1. Data establishing these patterns, from a 1982 survey in British Columbia, are reported in Donald A. Erickson, *Victoria's Secret: The Effects of British Columbia's Aid to Independent Schools,* Final Report to the British Columbia Ministry of Education and the (U.S.) National Institute of Education, preliminary draft (Los Angeles: Institute for the Study of Private Schools, 1984), Chapter 7.

2. Ibid.

3. "Characteristics of Households with Children Enrolled in Elementary and Secondary Schools," National Center for Education Statistics *Bulletin,* Sept. 1984, pp. 1–11.

4. M. D. Eldridge, "America's Nonpublic Schools: A Quantification of Their Contribution to American Education," *Private School Quarterly,* Fall 1980, pp. 4–7; D. H. McLaughlin and L. L. Wise, *Nonpublic Education of the Nation's Children* (Palo Alto, Cal.: American Institutes for Research, 1980).

5. Bruce S. Cooper, Donald L. McLaughlin, and Bruno V. Manno, "The Latest Word on Private School Growth," *Teachers College Record* 85 (Fall 1983), pp. 88–98.

6. Ibid.

7. Ibid.

8. The figures are only approximate indications of the distribution of enrollment from group to group, since the categories are not mutually exclusive (some schools belong to more than one group).

9. J. A. Burns and B. J. Kohlbrenner, *A History of Catholic Education in the United States* (New York: Bensinger Brothers, 1937); Harold A. Buetow, *Of Singular Benefit: The Story of Catholic Education in the United States* (New York: Macmillan, 1970); James W. Sanders, *The Education of an Urban Minority: Catholics in Chicago, 1833–1965* (New York: Oxford University Press, 1981); Thomas C. Hunt and Norlene M. Kunkel, "Catholic Schools: The Nation's Largest Alternative School System," in James C. Carper and Thomas C. Hunt, eds., *Religious Schooling in America* (Birmingham, Ala.: Religious Education Press, 1984), pp. 1–34.

10. Otto F. Kraushaar, *American Nonpublic Schools: Patterns of Diversity* (Baltimore: Johns Hopkins Press, 1972), p. 13.

11. Cooper, McLaughlin, and Manno, "The Latest Word."

12. Donald A. Erickson, "The Devil and Catholic Education," *America*, April 10, 1971, pp. 36–71; Donald A. Erickson and George F. Madaus, *Issues of Aid to Nonpublic Schools*, Report to the President's Commission on School Finance (Chestnut Hill, Mass.: Boston College, 1971).

13. Mary Perkins Ryan, *Are Parochial Schools the Answer? Catholic Education in the Light of the Council* (Chicago: Holt, Rinehart & Winston, 1963); also see discussion of this period in Hunt and Kunkel, "Catholic Schools."

14. Later in this article, we report data on this point from a British Columbia survey conducted in 1982.

15. Herbert J. Walberg, "Improving the Productivity of America's Schools," *Educational Leadership* 41 (May 1984), pp. 19–30; Henry M. Levin and Gail R. Meister, "Computers in the Balance: Weighing Costs and Effectiveness," *IFG Policy Perspectives*, Summer 1984, pp. 1–4.

16. Andrew Greeley, William McCready, and Katherine McCourt, *Catholic Schools in a Declining Church* (Kansas City, Mo.: Sheed and Ward, 1976).

17. James G. Cibulka, Timothy J. O'Brien, and Donald Zewe, *Inner-City Private Elementary Schools: A Study* (Milwaukee, Wisc.: Marquette University Press, 1982); Barbara L. Schneider, Diane T. Slaughter, and Robyn Kramer, "Blacks in Private Schools," paper presented at Annual Meeting of American Educational Research Association, Montreal, Canada, April 1983.

18. Goffman refers to mental hospitals, monasteries, and jails as "total institutions," since, among other things, their "clients" are under their control twenty-four hours a day. Erving Goffman, "The Characteristics of Total Institutions," in Amitai Etzioni, ed., *Complex Organizations* (New York: Holt, Rinehart, and Winston, 1964). Peshkin suggests that the same "totality" of impact may be achieved by a church and school working in close concert, especially when the school insists that students must live by its rules at all times. Alan Peshkin, *God's Choice: The Total World of a Fundamentalist Christian School* (Chicago: University of Chicago Press, 1986).

19. Ibid., p. 14 in manuscript.

20. By Bidwell's definition: "In moral socialization the person acquires values and goals for conduct, learns and becomes responsive to moral rules (norms), and gains a view of the world as a moral order. That is, he acquires culturally grounded goals and aspirations: he comes to know (though not always well) and observe (though not always willingly, scrupulously, or regularly) the rules that will govern his conduct in situations; he develops a view of the conduct of others as revealing motivations and contraints; he learns that social regulations and institutions embody values and are subject to moral regulations. Moral socialization thus involves an emerging capacity to make moral judgments of self, others, and society in the light of values and norms (and, indeed, of norms in the light of values)." Charles E. Bidwell, "Schooling and Socialization for Moral Commitment," *Interchange* 3, 4, (1972), pp. 1–

21. See, for example: George Edward Ballweg, Jr., "The Growth in the Number and Population of Christian Schools Since 1966: A Profile of Parental Views Concerning Factors Which Led Them to Enroll Their Children in a Christian School," Ed.D. disertation, School of Education, Boston University, 1980; Virginia D. Nordin and William L. Turner, "More Than Segregation Academies: The Growing Protestant Fundamentalist Schools," *Phi Delta Kappan* 61 (Feb. 1980), pp. 391–394; Peter Skerry, "Christian Schools Versus the IRS," *The Public Interest* 61 (1980), pp. 18–24; William Lloyd Turner, "Reasons for Enrollment in Religious Schools: A Case Study of Three Recently Established Fundamentalist Schools in Kentucky and Wisconsin," Ph.D. dissertation, University of Wisconsin-Madison, 1979.

22. Donald A. Erickson, "Differential Effects of Public and Sectarian Schooling on the Religiousness of the Child," Ph.D. dissertation, Department of Education, University of Chicago, 1962.

23. J. R. McQuilkin, "Public Schools: Equal Time for Evangelicals," *Christianity Today* 22 (1977), pp. 404–407; Nordin and Turner, "More Than Segregation Academies"; Skerry, "Christian Schools versus the IRS."

24. See: *State* v. *Whisner*, 351 N. E. 2d 750 (Ohio, 1976); *Kentucky State Board of Education* v. *Rudasill*, 589 S.W. 2d 877 (1979); *State ex rel. Douglas* v. *Faith Baptist Church*, 301 N.W. 2d 571 (1981), appeal dismissed, 454 U.S. 803 (1981); *Bangor Baptist Church* v. *State of Maine*, 549 F. Supp. 1208 (1982); *Prettyman* v. *State of Nebraska*, 537 F. Supp. 712 (1982); *Sheridan Road Baptist Church* v. *State of Michigan* (Ingraham Circuit Court, Docket No. 80-26205-AZ, December 29, 1982); *State* v. *Rivinius*, 328 N.W. 2d 220 (N.D., 1982).

25. The discussion that follows is based primarily on Alvin Irwin Schiff, *The Jewish Day School in America* (New York: Jewish Education Committee, 1966); and Eduardo Rauch, "The Jewish Day School in America: A Critical History and Contemporary Dilemmas," in Carper and Hunt, *Religious Schooling*, pp. 130–165.

26. Rauch, "The Jewish Day School," p. 141.

27. Ibid., p. 142

28. Ibid., pp. 147–148.

29. See, for example, "Decadence of the Pennsylvania, New York, and Scandinavian Systems," in Walter M. Beck, *Lutheran Elementary Schools in the United States* (St. Louis, Mo.: Concordia Publishing House, 1965), pp. 281†288.

30. John A. Hostetler and Gertrude Enders Huntington, *Children in Amish Society: Socialization and Community Education* (New York: Holt, Rinehart and Winston, 1971), pp. 35–36.

31. Lawrence A. Cremin, *The Transformation of the School: Progressivism in American Education: 1876–1957* (New York: Random House, 1961), pp. 277–291; Bruce S. Cooper, *Free School Survival* (Sarasota, Fla.: Omni-print, 1975); Alan Graubard, *Free the Children: Radical Reform and the Free School Movement* (New York: Pantheon Books, 1972).

32. Clemmont E. Vontress, "The Black Muslim Schools," *Phi Delta Kappan* 47 (Oct. 1965), pp. 86–90.

33. Peshkin, *God's Choice*.

34. See, as examples of the comparatively few conflicts (among the many that occurred) that reached the courts, the cases listed under note 24, above.

35. *Meyer* v. *Nebraska*, 262 U.S. 390 (Neb., 1923); *Pierce* v. *Society of Sisters*, 268 U.S. 510 (Ore., 1925); *Farrington* v. *Tokushige*, 273 U.S. 284 (Haw., 1927).

36. *Wisconsin* v. *Yoder*, 406 U.S. 205 (1972). Donald A. Erickson, "Showdown at an Amish Schoolhouse: A Description and Analysis of the Iowa Controversy," in Erickson, ed., *Public Controls for Nonpublic Schools* (Chicago: University of Chicago Press, 1968), pp. 15–59; Erickson, "The Plain People vs. the Common Schools," *Saturday Review* 49 (Nov. 19, 1966), pp. 85–87, 102–103; "The Persecution of Leroy Garber," *School Review* 78 (November 1969), pp. 81–90; Albert N. Keim, ed., *Compulsory Education and the Amish: The Right Not to Be Modern* (Boston: Beacon Press, 1975).

37. Erickson, *Victoria's Secret*, Chapter 10.

38. Summarized in ibid.

39. Whereas the term most commonly used in the United States to refer in general to nongovernmental schools is *private schools,* the Canadian term used in the same sense is *independent schools.* In the United States, the latter phrase is generally taken to refer to private schools not associated with the major denominational systems.

40. Erickson, *Victoria's Secret*.

II

Intersectoral Comparisons

4

Public Subsidies for Private and Public Education: The Dutch Case*

ESTELLE JAMES

The possibility of "privatizing" education and other quasi-public services has been widely discussed in the United States today, and in other chapters of this volume. Policies such as a voucher or tax credit system, which would give public subsidies to private schools, are examples of privatization proposals. Many people feel that such policies would bring variety, choice, consumer responsiveness, and greater efficiency to our schools. Others fear that they would increase social segmentation, damage the public schools, and enable wealthy people to receive a better education for their children privately, but (partially) at the public expense.

To expore these issues, this chapter examines the experience of the Netherlands, a country which, in effect, has had a voucher system in education for many years.[1] In Holland, education and most health and social services are financed by the government but delivered by private nonprofit organizations, often religious in nature. As shall become evident below, the Dutch educational system avoids many of the possible pitfalls of privatization. This is due partially to particular mechanisms the Dutch have adopted to avoid these problems, which could conceivably be replicated here, and partially to broader structural features of the Dutch educational system and its role within society, which could not readily be replicated.

The chapter proceeds as follows: The first section summarizes the historical background of the public-private division of responsibility for education in the Netherlands. The policy of privatization is seen as a response to diverse tastes about education, stemming from basic cultural (religious)

*This chapter is adapted from "Benefits and Costs of Privatized Public Services: Lessons from the Dutch Educational System," *Comparative Education Review* 28, 4 (1984). An earlier version of this chapter was Working Paper No. 47 of the Program on Non-Profit Organizations at Yale University.

differences, in a political setting where no one group was in a position to impose its preferred product variety on the others. This is consistent with a hypothesis I am testing in a multicountry study: that degree of reliance on private provision of quasi-public goods is positively related to cultural (particularly religious and linguistic) heterogeneity in democratic societies. It also is relevant to the discussions, found in several previous chapters, of why families choose private schooling.

The second section examines the source of entrepreneurship and entry of new private schools, virtually all of which are nonprofit in the Netherlands. Who starts them and what are the objectives of the founders, in the absence of a profit motive? The next section describes the unusual Dutch financing arrangement—public funding of private education and tied public-private budgets—which prevents a gross disparity in resources available to the two sectors. The fourth section sets forth the government regulations that accompany the government funding; as is often the case, these regulations tend to be input related rather than output related. The final two sections then analyze, respectively, efficiency and elitism in the Dutch system. Finally, the conclusion suggests some implications for the current American situation.

HISTORICAL ORIGINS OF THE DUTCH SYSTEM[2]

The evolution of the Dutch system of primary and secondary education is unusual for the Western world: We see a shift from a relatively secular public monopoly at the beginning of the nineteenth century to a highly pluralistic private religious-based system by the end. While secular public school systems were clearly in ascendancy in the rest of the West, the Dutch system was moving in the opposite direction and has remained there to the present day.[3]

The Education Act of 1806 gave the state a monopoly over education; private schools could only be established with the consent of the state, which was not readily granted. Public education was nondenominational, its secular cast, however, consistent with preferences of the dominant Dutch Reformed group. The main effect of the public monopoly was to prevent the formation of separate Catholic schools.

Catholics constituted a large minority (about 35%) of the Dutch population. Their right to practice their religion, as well as establish schools, had been severely restricted between the time of the Netherlands' war of independence from Spain in the sixteenth century and the French Revolution at the end of the eighteenth century. However, after the Napoleonic invasion, at the turn of the nineteenth century, Dutch Catholics began to enjoy greater religious freedom. In 1848 the situation was further liberalized and private groups were given the right to establish their own schools—using their own revenues. The state no longer had a monopoly, but did have advantageous access to resources. Nevertheless, we begin to see the appearance of separate Catholic schools, financed by voluntary contributions and free teaching services of monks and nuns, as soon as they became legal.

At the same time another religious group was developing in size and political power in the Netherlands—the Re-reformed Dutch Church, or Calvinists. These were orthodox Protestant sects that grew during the period of religious revivalism, dissatisfied with the secularism and liberalism of the Dutch Reformed Church. In addition to their purely religious functions, the Calvinists formed their own Anti-Revolutionary party and became a potent political force. Thus, instead of one dominant and one subordinate group, by the mid-nineteenth century Dutch society was split three ways, leaving room for the formation of coalitions and new policies.

Regarding the issue of education, each group had a different "first preference," the Dutch Reformed preferring a relatively secularized system of public education for everyone, the Calvinists preferring a public school system with a strong fundamentalist theology, and the Catholics preferring separate public and private systems, both with state support. Given the size and strength of the Catholics and liberal Protestants, however, it was clear that the Calvinists would not be able to achieve their first-best goal. Thus, they formed a political alliance with the Catholics to achieve their second-best goal: complete state subsidy of private schools, in which each group could teach its own religious philosophy. The Catholic-Calvinist coalition, with this educational program as its major issue, now had a small majority over the Dutch Reformed–dominated Liberal party and came to power in 1889, successfully obtaining limited state support for private schools.

Power seesawed back and forth between the Christian and Liberal parties over the next twenty-five years, with state support to private schools gradually increasing but still not complete. Concomitantly, still another political group was developing—the Socialists. Thus, in the 1913 election neither the Christian nor the Liberal parties could gain a clear majority, since the Socialists held the balance of power. The main political objective of the left was universal manhood suffrage, a change which would require a constitutional amendment, hence a two-thirds vote. In other words, a majority (of Socialists plus Christians) now favored some fundamental change in the system. And no one group was able to get what it wanted without reaching some agreement with the others. The 1913 electoral crisis was resolved by a "logrolling" arrangement in which each group got what it wanted most, giving in on the other issues: while the Liberal party formed the basis for the new government, the Socialists got universal manhood suffrage and the Christians got full financial parity for their private religious schools. Moreover, this principle was accepted as a long-term rather than a short-term decision, and was embodied in the Constitution of 1917.

"Separate but equal school systems" became a central component in a society which was sharply segmented along religious lines during the first half of the twentieth century. Not only education but also most other collective activities, such as health care, social services, media, political parties, and trade unions, were provided separately by and for each religious group, in a process known as *verzuiling* (columnization or pillarization) of society. Many of these activities were funded privately, initially often on a voluntary basis; but even when financing was taken over by the state, religious-based organizations continued to provide the service. In the following pages I examine how the separation of financing from service delivery worked in the field of education.

ENTREPRENEURSHIP AND THE SUPPLY RESPONSE

Most private schools both in Holland and the United States are nonprofit, so a major issue is a proposed voucher scheme would be: How do such organizations get started? In the absence of a profit motive, who will provide the entrepreneurship—the leadership and the venture capital for starting new enterprises or, in the case of education, new schools? Will the private sector respond rapidly to increases in demand? If government policy encourages privatization in order more fully to satisfy consumer preferences, the incentives and conditions for entry are obviously crucial. The Dutch system throws some light on how these mechanisms might work. Most notable is the key role of religious organizations in providing the entrepreneurial function—a common observation as well in other countries I have studied. In this respect, the Dutch situation is the norm, rather than a special case. Religion seems to be the major source of differentiated demand for education and private nonprofit supply, although Erickson's chapter has documented the changing complexity of the U.S. private sector.

The 1920 Law on Education, which implemented the 1917 Constitution, solved the entry problem by enabling relatively small groups of parents to start their own school and by requiring the government to provide almost all initial capital costs as well as ongoing current expenses. The law provided that if a specified number of parents got together in a formal nonprofit organization (a "foundation" or an "association") and requested an elementary school with a particular religious or pedagogical philosophy, the municipality had to provide them with a building and miscellaneous inputs, while the central government would pay teacher salaries. The requisite number of parents varied by size of municipality: 125, 100, 75, or 50 for municipalities with residents of more then 100,000, 50,000 to 100,000, 25,000 to 50,000, or less than 25,000, respectively.[4] Thus, only a minimum amount of organizational and political skills was needed to set up a private elementary school.

It is noteworthy, then, that most of this entrepreneurship came from the church; in general, unrelated groups of parents did not come together to form secular private schools, nor did secular organizers unite them. Instead, the parents involved already knew each other, and leadership was provided by their priest or minister. In the Catholic church, the foundation form, or *stichting*, was used: For each geographic area, a foundation, with a self-perpetuating board, was set up to determine where schools should be placed and to assemble the required number of parental signatures. The organization was, thus, "top-down" and hierarchical, with a representative of the bishop present on most *stichting* boards. The Protestant sects were more decentralized and variegated. Typically, a congregation would constitute an association, or *vereniging*, with all members electing a board that established and ran the school.

A few neutral private schools are also established, usually espousing a particular pedagogical technique, such as Montessori, Dalton, or Rudolph Steiner. These parents were brought together through word of mouth in their place of work or residence, or through newspaper advertising. The neutral schools are concentrated in large cities and are small in number (the private primary sector in Holland is 95% church related).

Further statistical evidence on the importance of religion as a motivating and organizing factor is provided if we examine the data disaggregated by province. The private-public division of responsibility for education varies widely by province, as does the representation of Catholics and Calvinists in the population. My expectation was that since these groups have the strongest "taste" for religious education, as well as the greatest entrepreneurial supply, the proportion of Catholics plus Calvinists would be positively correlated with the relative share of the private sector—that is, the higher the former, the higher would be the latter. When I tested this hypothesis using data on religious affiliation for 1977 and primary schools for 1979, I obtained a confirming r^2 of 0.85.[5]

In the case of secondary schools, where more capital resources are involved, the entry procedure is somewhat less automatic. Here, the minister of education is required to set forth an annual "plan," which specified the state, municipal, and private schools to be supported in each area, for the next three years. Negotiation and discretion, in which each group tries to convince the minister of the need for its own school, thus play a more important role. One mechanism used by private groups in the past was to self-finance for the first few years, to demonstrate that a demand existed; obviously some financial support from the church was particularly helpful here. However, in the end, the public-private configuration at the secondary level was very much like the elementary.

Given the ease of entry, the provision of entrepreneurship by organized religion, and the provision of capital and other costs by the government, the huge supply response of private school places is not surprising. Public schools were also provided directly by municipalities. Data on the public-private responsibility for education from 1850 to 1980 are provided in Table 4.1, which shows the dramatic shift that occurred at the primary and secondary levels when government subsidies became available.

As of 1880, 75% of all primary students were attending public schools. Between 1880 and 1925, as more children enrolled, the numbers grew in both the public and private sectors, but the relative share of the former

Table 4.1 Public and Private Enrollment Shares, 1850–1980

PRIMARY SCHOOL

Year	Total	Public	Private Total	Protestant	Catholic	Other
1850	100	77	23			
1900	100	69	31			
1910	100	62	38			
1920	100	55	45			
1930	100	38	62	25	36	2
1938	100	31	69	26	41	2
1950	100	27	73	28	43	2
1960	100	27	73	27	44	2
1970	100	28	72	27	43	2
1979	100	31	69	28	38	3

SECONDARY SCHOOL[a]

Year	Total	Public	Private Total	Protestant	Catholic	Other
1850	100	100				
1900	100	91	9			
1910	100	87	13			
1920	100	75	25			
1930	100	61	39	13	18	8
1938	100	53	47	17	22	8
1950	100	43	57	19	29	9
1960	100	35	65	22	35	7
1970	100	28	72	27	41	4
1980	100	28	72	27	39	6

[a]Data shown for 1850–1960 are for grammar schools; for 1970–80 (after an educational reorganization), general secondary schools.

SOURCES: 1850–1960: *de ontwikkeling van het onderwijs in nederlands,* editie 1966 (The Hague: Central Bureau of Statistics, 1966), pp. 65, 66, 119, 120, 148.

1970–1979: *Statistiek van het gewoon lager onderwijs* (The Hague: Central Bureau of Statistics, 1966–67, 1971–72, 1976–77, 1979–80).

1970–1980: *Statistiek van VWO, HAVO en MAVO,* (The Hague: Central Bureau of Statistics, 1966–67, 1971–72, 1976–77, 1980–81).

declined to less than 50%. After 1925, the number of public schools and students declined in both absolute and relative terms, with the private sector moving in the opposite direction, until World War II. By the end of the war, a new equilibrium had been reached. No longer were there substantial denominational or other groups of parents who felt that the benefits (i.e., the religious or pedagogical variety) outweighed the costs (i.e., the time, effort, and interest on the 10% bond) of establishing new schools. While absolute numbers in both sectors increased slightly after that in response to population growth and the opening of new neighborhoods, the sectoral shares had roughly stabilized, fluctuating only modestly in the range 27–31% public, 2% private secular, and 67–71% private religious—almost the mirror image of the situation a hundred years ago. The corresponding equilibrium distribution of school sizes yielded an average of only 160–175 students per school during this period.

A similar but more elongated pattern emerges for secondary grammar schools, with the public enrollment share 95% in 1880, but declining thereafter. General secondary school enrollments (junior secondary plus secondary grammar) have continuously increased in Holland over the past century as a larger proportion in the relevant age gruop has continued its education; but the private sector steadily increased its share until an equilibrium of 28% public, 6% private secular, and 66% private religious appeared to be reached by the early 1970s. The secondary schools, with larger capital requirements and program diversity, were much larger in size (an average of 545 students per school in 1980) than the primary schools. Whether these numbers, achieved through a decentralized cost-benefit analysis, are large enough for efficency is discussed in a later section.

The Dutch experience suggests that if greater public support for private schools were provided in other countries, the greatest beneficiaries would be the religious groups that are best able to set up new schools. In a more secularized society such as the United States, the supply elasticity of non-denominational schools would probably be somewhat greater, but the supply elasticity of the system as a whole would probably be much less than it was in Holland.

HOW SCHOOLS ARE FINANCED:
TIED PUBLIC AND PRIVATE BUDGETS

One of the concerns in this country is that if the private school system expands, financial support for public schools might decline. For example, if a community's public school budget is determined by the median voter, and if the median voter sends his child to a private school, he may opt for a very low public school budget, quality level, and tax rate. In Holland this danger is avoided simply by tying private school budgets to public budgets and by limiting the power to charge tuition. In effect, each family gets a voucher equivalent to the per capita cost in the local public school (approximately $1300 for current expenses in 1978)[6] and which must be spent on education. The school that receives the voucher is then entitled to funding that will cover specified amounts of teacher salaries and other expense. Private schools can and do supplement this voucher by charging ancillary fees; however, this right is severely limited, as discussed below. Municipal public schools collect similar vouchers from parents, but may not charge additional fees during the ten years of compulsory schooling, ages six to sixteen.

The actual process by which private school costs are covered is more complicated and has three fundamental characteristics: The central government has most of the taxing power and pays most of the costs; a limited degree of local government discretion is allowed; and substantial restrictions are imposed on the ability of private schools to raise and spend funds as they please.

First of all, the central government pays all teacher salaries directly, both for public and private schools. These salaries are based on fixed scales that take into account education and experience. Schools are not permitted to supplement the salaries, for example, to try to attract better teachers by paying higher salaries. The number of teachers to which a school is entitled depends on its number of students and is computed according to a schedule which embodies a faculty/student ratio of approximately 31/1. Additional teachers are provided for disadvantaged and other special student categories, on an equal basis to both public and private schools. (Municipalities may pay for extra teachers in their public schools, but if they do so, they must add an equivalent number to the local private schools; their limited taxing power means that few additional teachers are hired.) Since 80–90% of all current school expenditures are for teacher salaries, this immediately places the bulk of budgetary decisions in the hands of the central government.

As noted above, the buildings for both public and private primary schools are provided by the municipality—but with reimbursement by the central government for interest plus depreciation or for rent.

Remaining is a small fund for operating expenses, which the school may allocate at its discretion among activies such as maintenance, cleaning, heating, libraries, and teaching aids. This sum is determined separately by each municipality, which must then give all public and private schools the same per capita amount, usually about $200.

The financing procedure is somewhat different at the secondary level. Here, there are state as well as municipal and private schools. Once again, all teacher salaries and building costs are covered directly by the central government. In addition, municipal and private secondary general schools which are included in the minister of education's three-year plan get the same discretionary fund per capita as do comparable state schools. Secondary vocational schools have more individualized cost structures which are fully reimbursed by the central government, after a negotiated agreement on budget has been reached.

Private fees are only a minor source of financing. As noted above, the first ten years of public schooling are legally free, while small fees may be charged by higher secondary schools and universities. At all age levels, however, private schools are allowed to impose their own fees—ostensibly for "educational facilities" (e.g., libraries and swimming pools) rather than for "education" per se. Information about private fees is not relayed to the government and is jealously guarded, so I could not secure precise data. Parents and school authorities, however, indicated they range between $100 and $200 per year at most primary schools, and slightly higher at the secondary level—very modest by American standards.

Why have the fees remained so low? Since "education" itself is supposed to be free, many schools fear that an excessively large fee might disqualify them from receiving the large government subsidy, a risk they do not want to take. If the government subsidy were small, a larger number of schools might have opted out of the system, charging fees and retaining other authority. Thus, a voucher with low values may lead to a much more differentiated system than a high-valued voucher.

In addition, market competition keeps fees generally low, particularly in view of the easy entry conditions mandated by law. Even these low fees are not obligatory. In the past, in many schools, if a family could not afford the fee, it would usually be waived. If the school had some excess capacity, its revenue per student from the state would far exceed its marginal cost, so it was better off practicing downward price discrimination and accepting the child even if the parents paid nothing. In the future, this economically motivated rationale will be reinforced by the state under a new law which provides that failure to pay a school fee will not constitute legally acceptable grounds for excluding a child from a private school. Other reasons why elite selective schools, opting out of the publicly financed system and charging high fees, have not developed in the Netherlands (as they have in other countries) will be discussed later in this chapter.

Thus, from the budgetary point of view, every voter in a community is in the same school system. The voter must support the public school at the same time he or she supports his or her private school. It is unclear a priori whether total educational expenditures will be larger or smaller in such a publicly financed system as compared with one where private funding is permitted. It is also not certain, though probable, that per student expenditures in the public schools will be higher and the overall variance in per student expenditures will be lower in a tied system.[7] Under one plausible scenario, society faces a trade-off between the twin goals of maximizing educational equality and maximizing the total resources devoted to education. While the Dutch system avoids the possibility of a gross deterioration in the public schools, due to opting out and adverse selection, this comes at the cost of restricting the ability of the private schools to make their own spending decisions and the ability of parents to spend much more than average on the education of their children. Furthermore, since this arrangement requires that the voucher be set high enough to cover almost all educational costs, the tax burden of providing a given quality of education is greater than in a system where private schools are privately financed. These are the routes to and costs of financial educational equality, which the Dutch have accepted and which we would have to consider if we moved toward greater public funding of our private schools.

GOVERNMENTAL REGULATION

A major issue when privatizing education is discussed concerns the relationship between government funding and government regulation. Does more of the former imply more of the latter? The argument here is that the subsidies create a rent whose distribution politicians can control via regulations in ways which maximize their political benefit. In the case of the educational system in Holland, there is indeed a considerable amount of both funding and regulation, consistent with (but certainly not proving) a positive correlation between the two. The government controls could obviate some of the advantages (and disadvantages) of the private sector, which stem from its independence, flexibility, and differentiated product. Both society, in choosing its system, and private schools, in choosing where they fit into the system, would then face a trade-off between autonomy and more funds. In this trade-off, the Dutch private schools have clearly chosen the latter, so long as they can retain their specific denominational or pedagogical identity. Some American private schools might make divergent choices, depending on their degree of congruence with government policies and their access to alternative sources of funds.

Significantly, many of the regulations in the Dutch system apply to inputs rather than outputs. This appears even more in connection with their other quasi-public goods, such as health and social service. One rationale is that inputs are easier to measure and control than outputs. In addition, this observation is consistent with the well-known hypothesis that government financing is often a response to producer as well as (or instead of) consumer interests, and the regulations are designed in large part to protect the producers.

I have already noted some of the controls over inputs. Historically, teacher costs were the first inputs to be government financed and regulated. Teacher numbers (based on student/faculty ratios) and salaries, as well as required teacher credentials, are centrally determined, as are hours and other conditions of work. We also find rigid restrictions on the school's ability to fire teachers, stemming partially from the fact that their salaries are paid by the government and that hence they enjoy quasi–civil service status. The order of firing is specified, not discretionary, and depends on age and seniority, not competence.

The building cost is also separately determined, as is the small fund from the municipality for meeting other current expenditures.

While these regulations are justified as an attempt to achieve equality, they give the private school very limited discretion to choose the preferred point on its production function. It has no incentive, for example, to economize on building costs in order to buy more books. Nor can it hire three young teachers instead of two with more seniority, even though these alternatives might cost the same. In contrast, American private schools, which are privately funded, are more likely to have lump-sum budgets with transferability among input categories; they are likely to employ teachers with different credentials and salaries than public schools; and some would probably be reluctant to give up this flexibility in return for more state funding. If one argument in favor of decentralization and privatization is that the schools know more about their own teaching technology than does a central government official, then the Dutch arrangement does not allow them to exploit this potential advantage, since the schools cannot freely vary their factor proportions to minimize the costs of producing a given output.

Direct controls over outputs also exist. All schools must follow a uniform curriculum, which specifies the number of hours to be spent on each required subject each year. All students must take a uniform national exam at the end of elementary school, and in major subjects at the end of secondary school; these exams, which help determine admissibility to further education, serve as an important control mechanism, since all teaching must be geared to helping the student perform well. In addition, central inspectors periodically check on the activities of each school, to assure that all input and output regulations are being followed.

Controls extend, too, over the distribution of service and the criteria for selecting students. For example, as noted earlier, the government places de facto limits on the fees that schools can charge and on their right to exclude students who do not pay.

However, subject to these broad restrictions, educational institutions at all levels are permitted to teach in the manner they please. They can choose their own texts and their own teachers, including the possibility of using religion and life-style as criteria for hiring. Each denomination runs its own government-financed teacher-training colleges, which are empowered to grant certification providing the required curriculum is followed. Teachers can choose their own day-to-day classroom delivery. Certain subjects, such as history, have been taught in very different ways in different denominational schools.[8] Other school characteristics have also varied by religious group historically; for example, Catholic schools were more likely to be single sex rather than coed and to employ a high proportion of female teachers, probably nuns. However, these differences appear to be declining with the secularization of society.[9]

One of the most recent and interesting areas for government control is over the decision-making process at schools and other nonprofit organizations, the rationale being that if governmental funding is provided and authority is delegated to these organizations, society needs some assurance that their decision-making structure is democratic.

A second motivating factor has been the inconsistency between religious control of schools and secularization of society in the 1970s. Thus we have new laws mandating decision making by teachers, parents, and, at higher educational levels, by students as well.

Parental participation, however, appears difficult to mobilize; public apathy in Dutch society has frequently been noted.[10] Perhaps the apathy stems from the fact that parents who do not like the way their school is run can simply choose another and therefore take less trouble to change it (i.e., they exercise exit rather than voice). The net result of the new legislation, therefore, will probably be greater power to the teachers. This is consistent with the trend toward increased professional power in other social service fields and with the hypothesis that government regulations will have the effect of protecting producer, rather than consumer, interests.

The school founders and original decision makers, we have seen, were likely to be active members of the religious community, a characteristic they may have sought in their successors. The new decision makers—teachers, parents, and students—are likely to have different set of goals, with religion probably playing a smaller role. It will be interesting to observe whether in fact the decision-making structure changes as a result of government regulation, and whether this alters the basic nature of the schools.

COST AND EFFICIENCY

The evaluation of the Dutch system, and the desirability of using a voucher system in other countries, depends partially on its efficiency properties. The chief benefit of the system is that it provides product variety and gives consumers a choice, thereby enabling preferences about school characteristics to be satisfied. The corresponding costs of variety and privatization depend on a number of factors, including the existence of scale economies, the relative cost-effectiveness of public and private schools, transportation costs, the expenses of regulation, and the responsiveness of the system to disequilibrium and innovation. Each of these is dealt with briefly in this section.

Economies of Scale

The Dutch System is implicitly based on the assumption that there are few economies of scale, particularly in elementary schools, hence few cost disadvantages to having many small differentiated schools. As noted above, a new school can be started if desired by a few as fifty parents; the typical primary (secondary) school in Holland has only 160 (545) students, small by American standards. If the minimum point on the average cost curve is substantially above these numbers (or if higher quality can be achieved at lower average cost with larger numbers), the Dutch system may end up with "too many" private schools for cost efficiency or high quality; and the drain of students from the public schools would impose a similar cost there.

To study whether scale economies exist in the Dutch school system, we would ideally want to compare average costs at schools of different sizes, holding constant student inputs and quality of output (i.e., value added by the school) and assuming that all schools are free to choose the least-cost production technique for each size. In fact, however, schools are not free to choose their preferred technology; instead, as we have seen, they are assigned specific production factors, which may not be a least-cost combination, by the central government. Furthermore, small schools are found in rural areas and hence have a different student input from large schools;

and I was unable to ascertain whether educational quality is constant for schools of different sizes. Therefore, one cannot readily determine from the Dutch data whether real scale economies exist—although evidence from other countries suggest they do over the relevant range.[11]

We can, however, approach this question in another way: Do the reimbursement schedules followed by the central government imply lower or higher monetary costs for larger schools? If reimbursement schedules reflect the minimum resources needed to produce varying quantities of output, holding quality constant, we can use them to trace out the cost curves. One of the striking features is the discontinuities in these cost curves, stemming from the teacher assignment schedules. Because of this, it is clear that if municipalities were free to assign students to each school until a point of "full capacity" was reached, education could be provided as much lower cost.

For example, "full enrollment capacity" for a primary school with six teachers is defined by the government to be 199 students; this enables one class per grade. If, however, such a school is broken into halves (one public and one private), higher building costs are incurred and, in addition, each is entitled to four teachers—a cost increase of 33%. If it is instead broken into thirds (public, Protestant, and Catholic), each is entitled to three teachers, a 50% cost increase.[12] Similar calculations reveal that the "average" primary school in Holland today has 159 students and a student/faculty ratio of 27.5/1, compared with 199 and 33/1 at full capacity. If all schools were "average," this would increase teacher costs by 20%, and the number of buildings by 25%, as compared with a "full capacity" situation.

Of course, even a 100% public system would have some schools operating at less than full capacity, because of constraints stemming from fixed community boundaries and size. Nevertheless, with teacher salaries 80–90% of all current expenditures and building costs the largest component of capital expenditure, the cost savings from rearranging and concentrating students would obviously be substantial, and this process is hampered by the privatized system.[13] Moreover, the "small size" problem will be exacerbated as the school-age population declines in the coming decade.

Real economies of scale are likely to be particularly great at the secondary level, because of their higher equipment needs and program diversity. The Dutch government has, consequently, encouraged the development of larger secondary schools, by giving more facilities to such schools. Ironically, such an incentive system tends to make larger schools more expensive than the smaller ones and creates the appearance of diseconomies rather than economies of scale. Moreover, school mergers eliminate choice and create natural monopolies at the secondary level in many (small) municipalities, raising questions about the justification for delegating authority to a private group that is not ultimately chosen by and accountable to the public at large.

Suppose that the management of each private school had the sole objective of maximizing quality for any given cost. Then, if schools are operating with excess capacity (i.e., below the minimum point on their cost curve or the maximum point on the quality curve, feasible for the given per capita funding), they will have an incentive to merge with each other to achieve greater efficiency. Similarly, the public schools from two small municipalities might merge. Indeed, as enrollments decline due to the declining school-age population, such mergers are taking place.

However, it is likely that school managers have other goals in addition to school quality—for example, perpetuation of religious tradition and local autonomy—which may cause them to prefer separateness even though merger would otherwise be efficient for cost and quality reasons. (This may be particularly true for the many small Protestant sects; it is interesting to note that their schools tend to be smaller than those for Catholics, on average.) These other considerations may also be deemed socially worthwhile—that is, society may indeed be willing to pay for them, in terms of higher funding or quality foregone. To the extent that the preferences of school managers simply reflect these nonmeasured collective preferences, their decisions about the desirability of merger will be socially optimal. On the other hand, if school managers place a greater value on religious and local differentiation than does society at large, as is probably the case, their private cost-benefit analysis will differ from the social cost-benefit analysis, and they will opt for schools that are too numerous and too small.

Relative Efficiency of Public and Private Schools

In evaluating the efficiency of a privatized system it would be useful to compare the relative costs of public and private schools. Small schools may be less efficient than large, but if private management is more efficient than public, the latter advantage may outweigh the former disadvantage. Unfortunately, given the method of funding in Holland, it is difficult to make this comparison by the methods usually employed in econometric analyses. As described above, private schools are given the same government funds per capita, and similar factor combinations, as public schools in their own community; they spend it all, plus the small additional fee received from parents. Thus, the private schools are slightly more costly than the publics, and to analyze their relative efficiency we would have to compare outputs, rather than just inputs. To raise a question discussed in the two ensuing chapters by Murnane: What is the "value added" by the two school types, controlling for any differences in the entering student raw material? The problem here is that the student inputs are, by definition, differentiated along religious lines. For example, relatively few Catholics have historically gone on to the university; is this due to a Catholic school effect or an effect stemming from the student's cultural background?

We can, however, use a more direct market-based test to examine public-private differences in school quality and efficiency in the Netherlands. Since people have a choice, we can simply observe their actions to make inferences about perceived benefits and costs. The fact that 70% of all parents choose to send their children to private schools, which charge a positive fee, suggests they believe they are getting more for their money there. Given the smallness of the fee, this cannot be interpreted as a preference for "more" education which may, however, be inefficiently provided, nor as a device for socioeconomic class segmentation. Instead, it appears that, for most parents, for approximately the same cost, private schools provide a "better" mix of school characteristics.

Part of this preference, of course, comes from religious identification and from the desire for religious segmentation. However, since the proportion attending private schools has not declined with the increasing secularization of Dutch society, other forces must also be at work. Many people with whom I discussed this issue attributed part of this preference to the fact that private schools label their ideology ahead of time, so parents know what they are getting, in contrast to public schools, whose treatment of values is left to the discretion of the individual teacher—a kind of "truth in packaging" advantage. In addition, most educators and parents believe that the private schools are more personal and responsive to consumer wishes, more careful about how they spend their funds than the publics. Private schools are considered more flexible, less bureaucratic, and effectively overseen by a board of directors specifically concerned about the welfare of the school, rather than by a generalized municipal administration. We do know that, on the average, private and public schools spend their "discretionary funds" somewhat differently, the latter paying more for "maintenance and cleaning," the former having more left over for various "educational facilities."[14] This may be due to the fact that private schools can hire the cheapest available services in the marketplace while public schools are constrained by arrangements made at the municipal level, which may be costlier. An OECD study of preprimary education in Holland suggested that private nurseries were less expensive than public nurseries.[15] However, the full evidence on this issue is as yet unavailable.

Transportation Costs

Besides the potential loss of scale economies which may be offset by public-private differences in efficiency, the Dutch system imposes higher transportation costs than would a neighborhood school monopoly system. Children must travel, sometimes long distances, to the school of their choice. These transportation costs include the resource costs of busing (equipment, gasoline, etc.) and the time cost of the children. It would appear, however, that these costs do not create an inefficiency in Holland—although they might in other countries. Much of Holland is densely populated and its system of public transportation is highly developed; hence the marginal cost of additional riders getting to and from schools is relatively low and probably covered by the small fee which the children must pay. Similarly, the real cost of the children's time is presumably taken into account by the family in making the decision about whether to send them to a nearby school or to one which is farther away but preferred. The fact that most of the marginal transportation expenses are borne by the household involved, at its own choice, suggests that the benefits outweigh the costs, both privately and socially.

Costs of Regulation

Privatization of a compulsory publicly funded service also involves regulation, and this is one of its costs. Not only do the schools incur their own managerial expenses, but the government authorities also incur the expense of looking over their shoulders, imposing rules, and checking to see that the rules are obeyed. For example, an extensive system of state inspectors visits each primary school periodically. The Ministry of Education must negotiate with and audit the books of approved secondary schools annually. As a corollary, schools must pay the expenses of regional and central organizations, at least one for each denomination, to provide them with legal and political assistance in this process.

While this is a real cost of the Dutch system, it should be noted that similar costs would be incurred if most schools were run by the municipalities with central government funding; in that case, the state would have to check up on the local authorities rather than on the private schools. This is the situation, for example, in Sweden, where a large state bureaucracy oversees the system of local public schools. And direct provision by the central government would require the cumbersome monitoring of lower by upper bureaucratic levels. It is not clear that any one of these three systems necessarily entails higher administrative costs than the others.

Adjustment to Disequilibrium

Finally, it is important to evaluate the flexibility of the system, that is, its responsiveness to changing economic-demographic conditions and to educational innovation. Specifically, what happens when the number of school-age children declines, as is the case now? If the size and distribution of schools was optimal before, it no longer is; how does the system adjust to this disequilibrium situation?

The problem of underutilized schools, and the difficulties involved in shutting them down, are certainly present in public systems, as we see in the United States today. However, they are probably exacerbated in the Dutch system, where each group is anxious to keep its own school open, and uses its political power to do so. Officially, once enrollment in a school falls below a specified point, it may be closed by a municipality. However, the minimum required enrollments are very low and, moreover, municipalities are reluctant to close them down even when that point is reached. In the meantime, the school operates with excess capacity and underutilized space, in a building which is technically "owned" by the school board even though it was built by the local authorities. The inefficiency is even more evident if a new religious sect has moved into the neighborhood and is demanding its own school and building, at the same time.

Until recently, private-school boards had complete control over their building, so long as the school was operating. However, recurrences of the situation described above led to a change in the law, so that municipalities now have the right to allocate underutilized space to some other educational purpose. Furthermore, once a school is closed down, the entire building reverts to the municipality—that is, the school board cannot sell it and make a profit. Thus, "private ownership" means specified "use rights" but not "rental rights" or "exchange rights" over the school building.

The private schools themselves are adjusting in other ways to the declining demand. For example, some secondary schools are using their excess capacity to offer classes for adults, particularly housewives, who did not secure an equivalent education in their youth. The regional Catholic organizations are drawing up plans for closing schools in ways which would minimize disruption to their clientele, and are temporarily subsidizing, from endowment funds, some of those in the worst financial difficulty. Mergers of Catholic and Protestant schools into unified Christian schools are beginning to take place. Given the small size of the schools to begin with, however, and the pressure against merger, as discussed earlier, it would seem that the highly fragmented and privatized Dutch system is particularly subject to inefficiencies during a period of contracting disequilibrium.

Responsiveness to Innovation

Finally, I conclude with a few comments on responsiveness to educational innovation. The big advantage of the school system in Holland is its potential diversity. Much of this diversity, we have seen, is based on religious rather than pedagogical differences. Nevertheless, we do find secular private schools that emphasize and experiment with particular educational philosophies, such as Montessori, Dalton, and Rudolph Steiner, and parents who prefer these techniques are able to start their own school, if one does not already exist. Thus, there is great potential for innovation in individual schools.

On the other hand, systemwide innovation is inhibited by its fragmentation and heterogeneity. For example, when the minister of education wants to combine nursery and primary schools, or to introduce the concept of "comprehensive middle schools" in order to postpone the streaming which now takes place at age twelve, he faces a difficult job of persuasion. He must secure the concurrence not only of the state and municipal authorities, but also of the central organizations representing each of the denominations, which wield considerable political power. Unless all of these parties agree, systemwide change cannot go forward—leading to a sluggishness which is one of its costs. This may help account for the fact that, while the Dutch system of funding education might be termed innovative, the Dutch educational structure remains one of the most traditional in Europe.

Efficiency: Summary

In summary, teacher costs and costs of buildings and other indivisible, specialized, educational facilities in the Netherlands are probably 10–20% higher than they would be in a more monolithic efficiency-oriented system. This is the main price paid for product variety, and it is exacerbated in the present environment of declining enrollments—although some mechanisms are being developed to mitigate these effects. Higher transportation expenses are also implied, but are largely taken into account by private cost-benefit calculations. Costs of regulation exist, but may not be greater than in any other publicly funded system. Ironically, while the Dutch system encourages diversity among schools and innovation in individual schools, it makes overall structural change very difficult to achieve; and for people who oppose the social stratification inherent in the present system, this is one of its costs.

SELECTIVITY AND ELITISM

In the United States, one of the arguments against privatization is that the rich and middle classes would vote for low-cost, low-quality public schools, thereby saving on taxes, and would send their own children to high-quality private schools. We would therefore get a segmentation of education along class lines and a perpetuation of class differentials. Has this occurred in Holland?

It is true that certain "problem" and "special" groups, such as the children of the guest workers from Turkey and Morocco, are heavily concentrated in the public schools.[16] It is also true that residential segregation by class has produced some educational segregation by class, as in the United States. However, for most communities, and for the country as a whole, the entire class spectrum is represented in both the public and private sectors of the educational system.[17] Moreover, at the elementary level, selective or exclusive schools seem rare.

Why has the private school system not become the elite school system, attracting the upper classes into higher-quality, more expensive institutions? Part of the answer lies in specific restrictions imposed by the government for schools which accept its subsidy. For example, such schools are not supposed to charge for "education," only for "educational facilities," and in the future will not be able to exclude students for nonpayment. Therefore, price rationing as a method of achieving educational differentiation by class is legally limited. Relatedly, schools are not able to attract better teachers by paying them higher wages, since salary scales are determined by the central government.[18] These kinds of rules could be replicated in the United States if we moved toward public funding of private schools; we would probably find that some private schools would be willing to accept the rules together with the funds, while others would prefer to forgo both and retain their autonomy. We would probably also find that, even if these rules were imposed, class segmentation would result if private schools were permitted to select their own students. Thus, we need a more fundamental explanation for the absence of elite private schools in Holland, and I believe the explanation lies in the overall structure of the educational system as well as the relationship between education and society.

First of all, I have discussed above the religious basis for most private schools, which tends to make them "inclusive" rather than "exclusive." In particular, in small communities where only one primary school from each denomination may exist, it cannot be selective along class or ability lines.

Further insight is obtained if we examine the internal structure of the educational system, that is, the high degree of "streaming" or "tracking" within the public and private sectors and the interrelationship between the higher and lower levels of education. Education in Holland is still characterized by a low proportion of university attendance and a streaming system which determines at an early age who will occupy those places—a system which gives an advantage to students coming from high socioeconomic backgrounds and which most other European countries have gradually abandoned during the post–World War II period.

At the age of twelve or thirteen, upon leaving primary school, most Dutch children make choices that determine their future access to further education. Approximately one-third (30% in 1979) go into "junior vocational training," preparation for occupations such as agriculture, domestic service, and retail trade. The remaining 70% go into secondary general education.[19] However, a multiplicity of tracks exist at this level, including a junior secondary track known as MAVO, which primarily prepares students for senior vocational training; HAVO, which prepares them mainly for higher technical training; and VWO, the major preuniversity route. Most general secondary students opt for MAVO. In 1979 only 11% of students at the lower secondary stage were enrolled in VWO, and only 5% of all nineteen-year-olds were attending university. It is true that another 11% attended various technical colleges and a still larger group attended senior vocational training (which is roughly equivalent to community college in the United States), so that the proportion receiving some kind of higher education is not very different from that in the United States. Nevertheless, the fact remains that different secondary school tracks led to each of these higher educational institutions and occupations, with the basic choice made at a very early age.[20]

Moreover, these choices are highly correlated with a family's socioeconomic status, both historically and currently. For example, in 1954 the ratio of lower- to upper-class students enrolled in junior secondary schools, secondary grammar schools, and universities were 8/1, 1/1, and 1/5, respectively.[21] More recent data are somewhat less exaggerated but still consistent with this pattern.

Although the final choice of secondary-school type is made by parents, it is heavily influenced by the advice of the primary-school headmaster, which in turn depends partially on the student's score on the sixth-grade national exam. Students coming from upper-class backgrounds are more likely to receive higher test scores and, for any given score, their headmaster is more likely to recommend a higher-track secondary school. In addition, upper-class parents are more likely to send their children to VWO despite negative headmaster advice. The net result is a heavy bias in the class distribution of preuniversity students. For example, over half of all high-salaried employees send their children to a school offering VWO or VWO plus HAVO and only 7% go into junior vocational training, while for the working class these numbers are 16% and 43%, respectively.[22] Thus, Dutch upper-class families need not look for elite private schools if they want their children to associate with other achievement-oriented students from similar backgrounds; they can accomplish the same thing simply by utilizing the highly selective preuniversity track which is found both in the public and private sectors.

This conclusion is further reinforced by a variety of procedures within the educational system which have the consequence of minimizing the importance of the particular school attended. For example, universities (even the private ones) do not select their own students. Instead, students are centrally assigned, with a lottery used in cases of excess demand and without taking identity of secondary school into account. Thus, one university cannot develop a reputation for having a "better" student body than another, nor can admission to such a university be an inducement for attending a "better" secondary school. Moreover, if prestige of secondary school does not matter, it follows that prestige of primary school is also relatively unimportant: You don't need an elite elementary school to get into an elite secondary school to get into an elite university to get a good job. Under these circumstances, parents may be unwilling to pay high tuition for a private education, since they can achieve (almost) the same results by attending a free public school; this in turn keeps private tuition low and private schools available to all classes.

In conclusion, in the United States we are concerned that privatization may lead to class segmentation in education. The Dutch experience suggests that this will not happen, under certain circumstances. Some of these circumstances, including restrictions on tuition and salaries, could be transferred to the American scene (although many private schools would be unhappy about such a development). Other conditions could not easily be replicated, since they involve a complex set of interrelationships among the various parts of the educational system and its broader role within society. Two such conditions are particularly important: the existence of a highly selective secondary educational system, which itself segregates along class lines at an early age, and a university system equally accessible to all those who have passed through the preuniversity screening, in both the public and private sectors. Privatization does not necessarily contribute to class segregation in education, but it would be dangerous to extrapolate from the Dutch to the American scene without taking this complex confluence of regulatory and broader societal factors into account.

CONCLUSION

In summary, I have described the Dutch system of publicly funded private education as an alternative mode of delivering quasi-public services, services that provide private as well as collective benefits. This analysis suggests that private organizations and local governments are competing institutional arrangements for providing quasi-public goods. Privatization may have a comparative advantage in cases where product variety is possible, tastes are differentiated, and economies of scale are relatively small. Diverse organizations may be better able than government to offer a heterogeneous product mix and enable people to make separate choices about different services, rather than tying together a bundle of public goods, as is done through local governmental provision.

In the Netherlands, where peoples' choices about schools, hospitals, social services, trade unions, and many other "collective" activities were traditionally church related, through the process of *verzuiling*, this potential for separate choices was not realized. In effect, membership in a church community had many of the same economic implications as membership in a geographic community has in other systems: Each person had to utilize the services offered by his group, rather than making his own individual choice. However, as secularization proceeds, people may be able to make separate decisions about different quasi-public goods, independent of their choices about residence and religious affiliation.

Another potential advantage of private service provision is that this often permits some reliance on voluntary payments, thereby revealing peoples' intensity of preferences and reducing the necessary amount of taxation and tax-induced disincentive effects. The corresponding disadvantage is the free-rider problem, leading to underprovision, unless the private benefit component is very large. In the Dutch system we find little scope for this advantage or disadvantage, since most costs of both private and public schools are covered by the central government. Choice exists with respect to the philosophy of education but only slightly with respect to funding or quality components which are dependent on funding.

I have used the Dutch system as a laboratory to investigate the impact of a policy favoring private schools on important educational characteristics such as: supply of schools and school places, cost efficiency, political support for school budgets, and social segmentation along religious, class, or other lines. The supply response to government funding was clearly very positive in the Netherlands, with the entry problem solved mainly by religious organizations. The cost-efficiency of the system depends largely on the existence and size of scale economies and the relative effectiveness of public and private schools. Some scale economies can and have been realized by sharing indivisible specialized facilities across schools. However, current data suggest that many schools have excess capacity with respect to teacher costs and space as a result of the privatization policy, so that substantial savings could be realized if entry and variety were reduced. Moreover, because a privatized system is probably slow and cumbersome to adapt to change, these inefficiencies will probably grow in the near future as a consequence of the demographic decline.

The extensive reliance on private schools in Holland has reinforced the religious segmentation within society. If all groups prefer such segmentation, it is Pareto-efficient; but a social dilemma exists if one group prefers segmentation while another group prefers integration. Then, a choice between the two policies also implies a choice about the distribution of utility between the two groups. In Holland, the separatists won a clear victory in this struggle.

The separatist-integrationist division did not, however, correspond to a class division, nor has the private school system contributed to class segmentation. This is partially because specific mechanisms, such as restrictions on tuition charges and teacher salaries, have been adopted to maintain equality and partially because class segmentation is, instead, provided by other structures within the educational system. Relatedly, the Dutch system has probably strengthened rather than weakened the political willingness to support public education, since private school budgets are directly tied to public school budgets and nongovernmental financing sources are limited. This suggests that privatization does not necessarily contribute to elitism, perpetuation of class differences, and weak public schools; but elaborate structural differences between the Dutch and American educational systems and their role in society preclude easy transferability of this result.

We have seen that private schools in the Netherlands are heavily regulated by the government with respect to inputs. Disguised profit distribution through factor payments is thereby limited; it may, however, take place in nonpecuniary forms such as the preservation of inefficient underutilized schools to satisfy the objective functions of their managers. Also, but to a lesser extent, we find regulations over output characteristics (e.g., curriculum, examinations, and degree requirements) and service distribution (e.g., tuition and exclusion criteria). These are partially designed to achieve equality, but they come at the expense of the choice which the system was designed to ensure. The concern over democracy and social control has led, furthermore, to recent regulation of the decision-making structure in schools. These rules are consistent with the expectation that government financing can easily lead to government control, that there is a trade-off between more autonomy and more funds.

Cultural heterogeneity often generates a demand for private education and for government subsidies to help cover the associated costs. The subsidies facilitate private sector growth, but they also allow the government to impose regulations, particularly over inputs but also over outputs and other behavioral characteristics. Thus, the initial demand for differentiation, if successful, sets in motion forces which make the private sector quasi-governmental; subsidized private sectors are very much like public sectors. If we institute a voucher scheme or other privatization policies, we may end up with a private sector which is larger but less distinctive than the one we have now.

NOTES

1. This chapter is based on published material as well as statistical data collected and interviews held with numerous government officials, educators, and scholars during a research visit to the Netherlands in 1981–82. I wish to thank all of these people, in addition to the many staff members at the Central Bureau of Statistics, who were so generous with their time. My research assistant, James Sinclair, was very helpful in assembling the tables and performing related calculations. I also appreciate the financial assistance from the Social Science Research Council and the Exxon Education Foundation for this trip and the facilities provided by the Netherlands Institute for Advanced Study during my stay in Holland. Support has been received from the National Endowment for the Humanities, the Program on Non-profit Organizations at Yale University, and the Research Foundation, S.U.N.Y., on broader aspects of this project. An earlier version of this paper was written while the author was a Fellow at the Woodrow Wilson International Center for Scholars, Washington, D.C.

2. The best historical summary is presented in Arend Lijphart, *The Politics of Accommodation: Pluralism and Democracy in the Netherlands* (Berkeley: Univ. of California Press, 1968).

3. For interesting higher-education parallels and contrasts to policies for Dutch schools, see the discussion of "parallel" private and public universities in Roger L. Geiger, *Private Sectors in Higher Education: Structure, Function and Change in Eight Countries* (Ann Arbor: University of Michigan, 1986). Also see Levy's "Homogenized" private-public financial pattern in his last chapter in this volume.

4. See Rein van Gendt, "Netherlands," in *Educational Financing and Policy Goals for Primary Schools*, Vol. 3 (Paris: OECD, CERI, 1979). This piece is the best single source on financing primary education in Holland.

5. See *Statistiek van gewoon lager onderwijs* (The Hague: Central Bureau of Statistics, 1980), p. 14; and *Voortgezet Onderwijs en Verzuiling c.g. Ontzuiling in Nederland 1953–1978;* KASKI, rapport no. 366 (The Hague: 1981).

6. *Pocketbook of Educational Statistics* (The Hague: Central Bureau of Statistics, 1981), p. 89.

7. In a publicly financed system, under a majority voting scheme, with single-peaked preferences, the entire system ends up with the quality level preferred by the median voter—great uniformity. If supplementary private financing is permitted, some people opt out and choose their preferred quality-expenditure level, immediately introducing greater diversity. If the people who opt out prefer higher quality, this implies a higher rate of expenditure in the private sector. The adverse selection-voting problem may lead to lower expenditures per student in the public schools. On the other hand, the tax cost per unit of quality improvement in the public schools is now less, because there are fewer public school places; hence this is a counteracting force which may lead to higher expenditures per student, particularly if people outside the system derive some external benefit from having a well-educated citizenry. The net outcome regarding total expenditure in the system as a whole and expenditure per student in

the public schools is therefore uncertain, although one plausible outcome is that the former will go up while the latter goes down. For a more rigorous development of this point, see E. James, "Benefits and Costs of Privatized Public Services," mimeo, 1983.

8. See, for example, Lijphart, op. cit., p. 53, and E. Gadourek, *A Dutch Community* (Groningen: Walters, 1961), pp. 544–547. Gadourek quotes from texts used by each of the groups on sensitive subjects such as the Reformation and the War of independence from Spain; the contrasts are striking.

9. *de ontwikkeling van het underwijs in nederland,* editie 1966 (The Hague: Central Bureau of Statistics, 1966), p. 69.

10. See Lijphart, op. cit., pp. 155–162, for a discussion of deference and passivity among the Dutch rank and file. See Ralph Kramer, *Voluntary Agencies in the Welfare State* (Berkeley: University of California Press, 1981), p. 25, for references to the apathy problem. This "problem" was also raised by many of the people I interviewed.

11. The evidence is inconclusive on the shape of cost functions in education. Probably, scale economies are greater in secondary education than in primary education; they probably continue until enrollments reach 200 or 300 in the latter, 500 or 600 in the former. However, difficulties in measuring educational output, particularly quality, make these calculations particularly difficult and suspect. See, for example, Elchanan Cohn, *The Economics of Education* (Cambridge, Mass.: Ballinger, 1975), pp. 263–269; and Martin O'Donoghue, *Economic Dimensions in Education* (Chicago: Aldine, 1971), pp. 154–160, for reference to American and OECD studies, respectively.

12. The schedule relating numbers of students to teachers is as follows: up to 26 pupils = 2; 91 = 3; 125 = 4; 156 = 5; 196 = 6. See van Gendt, op. cit., p. 20.

13. Offset against this are possible positive effects on quality of education, stemming from the lower student faculty ratio. The point is, however, that the higher costs are not being incurred because of a policy decision to purchase higher quality, but rather as a consequence of a policy encouraging private schools and easy entry, without serious study of the trade-offs between costs, quality, and product variety. For a discussion of the indecisive evidence on whether student/faculty ratios and class size affect education achievement, see Cohn, op. cit., pp. 240–256; O'Donoghue, op. cit., pp. 163–172; and Eric Hanushek, "Throwing Money at Schools," *Journal of Policy Analysis and Management,* (Fall 1981), pp. 19–41. A recent study in the Netherlands indicated that the faculty/student ratio does not have a statistically significant influence on student achievement within the relevant range for Holland. See *Social and Cultural Report,* (Rijswijki: Social and Cultural Planning Office, 1981$, p. 198.

14. See *Tweede Interimadvies van de Interdepartementale Werkgroep Regeling Rijksuitkeringen Kleuter-En Lager Onderwijs* (Werkgroep LONDO) (The Hague: Ministry of Education, 1981), pp. 79†84.

15. See van Gendt, op. cit., p. 29.

16. See *Statistiek van het gewoon lager onderwijs* (The Hague: Central Bureau of Statistics), p. 19.

17. Data on current class breakdowns of various schools are difficult to secure. However, some historical data are available. For example, during the 1950s enrollments in the public junior secondary schools were 6% upper class, 51% middle class, and 43% lower class, while in the private sector these numbers were 5%, 55%, and 40%, respectively. Enrollments in public secondary grammar schools were 27% upper class, 50% middle class, and 23% lower class, compared with 21%, 54%, and 25%, respectively, in the private sector. These numbers suggest a slight tendency for the upper classes to attend public schools, the middle classes, private schools. However, the aggregated data do not allow us to test whether these small differences were statistically significant. See *de ontwikkeling . . . .,* p. 46.

18. This also means that inner-city schools cannot use higher salaries to compensate for their disadvantageous position; salary equality can sometimes imply competitive inequality overall. In a few cases, private schools in wealthy communities tried to attract superior teachers by offering subsidized housing or small class sizes; however, these were usual and temporary situations.

19. *Pocketbook of Educational Statistics,* pp. 62–66.

20. Ibid., p. 36, 60–65.

21. See *de ontwikkeling* . . . , p. 46.

22. See *Pocketbook of Educational Statistics*, pp. 110–113; and E. James, op. cit., pp. 50–52.

5

Comparisons of Private and Public Schools: The Critical Role of Regulations*

RICHARD J. MURNANE

The rising cost of publicly provided social services had led many analysts to conclude that government agencies are inefficient suppliers of services, both because they do not maximize output from existing resources and because they respond only very sluggishly to changes in the level and composition of demand. These analysts often couple this diagnosis with the prescription that private nonprofit organizations should play a larger role in delivering many social services.

In debates over the wisdom of this type of reform, advocates often introduce statistical evidence on the comparative performance of public and private organizations, concluding as a rule that the performance of the private providers is superior.[1] The central theme of this chapter is that much of the performance differences between public and private providers of social services stems from differences in the regulations they face, and the resulting differences in the characteristics of the clients they serve.

The evidence in support of that conclusion presented here focuses on one social service, education. The reasons are twofold: The data on the determinants of performance in that sector are of relatively high quality and the issue of governmental policy toward private sector providers of educational services is currently a topic of much public interest. But, as I intend

*This chapter is adapted from "How Clients' Characteristics Affect Organizational Performance: Lessons from Education," *Journal of Policy Analysis and Management* 2, 3 (1983). An earlier version was Working Paper No. 46 of the Program on Non-Profit Organizations at Yale University. It is based on research supported by the Institute for Research on Educational Finance and Governance, Stanford University; by the Program on Non-Profit Organizations, Yale University; and by Grant Number NIE-G-79-0084 from the National Institute of Education. The author would like to thank Marc Chupka, George Cohen, and Stuart Newstead for first-rate research assistance; Randall Olsen and Jon Peck for statistical advice; and Paul Di-Maggio, Michelle Hirschoff, Estelle James, Richard Nelson, Edward Pauly, Susan Rose-Ackerman, and John Simon for helpful comments on earlier drafts.

to show, the themes developed in the context of the education sector have relevance in other sectors as well, especially as one confronts the problem of designing an appropriate set of regulatory policies.

STUDENT BODY COMPOSITION AND THE SORTING PROCESS

A recent, highly publicized study reported that the education offered in private high schools is of higher average quality than the education offered in public high schools.[2] The analysis in this section demonstrates that a large part of the observed quality difference is due to differences in the composition of student bodies, and that these differences stem to a significant extent from differences in the regulations pertaining to public and private schools.

Student Body Composition

The finding that student body composition is an important determinant of school effectiveness first gained prominence with the publication in 1966 of the Coleman Report, which emphasized the positive relationship between the average socioeconomic status of the students in a school and the academic achievement of individual students.[3] Subsequent studies either replicated that finding or found the achievement of individual students to be related to other characteristics of the student body such as racial composition or the average achievement level of the students in the class or school.[4]

Experts differ in their explanations of these relationships. However, an important fact is that parents and school officials know that student body composition matters, and this knowledge influences their actions. In particular, when parents choose schools for their children, they pay attention to who the classmates will be; and when school officials admit students, they pay attention to the attributes of those they admit. The actions of parents and school officials, taken in the context of a number of institutional constraints, result in significant sorting of students among schools. This sorting creates differences in the characteristics of the student bodies of different schools, and it influences the achievement of students attending different schools.

Sorting Within Each Sector

The problem facing parents is to find a school for their child that has a student body that will enhance their child's education—as they define it. The problem is made complex by the difficulty of collecting reliable information about students in particular schools. With information scarce, many parents in making school choices pay attention to variables, such as the socioeconomic status of the students, that are quite easily observed and that are correlated, albeit imperfectly, with variables that are more critical but less easily observed, such as the skills and attitudes of students.

Of course, not all families succeed in placing their child in the type of school they desire. There are three types of sorting mechanisms at work in both the public and private sectors that determine which families succeed in placing their children in the schools they are aiming for—schools that are usually, but not always, characterized by student bodies with relatively high socioeconomic status. These sorting mechanisms include self-selection by families, admission policies of individual schools, and dismissal policies of schools.[5]

For parents who intend to send their children to public schools, self-selection usually takes place through residential location; this is because in the majority of public school districts in this country, the family's residential location determines which school the child attends. There is compelling evidence that families pay premiums for housing in school districts with reputations for good schools.[6] There is also evidence that within a given school district families pay premiums to live in neighborhoods that are served by schools in which the average achievement of the students is high.[7] (The Kutner-Sherman-Williams article in this volume discusses in more detail the role of schools in families' residential location decisions.)

Selective admission policies are used by some public schools. In addition to well-known examples such as the Bronx High School of Science, there are now many schools in low-income areas that employ achievement criteria for admission.[8]

Dismissal of disruptive students is also a method of sorting that is used in the public sector. All public school districts have procedures that school administrators can use to suspend and, if necessary, to expel students who consistently violate school rules. All of these mechanisms influence the distribution of student achievement because they influence the nature of the student body with which individual students interact.

Many parents who do not find in the public schools available to them the educational environment that they want for their child choose private schools. Parents' choices of private schools, as constrained by family incomes and by the tuition, admission, and dismissal policies of individual private schools, also lead to significant sorting of students among private schools. And, even more than in the public sector (as I demonstrate below), this sorting results in differences in the quality of education offered by different private schools.

Sorting Between the School Sectors

Clearly, sorting takes place not only within the public and private school sectors, but also between the two sectors. The nature of this sorting, which is critical in understanding differences between public and private schools, is influenced not only by the three types of sorting mechanisms described above, but also by two sets of regulations. The first set consists of compulsory education statutes which require that all children up to a certain age receive formal schooling. The second set consists of laws that guarantee the right of all students to a free education in a public school. A consequence of these regulations is that all students who are not sorted into private schools must be educated in public schools.

The effects of these regulations on the sorting process are particularly evident when students are dismissed from schools. Schools in both the public and private sectors dismiss troublesome students (although dismissals are probably less common in private schools, since these schools have more control over whom they admit). The difference is that students dismissed from a private school need not be accepted by another private school. However, these students, like students dismissed from a public school, are entitled to an education in a public school.

All told, therefore, students tend to be sorted out into different schools by a number of factors. And the sorting produces student bodies in private schools that are different on average from those in public schools. One could argue by analogy that just as sorting within the public sector creates differences in the relative performance of public schools, sorting between the public and private sectors is an important reason for the superior average performance of private schools. Fortunately, one can do better than argue by analogy. New data permit a direct test of this proposition.

EFFECTS OF SORTING

In 1982, James Coleman and two colleagues completed a highly publicized study of the relative quality of public and private high schools (henceforth referred to as the CHK study).[9] The analysis was based on the first wave of data from a large, federally funded study of students attending public, Catholic, and non-Catholic private schools in the United States, known as the High School and Beyond (HSB) project. CHK interpret their analysis as providing answers to the following hypothetical questions:

> What would the achievement level of the average *public* school student be if he or she attended a Catholic school? A non-Catholic private school?[10]

I began my work by essentially replicating CHK's analysis for a subset of the HSB data. I then extended CHK's methodology to address a second set of hypothetical questions:

> What would the achievement of the average *public* school student be if he or she attended a Catholic school or other private school *and took along his or her public school classmates?*

A comparison of the answers to these two sets of questions is informative because it focuses attention on a somewhat elusive, but potentially critical fallacy of composition—while individual students may be able to improve their education by moving to a school attended by students of above average ability or socioeconomic status, it is impossible for all students to attend such schools.

My sample, drawn from the HSB data base, includes all seniors attending Catholic schools, all seniors in nonelite other private schools, and all seniors in a random sample of 123 public schools.[11] The size of the public school subsample was chosen to make the number of public school students roughly comparable to the total number of Catholic and other private school students in the sample. Only students for whom complete data could be obtained were included in the analysis.

Table 5.1 presents summary statistics describing the samples of public, Catholic and other private school students that I drew from the HSB data base. This table also presents estimates for the nation of the average characteristics of high school students attending different types of schools. The national estimates were obtained by weighting the observations in the HSB study in a manner that takes account of the overrepresentation in the HSB sample of students in schools with particular characteristics, such as the presence of a large proportion of minority students.

The statistics in Table 5.1 describing my sample and the national population of U.S. high school students present few surprises. Public high school students perform less well on standardized tests of achievement than do students in Catholic schools, who in turn perform less well than do students in other private schools. An index of the socioeconomic status of the students in each group of schools runs in the same order. Black students and those of Hispanic origin are more heavily represented in the public schools. Fewer students in the public schools perceive that their parents want them to attend college; fewer students in the public schools come from two-parent households.

Obviously, these data by themselves say nothing about the effects of the schools themselves on student scores. Before drawing any conclusions on the effects of the schools, it is necessary first of all to determine what role student characteristics have played in determining the scores of students in each of the three types of schools.

Following CHK's general strategy, I sought to determine for each of the three groups of students what relation existed between the scores on a test of vocabulary and reading skills on the one hand and ten different characteristics of the students on the other. For that purpose, I estimated equation 1 separately for each of the three subsamples:

where
$$A_i = \sum_{j=1}^{10} d_j D_{ij} + a_i \qquad (1)$$

A_i = the ith school senior's raw score (total number of correct answers) on a forty-seven-item test of vocabulary and reading skills

D_{ij} = the jth characteristic of the ith student (the ten characteristics being listed in Table 5.1)

Table 5.1 Means (with standard deviations in parentheses) of Student Skills, Student Characteristics and Student Body Socioeconomic Status for my Sample and the Nation[a]

	Public Schools		Catholic Schools		Other Private School	
	Sample	Nation	Sample	Nation	Sample	Nation
Student Achievement						
Student's Score on Test of Reading and Vocabulary Skills	23.72 (8.50)	24.44 (8.39)	26.41 (8.26)	27.83 (8.00)	28.50 (8.95)	29.14 (9.20)
Ten Student Characteristics						
Index of Student's Socioeconomic Status	−0.14 (0.72)	−0.05 (0.70)	0.10 (0.72)	0.23 (0.67)	0.45 (0.74)	0.50 (0.76)
Student is Black	0.10 (0.30)	0.07 (0.27)	0.13 (0.34)	0.05 (0.24)	0.02 (0.16)	0.02 (0.15)
Student is Male	0.46 (0.50)	0.46 (0.50)	0.41 (0.49)	0.40 (0.49)	0.46 (0.50)	0.44 (0.50)
Mother wants Student to Attend College (Student's Perception)	0.65 (0.48)	0.64 (0.48)	0.83 (0.38)	0.81 (0.39)	0.77 (0.42)	0.77 (0.42)
Father wants Student to Attend College (Student's Perception)	0.57 (0.49)	0.58 (0.49)	0.75 (0.43)	0.76 (0.43)	0.74 (0.44)	0.74 (0.44)
Student is of Hispanic Background	0.14 (0.34)	0.08 (0.27)	0.20 (0.40)	0.07 (0.25)	0.01 (0.07)	0.01 (0.07)
Student has Two Parents Living at Home	0.73 (0.44)	0.75 (0.43)	0.79 (0.41)	0.84 (0.37)	0.81 (0.39)	0.79 (0.40)
Student Lives in Northeast Region of U.S.	0.12 (0.32)	0.13 (0.33)	0.35 (0.48)	0.37 (0.49)	0.16 (0.37)	0.27 (0.44)
Student Lives in North Central Region of U.S.	0.29 (0.45)	0.32 (0.47)	0.32 (0.47)	0.39 (0.49)	0.20 (0.40)	0.13 (0.34)
Student Lives in Southern Region of U.S.	0.38 (0.49)	0.34 (0.47)	0.18 (0.38)	0.13 (0.33)	0.46 (0.50)	0.39 (0.49)
Student Body Characteristics						
Average Socioeconomic Status of Students in the School	−0.15 (0.35)	−0.07 (0.33)	0.14 (0.40)	0.26 (0.33)	0.48 (0.44)	0.53 (0.46)
Number of Students in Sample	2464		2026		361	
Number of Schools in Sample	123		79		21	

[a]The estimates for the nation as a whole were calculated by weighting the observations in the HSB sample in a manner that take account of the overrepresentation in the sample of students attending schools with particular characteristics.

(The small differences between my strategy and CHK's are described in the appendix.) In effect, equation 1 posits that a student's achievement depends on personal characteristics and family background. An implicit assumption is that, while being in school in a particular sector affects achievement (as represented by the intercept term), no characteristics of the particular school the student attends affect achievement.

At the same time I also produced a second set of estimates aimed at testing the hypothesis that one attribute of a school, namely, the average socioeconomic status of *fellow students,* affects the achievement of individual students in the school. This hypothesis was tested by estimating a second equation, which was specified as follows:

$$\text{where} \qquad A_i = \sum_{j=1}^{10} d_j D_{ij} + s(\text{SESM}_i) + a_2 \qquad (2)$$

SESM$_i$ = the average socioeconomic status of the students in the ith student's high school (This value was calculated using the information on all students in the HSB sample, both sophomores and seniors, who attended the ith student's high school.)

Notice that equation 2 includes all of the individual student characteristics present in equation 1, as well as the average socioeconomic status of the students in the school.

The estimates for both sets of equations are presented in Table 5.2. Once again, they present no great surprises. Both equations indicate that students with high socioeconomic status do relatively well in all three types of school, that blacks and those of Hispanic background do relatively poorly, and that students who report that their mothers want them to go to college do relatively well.[12] But the results of equation 2 provide one more important piece of information: They support the view that the socioeconomic status of fellow students plays a significant contributing role in determining students' scores. The effect is particularly strong in non-Catholic private schools, but it is present in schools of all three types. Thus analysis of the HSB data reveals the same patterns found in earlier studies.[13]

It is possible to use the estimates of equation 1 to address CHK's hypothetical questions, which concern what would happen if a student in a public school were moved to one of the other two types of school. My estimates of the answers to CHK's questions are as follows:

	Predicted Test Score
When public school students remain in their public schools	24.3
If public school students were placed in Catholic schools	26.1
If public school students were placed in other private schools	25.3

The scores that would be achieved if public school students were placed in Catholic schools or in other private schools are clearly higher than their actual scores in public schools, and the differences are sufficiently large that the probability of their occurring by chance is less than 0.05.

Comparison of these predicted scores with the average test scores of the students in each sector that are displayed in Table 5.1 is informative. It indicates that one reason (but not the only reason) students in private schools score higher than students in public schools is that on average they come from more advantaged homes and consequently bring more skills to school with them.

Table 5.2 Regression Coefficients (with Standard Errors in Parentheses) from Equations Estimating Students' Test Scores

	Equation 1			Equation 2		
	Public Schools	Catholic Schools	Other Private Schools	Public Schools	Catholic Schools	Other Private Schools
Index of Socioeconomic Status	2.32 (0.24)	1.96 (0.27)	4.15 (0.63)	1.96 (0.26)	1.14 (0.30)	2.16 (0.76)
Student is Black	−6.07 (0.53)	−4.57 (0.54)	−5.49 (2.72)	−5.84 (0.53)	−4.06 (0.54)	−4.51 (2.66)
Student is Male	0.84 (0.30)	1.39 (0.35)	0.89 (0.84)	0.85 (0.30)	1.16 (0.35)	0.61 (0.82)
Mother Wants Student to Attend College[a]	2.31 (0.45)	2.58 (0.59)	3.82 (1.57)	2.32 (0.45)	2.44 (0.58)	3.49 (1.53)
Father wants Student to Attend College[a]	1.76 (0.45)	0.78 (0.54)	0.22 (1.54)	1.75 (0.44)	0.68 (0.53)	0.09 (1.50)
Student is of Hispanic Background	−4.23 (0.48)	−3.61 (0.48)	−3.35 (5.69)	−3.78 (0.50)	−2.82 (0.49)	−3.16 (5.54)
Student has Two Parents Living at Home	−0.50 (0.35)	−0.00 (0.46)	0.99 (1.11)	−0.47 (0.35)	0.02 (0.45)	1.65 (1.09)
Student Lives in Northeast Region of U.S.	−0.35 (0.55)	0.24 (0.55)	3.70 (1.46)	−0.21 (0.55)	1.05 (0.56)	5.34 (1.47)
Student Lives in North Central Region of U.S.	0.06 (0.45)	−0.29 (0.56)	2.54 (1.42)	0.09 (0.44)	−0.04 (0.56)	4.67 (1.46)
Student Lives in Southern Region of U.S.	−1.26 (0.41)	−0.17 (0.62)	−0.15 (1.21)	−0.92 (0.42)	−0.80 (0.62)	1.11 (1.21)
Average Socioeconomic Status of Students in the School				1.93 (0.53)	3.53 (0.58)	5.89 (1.31)
Intercept	23.19 (0.50)	24.26 (0.72)	21.45 (1.52)	23.17 (0.50)	23.62 (0.73)	18.16 (1.65)
R^2	0.23	0.14	0.25	0.24	0.15	0.29
Number of Students	2464	2026	361	2464	2026	361
Number of Schools	123	79	21	123	79	21

[a] As CHK point out, this may not be an exogenous variable. Using CHK's rationale, it was included to control as completely as possible for student background.

Now I present estimates indicating the extent to which the advantage of attending a private school stems from the presence in school of other children from advantaged backgrounds. The predicted test scores are as follows:

	Predicted Test Score
When public school students remain in their public schools	24.4
If public school students and their schoolmates were placed in Catholic schools	25.1
If public school students and their schoolmates were placed in other private schools	23.4

Note some of the substantial differences between this pattern of predicted test scores and the pattern presented earlier. The scores that public
school students would achieve in Catholic schools if placed there with their
schoolmates are considerably lower than those that would be attained in
the absence of their school classmates. The Catholic school–public school
gap shrinks by 60%. The gap that remains is statistically significant at the
0.05 level, but this gap is very much smaller. The scores that public school
students would achieve in other private schools if placed there with their
public school classmates are actually lower than the public school scores,
although the difference is not statistically significant.

The significant role student body composition plays in determining school
effectiveness implies an important distinction between the schooling options of individual families and the options for public policy. Parents may
succeed in raising their child's achievement by placing the child in a school
with a socioeconomically advantaged student body. In contrast, however,
the public policy goal of providing all children with a good education cannot be achieved by providing all students with the option of attending a
school with a socioeconomically advantaged student body. The next section develops in more detail the public policy dilemmas created by the importance of "client composition" in determining "organizations' performance."

DESIGNING PUBLIC POLICIES

In recent years, many observers of American education, frustrated by
problems with the public educational system, have suggested that government follow the path taken for other social services and rely more heavily
on nonprofit private organizations for the delivery of services. Vouchers
and tuition tax credits have been the most prominent proposals for encouraging the use of private schools. Under a simple voucher system, every
family would receive for each school-age child a voucher that would have
a specified dollar value when used to pay for educational services at either
a public or private school. Under a tuition tax credit system, parents would
subtract from their federal income tax bill a part of the amount that they
paid in private school tuitions. Current proposals suggest credits ranging
from $250 to $500 per child. (See the Kutner-Sherman-Williams chapter
in this volume.)

While the arguments in favor of vouchers and tuition tax credits vary, a
common theme is that these proposals would improve the efficiency of the
education sector by placing greater reliance on market forces for the allocation of educational resources. At the same time, it is argued, the proposals would promote equality of educational opportunity by increasing the
access of low-income families to high-quality private education. The fact
that the composition of the student body influences the quality of the student's educational experience, however, has important implications for
thinking about such public policies toward private schools.

Limitations of the Market Model

One of the valued properties of competitive markets is that consumers are normally free to purchase any good provided they are prepared to pay the announced price. In the case of educational services, however, families find that their options depend not only on their willingness to pay, but also on the attributes of their children. Children who lack the attributes that particular private school managers feel will contribute to the skills of the other students in the school find it difficult to gain acceptance to those schools. One reason stems from the importance of the composition of the student body in determining school effectiveness. If schools charge all students the same price, schools that do not discriminate among applicants on the basis of their effects on other students will lose desirable students to schools that do discriminate.

To understand why a student who does not have attributes valued by other families has limited educational options in a competitive market, think about the incentives for the parents of a child who does have valued attributes, and consequently is viewed as an asset to his or her classmates. How will these parents be compensated for the benefits such a child bestows on classmates? One method of compensation is a scholarship, which reduces the cost of the education for that child. Many schools do offer scholarships to sought-after students. A second method of compensation, however, is for the child to be admitted to a school that accepts only students who provide clear positive benefits to other students; in this case, the family is compensated by those positive benefits. Accordingly, in simple markets for educational services in which all potential consumers are charged the same dollar price, freedom to choose implicitly has a much more restrictive definition than that usually associated with competitive markets.

Regulations Dealing with Access

As a result of client group composition effects, regulations dealing with the access of individual families to particular private schools would play a critical role in determining the outcomes of a tuition tax credit or voucher system. To understand this, compare two alternative systems: one with no regulations relating to access; the other with regulations that totally specify the student body composition—by lottery, for example—of all schools for which the demand for places exceeds supply. In the case of no regulations, one would expect to find that despite the existence of a public subsidy, access to high-quality private schools would be denied to many families because the incentives for student sorting would continue to exist just as they do under the current system. One would also expect that private schools would provide higher-quality education on average than public schools, inasmuch as the public schools would be obliged to provide services for anyone who could not find a place in a private school.

Under a system in which places in oversubscribed schools were rationed by lottery, inequality of access would be ameliorated in the sense that all students would have an equal probability of admission to the sought-after schools. However, given the importance of student body composition in determining school effectiveness, eliminating private schools' control over admission and dismissal practices would reduce the quality of education provided in many private schools while probably improving the average quality of public education.

Thus, a central problem in the design of a voucher or tuition tax credit system is the trade-off between access and quality. Regulations that insure access undermine the quality of private schools by prescribing the composition of each school's clientele; regulations that protect the private school's capacity to control the composition of their student body undermine citizens' equality of access to those schools.

CLIENT COMPOSITION AND OTHER SOCIAL SERVICES

The same trade-offs and the same regulatory dilemmas apply to any social services in which client composition affects outcomes.

Recently the *New York Times* reported that nursing homes in New York State were not willing to admit applicants with organic brain disorders. The reason given was that such patients caused problems for other residents of the nursing homes.[14] A continuing challenge for New York City government is to find adequate foster care for the significant portion of the clientele of homeless children that private foster care homes, operating with public funds, refuse to admit on the grounds that the children disrupt their programs.[15] Just as in the case of education, these private providers perceive strong incentives to sort clients in order to produce "quality" services.

In all service areas where client group composition affects outcomes, attempts to regulate private providers of social services will continually confront painful choices between the goals of access and service quality. Job training, mental health services, nursing homes, foster care—the list is endless. The attractiveness of the private provider option will depend to a large extent on the ability of policymakers to design incentives that mediate the conflict between access and service quality. There are many options, including differential subsidies and multitiered delivery systems.

THE OEO EXPERIENCE WITH EDUCATION VOUCHERS

The richness of possible regulatory frameworks and the importance of politics in shaping actual regulations are illustrated by the Office of Economic Opportunity's (OEO) experience with education vouchers.[16] In the late 1960s OEO commissioned a study of possible voucher plans. The study recommended what came to be called the regulated compensatory voucher plan. Under this plan students from low-income families would receive vouchers with a value greater than the vouchers issued to other families, in order to provide an incentive to private schools to accept such children. In oversubscribed schools, one-half of the places would be allocated by lottery; the other half could be allocated by the school in any manner that did not discriminate on the basis of race. A regulatory agency would not only monitor compliance with the regulations, but also would provide parents with information about the attributes and accomplishments of the available school programs.[17] This creative regulatory proposal offered the potential of providing families widespread access to private schools and also leaving private schools with sufficient control over admission policies to retain the character and quality of their programs.

During the early 1970s OEO attempted to initiate a trial of the regulated compensatory voucher plan. While many localities were initially interested, all ultimately withdrew when the details of the plan became clear. In effect, there was no constituency for a plan that threatened the job security of teachers, compromised the independence of private schools, and had the possibility of denying families' access to their neighborhood schools, if the school should be oversubscribed.

Eventually OEO was successful in finding a school district in Alum Rock, California, that was willing to try out a modified version of the regulated compensatory voucher plan. However, the process of negotiation between federal sponsors and local interest groups resulted in a dramatic alteration of the voucher plan. Ultimately, no private schools participated in the Alum Rock voucher demonstration. No teachers in unpopular programs lost their jobs. No teachers in popular programs received additional compensation. In fact, none of the incentives usually thought to spur initiative in the private sector was present in Alum Rock.[18]

Perhaps the most important lesson from the OEO experience with vouchers is that implementation of a regulatory strategy that successfully balances demands for access and quality requires not only creative design, but also extraordinary political skills in building support for the proposed design. Without the exercise of significant political skills, the final regulatory policy is more likely to reflect the balance of power among the participants than the original regulatory design.

MANY ALTERNATIVES, ALWAYS DIFFICULT TRADE-OFFS

The regulated compensatory voucher plan is not the only means of encouraging a larger role for private sector providers of social services while protecting access for disadvantaged children. For example, the first article by Estelle James in this volume describes the Dutch educational system, a system in which private nonprofit organizations play a large role in providing services and students from different backgrounds appear to have access to both private and public schools. The Dutch experience suggests that it is possible to design a regulatory system that both provides a large role for private schools and provides access to these schools for students from different backgrounds. However, it is ironic that these goals are achieved in the Dutch system by heavily regulating the behaviors of private schools—for example, these schools have no flexibility in determining teachers' salaries. The regulations bring about precisely the kinds of inefficiencies in production that, observers claim, plague U.S. public schools and that spurred the call for a larger private sector role.

The Dutch experience provides yet another example of what may be a critical theorem of regulatory design: The range of regulatory options is wide, but the design process will inevitably be characterized by trade-offs among access, quality, and efficiency.

APPENDIX

There are a number of small differences between my methodology and CHK's.

1. In estimating equation 1, CHK pooled the Catholic school and other private school subsamples. (Their equation included separate intercepts for the two subsamples.) The reason they did not pool the private school subsamples with the public school subsample and conduct a simple analysis of covariance was that the coefficients on the background variables differed for the public school and private school subsamples. My F test results indicate that the coefficients on the background variables for the Catholic school subsample are different from those for the other private school subsample. Consequently, extending CHK's logic, I estimated equation 1 separately for the three subsamples.

It is important to keep in mind that the "other private school" subsample drawn from the HSB data base is extremely small (361 students in twenty-one schools). Moreover, the limited evidence available in the data indicates that schools in this sector are extremely diverse—in tuitions, in academic programs, and in student achievement.[19] Consequently very little can be learned from the HSB data about schools in this sector.

2. The HSB sample is a stratified sample that oversamples students in certain types of schools, including public and private schools attended by large numbers of minority students. In estimating equation 1, CHK weighted their observations by the design weights. I used unweighted data on individual students in order to preserve the homoscedastic property of the error terms. However, CHK and I both used the design weights in calculating the average characteristics of high school seniors attending public schools in the United States. These characteristics were then attributed to the hypothetical average public school senior whose performance was examined in the two experiments.

The results of the two experiments are somewhat sensitive to the choice of ordinary least squares or weighted least squares in estimating equations 1 and 2. When the experiments are based on the weighted least squares estimates (CHK's procedure), 25% of the advantage of Catholic schools over public schools is estimated to be the result of student body composition effects (as opposed to 60% when the experiments are based on the ordinary least square estimates). The results of the "public school"–"other private school" comparison are not sensitive to the choice of estimation technique. Using either technique, the predicted test scores indicate that all the advantage of other private schools over public schools is due to student body composition effects.

3. CHK used seventeen background variables in estimating equation 1. I used only ten in order to minimize the missing data problem that led CHK to employ the method of pairwise deletion of missing data—a method that many statisticians find troubling.

4. Unlike CHK, I calculated the standard errors appropriate for testing whether the achievement of the average public school student would be different if he or she attended a Catholic or other private school. A description of the method used to calculate these standard errors is available from the author on request.

5. A final methodological issue concerns the specification of equation 2, which does not contain variables describing the quality of teachers and school programs—both of which are determinants of school quality. If these variables are correlated with the average SES of the students in the school, their influence will be attributed to SES. It can be argued that this is not a specification error, since a school's ability to attract high-quality teachers and to implement effective homework and discipline practices depends on the composition of the student body. However, it would have been desirable to investigate whether the predictions for the second hypothetical experiment would be different if equation 2 included teacher and program characteristics. This was not done for two reasons: First, the HSB data set includes no information on the characteristics of teachers that have been found to be related to teaching performance—variables such as verbal ability and the quality of the teacher's undergraduate college. Second, the information in the data set on homework and discipline refers to the policy outcomes, not the policies themselves. Since the outcomes (what the disciplinary environment is like and how much homework is completed) are endogenous, they do not belong on the right-hand side of equation 2 unless this equation is embedded in a larger system that includes equations explaining the determinants of these outcomes.

NOTES

1. See the references in E. S. Savas, *How to Shrink Government: Privatizing the Public Sector* (Chatham, N.J.: Chatham House, 1982).

2. James S. Coleman, Thomas Hoffer, and Sally Kilgore, *High School Achievement: Public, Catholic, and Private Schools Compared* (New York: Basic Books, 1982).

3. James S. Coleman, Ernest Q. Campbell, Carol J. Holson, James McPartland, Alexander Mood, Frederic D. Weinfield, and Robert L. York, *Equality of Educational Opportunity* (Washington, D.C.: U.S. Government Printing Office, 1966).

4. Eric A. Hanushek, *Education and Race* (Lexington, Mass.: D. C. Heath, 1972); Vernon Henderson, Peter Mieszkowski, and Yvon Sauvageau, "Peer Group Effects and Educational Production Functions," *Journal of Public Economics* 10 (August 1978), pp. 97–106; Anita A. Summers and Barbara L. Wolfe, "Do Schools Make a Difference?" *American Economic Review* 67 (September 1977); and Donald R. Winkler, "Educational Achievement and School Peer Group Composition," *Journal of Human Resources* 10 (Winter 1975), pp. 189–204.

5. Student transfers constitute an additional sorting mechanism, the significance of which is not known for elementary and secondary education. Transfers are an important sorting mechanism in higher education. It is possible that future research based on follow-ups of the High School and Beyond sample (defined below) will increase our knowledge of the role of transfers in influencing the education received by high school students from different backgrounds.

6. Matthew Edel and Elliott Sklar, "Taxes, Spending and Property Values: Supply Adjustment in a Tiebout-Oates Model," *Journal of Political Economy* 82 (September–October 1974); Wallace Oates, "The Effects of Property Taxes and Local Public Spending on Property Values: An Empirical Study of Tax Capitalization and the Tiebout Hypothesis," *Journal of Political Economy* 77 (November–December 1969); Raymond M. Reinhard, "Estimating Property Tax Capitalization: A Further Comment," *Journal of Political Economy* 89 (December 1981), pp. 1251–1260.

7. David Grether and Peter Mieszkowski, "Determinants of Real Estate Values," *Journal of Urban Economics* (April 1974).

8. J. S. Fuerst, "Report Card: Chicago's All-Black Schools," *Public Interst* 64 (Summer 1981).

9. Coleman, Hoffer, and Kilgore, *High School Achievement*.

10. Several critics have argued that CHK do not provide reliable answers to these hypothetical questions, primarily because their analysis strategy does not adequately control selectivity bias. For a detailed discussion of this issue, see my other paper in this volume (Chapter 6).

11. The "elite" other private schools excluded from the sample are a small number of private schools characterized by very high tuitions and very high student performance.

12. The positive correlation between mothers' expectations concerning their children's education and the children's achievement could reflect either of two causal mechanisms: Students work hard and do well when their parents expect a lot of them, or high achievement by students makes their parent think that the students should go on to college.

13. See, for example, Coleman, Campbell et al., *Equality of Educational Opportunity*.

14. "Nursing Home Care Being Denied to Thousands of Mental Patients," *New York Times,* November 1, 1982, p. B1.

15. Dennis Young and Stephen Finch, *Foster Care and Nonprofit Agencies* (Lexington, Mass.: Lexington Books, 1977).

16. See the Kutner-Sherman-Williams chapter in this volume for more discussion of alternative regulatory policies toward private schools.

17. Center for the Study of Public Policy, *Education Vouchers: A Report on Financing Education by Grants to Parents* (Cambridge, Mass.: CSSP, 1970).

18. David Cohen and Eleanor Farrar, "Power to the Parents?—The Study of Education Vouchers," *The Public Interest* 48 (Summer 1977), pp. 72–97.

19. The extraordinary diversity among private schools was discussed in Donald Erickson's chapter in this volume.

6

Comparisons of Private and Public Schools: What Can We Learn?*

RICHARD J. MURNANE

INTRODUCTION

The previous chapter argues that comparisons of the performance of public and private schools can be misleading. This chapter examines in detail recent research providing such comparisons with the goal of clarifying what lessons can be drawn. The chapter also explains why the recent comparisons have puzzled, and in some cases infuriated, many public school educators. I begin by providing background on the best known of the recent studies.

On April 7, 1981, at a conference attended by more than four hundred educators and the press, James Coleman announced the findings of research that he had conducted with Thomas Hoffer and Sally Kilgore on public and private high schools in the United States. Their principal finding was that Catholic schools and non-Catholic private schools are more effective in helping students to acquire cognitive skills than public schools are.

Coming at a time of widespread criticism of public education and presidential support for tuition tax credits for families that use private schools, this finding was widely reported in the press and evoked a range of spirited reactions. Critics and supporters responded to Coleman, Hoffer, and Kilgore's (henceforth CHK) work with articles and editorials with lively titles

*This chapter is adpated from "A Review Essay—Comparisons of Public and Private Schools: Lessons from the Uproar," *Journal of Human Resources* 19, 2 (1984). An earlier version was Working Paper No. 73 of the Program on Non-Profit Organizations at Yale University. Helpful comments on various drafts were provided by Anthony Bryk, Glen Cain, David Cohen, Paul DiMaggio, Dan Levy, Richard Nelson, and Barbara Neufeld. I would particularly like to acknowledge the help of Edward Pauly, who read several drafts of this chapter and provided many important ideas.

such as: "Coleman Goes Private (in Public)," "Lessons for the Public Schools," "Coleman's Bad Report," and "Private Schools Win a Public Vote."[1]

Over the succeeding months CHK's work remained visible as critiques of their research and reanalyses of the data they used appeared in a variety of journals, in some cases accompanied by lengthy responses by CHK. Another wave of interest was sparked by the publication and subsequent reviews of CHK's *High School Achievement: Public, Catholic, and Private Schools Compared*,[2] in which they presented their final research findings.

As a result of the wide range of responses to CHK's work and the numerous symposia in which CHK have debated their critics in print, there is now ample material available to any reader interested in forming a judgment about the quality of the research that produced their main conclusion.[3] Therefore, this chapter does not provide yet another critique of their methodology. Instead, its purpose is to step back from the debates concerning the appropriateness of the methodologies CHK used to generate their findings, and to examine three kinds of significant, but neglected, lessons to be drawn from CHK's work and the critiques and reanalyses it provoked.

The first set of lessons concerns unrecognized differences in perspectives that underlie debates about how the research on public and private schools should be conducted and how the results should be interpreted. The second set concerns neglected substantive findings, including findings about which all analysts agree, but the significance of which has been neglected, and anomalies and puzzles that have been relegated to asides or footnotes, but should not be. The third set of lessons concerns the strengths and weaknesses of the particular philosophy that has guided CHK's interpretation of their research findings.

Before turning to these lessons, I want to describe briefly the data base used to generate the recent public school–private school comparisons and to clarify the meaning of certain terms. The data base used by CHK and their critics is the first wave of data generated by the High School and Beyond (HSB) project, a longitudinal study of 58,728 U.S. high school students. The sample includes students who were either sophomores or seniors in 1980 in one of 893 public schools, 84 Catholic schools, or 38 non-Catholic private schools, 11 of which were selected as representatives of high-performance private schools. The HSB data base has a stratified sample design with an oversampling of students in certain types of schools, including public and Catholic schools in which more than 30% of the students were minority group members. The data base includes design weights that in principle permit estimation of the characteristics of the U.S. high school student population.

The small number of non-Catholic private schools in the sample and the wide variation across these schools in institutional characteristics, student characteristics, and student performance have led most analysts to conclude that there are insufficient data to derive reliable conclusions about the population of such schools. As a result, attention has focused primarily on public school–Catholic school comparisons, especially on whether Catholic schools are more effective in imparting cognitive skills to students than public schools are. I will refer to this as the question of whether there is a Catholic school advantage.

UNSTATED DIFFERENCES IN PERSPECTIVES UNDERLIE METHODOLOGICAL DEBATES

Families' School Choices and School Effectiveness

Can CHK's research findings be used to predict the consequences of policies that would induce students to move from public schools to Catholic schools? This question has been ardently debated by CHK and their critics, with the discussion focused primarily on whether CHK's finding of a Catholic school advantage is contaminated by selectivity bias. As explained in more detail below, selectivity bias in this context refers to the notion that at least part of the estimated Catholic school advantage is actually a reflection of an unobserved differential in the average skill level of Catholic school and public school students. The selectivity bias issue clearly merits attention because it influences the interpretation of CHK's central finding. However, preoccupation with this issue has diverted attention from another important issue, namely, whether the effectiveness of school programs depends on the factors that influence families' schooling choices. This issue also influences in a critical way the interpretation of CHK's central finding.

Let me begin my explanation by summarizing briefly CHK's methodology. CHK used multiple regression analysis to estimate the impact of seventeen student background variables on the achievement of students in public schools. In a separate regression, they estimated the impact of these same variables on the achievement of students in Catholic schools. They then used the regression results to predict the achievement that a hypothetical student with the characteristics of the average public school student would have if he or she attended a public school or a Catholic school. The predictions indicated that the hypothetical student would have higher achievement in a Catholic school; hence, the conclusion of a Catholic school advantage.[4]

Critics immediately pointed out that the seventeen student background variables may not fully account for differences in the skill and motivation levels that Catholic school students and public school students bring to school. Consequently, CHK's finding may be contiminated by selectivity bias. In response to these criticisms, CHK and other analysts employed a variety of alternative techniques to investigate the selectivity bias question.[5] An explicit assumption common to all of these techniques is that the factors that influence family schooling choices, such as family incomes, schools' tuitions, and schools' admission and dismissal policies, make it difficult to compare school programs because they result in nonrandom assignment of students to schools. Techniques for controlling selectivity bias attempt to control statistically for the differences in skills and motivations that students bring to different schools.

There is a second assumption implicit in the strategies for controlling selectivity bias that has not received much attention, namely, that the factors affecting families' school choices do not themselves influence the effectiveness of school programs. In fact, it is the assumption of a conceptual distinction between the determinants of school effectiveness and the factors that influence families' schooling choices that justified framing the evaluation question in terms of asking what the relative effectiveness of public schools and Catholic schools would be in educating randomly assigned samples of students.

An alternative view of the relationship between families' schooling choices and school effectiveness (also discussed in Erickson's chapter in this book) is that at least some of the factors that influence families' schooling choices also influence the effectiveness of school programs. For example, control over admission and dismissal policies may not only help a school to attract talented students; it may also improve a school's program by making it easier to attract high-quality teachers, many of whom do not want to work with disruptive students.[6] Similarly, charging tuition may not only result in a school attracting primarily students from high-income families; it may also strengthen a school's program by stimulating parental supervision of students' homework.

Viewed from this perspective, comparing the effectiveness of public and Catholic schools in educating randomly assigned students is not the appropriate conceptual experiment for learning about the consequences of policies that would induce students to move from public schools to Catholic schools. Instead, we must learn the extent to which each of the many factors that influence families' school choices also influence schools' effectiveness. This is necessary because policies designed to change families' school choices may themselves alter the relative effectiveness of different schools.

At several points in their book, CHK endorse the view that many of the factors that influence families' school choices also influence the effectiveness of school programs. For example, they discuss the impact that control over admissions and dismissals may have on the quality of school programs.[7] A weakness of CHK's book, however, is that they do not explain clearly the implications of this view for the interpretation of their results. I will try to provide this explanation.

CHK's research compares Catholic schools as a group with public schools as a group. They find that the package typically associated with Catholic schools (tuition charged; significant control over admission and dismissal of students) is associated with higher student achievement than is the package typically associated with public schools (no tuition; no control over admissions; limited control over dismissals). If one believes that CHK's methods eliminate selectivity bias, then one might predict from their findings that a public school that adopted the entire Catholic school package would be able to increase its effectiveness.

These are not the types of policy changes currently being debated, however. Instead, the changes under discussion concern the introduction of policies such as tuition tax credits or education vouchers that would induce more students to attend private schools. To predict the consequences of these policies, we would need to know, first, exactly how they would impact on the incentives that influence family schooling choices and on the control that individual schools have over student admissions and dismissals. Then we would need to know how each of these changes in the determinants of families' school choices influences the effectiveness of school programs. CHK do not address either of these questions. In particular, they do not explore whether the variation among schools in the private sector in tuitions and in control over student admissions and dismissals explains the variation in the effectiveness of individual school programs. Since these are the types of variables that would be affected by policies designed to induce students to move to private schools, we need to know how these variables influence school effectiveness to know how such policies would influence the distribution of student achievement. Studies of the school systems of other countries (see the first James essay in this volume) may provide information on the role of admission and dismissal policies in determining school effectiveness.

School Policies

To what extent are school policies responsible for differences in the achievement of students attending public and Catholic schools? CHK claim that school policies, defined as "homework, curriculum, and disciplinary practices,"[8] do play a significant role in contributing to a Catholic school advantage. Moreover, they conclude:

> . . . where such things as curriculum and disciplinary practices have effects on student behavior and achievement that are independent of school type and student background, we can institute changes in any school that would affect achievement. It is for this reason that the results in this chapter are as relevant to public schools as they are to private schools.[9]

These findings and CHK's interpretation of them have been highlighted in articles with names like "How to Save Our Public Schools,"[10] and have troubled many public school educators, leaving them wondering what the research really means.

How should we interpret CHK's statement that a school's homework and discipline practices have an effect on student achievement, independent of student body composition? Does this mean that the faculties of public schools could raise student achievement if they simply altered practices, and that these practices are unambiguously subject to their control? If this is the correct interpretation, then one must ask why these steps have not already been taken. Is the reason laziness? A lack of awareness that these things matter? In effect, this interpretation implies an extraordinary indictment of teachers and administrators in public schools characterized by low student achievement. Do CHK intend such an indictment? At no point in their book do they directly criticize public school educators. But what other interpretation can there be?

I believe that the answer lies in alternative definitions of the term *school policy*. To my mind a school policy should be defined as a set of instructions that tells the personnel responsible for carrying out the policy what they should do. It is crucial that the mandated actions are actually subject to the control of those responsible for the policy's execution. An example of a school policy that would satisfy this definition is a rule that teachers must assign one hour of homework every night and that any student who does not complete the homework must be kept after school for a period of one hour. If CHK had found that clearly defined school policies such as this were systematically related to student achievement, then it would be appropriate, indeed important, to ask school personnel why such policies were not in effect in all schools.

CHK's results are not of this sort, however. They analyzed no variables that are school policies in the sense of the definition described above. Instead, CHK's analyses were directed at a somewhat different, more diffuse, objective. They wanted to investigate whether the difference between the average achievement of students attending public schools and Catholic schools was due in part to differences in what happened in these schools. In other words, they wanted to challenge the allegation that the Catholic school advantage was due solely to selectivity bias. To investigate this issue, they adopted the term *school functioning* to characterize what went on in schools. The evidence they collected on school functioning consisted of students' reports on such things as how much homework they completed and their perceptions of the quality of the disciplinary environment. CHK standardized these results to account for observed differences in students' background.[11] They found that the standardized student reports, aggregated to the school level, explained part of the difference between the average achievement of students attending public schools and Catholic schools.[12] These variables also explained part of the variation in the average achievement of students attending different public schools. CHK rely heavily on this second set of findings to support their conclusion that "we can institute changes in any school that would affect achievement."[13]

But what are these changes? CHK do not tell us. Throughout much of the book, CHK seem implicitly aware that they have presented no *evidence* about what clearly defined actions would improve schools. I presume that this explains their tendency to use the term *school functioning*, rather than the term *school policies*, to describe their homework and discipline variables. However, they do not consistently retain this distinction. For example, in describing their empirical work relating the homework and discipline variables to student achievement, CHK state, "This will allow us to identify school policies which increase achievement within each sector."[14]

I believe that CHK's ambiguity about the meaning of the term *school policy* underlies the frustration that many public school educators feel toward their work. The experiences of many educators lead them to believe that there are no well-defined school policies that consistently produce high levels of homework and an orderly disciplinary environment. Had CHK made clear that these dimensions of school functioning are not policies, but rather intermediate outcomes that are consistently related to student achievement, then I believe that the reactions of educators to this work would have been more positive. Many educators would have embraced such findings as much-needed documentation of the importance to school effectiveness of struggling and searching for ways to improve school discipline and to increase the amount of homework students complete.

Design Weights

In addressing such questions as whether there is a Catholic school advantage and, if so, what are its sources, should the observations in the HSB data base be weighted by the design weights or should all observations be assigned the same weight? In many analyses, the decision makes a difference. For example, in the analysis described in the previous chapter, in which I weighted all observations equally (i.e., did not use the design weights), I found that a variable describing the composition of a school's student body (sometimes referred to as a peer group variable) explained more of the variation in the achievement of students in Catholic schools than it explained the variation in the achievement of students in public schools.[15] Kilgore,[16] who used the design weights to weight observations, found the opposite. Understanding the role that student body composition plays in determining school effectiveness is important in understanding the meaning of CHK's finding of a Catholic school advantage. (This is the central theme of the previous chapter.) Consequently, it is important to explore the weighting question.

Underlying the decision about whether to use the design weights in conducting empirical work with the HSB data is an implicit assumption about the degree of confidence one has in the specification of one's model: If the model is specified correctly, then equal weighting is the desirable strategy. The reason is that, under the plausible assumption that the variances of the disturbance terms associated with individual students are equal, weighting all observations equally preserves the homoscedastic (i.e., equal variance) property of the error terms and provides efficient estimation of the model's parameters.

The case for using the design weights rests on the assumption that the model may be misspecified. In this case, equal weighting of observations in a stratified random sample can exaggerate the effects of any misspecification on the estimated model parameters. This is an especially important consideration in working with the HSB data base because the extent of oversampling of students with particular characteristics is so great. For example, the design weights for sophomores, which indicate how many sophomores in the U.S. population are represented by a particular observation in the HSB data base, range from less than 3 to more than 700. The *average* design weights for white, black, and Hispanic students attending public schools are 136, 137, and 85, respectively.[17] The *average* design weights for white, black, and Hispanic students attending Catholic schools are 110, 34, and 33, respectively. Thus, weighting all observations equally gives greater weight to minority group students, especially those in Catholic schools, than using the design weights does.

To illustrate the influence that the weighting decision can have on the parameter estimates of a misspecified model, consider Murnane's and Kilgore's work on the role of student body composition in explaining the achievement of students in Catholic schools. Both researchers estimated a model that is described in simplified form by equation 1:

$$A_{ij} = a_0 + a_1 M_i + a_2 S_j + e_i \qquad (1)$$

where

A_{ij} = the achievement of the ith student attending the jth Catholic school

M_i = 1, if the ith student is a minority group member
    0, otherwise

S_j = the average socioeconomic status of the students attending the jth school

e_i = a student-specific disturbance term

$a_1 < 0$

$a_2 > 0$

Let us now assume that the true model is described by equation 2:

$$A_{ij} = b_0 + b_1 M_i + b_2 S_j + b_3[(S_j)(M_i)] + e_i \qquad (2)$$

with $b_2 > 0$ and $b_3 > 0$

In other words, the average socioeconomic status of a school's student body has a larger effect on the achievement of minority group students than it has on the achievement of white students.

Both Murnane's and Kilgore's estimates of a_2 can be viewed as weighted averages of the true coefficient for white students (b_2) and the true coefficient for minority group students ($b_2 + b_3$). However, Murnane's estimate will be larger because, as a result of weighting all observations equally, his weights correspond to the relative numbers of minority group students and white students in Catholic schools in the HSB sample, while Kilgore's weights correspond to the relative numbers of minority group students and white students in the U.S. Catholic high school population.

If one were to use estimates of equation 1 to predict the effect on the average achievement of a random sample of Catholic school students of moving from a Catholic school with a low value of S to a Catholic school with a high value of S, then the prediction based on Kilgore's estimate would be more accurate. This, I believe, is the essence of the case for using the design weights.

In one respect, the case for using the design weights is compelling because the potential for misspecifying models of student achievement is great—particularly because, as Erickson documents in this volume, there is an extraordinary range of school types in the United States. In another respect, however, framing the discussion of design weights in terms of an either/or choice, use them or not, is the wrong way to consider the issue. Neither choice eliminates model misspecification: consequently, neither choice would permit accurate predictions of the achievement consequences of moving white students or minority students from one Catholic school to another. Thus, it seems important to reframe the discussion to focus on how the design weights can be used to inform model specification.

I would argue that examination of the sensitivity of empirical results to the weighting decision should be a part of all empirical work based on stratified samples such as the HSB data base. The reason is that sensitivity of results to the weighting decision is per se evidence of misspecification. As a result, such sensitivity analyses can be useful procedures in attempting to go beyond the question of whether there is a Catholic school advantage and to begin to learn from the HSB data about the schooling options available to American families from different backgrounds, the schooling choices families make, and the extent to which differences in options and choices explain the distribution of student achievement in the United States.

NEGLECTED FINDINGS

The publicity surrounding a few of CHK's findings has resulted in neglect of several patterns in the HSB data about which all analysts agree, but the significance of which has not been appreciated. The first of these is that there are important differences in the quality of education offered in different American schools. In light of the debate over the relative quality of public and private schools, this might seem obvious and not worth emphasizing. However, recall the press reports following the publication of *Equality of Educational Opportunity*[18] in 1966, which might be summarized as: Schools don't matter, families do.[19] The evidence from the HSB data is that differences among schools do matter.

The second finding concerns diversity among public schools and among private schools. While there is considerable disagreement about whether Catholic schools and other private schools are more effective on average than public schools, there is agreement that even the largest estimates of a private school advantage are small relative to the variation in quality among different public schools, among different Catholic schools, and among different non-Catholic private schools. Consequently, in predicting the quality of a student's education, it is less important to know whether the student attended a public school or a private school than it is to know which school within a particular sector the student attended. A related implication is that in trying to understand why families make particular schooling choices we should pay great attention to the nature of the option set—that is, to the qualities of the public and private schools available to the family.

A third set of findings about which analysts agree (and which is a central theme in the previous chapter) is that variables describing the composition of the student body in a school are systematically related to the achievement of individual students in the school.[20] To date, student body composition has been characterized in terms of the average values of demographic characteristics of the students in a school. However, no analyst has asserted that the averages themselves are the critical variables. One plausible interpretation for why variables describing student body composition matter is that they serve as proxies for the number of students in a school who do not want to be in school, who come to school without motivation to succeed in school, and who come without the parental support that typically accompanies academic success. I believe that an important interpretation of CHK's book is that it provides documentation of the paths through which such troubled and indifferent students influence the quality of education provided to their fellow students. As CHK explain, these students reduce the achievement of their peers through their impact on teacher morale, through their effects on the implementation of school policies, and through their effects on the behavior of other students.

Viewed in this light, CHK's research demonstrates the significant tension that exists in our society between honoring the commitment to educate all citizens and developing high-quality educational programs. Finding ways to resolve this tension is perhaps the greatest challenge that public educators face.

CHK interpret some of the patterns in the HSB baseline data—compared to Catholic school students, public school students feel discipline is less fair and teachers are less interested—as indicating that the trends in public education over the last fifteen years toward more state and federal regulation of schools and greater legal protection of student rights have not been an effective strategy for meeting this challenge.[21] CHK also speculate that alternative strategies would be more effective—in particular, strategies that "involve more choice by parents and students and more leverage for the school to make demands and exercise authority."[22]

CHK's suggestions can only be viewed as untested hypotheses, since their research does not examine the effect on student achievement of either state and federal regulations or student choice plans. However, these are interesting hypotheses, and it is important to ask how research might throw light on the consequences of policies that would increase student choice and/or increase the authority of schools to select and dismiss students.

In particular, it is important to learn whether such policies would bring about beneficial changes in the in-school behaviors of troubled and indifferent students or whether the policies would only make it easier for individual schools to avoid working with such students (thereby relegating them to another school whose effectiveness would suffer as a result). This distinction is not critical in predicting how the effectiveness of an *individual* school would be influenced by a policy change. However, the distinction is critical in evaluating whether a particular policy change would be a useful strategy for reforming a school *system* committed to educating all students. I believe there are three areas of research that might increase our knowledge of these issues.

The first explores the role of admission and dismissal policies in public high schools in explaining the variation in student achievement among schools. More than one-fourth of the public school districts in the United States provide students with choice of school, including many programs that are as rich and distinctive as those of much-admired private schools.[23] Yet we know very little about the factors that influence the choices families make among alternative public schools. There also appears to be significant variation across schools concerning what happens to students who do not meet academic or disciplinary standards. Learning more about the variation in admission and dismissal policies of the schools in the HSB study and whether these policies only serve to allocate students among schools or whether they influence student behaviors may be a fruitful approach for learning about the extent to which organizational reforms can lead to improvements in the efficacy of public schools.

A second potentially fruitful area of research is to learn more about the practices of Catholic schools, which appear (on the basis of the cross-sectional data available from the HSB study) to be effective in helping many minority group students and students from low-income families to acquire cognitive skills. In many respects—student/teacher ratios, income distribution of students—Catholic schools are more similar to public schools than to other private schools.

Of course, Catholic schools do have more control over the composition of their student bodies than public schools typically do. In the past, this may have dissuaded researchers interested in improving public schools from examining Catholic schools. However, as public school districts explore the merits of a variety of plans—magnet schools, open enrollments, mini-schools within schools—that involve matching students with programs, the Catholic schools' experiences may be relevant. For example, it would be valuable to explore whether admissions interviews with students and parents, a common practice in Catholic schools, not only serve to select students, but also to inform families about how a particular school works. Such interviews might be a first step in helping students to adopt behavior patterns that lead to high achievement for them and their peers.

Another area in which there may be important things to be learned from Catholic schools concerns the recruitment of teachers. How are Catholic schools able to attract teachers at modest salaries who demonstrate great interest in and commitment to students, as reflected in student responses to the HSB questionnaires? Is part of the answer a willingness among Catholic schools to hire new college graduates who are interested in teaching for a few years but do not plan to make teaching a long-term career? Does control over student admissions make teaching in Catholic schools more satisfying than teaching in many public schools? Is it important that hiring of teachers is done by the individual Catholic school while most public sector hiring is done at the school district level, often without input from individual school administrators and without applicants' knowledge of where he or she will be assigned? Learning the answers to these questions might provide ideas for dealing with an issue raised in all the recent reports on the crisis in American education—namely, how do we attract talented college graduates into teaching?

Finally, a third research approach for learning more about how schooling works in America is to explore the many puzzles and anomalies that analyses of the HSB data have produced. These puzzles are present both in CHK's book and in a book by Andrew Greeley that examines the experiences of minority group students in Catholic schools and public schools.[24] The logic underlying this approach is that if we are going to take seriously the implications of CHK's most highly publicized findings, we should also examine the meaning of other statistically significant patterns in the data, puzzling as the patterns may appear. Two of these puzzles deal with the achievement of students in non-Catholic private schools and may possibly be artifacts of the small number of such schools in the HSB data base. However, I include them in the list because they suggest how different non-Catholic private schools are from Catholic schools.

The puzzles and anomalies include:

1. Although attendance is positively related to performance for students attending most schools in the HSB data base, students in high-performance public schools have poorer attendance records than do students attending any other type of school identified in the HSB data base.[25]
2. Although student reports of the quality of the disciplinary environment are positively related to student achievement in most schools, reports of the quality of the disciplinary environment in Catholic schools are negatively related to the achievement of sophomores.[26]
3. Although the education provided by different Catholic schools appears to be relatively homogeneous in quality (compared to public schools or non-Catholic private schools), students attending Catholic schools run by religious orders have higher achievement, controlling for student backgrounds, than do students attending Catholic schools run by dioceses and parishes.[27]
4. Although Catholic schools appear to be more effective than public schools in educating many types of students (according to CHK and Greeley), students in Catholic schools who plan to graduate from college and whose fathers attended college have lower achievement than students with these same backgrounds and aspirations who attend public schools.[28]

5. The achievement of students in non-Catholic private schools is more dependent on family background than is the achievement of students in public schools. This is in contrast to CHK's finding that the achievement of students in Catholic schools is less dependent on family background than is the achievement of students in public schools.[29]
6. Although CHK emphasize the importance of the disciplinary environment and the amount of student homework completed in explaining the achievement of students attending different public schools, these variables explain an even larger part of the variation in achievement among students attending different non-Catholic private schools.[30]
7. Although black students in private schools in most parts of the country are less segregated into schools serving primarily black students than is the case for black students in public schools, minority students in private schools in the western part of the United States are more segregated into schools serving primarily minority students than is true of minority students in public schools in that part of the country.[31]

Understanding the sources of these statistically significant patterns in the HSB data may improve our understanding of the schooling options available to different American families, the choices families make, and the effects that different types of schools have on students from different backgrounds.

HOW DOES RESEARCH INFORM THE POLICY PROCESS?

In the last section of the final chapter of their book,[32] CHK articulate their view of the role of research in informing public policy:

> Policy is the resultant of pressures from a multitude of interests. . . . The role of policy research is to inform these interests. . . . The proper function of policy research is to make it possible for each of these interested parties to better see the lines along which to pursue its interest. . . .
>
> research results do not replace interest groups—they are used by interest groups. . . . results should be available to all and in full view, and . . . the very openness of the process will lead to disputes over what the research data really show.[33]

The debate concerning the interpretation of recent research comparing public and private schools has been carried out very much along the lines James Coleman and his associates advocate. To a large extent this is because Coleman has been extraordinarily energetic in participating in this debate, in publicizing the implications of his research, in responding to critics at great length and in a variety of publications, and in facilitating continuation of the debate by providing potential critics with data, computer printouts, and explanations of his statistical methods.

In concluding this essay it may be useful to examine briefly the strengths and weaknesses of the research philosophy that has shaped the manner in which the debate about research on public and private schools has been conducted.

One significant strength of this research philosophy is that it does stimulate criticism and further research. In the first two years following the April 1981 conference at which Coleman first announced his research findings concerning public and private schools, more than thirty articles were published that either criticized CHK's research or provided reanalyses of the HSB data. Thus, only a short time after the first wave of HSB data became available for analysis, sufficient research was published to support an essay such as this, which tries to sort out the important lessons. And the research flow has continued.

A second implication of this philosophy is that it does push researchers to emphasize the policy implications of their work, since that is, after all, what interest groups want to know about. To the extent that there really are policy implications that stem from research, the fact that they will receive attention is a strength.

At the same time, the emphasis on policy implications is a significant weakness of this research philosophy. The reason is that research based on data from a natural experiment, particularly cross-sectional data, rarely provides reliable evidence about the effects of a policy change; CHK's research is not an exception to this general rule. In my view, the weakest parts of CHK's book are those parts that emphasize policy implications. One example is the section emphasizing the importance of homework and discipline, in which CHK's language implies that these attributes of schools can be produced by policies, but no documentation of what these policies are is presented.

Another example is a section that projects the effects on private school enrollments of providing families with an additional $1000 of income.[34] The projections are based on income elasticities estimated from demand equations that contain no variables describing the availability or prices of alternative schooling options. If the omitted variables are correlated with family incomes, the estimates of the income elasticities will be inconsistent, and consequently the enrollment projections will be inaccurate.

Not all of CHK's book emphasizes policy implications. There are sections that have a very different emphasis and a different tone. These sections try to educate the reader about the variation in school programs, student bodies, and student achievement that exists in an educational system requiring universal participation of students, but permitting extensive choice among schooling alternatives, with the range and quality of the options very sensitive to family income.

CHK show that the choices families make, as constrained by their incomes and locations, result in a large variation in the quality of education provided by different schools. There are many high-quality schools, both public and private. Although there are exceptions, these schools tend to be attended by students from above-average-income families. There are also many schools that are not successful in helping students to acquire cognitive skills. These schools, again with exceptions, tend to be attended by students from families that either have below average income, are of minority group status, or both.

CHK also show that life in high-quality schools is characterized by an orderly disciplinary environment, by the presence of concerned teachers, and by high levels of student homework. This is true not only in the typical high-quality schools that serve primarily students from affluent families; it is also true in the exceptional high-quality schools attended by students from lower-income families.

I find extremely interesting and informative the parts of CHK's book that emphasize the patterns present in U.S. schools today. To my mind, CHK's book would have been a stronger piece of social science research if the authors had explicated these patterns more completely and had made a sharper distinction between the statistical evidence documenting these patterns and their speculations, unsupported by evidence, about what should be done to improve American education.

I believe that such a redirection of emphasis is consistent with CHK's goal of informing the policy process. For example, their findings are rich in evidence supporting the notion that the consequences of any policy designed to increase the number of students attending private schools will be very sensitive to the details of the policy. Moreover, their findings suggest that there are trade-offs in policy design between enhancing the options of families currently without good schooling options and protecting the freedom of action of private schools that is critical to their effectiveness. Making participants in the policy process aware of these trade-offs may be important in producing good public policy.

CHK's findings also provide important lessons for school principals and teachers about improving school quality. The lessons include encouragement that schools can be improved and the significant suggestion that educators focus their attention on what they can do to improve discipline and to get students to do more homework.

Clearly, these lessons are modest, particularly when contrasted with predictions about the consequences of particular well-defined policies. However, the modest lessons are important. Moreover, I believe that they are the only kind of lessons stemming from analysis of cross-sectional data that have the potential for weathering well the test of time.

NOTES

1. Arthur S. Goldberger, "Coleman Goes Private (in Public)," unpublished paper cited in Albert Shanker, "Another Attack on the Coleman Report," *New York Times,* July 26, 1981, p. E7; Phil Keisling, "Lessons for the Public Schools," *New Republic,* November 1, 1982, pp. 27–32; James P. Comer, "Coleman's Bad Report," *New York Times,* April 19, 1981, p. E11; and "Private Schools Win a Public Vote," *Newsweek,* April 13, 1981, p. 107.

2. James S. Coleman, Thomas Hoffer, and Sally Kilgore, *High School Achievement: Public, Catholic, and Private Schools Compared* (New York: Basic Books, 1982).

3. See, for example, the symposia in *Harvard Educational Review* 51 (November 1981) and *Sociology of Education* 55 (April–July 1982), and my other chapter in this volume.

4. See Arthur S. Goldberger and Glen G. Cain, "The Causal analysis of Cognitive Outcomes in the Coleman, Hoffer and Kilgore Report," *Sociology of Education* 55 (April–July 1982), pp. 103–122, for a more detailed explanation of CHK's methodology.

5. For example, see Karl Alexander and Aaron M. Pallas, "Private Schools and Public Policy: New Evidence on Cognitive Achievement in Public and Private Schools," *Sociology of Education* 56, 4 (October 1983), pp. 170–182; Coleman et al., *High School Achievement;* William Fetters, F. Owings, S. Peng, and Ricky Takai, "Review of NORC Report, Public and Private Schools," National Center for Education Statistics, Memorandum (June 26, 1981); Richard J. Murnane, Stuart Newstead, and Randall J. Olsen, "Comparing Public and Private Schools: The Puzzling Role of Selectivity Bias," *Journal of Business and Economic Statistics* 3 (January 1985), pp. 23–35. Jay Noell, "Public and Catholic Schools: A Reanalysis of Public and Private Schools," *Sociology of Education* 55 (April–July 1982), pp. 123–132; Ellis B. Page and Timothy Z. Keith, "Effects of U.S. Private Schools: A Technical Analysis of Two Recent Claims," *Educational Researcher* 10, 7 (August–September 1981), pp. 7–17.

6. Joseph R. Antos and Sherwin Rosen, "Discrimination in the Market for Public School Teachers," *Journal of Econometrics* 3 (May 1975), pp. 123–150.

7. Coleman et al., *High School Achievement*, p. 100.

8. Ibid., p. 205.

9. Ibid., p. 207.

10. Phil Keisling, "How to Save Our Public Schools, *"Readers Digest* (February 1983), pp. 181–188.

11. CHK's methodology, which is based on regression analysis, is analogous to the methodology they used in calculating the relative effectiveness of public schools and Catholic schools in raising student achievement. See Cathleen J. Macias, "Reactions to Coleman," *Private School Monitor*, 4, 1 and 2 (1982), pp. 1–11, for other potential problems with the student reports.

12. Coleman et al., *High School Achievement,* pp. 166–175.

13. Ibid., p. 207.

14. Ibid., p. 159.

15. Richard J. Murnane, Chapter 5 of this volume.

16. Sally Kilgore, "School Policy and Cognitive Growth in Public and Catholic Secondary Schools," unpublished Ph. D. dissertation, University of Chicago (1982).

17. These averages were computed from a sample that contained all sophomores in the HSB database for whom test scores and basic demographic information were available.

18. James S. Coleman, Ernest C. Campbell, Carol J. Hobson, James Mc McPartland, Alexander M. Mood, Frederic Weinfeld, and Robert L. York, *Equality of Educational Opportunity* (Washington, D.C.: Government Printing Office, 1966).

19. It is important to distinguish between the findings that were published in *Equality of Education Opportunity* and the press reports describing and interpreting these findings. See Richard J. Murnane, "Evidence, Analysis, and Unanswered Questions," *Harvard Educational Review* 51, 4 (November 1981), pp. 483–489.

20. Coleman et al., *High School Achievement:* Robert L. Crain and Robert L. Ferrer, "Achievement Prediction with School Level Equations: A Non-Technical Example Using the Public and Private Schools Data," Report No. 323, Center or Social Organization of Schools, John Hopkins University (March 1982); Kilgore "School Policy and Cognitive Growth."

21. Coleman et al., *High School Achievement*, p. 100. These trends are discussed in the chapters by Hirschoff and Kutner-Sherman-Williams in this volume.

22. Ibid., p. 193.

23. R. Gary Bridge and Julie Blackman, *A Study of Alternatives in American Education, Family Choice in Schooling* 4 (Santa Monica, Cal.: The Rand Corporation, 1978).

24. Andrew M. Greeley, *Catholic High Schools and Minority Students* (New Brunswick, N.J.: Transaction Books, 1982).

25. Coleman et al., *High School Achievement*, p. 108.

26. Ibid., pp. 171–172.

27. Andrew Greeley, *Catholic High Schools and Minority Students*, p. 68.
28. Ibid., pp. 83–84.
29. Coleman et al., *High School Achievement*, p. 195.
30. Ibid., p. 172.
31. Ibid., p. 220.
32. Ibid., pp. 220–227.
33. Ibid., p. 221.
34. Ibid., pp. 65–71.

7

"Private" and "Public": Analysis Amid Ambiguity in Higher Education*

DANIEL C. LEVY

PUBLIC BY ANY OTHER NAME?

When a well-bred Yale alumnus like William F. Buckley, Jr., sardonically suggests that his alma mater donate itself to the state of Connecticut ("To tell the truth, I don't know that anything much would happen."), some conventional assumptions require reexamination.[1] Chief among these is the much ballyhooed distinction between "private" and "public." Analysis reveals serious ambiguities. We lack an agreed-upon notion of what defines our types. Different observers define the private-public split by different criteria. In fact, criteria are usually implicit and fuzzy, but even when they are explicit and clear, they vary. What defines a private institution for one observer does not do so for another. And the problem goes beyond this definitional conflict. As will be shown at least for higher education, *no* behavioral criterion or set of criteria consistently distinguishes institutions legally designated private from institutions legally designated public. Surely this volume's chapters, on both schools and universities, arrive at no such criteria; instead, as discussed below, several provide evidence of increasing private-public blurring.

In a desperate attempt to reassert its distinctiveness, the U.S. private higher-education sector has recently rebaptized itself "the independent sector." The new nomenclature, while it brings private higher education under a terminological umbrella widely used by the U.S. nonprofit world, contributes

*I thank Burton R. Clark, John Whitehead, and other members of Yale University's Higher Education Research Group who helped me prepare, as Working Paper No. 37 (1979) for that group, the first draft of this article. I also thank John Simon and other members of Yale's Program on Non-Profit Organizations for subsequent comments. The Andrew W. Mellon Foundation provided financial assistance.

nothing to definitional clarity. It is simultaneously intended to legitimize the private sector's claim to the public dollar (by downplaying privateness) and yet to distinguish that sector from the public sector by emphasizing its autonomy from government. The first aim, of course, undermines the second.

Looking abroad seems to frustrate yearnings for clear definitional usage. England, for example, long noted for its paradoxical labeling of private and public secondary education, offers an ambiguous picture at higher levels as well. *All* the universities, even those financed over 90% by the government, form what is still frequently called the autonomous or private sector, distinct not from public universities but from the technical sector of higher education (which is consensually considered public). Increasingly, however, one hears England's universities identified as public.

If the private-public muddle is not particular to the United States, it is not, as sometimes supposed, a new phenomenon. Scholarship has exposed the myth of pure privateness in the early development of such private luminaries as Harvard, Dartmouth, Columbia—and Yale. All received substantial government funds, indeed regarded them as a public responsibility. This perception was often shared by state legislatures. Meanwhile, some legislatures declined to give funds to their new *public* universities. Even when funding to the private colleges declined, from 1820 to 1850, legislators remained on college governing boards, and by the time they stepped down, funds had again increased. Later in the nineteenth century, when Harvard's Charles Eliot successfully championed the idea of a definite split between private higher education and state, he did so somewhat ahistorically, since a clear "distinction between 'private' and 'public' did not exist in the century between 1776 and 1876."[2]

Such ambiguity obviously poses problems for scholarly analysis, where a premium is placed on clarity, communicability, and causality. If we lack explicit and standard criteria, it is difficult to interpret evidence or make comparative statements. What does it mean to say that a nation's private higher-education sector is large or vibrant? It becomes dangerous to extract conclusions about, for example, what purposes private universities serve, what their differential output is, how adaptable they are, or what the implications are of dual public-private sectors versus unitary structures.

Naturally, the problem is far from a purely academic one. As the volume's introduction suggested and as several preceding chapters have attested, so many policy issues turn largely on private-public considerations, often highly contentious ones in times of change.[3]

Before proceeding to the heart of the analysis, however, the rationale for this essay should be developed more fully, especially because there are certain typical, perhaps inherent, problems in an exercise of this type—problems admittedly manifested below. For one thing, it can be tedious and quarrelsome. It is an excursion into what Robert Dahl calls "conceptual analysis," defining terms and categories.[4] While many of us willingly read such analyses as parts of works, few get animated about works that are basically definitional. Another problem with such analyses is that they may exaggerate the confusion. Public officials and individual actors have some sense, frequently as much as needed in order to make reasonable choices, about the sorts of privateness and publicness that exist at certain institutions, even if they could not articulate a set of consistent criteria for distinguishing private and public in general. For example, they know that the private institution they are considering charges higher tuition than their local public institution. Besides, whatever the level of confusion that actually does exist in distinguishing private and public, a related problem with this sort of essay is that it cannot hope to untangle most of the ambiguities it identifies. Neither can it expect to develop fully consistent categories; and even if it could, they probably would not be simple, parsimonious, manageable, and attractive enough to be widely used in private-public analysis and policy-making. Instead, the realistic hope is only to improve analytical tools and choice criteria by a matter of limited degree.

But if the issues are important enough in the United States and elsewhere, then a more *explicit recognition* of significant but contrasting usage— of how private and public are commonly conceived, often implicitly, often ad hoc—is worth pursuing; beyond that recognition, even a marginal improvement in our definitional understanding and usage is another worthwhile goal. And while the scholarly pursuit of more accurate understanding could alone warrant this exercise, the policy relevance builds the rationale further. As illustrated later by the Geiger chapter, the private sector contributes an enormous degree of choice for various actors, yet that choice increases in value to the extent that it is based on accurate perceptions. This essay, therefore, deals with and tries to improve modestly on the principal perceptions held by those who make important choices at least partly dependent on private-public distinctions.[5] In other words, relevant to the themes of this volume, our notions of private and public are critical to notions about the range and contour of choices available to various actors and susceptible to shaping by public policy. Greater definitional clarity may help us better assess what differences private-public distinctions make, how actors can take advantage of them, and how public policy can affect them. Greater definitional clarity also can help focus attention on not just private-public enrollment percentages but also on components of privateness and publicness.

A corollary reason for pursuing this exercise is that many of its concerns are relevant beyond higher education. Indeed, they may relate to virtually all policy fields where both public and nonprofit private institutions exist, and therefore to wide-ranging issues treated in other volumes in this series on the nonprofit world.[6] In fact, the question of how distinct private and public institutions are has historically intrigued political theorists, political economists, organizational sociologists, and others, though they have often neglected the nonprofit part of the private side. We are in a better position to evaluate what difference private and public make, what causes growth in a given sector, what the ramifications of various public policies are, and so forth, if we are as clear as reasonably possible about our concepts.

To take the example most obviously relevant to this volume, private-public definitional questions and ambiguity arise not only for higher education but for other educational levels as well. In what sense, for example, are the (publicly subsidized) Dutch private schools analyzed by James comparable to private schools elsewhere? To what extent can the longitudinally varying private percentage of total U.S. school enrollments, as analyzed by Erickson, be taken as a measure of varying privateness in the overall educational system? Or, to raise a question pertinent to both Murnane chapters, are the putatively superior outputs of private schools properly attributable to their privateness? And, to take one final example among numerous other possibilities, how would the voucher proposals discussed by Hirschoff and Kutner-Sherman-Williams alter the educational system's present private-public balance? In light of such questions, it comes as no surprise that several works dealing with elementary and high school education have tried, at least in passing, to define or redefine private and public.[7]

With this background in mind, we can move ahead. I will consider each of four major sets of criteria—finance, control, mission, and extant usage—most commonly invoked to distinguish private and public. As stated, I want first to identify the criteria and then to explore their shortcomings and underscore how prevailing dichotomies based on these criteria are simplifications and how policy analysis should be more sensitive to vast differences in degree. Furthermore, I will argue that it is not just a matter of degree (that private institutions are simply more private than the public ones while not thoroughly private). Things would be more manageable than they presently are if private and public explicitly designated ideal types between which actual universities were labeled more or less private. Instead, we do not use criteria that consistently work, even for purposes of more or less, to distinguish those universities which we call private from those which we call public. Again, this is not to spurn completely the criteria used most commonly. On the contrary, the concluding sections try to build on the most promising of these.

In sum, the essay has three major purposes: (1) to identify, make explicit, and differentiate among the major criteria often used ad hoc, implicitly, undefined, and in isolation in distinguishing private from public universities; (2) to show that these criteria often conflict with one another and that none of them consistently distinguishes universities legally or commonly labeled private from those legally or commonly labeled public; (3) to explore more explicit, systematic approaches to building on those criteria that do point us toward meaningful tendencies. (Unless otherwise stated, I use the terms *private university* and *public university* according to the institutions' legal designations, avoiding continual use of *so-called* or of quotation marks to cast doubt on the degree of privateness or publicness.)

FINANCIAL SOURCE

A commonly used criterion to distinguish universities called private and public is the source of funds. It is an appealing *and helpful* one. The State University of New York gets more of its income from the state legislature than Columbia University does; the National University of Colombia gets more of its income from the national ministry than the private University of the Andes does; and so forth.[8]

One difficulty, however, concerns the complexity of the source. The advent of strong U.S. federal research aid provides an important illustration. As a Sloan Commission report points out, "federal policy for academic R and D is neutral between the public and private sectors."[9] In fact, given the strength of private research universities, this "neutrality" means more federal support per capita for the private sector—nearly 50% more. Some research-oriented private universities get most of their income from the government. Thus, even within government, sources are not always preferentially tilted toward public universities. As Edward Shils and others have noted, only the *state* subsidy to institutions provides a sharp U.S. financial distinction between private and public.[10] Moreover, institutional grants, more than student loans (especially characteristic of federal financial policies), are likely to connote government control, and state grants may place greater demands on institutions than federal research grants do. Yet federal funds also carry some government control. Decisions on federal scholarships often become crucial to institutional survival, and federal research funds help shape the direction of professional tasks. And even at the state level itself, matters are confused when we look beyond institutional aid to student aid. California's constitution prohibits direct state support for private institutions, but about 85% to 90% of state scholarship money goes to students attending private universities, while private enrollments amount to only 10% to 12% of the state's total.[11] In other words, state funding of students is much less pro-public university than the same state's direct subsidization of institutions; indeed, the former would identify private more than public higher education with the state as financial source.

A second difficulty concerns the lack of a cutoff point. There are, for the most eye-catching problems, notoriously ambiguous hybrids, such as Temple University or the University of Pittsburgh. Moreover, the lack of an accepted cutoff point becomes especially troublesome as we move to longitudinal and international analysis. University education in much of the world is increasingly government subsidized, as shown in the "Public-Autonomous" and "Homogenized" patterns discussed in my ensuing higher-education chapter. At the extreme, some private sectors (as in Belgium, Chile, and the Netherlands) are funded almost fully by the government. Thus the criterion of government financial support, even with a cutoff point, would not separate private from public universities consistently.

Nor does nongovernmental support turn the trick. For one thing, deductible contributions by alumni, foundations, corporations, and other essentially private donors involve a muddling sort of governmental assistance insofar as there is forgone governmental income. But even if we identify these donations as coming exclusively from private sources, consider the objects of donor choice in the United States. Within given states, a prestigious public research university, as opposed to an unprestigious private liberal arts college, is likely to receive more funds both in absolute terms and as a share of its total income. Or consider some related points concerning tuition. Even if private institutions would always set higher tuitions than public ones within the same system, problems of cutoff points and interstate and international comparability remain. Moreover, public universities in many U.S. states and several nations are raising tuition while private universities in many of the same states and nations are meeting decreasing shares of their costs with tuition. If the trend established by the U.S. Educational Amendments Act of 1972 continues, then government grants to students rather than institutions will, on the one hand, strengthen the "market" by allowing students to choose institutions, but, on the other, will increasingly *subsidize* the private sector by removing a major obstacle to student choice of private institutions.

A related approach to distinguishing private from public concerns the financial character of the university. Is it a consumer-oriented, even profit-oriented, enterprise or a nonprofit institution? Private universities might seek to operate at a profit, while public ones would operate more like public schools, fulfilling responsibilities for nonpaying students. However, as several chapters in this volume make clear—indeed, as made clear by the entire book series of which this volume forms only a part—a significant amount of private activity occurs in the nonprofit sector; specifically in higher education, the great majority of private universities worldwide are nonprofit. Reformulating the private-public dichotomy as a for-profit–nonprofit dichotomy or as a trichotomy of private for-profit versus private nonprofit versus public does not resolve nagging ambiguities.[12]

In attempting to distinguish private and public, therefore, notions about an institution's financial character appear to offer less promise than do notions related to financial source. To the latter only will this essay return when trying to build toward improved criteria. I conclude this section on financial criteria by considering one criterion that has problems but that moves us closer to such improvement. It retreats from the 100% or 50% or 0% cutoff points. Instead, within a given nation or state, policymakers could choose a certain percentage of government support to total income above which institutions would be considered and treated as public, and below which they would be considered and treated as private. Still, where will a line be drawn between private and public if not at 100% or 50%? For example, it seems arbitrary to draw it at, say, 70% just in order to make perhaps half a system's universities private. Additionally, even if we could establish reasonable demarcation points, and therefore dichotomies, within each nation or state, we could not easily move toward cross-national or cross-state discourse. In the extreme, a private Dutch university could receive a greater share of its income from its government than many U.S. public universities receive from theirs. We would be dealing in somewhat dissimilar concepts: Chilean privateness, often representing roughly 10% government financing, could not be equated with Mexican privateness, usually achieved at 100% nongovernment financing. Similarly, for U.S. policy makers at the federal level, criteria that differed by state would be unwieldy, to say the least.

CONTROL

As with finance, so with control, the discussion is not meant to trivialize intersectoral tendencies and often important differences of degree. Instead, the idea is to identify, and make explicit, common usage and to explore both the difficulties and potentialities tied to that usage.

Beyond the obvious difficulties of accurately gauging degrees of control, even *form* of control would not distinguish consistently between universities labeled private and public. Private universities are not necessarily autonomous; more to the point here, they are not even necessarily autonomous from government. Nor do public universities necessarily lack such autonomy, however great actual and potential government control often is. U.S. state universities generally enjoy substantial (though quite variable) autonomy from state government, as British universities have from national government.

In Latin America also there is a juxtaposition of public to autonomous. Many of the most autonomous universities, such as the National Autonomous University of Mexico (UNAM) and the Central University of Venezuela (UCV), have been public as determined by probably every major criterion *except* control. They are legally public and expected to spend public funds for public purposes. Very few observers, of any political stripe, within those nations would consider UNAM or the UCV private. Yet they enjoy enviable power to rule themselves. They are accountable to the public only in the broadest sense, even insofar as expenditures are concerned. The same factors applied, in certain eras, to such institutions as Argentina's University of Buenos Aires and Uruguay's University of the Republic. In fact, nearly all Latin American public-autonomous universities depend almost exclusively on government finance. In short, it is not uncommon for governments to delegate substantial self-rule to public universities, even if these universities depend heavily on government finance. Nor is it simply a matter of governments choosing to delegate while maintaining a ready capability to impose control when autonomy produces distasteful results; on the contrary, autonomy often rests heavily on enviable university power. He who pays the piper does not necessarily call the tune. Moreover, some governments control certain important decisions in private *more* than public universities even within given nations. In Argentina and Brazil (as well as the Philippines), education ministries have often used tougher criteria in evaluating private than public university proposals for structural and curriculum changes.

A corollary criterion should likewise be treated skeptically: We cannot consistently go by who appoints the administrators. This approach would concede that public universities could be highly autonomous in academic or even financial matters but would at least be administered by publicly appointed officials. There are too many exceptions. Most major twentieth-century Latin American public universities won (at least for some time) the right to appoint their own high officials. Even in Western Europe, where ministerial appointment is often the formal rule, professional appointment is often the actual practice. Similarly, we cannot confidently distinguish legally private and public universities according to whether university employees are civil servants. In some public universities they are; in others they are not. And besides, that may just tell us whether the university is defined as public or may depend on particular labor laws. True, privately appointed boards of trustees are the executive authorities in many U.S., Japanese, and Mexican private universities, but some autonomous public universities also entrust appointments to such boards.

Just as knowledge of who appoints administrators does not allow policymakers, donors, students, and others to distinguish consistently between private and public universities, neither does knowledge of who is appointed. There is a tendency for private persons to be on private boards and public functionaries to be on public boards, but private persons or representatives of private economic or social groups may comprise lay boards to hold public universities responsible to extrauniversity interests. This has been a historic practice in the United States and England in higher education as well as other fields. It is also a notable practice even in Sweden, the democratic nation probably taken more frequently than any other as a model of governmentally administered higher education.[13]

Another related criterion—ultimate authority—suggests itself. Whatever ongoing self-rule a public autonomous university may enjoy, the government retains the prerogative to exert its will in extreme circumstances, while private universities are ultimately accountable to private authorities; relatedly, government is likely to set the bounds that limit the freedom of a public university, more than that of a private university, to alter basic missions. Again, there appear to be different tendencies by sector. Yet we have already seen that public autonomy can go beyond mere government delegation. Additionally, consider the example of New York State, where the regents selected by the legislature have great authority over the private university and can force it to "close its doors."[14] Governments usually retain ultimate authority over *all* institutions. Where there is severe conflict, clubs are ultimately trump. In many nations, all higher-education institutions come under the jurisdiction of an overall law of education. The most striking exceptions to the government's ultimate authority occur where universities take effective refuge behind the principle of "extraterritoriality." Probably the best-known illustrations have been found in Latin America—and these have involved *public* universities!

MISSION

For some analysts, policymakers, and actors who choose among institutions, funding and control are only procedural factors, while what matters is whether private and public universities *do* different things. What, then, about the notion of distinct institutional mission? What do private and public institutions, legally defined, attempt differently and what do they actually produce that is distinct? Unfortunately for the search for clear distinctions, evidence from many policy fields casts doubt on whether privately and publicly effected policies are distinguishable in terms of such factors as social change, equality, and welfare.[15] Moreover, since identifying missions as private or public would be a tricky and highly subjective undertaking (e.g., what is the "public interest"?), I search here for any consistently distinguishing missions separating private and private institutions, not worrying for the moment whether those missions are intrinsic to privateness or publicness per se.

Two often-cited criteria are clientele and quality. As at the school level, the two are powerfully related. A great deal of debate has turned on whether institutions of higher quality are really producing more "value added" than other institutions or simply attracting a better-prepared, more socially exclusive clientele. This debate over the determinants or quality clearly has important policy ramifications for many actors, as shown in the Murnane contributions to this volume. However, putting that debate aside here, can we make the more modest claim that private and public universities can be distinguished by clientele and quality characteristics?

Probably most observers who would answer yes would associate private universities with privileged clientele and high quality. And in those places where private universities are perceptibly superior they indeed tend to attract a privileged student clientele; but superiority is not a rule. Clark and Youn have identified six distinct U.S. private types, differing from the University of Chicago to Bob Jones, while the public sector encompasses three distinct types, ranging from Berkeley to Los Angeles City College.[16] If the private sector clings to an edge in several northeastern states, this is not a clear pattern in much of the rest of the nation. Very often, private-public overlap is dominant within states. Furthermore, such overlap is common in many national systems. Most Latin American nations are characterized by an average private advantage, yet one strongly qualified by a great deal of overlap, especially (as in Colombia, Peru, and the Dominican Republic) where the majority of private institutions are low-quality attractions for a clientele very distinct from that gaining entry to the most prestigious private universities. Furthermore, rough parity has characterized Argentina recently, as it has characterized Chile for decades. Add to all this the fact that strong *public* advantages (in clientele and quality) are found in Brazil. The Brazilian pattern parallels the Japanese, though some private-public overlap is found in both. In fact, several Asian systems exemplify public superiority. Besides all this, "quality" often depends on widely varying subjective notions. The claim to private distinctiveness based on superior status lacks cross-national consistency.[17]

If the uniqueness of the private sector does not derive from the pursuit of excellence or elitism, it might at least derive from the pursuit of *some* special values. It is the absence of these values, however, that is precisely what Buckley laments in his *God and Man at Yale*. If other criteria fail to distinguish his university from great public universities, mission should:

> The critical difference is the corporate sense of mission. At Berkeley that sense of mission is as diffuse and inchoate—and unspecified and unspecifiable—as the resolute pluralism of California society. At the private college, the sense of mission is distinguishing. . . . It is, however, strangled by what goes under the presumptuous designation of academic freedom. It is a terrible loss, the loss of the sense of mission. It makes the private university, sad to say, incoherent.[18]

In short, let academic freedom in the public universities promote pluralist exploration of "all" values, but let the private universities corporately identify with the particular moral values of their alumni. Sticking to reality rather than plea, however, such distinctions were more effective in identifying private institutions in the nineteenth century, when more were pursuing religious ends—some would say "the pursuit of truth" as opposed to "free inquiry." In many nations, conflict between private (often religious) and public (often secular) education was a central political issue—the antagonistic poles around which political parties often revolved. In fact, private-public has often been fundamentally a reflection of sectarian-secular. But institutions such as the Catholic University of Chile or early American Protestant colleges have generally become more secular or less common. The decline of religious identity in U.S. Catholic higher education is amply documented, paralleling trends in Catholic schools.[19] Naturally, this loss of religious distinctiveness affects the range of choice available to prospective students and their families. Besides, many public institutions have had pointedly religious profiles. For example, a concordat between the Vatican and the Colombian government had a major effect on Colombian public universities well into the twentieth century.

Moving from values to material missions, one possible distinction is that private universities meet the needs of private enterprise while public ones glut the civil service. The pattern seems to hold in such diverse nations as Mexico and Japan and demands more exploration. In contrast, however, U.S. private institutions' emphasis on liberal arts belies it. Furthermore, in large countries the elite private universities may concentrate in one region (the U.S. Northeast, Brazil's Southeast), disproportionately serving the pri-

vate *and* public market there while leaving public universities more latitude to fill jobs in both markets elsewhere. Cross-nationally, the problem
is more severe. It is easy to associate public universities with the public
economic sector in the Communist bloc, where there is no private sector;
yet what about Western European countries with vibrant private enterprises but practically no private universities? In the latter cases, the public
universities may not be so clearly public after all—even if funded and controlled centrally by a highly bureaucratized ministry.

Nor is mission decisive if we pose more broadly the question of whom
the universities serve. Albornoz believes that the Venezuelan government
serves the private economic sector more than the public one; consequently,
its newly created, publicly financed universities are really more private than
public.[20] He even implies that all Venezuelan universities are somewhat
private insofar as they strengthen the status quo, which itself favors private
interests. Pushing further, Marxists could well downplay any apparent
private-public differences in mission, emphasizing instead how both institutional types serve similar interests, reflecting and reproducing society's
dominant economic and power relationships. (Just as, according to Buckley, a legally private university may betray its privateness, so a legally public university may betray its claim to publicness.)

At the same time, others see the blurring of private and public missions
in a more positive light. There are intercontinental echoes of the claim by
Boston University President John Silber that legally private universities are
truly public because of the public purposes they serve.[21] Virtually all universities claim to benefit the general public, though public universities may
claim that their benefit is more direct. Harvard rightfully emphasizes its
contributions to public leadership and social research and, through public
tax laws and research grants, government policy affirms such claims.
Moreover, both types of universities may strive to gratify their clients' (private) demands, even while both may also strive to meet publicly defined
needs in a given region.[22] In sum, performance of what may commonly be
considered private missions is neither an inevitable nor unique hallmark of
the private university, and performance of what may commonly be considered public missions is neither an inevitable nor unique hallmark of the
public university.

EXTANT USAGE

Finally, beyond the variables of finance, control, and mission, there is definition of the last resort—a private university is, tautologically, whatever
is called a private university. Any flower called a rose is a rose, and a rose
by any other name is not a rose. Such definition is the most commonly
used "criterion." It may derive from legal labels or subjective perceptions.

It is indeed legal designation that has provided the working nomenclature used thus far in this essay. Yet that only illustrates how legal desig-

nations do not consistently define private-public distinctions in finance, control, or mission. Like other criteria, legal ones are not wrong but inadequate. Statutes and laws may give only glimpses as to *why* the institution is labeled private or public. It often depends simply on who created it; even in that connection, governments can create legally private institutions, as the Dominican Republic did in the 1960s, when it was fed up with its public Autonomous University of Santo Domingo. Much more important, even where labels reflect the character of the institution at its *inception*, institutions often change their character. Again, many Catholic institutions provide good examples. Therefore, some laws and policies that appear clear-cut may really be fuzzy. Moreover, following a pattern for schools, some laws concerning private and public in higher education are notoriously ambiguous. There has been a good deal of confusion, for example, in states (such as New York) where the law forbids public funding of religious education but allows public funding of religiously "affiliated" colleges. Laws cannot be expected to provide reliable definitional criteria if we do not have consistent criteria on which to build clear laws.[23]

An obvious problem with resorting to popular perception is that it eschews consistent use of objective criteria. Two similar universities may be perceived as public and private by their respective constituencies, either because those who perceive are fallible or because some emphasize criteria that others do not. Moreover, university partisans may carry biased perceptions or even deliberately try to distort others' perceptions. They claim the label private in order to attract funds for their distinctiveness or importance to the free market or to assert their academic freedom. Sometimes they may claim it simply to feel different—and superior. Others declare themselves public to stake their claim to the public dollar or perhaps to progressive egalitarian goals. New institutions may adopt whatever designation existing institutions do *not* have, especially when the new ones emerge as a backlash to the others. This is not to underestimate the importance of perceptions.[24] But, naturally, they do not necessarily reflect what actually exists.

REBUILDING: ONE APPROACH

No criteria have appeared that consistently distinguish universities considered private from those considered public. Nor is it "just a matter of degree." A continuum, even based on an admittedly ideal typical dichotomy, supposes some explicit criteria on which more private institutions distinguish themselves from less private ones, if only by degree.

Unfortunately, no fully satisfactory substitute emerges, at least at this point. The absence of a dichotomy involves a big cost. That cost falls hard on comparative analysis. If we use some criteria to conclude that university A is more private than university B in one system and other criteria to decide between universities X and Y in another system, then we must be very careful in making intersystem comparisons. These may be asymmetrical relationships. A and X are not necessarily private in the same sense or degree, B is conceivably more private than X, etc. Consequently, it becomes difficult to assess the ramifications of larger or smaller, expanding or shrinking, private sectors. Complications for policy analysis and choice are manifold.

There are, however, always more and less adequate alternatives. Less adequate would be to ignore the inexplicitness, inconsistency, and variability of present usage or to cling to a fictitious dichotomy. The challenge is to find the best routes towards establishing what we really do know about identifying private and public and proceeding to conceptualize and build on that knowledge. We need not write off the private-public distinction so much as induce a molting process wherein it sheds its false exterior and begins to renew itself in more modest form.

One useful alternative—by no means novel—would be an inductive, bottom-up approach. Scholars and policy analysts would study what private and public universities (labeled only by legal or other extant definition) actually do. No a priori assumptions would be made. Knowledge would accumulate piece by piece. Patterns might emerge in relation to certain factors, not others, discussed above. The advantages of this approach are fairly obvious. It is careful, unassuming. It is based on close factual analysis of individual cases. Knowledge accumulates every step of the way, and subsequent generalizations are built on facts. We would be testing which of the factors discussed above and commonly cited as distinguishing private from public institutions in fact "work" to substantial degrees, even though none "works" completely or consistently. Additionally, this inductive approach can be quite useful for policy analysts, policymakers, and others, as it builds on the relevance of legal identifications. This is because it deals with how institutions legally labeled and legally treated differently may (or may not) be different, because it invites consideration of differences between legal constructions of private and public and empirical reality.

Disadvantages also emerge, however. Demands on time and effort are paramount. A great commitment would be necessary before knowledge might accumulate beyond the idiosyncratic case-study stage. A good deal of effort would be invested in analyzing factors that really have little to do with privateness and publicness. Moreover, if such considerations affect "pure scholarship," they affect even more policy analysis by government officials and other individual actors. It therefore seems prudent to blend this inductive approach with some a priori notions of what sorts of variables (associated with privateness and publicness) interest us;[25] for an example, see note 5.

REBUILDING: IDEAL TYPES OF PRIVATE AND PUBLIC

Another alternative approach might start by postulating ideal types of private and public. Individual universities would then be analyzed in comparison to these types. An institution would be private to the extent it approximates the private ideal type. And the ideal types would offer explicit criteria by which to compare individual institutions and systems. Between two institutions or systems, the more private one is the one which has more in common with the private ideal type.

Rather than building piece by piece from the factual, this approach makes certain a priori assumptions about what private and public really mean or should mean. Whereas the inductive approach starts from the legally (or perceived) private and public cases and seeks to discover what in practice may distinguish them, this approach starts from some postulated essence of the private-public distinction and seeks to discover how it may manifest itself. It does not, therefore, presume that its definition of private and public will consistently distinguish between legally private and public institutions. Obviously, much depends on whether we ultimately want to know what institutions labeled private and public are really like or where true private and public characteristics are really found. Both are vital questions for public policy and choice, but they are different questions.

The relative advantages and disadvantages of the ideal typical approach parallel those usually associated with ideal typical social science approaches. The ideal type is a guide for research, orients data collection, provides a context for otherwise particularistic findings, and increases the possibilities of comparative statements. It also runs the danger of arbitrarily choosing and coloring the data in accordance with our preconceptions.[26]

In practice, of course, the two alternative approaches can blend. Just as some a priori notion of what may be important can guide the inductive approach, so ideal types derive largely from empirical reality, albeit abstracted and idealized. Following Weber, Rudolph and Rudolph write that ideal types are heuristic, formal constructs which "emphasize by accentuation factors that are considered prominent or distinct."[27] Such types deal with relationships and regularities, not necessities. Thus privateness and publicness would derive from an abstracted accentuation of traits which we think of as naturally or inherently private or public. The goal is to clarify, emphasize, make explicit, and purify as much as possible while at the same time distorting reality as little as possible. No pretense need be made about discovering the truest criteria. Ideal types depend on their utility, and different ones are more adequate for different analytical purposes. Furthermore, ideal types may focus our attention on central, comparable variables while in no way barring citation of other relevant factors.

Rather than pursuing a single ideal typical private-public continuum, we may push toward *continua*. Private and public would be based on multiple variables. More private funding would not necessarily correlate with more private mission, for example. Instead, at least we could create composites of different variables. Such composites would show how each variable itself appears, how the variables relate, and how attempts at brief overall evaluations might look.

The component ideal typical dimensions can be derived in part from empirical tendencies. Again, few of the criteria considered earlier are "wrong" so much as misleading or inconsistent when interchanged with legal or other extant nomenclature. That they are nondeterminative does not mean that they are not at all indicative. Showing that financing, control, and mission do not determine a definite distinction does not mean that they are irrelevant. As Abraham Kaplan argues, the fact that we require different indicators to measure something in different contexts does not make the indicators totally invalid, but instead may show that our concept is complex.[28] Once we surrender the claim or even hope of defining two categories, public and private, we are dealing in complex concepts. We can lucidly observe that some institutions are more private than others *according to certain criteria*. Were Yale to become part of the University of Connecticut, something private would be lost. The search, then, is to establish meaningful continua *along multiple ideal types*.[29]

This search for continua may be facilitated by consecutive reference to the first three variables discussed earlier: finance, control, and mission. The idea is to construct ideal types from abstracted notions of privateness and publicness on each variable.[30] To repeat, these criteria need not always distinguish universities presently called private from those presently called public. Rather, universities commonly called private and public could be compared on each ideal typic criterion.

The earlier analysis of *financial source* dealt with the degree of government funding, institutional versus indirect aid, self-generated income, and for-profit versus nonprofit goals. Any of these might be cited, acknowledging the qualifications, as indicating a degree or kind of privateness or publicness. For example, government subsidies to institutions could indicate more publicness than indirect government support via student aid or tax exemptions, since indirect subsidies allow for some nongovernment choice over which institutions get what. The single most powerful and manageable defining criterion, however, might concern financial source as measured by the share of governmental involvement. A private institution, defined by the ideal type, would receive no government finance; a public ideal type would receive nothing but government finance. Between these two extremes, institutions would be ranked as more or less private according to the ratio of nongovernment to total income. This admittedly ignores whether an institution receives more or less government funding per student. University A may get more such funding than university B but still be more private if it receives proportionally more nongovernment funds than that university. This approach also fails to solve some of the comparative problems raised earlier, but at least it ameliorates them a little. No longer would we label universities private and public and then encounter situations where a private university may be more financially dependent on government than a public one. Instead, across systems, universities are placed along a continuum that gauges the extent of privateness and publicness without pressing for dichotomous designations. In sum, this financial criterion, for all its shortcomings, has some virtues of simplicity, consistency, and relevance to characteristics that most of us would probably include in our ideal typical notions of private and public. It could rather easily accommodate much of the data found in the ensuing higher-education chapters.

Control can be similarly used to define a dimension of privateness and publicness, even though it is usually more difficult (than financial source) to assess.[31] It involves decision-making power over such concerns as admissions, personnel appointments, curriculum, discipline, intrauniversity resource allocation, and so forth. In any case, autonomy alone is an inadequate criterion if we acknowledge that truly private universities may be closely controlled by externally appointed boards, financiers, or alumni. The overriding issue, then, should be institutional autonomy *from government control*. I need not repeat how even this criterion does not in fact consistently distinguish what are commonly called private and public universities. As with financial source, it might be good to think in terms of ratios, the part of the total university-related policy process that is dominated by government. For example, in comparison with a neighboring institution, a university with proportionally less government representation on its governing board might be considered more private in that respect.

Institutional *mission* probably presents the greatest difficulty for establishing ideal types.[32] Here we should be especially careful to avoid basing ideal types on normatively glorified ideals, as opposed to actual undertakings. And I have already shied away from trying to identify missions as intrinsically private or public. Perhaps ideal types could deal with functions that universities perform for clearly private and public actors, institutions, and purposes.

But only sometimes are a university's pursuits in terms of clientele, curriculum, course content, research, graduate studies, and the like clearly oriented more toward one sector than the other. An area worth investigation is job market placement (in private enterprise versus the governmental bureaucracy, for example). Another idea worth considering relates to the clientele criteria discussed earlier. Definitionally, public institutions could be considered those open to all on a nondiscriminating basis (with no tuition and with full information available), while institutions that impose restrictions against certain groups could be considered private. This is the approach advocated by Aveen and Jencks, for example, in pushing their school voucher plans. The policy relevance of their private-public definitional distinction is that private institutions would be excluded from their voucher system, one financially dependent on government.[33] Apart from the practical difficulties of defining what is discriminatory, however, a major problem with this definitional distinction flows naturally from the voucher effect of extinguishing many present private-public differences; few institutions would be left in the private sector. This is precisely what would happen if we followed John Silber's advice, cited above, and defined as public all higher-education institutions performing missions for society at large. Such proposals for ideal typical private-public distinctions are definitionally legitimate but only questionably useful. In lieu of more persuasive ways to define missions as private or public, therefore, we might prudently fall back, at least in part, on the inductive approach. What missions are in fact pursued by universities that are more private than others in ideal typical terms of finance and control? Geiger's "Finance and Function" chapter may provide some helpful insights for such an approach.

SYSTEM PROFILES

Most of the discussion of alternatives has focused thus far on distinctions among individual universities. It is also relevant, however, to systems. With universities identified as not just private or public but more or less private or public according to multiple criteria, systems would not simply be labelled x% private. By contrast, systems would be composed of institutions that are more or less private in different ways. System *profiles* would emerge from some aggregation of universities assessed by multiple criteria.

Cross-system comparisons are affected by loss of the dichotomy. Working from a dichotomy, scholars and policymakers can say how private or public a system is merely by aggregating the individual institutions in each sector. Simple addition reveals that according to enrollments, for example, a system is x% private. Intersystem comparison follows easily. A system with 10% enrollment in private institutions is less private than one with 25% private enrollment. However, once we acknowledge that relatively private universities may be private by different criteria and that some nominally private universities are less private than others, this does not hold. It is not easy to judge which of two systems is more private, to make invidious comparisons, for scholarly or policy purposes.[34]

A significant implication for intersystem comparison is that some sort of weighting would be helpful. Two systems with 15% private enrollment probably are not equally private.[35] What is required is an evaluation of *how* private the individual universities are, perhaps as a composite of our three continua "multiplied" by the percentage of enrollments in those institutions. Precise "weighting" obviously lies well beyond at least our present capability, but some sort of explicit, if crude, estimation could be envisioned for system-level comparisons. Also worth figuring in is the relative importance of the private institutions. Two nations may have similarly private institutions comprising 10% of total enrollments, while in only one system are those institutions academically prestigious, with substantial budgets, more influence on national policy, and so forth. Japan's (80%) enrollments in private institutions do not make its system four times as private as the U.S. system. Nor does Brazil's private sector really hold two-thirds of its system's "weight." Venezuela's system is more private than its 10% private enrollments might indicate.

Figure 7.1 illustrates, albeit *very* tentatively and crudely, one small step that could be taken toward summarizing how private a system is. It plots percentage enrollments against the degree of private-public distinction.[36] It

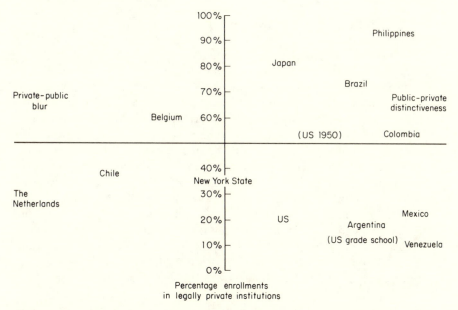

Figure 7.1: Privateness and Publicness in Higher Education Systems.

NOTE: I rather arbitrarily set New York State as the midpoint in private-public distinctiveness; I then put the most blurred and distinctive cases at the left and right extremes, respectively.

SOURCES: Very loosely drawn from Roger L. Geiger, *Private Sectors in Higher Education: Structure Function and Change in Eight Countries* (Ann Arbor: University of Michigan, 1986) and Daniel C. Levy, *The State and Higher Education in Latin American: Private Challenges to Public Dominance* (Chicago: University of Chicago Press, 1986).

suggests, for example, the very different basis of Mexican and Chilean privateness. While both nations have public universities that approximate our ideal typical public criteria in most respects, private-public distinctiveness is greater in Mexico, where the private sector holds 15% of enrollments, because only its private universities approximate our ideal typical private criteria. These private universities are financed nearly 100% by nongovernment sources, ruled by private boards free from government control, and strongly linked to the business enterprises toward which they funnel their graduates. By contrast, Chile educates roughly 35% of its university students in the private sector, but this sector has long been far less distinguishable from the public sector, receiving most of its funds from the education ministry and offering only a limited choice for matriculating students. I would consider Mexico's system more private; more important, we begin to capture the different ways in which each system is private. Similarly, at the state level, New York may have the third highest proportion of students in a legally private sector, but that need not automatically persuade us that New York has the third most private system. One would have to plug into the assessment such factors as the private sector's unusually great dependence on both state funds and state directives.

A much better graphic representation than that offered in Figure 7.1 would plot each system along at least three separate dimensions of privateness and publicness. Such a representation would indicate, for example, that Argentina's private-public distinction is greater in finance than mission. In Figure 7.1 distinctiveness is represented only as a very rough composite based on factors of finance, control, and mission. Furthermore, distinctiveness does not necessarily indicate how private given private sectors are, only how much they differ from public sectors in the same nation. Nor does it indicate how private or public whole systems may be; for example, if the Chilean military regime (since 1973) with its enthusiasm for "Chicago Boys" economics had succeeded in forcing all universities to become self-financing, there would be little private-public distinctiveness, but all universities would have become quite financially private.[37] Figure 7.1 shows some pattern of increasing privateness as we move to the right and upward, with the lower left clearly the least private (and the upper left probably next). Numerous additional qualifications to Figure 7.1 are warranted, but the point here is simply to give an example of how we can explore alternative ways to make private-public distinctions.

Although broad comparisons do not flow as easily from complex continua and profiles as they do from a simple dichotomy, perhaps more defensibly meaningful statements can be made. Due to the complexity of variables, research may seek out cases where many factors can be held constant. Longitudinal analysis within a given system is one possibility. Even intersystem comparisons need not deal with whole systems; that is the most ambitious enterprise, required to address issues such as the performance of more and less, or increasingly and decreasingly, private systems. Instead, or at least separately, research can purposefully address issues linked to, for example, different degrees of private financing. And where we do compare whole systems, piece-by-piece breakdowns are appropriate. Research may report that compared to system A, system B has a smaller private sector which, however, has greater importance in the system and which is more private with respect to funds generated from nongovernment sources and autonomy from government control. The key is to substantiate why and how certain systems are more or less private. Such discriminating comparisons, whatever difficulties they pose for broad generalizations, may offer appropriate information to decisionmakers, governmental or individual.

SUMMARY

Compared to reliance on a dichotomy, or on some (often not explicit) criterion to the unaccounted disregard of others, the more detailed and self-conscious approaches tentatively probed here obviously have their disadvantages. The research burden may be weightier, parsimonious conclusions more difficult to achieve. Such trade-offs seem necessary, however, to produce more accurate statements of what we know—and do not know.[38]

From the ruins of both a too prevalent dichotomy and ad hoc criteria come not only serious costs but also potentially helpful clues for research. Limited and careful conclusions are better than bold ones based on misleading dichotomies.

This essay has explored two alternatives. One is an inductive approach. It would establish how well different behavioral characteristics could be correlated with universities legally (or otherwise) called private and public. The second relies more on ideal typical constructions of privateness and publicness. Eventually, universities could be categorized and compared according to multiple continua. Beyond that, complex system profiles could be established. Although this complexity may seem particularly suited to scholarly analysis, it may also be helpful in making policy decisions. This is because the complexity is based on separate criteria. Government policymakers and individuals who confront important choices need not deal with the aggregations but instead could work with discriminating comparisons based on the factors that most concern them. In sum, discriminating profiles, as opposed to dichotomies based on variously selected factors, may facilitate policy choices, providing not only accurate but "usable" knowledge.[39]

There are, of course, other valid ways in which private and public could be assessed. Indeed, we will surely find better ways than those discussed here. With that in mind, all approaches are transitional, not definitive, as a dialectic develops between better conceptualizations, which facilitate empirical research, and that research, which contributes to better conceptualizations.

NOTES

1. William F. Buckley, Jr., *God and Man at Yale* (South Bend, Ind.: Gateway Editions, 1951, Introduction 1977), p. xlviii.

2. John S. Whitehead, *The Separation of College and State* (New Haven: Yale University Press, 1973), p. 238 and passim. Some historians would argue that a substantial private-public distinction arose as early as 1819, with the Dartmouth decision. For a discussion and a comparative treatment of how "fused" private-public institutions in the United States became private, while fused counterparts in Latin America became public, see Daniel C. Levy, "The Rise of Private Universities in Latin America and the United States," in Margaret Archer, ed., *The Sociology of Educational Expansion: Take-off, Growth, and Inflation in Educational Systems* (London: Sage Publications, 1982), pp. 93–132.

3. For one of the best contemporary analyses of relevant policy issues in the United States, see David W. Breneman and Chester E. Finn, eds., *Public Policy and Private Higher Education* (Washington, D.C.: Brookings, 1978). Like virtually all works on the private question, the book does not deal explicitly with the meaning of the term *private*. It differentiates within the heterogeneous private sector but on such bases as size, quality, staff, etc.—not on degrees of privateness versus publicness.

4. Robert Dahl, *Modern Political Analysis* (Englewood Cliffs, N.J.: Prentice-Hall, 1976).

5. We start here with the definitional distinctions between private and public higher education, not with the empirical differences that could be associated with institutions called private and public. The latter approach is suggested later in the chapter as a potentially useful alternative. It is pursued (for all educational levels) in Daniel C. Levy, "A Comparison of

Private and Public Educational Organizations," in Walter W. Powell, ed., *Between the Public and the Private: The Nonprofit Sector* (New Haven: Yale University Press, 1986).

6. Even where there is only one sector or where we focus on only one, it is important to know whether it has any characteristics more definitionally associated with the other sector. Illustratively, U.S. public higher education has more private characteristics than Swedish public higher education, just as Dutch private schools have more public characteristics than U.S. private schools. In other words, there are questions of privateness and publicness even when we do not compare across sectors.

7. For example, the opening chapter of Richard J. Gabel's mammoth work, *Public Funds for Church and Private Schools* (Toledo, Ohio: Times and News Publishing, 1937), is devoted to defining private and public. Gabel notes (pp. 12–13) how private-public usage has sometimes changed yearly. For Guy Neave, private schools are those nonpublic schools that do not receive public funds: "The Non State Sector in the Education Provision of Member States of the European Community," an internal memo to the Educational Services of the Commission of the European Communities (Brussels: 1983). For Gordon Robinson, however, private schools are proprietary schools pursuing profits much as other commercial enterprises do: *Private Schools and Public Policy* (Loughborough, England: Loughborough University of Technology, 1971).

8. Except where otherwise noted, all references to Latin America are based on Daniel C. Levy, *Higher Education and the State in Latin America: Private Challenges to Public Dominance* (University of Chicago Press, 1986).

9. Edward S. Gruson, "The National Politics of Higher Education," report of the Sloan Commission on Government and Higher Education, November 1977, mimeo, p. 30. Also see the informative annual reports by Howard Bowen and John Minter, *Private Higher Education* (retitled *Independent Higher Education* in 1978) (Washington, D.C.: Association of American Colleges).

10. Edward Shils, "The American Private University," *Minerva* 11, 1 (1973), p. 14 and pp. 6–29 passim. This is one of the best attempts to identify what is special about U.S. private higher education.

11. Robert M. O'Neil, "Law and Higher Education in California," in Neil J. Smelser and Gabriel Almond, eds., *Public Higher Education in California* (Berkeley: University of California, 1974), p. 205.

12. The status of public universities also appears ambiguous. They are probably best categorized in the public sector, but may be placed in the nonprofit sector. The more they are run as parts of the government bureaucracy, the more they could be considered public; the more they are run as separate institutions pursuing public purposes with a substantial degree of nongovernment control and funding, the more they could be considered nonprofit. Like charitable organizations, political parties, and other nonprofits, and unlike public bureaucracies, public universities may well receive private donations. (Nonprofits often have explicitly public missions.) Most U.S. public universities could be considered public-nonprofit hybrids, while public universities in more centralized systems are more clearly in the public sector. Usually it is the universities referred to as private that best describe the nonprofit sector, as that sector is generally defined. Analysis of private universities, therefore, is largely analysis of the nonprofit sector.

13. See Rune I. T. Premfors, "The Politics of Higher Education in Sweden: Recent Developments, 1976–78," *European Journal of Education* 14, 1 (1979), p. 89.

14. O'Neil, "Law and Higher Education," pp. 204–205.

15. For example, see Theodore I. Lowi, *The End of Liberalism: The Second Republic of the United States* (New York: W. W. Norton, 1979) 2nd. ed., pp. 44–47.

16. Burton R. Clark and Ted I. K. Youn, *Academic Power in the United States* (Washington, D.C.: American Association of Higher Education, ERIC/Higher Education Research Report No. 3, 1976), p. 14.

17. Another possible criterion related to distinct clientele probably correlates significantly with academic excellence. Many of the better U.S. private universities attract a national or at least regional constituency, while most state universities are more limited, at least at the un-

dergraduate level. This applies not just to admissions but to financial contributions. Yet in most nations it is the public university, often *the* national university, which boasts the broadest magnetic field.

18. Buckley, *God and Man*, p. 1.

19. See Christopher Jencks and David Riesman, *The Academic Revolution* (Garden City, N.Y.: Doubleday, 1968).

20. Orlando Albornoz, *La educación superior en Venezuela* (Caracas: FUNDARTE, n.d.), pp. 40–43.

21. John Silber, "Paying the Bill for College: The Private Sector and the Public Interest," *Atlantic Monthly* 235 (1975), pp. 33–40. One purpose of such definitions is to attract government funds; another, common in Latin America, is to shore up the legitimacy of private institutions.

22. Another criterion relevant to mission could be the university's service function. It might be argued that the public university has a greater responsibility to provide cultural, legal, and technical services to its community, but this is debatable where private universities also claim to serve the public. Perhaps, just to offer one hypothesis, public institutions would be bound to provide a plurality of services, demanded by the community, or perhaps they would provide those mandated by publicly elected politicians. By contrast, private institutions would be freer to choose those services which they deem proper.

23. Some of the problems with using legal ownership as the criterion overlap the problems (discussed earlier) with using "ultimate authority."

24. Perceptions can influence legal stipulations, student choice, donor generosity, and so forth. Thus even a kernel of truth may contribute to greater distinctiveness. Research could usefully probe the perceptions as well as choices of relevant actors.

25. To use language from the policy literature, we would not claim to follow a "rational comprehensive" approach but perhaps a "mixed-scanning" or other, more limited approach.

26. Very generally speaking, historians may be more at home working inductively from the bottom up, social scientists from ideal types. Also very generally, the inductive approach may be more suitable for some intensive firsthand research, while ideal types may help us order and compare knowledge as it accumulates, but both approaches can be used at both stages.

27. Lloyd Rudolph and Susanne Hoeber Rudolph, "Authority and Power in Bureaucratic and Patrimonial Administration," *World Politics* 31, 2 (1979), p. 200.

28. Abraham Kaplan, *The Conduct of Inquiry* (San Francisco: Chandler Publishing, 1964), p. 52.

29. An important question in defining private and public, whether in higher education or other policy fields, concerns the distinction between characteristics (definitionally) intrinsic to one or another type and characteristics merely very associated, logically or empirically, with one type or the other. On associated characteristics, see Levy, "A Comparison."

30. This essay does not deal with many issues related to the private sector that would be important to a *theory* of the private sector. These include the causes of private sector creation and evolution and more on the consequences of private sectors.

31. In other works (such as *Higher Education*), which analyze the complexities of how institutions are run politically, I have gone beyond control to the broader concept of governance. For establishing definitional distinctiveness between privateness and publicness, however, "control" may capture the essence.

32. Following up on the previous footnote, I have generally found function a more suitable concept than mission for complex comparisons of private and public institutions. However, this essay has stuck with mission because of its more frequent use in the higher-education literature.

33. Judith Areen and Christopher Jencks, "Educational Vouchers: A Proposal for Diversity and Change," in George R. La Noue, ed., *Educational Vouchers: Concepts and Controversies* (New York: Teachers College Press, 1972), pp. 47–57. Aveen and Jencks pointedly reject defining private and public by ownership and administration, which they take to be the basic criteria presently used.

34. Obviously, the point is not to reject all intersystem comparisons. Limited comparisons are better than bold ones based on false dichotomies, and transitions from assessments of individual universities to systemwide profiles and then to intersystem comparisons must be made carefully. Just as with any statement on how two systems compare, one must make the supporting criteria explicit. Matters are helped some where consistent ideal types have been used. Criteria are then fairly consistent on each variable. But universities would still be defined according to different combinations of the three variables. And then some systems profiles would grow from these composites.

35. In addition to enrollments, full-time teaching equivalents, or financial expenditures, could give some quantitative weight.

36. It also blurs by aggregation. The United States, for example, has many very private institutions, but also some very ambiguously private ones. (I tend to see the U.S. private sector today as less private than its 1950 counterpart, as a result of increased public finance and regulation/control.)

37. The self-financing plan did not go nearly as far in practice. Had it, Chile's system would have come closer than any other national system to approximating the private ideal type in finance.

38. Scope is important. The more limited our comparisons, the more precise they can and should be. Broader scope risks oversimplification. National systems aggregate state systems, where there are federalist structures. For example, Massachusetts has majority private enrollments, Wyoming none. Systems also aggregate individual universities, which themselves aggregate undergraduate and graduate levels (see the James chapter on higher education in this volume), pedagogical departments, and research institutes. Within systems, which components are more private? With what consequences? A more detailed dialogue on privateness and publicness could be sensitive to such questions.

39. On the common difficulties of using social science knowledge, see, for example, Charles E. Lindblom and David K. Cohen, *Usable Knowledge: Social Science and Social Problem Solving* (New Haven: Yale University Press, 1979).

III

Private Choice and Financial Policy in Higher Education

8

Alternative Private-Public Blends in Higher-Education Finance: International Patterns*

DANIEL C. LEVY

ALTERNATIVE POLICIES

Several of the preceding pieces in this volume have analyzed policy debates concerning the financing of school systems. The policy debates are no less intense when the focus turns to higher education. Many arguments run in parallel fashion between educational levels. Some differ by matters of degree, while others differ fundamentally. Whatever the parallels in argumentation, there are striking differences in actual practice between levels. In the United States, private schools depend much more on private finance than private higher education does, while public schools depend much more exclusively on public finance than public higher education does. The panorama appears to be different in many other nations that have both private and public sectors. Their private schools seem more likely than private universities to receive public funds and their public universities seem nearly as likely as public schools to depend almost exclusively on public funds.

In U.S. higher education there is considerable debate concerning the appropriate blend of private and public financing for each sector. The problem has become especially acute as enrollments decline, federal and state governments seek to cut costs, and concern spreads about higher education's equity effects in serving privileged groups out of general revenues. There is a good deal of reference to different economic theories, social val-

*I thank John Simon, Roger Geiger, and other members of the Institution for Social and Policy Studies, Yale University, for their comments, and I thank the institution's Program on Non-Profit Organizations and the Andrew W. Mellon Foundation for institutional and financial support. This chapter is a revised version of a contribution to *Higher Education* (Amsterdam) 11, 6 (1982), which itself was a revised version of Working Paper No. 38 of Yale's Program on Non-Profit Organizations.

ues, and political constraints. But there is almost no consideration of how policymakers elsewhere have approached the problem.

Of course, financial policy outside the United States is made within private-public parameters that are different from those faced by U.S. policymakers, but cross-national comparisons may help stimulate, or even orient, cross-state comparisons within the United States. More importantly, cross-national experience could at least help put our policy choices into perspective. For example, few in the United States support either 100% private or 100% public funding. An economic theory that tends to favor private over public funding may simply tell us to increase our present private share if that share is "low." But how do we decide whether it is low or high? One approach, among various others, is to see how our formulas and rationales compare to those found in other systems.[1]

Certain basic themes run through the international private-public debate at the higher-education level. While this chapter cannot analyze them in depth, nor assess the objective validity of opposing viewpoints, it can briefly outline the themes and viewpoints, indicating as it goes along how they play themselves out in different contexts. Naturally, those who tend to favor one blend of financing over another do not necessarily endorse all the arguments often associated with that blend.

Advocates of private financing often claim that education yields private, or individual, as well as social returns. This is especially true of *higher* education. Income is the key example, as youngsters privileged enough to receive more years of formal education are generally those who earn high salaries. Furthermore, higher education's privileged clientele draws on tax revenue paid by society at large. Consequently, according to this view, public funds should be more justly invested at the primary and secondary levels. Beyond these equity issues, advocates of private financing claim that plural income sources help insure university autonomy, pluralism, efficiency, accountability, and client responsibility. All these advantages are intimately related to consumer choice. For example, students, as paying clients choosing their institutions, limit the government's financial and therefore governance role, promote a diversity among institutions sufficient to attract the diversity of client preferences, encourage healthy competition among institutions dependent on not only attracting but holding consumer allegiance, and encourage student industry partly because students can choose what they truly want, partly because they pay for their choices. At an extreme, followers of Milton Friedman regard public subsidies as another "indiscriminate extension of governmental responsibility."[2]

Advocates of public funding, on the other hand, tend to distinguish somewhat less between the benefits of higher and other education. They argue that the state has responsibilities for all education levels. "Neighborhood effects," "social effects," or "externalities," both economic and noneconomic, make higher education mostly a public good. In this view, good public policy should not promote privileged choice for the few who can either afford high tuitions or the luxury of making donations and thereby influencing university policy. Instead, publicly financed institutions ought to uphold a more equitable distribution of both access and voice. Such a financial pattern is associated with public more than private choice, or with choice only when manifested through the public policy process, not through privately financed sanctuaries.

Thus, this chapter deals with alternative policies. The alternatives in question clearly involve governmental policy, as decisions are made over both the size and shape of the government role. Yet the alternatives also involve private choices, not only insofar as private preferences influence government policy but also insofar as the size and shape of the government role affects the range and type of private choices available. As will be seen in the rationales offered for various existing private-public patterns, and in the debates swirling over each, one's assessments depend very much on one's views of the proper roles of both government and private choice.

Harkening back to this volume's treatment of school financing, we could appreciate that the policy patterns, rationales, and critiques are not unique to higher education; neither are they unique to education more broadly conceived. In fact, some parallels can be found in numerous policy fields where institutions vary in terms of how much they are privately or publicly financed. Thus, many of the points raised here are broadly relevant to the study of nonprofit (and, to a lesser extent, for-profit) organizations in comparison to public organizations. Indeed, one of the major questions in the study of nonprofit organizations concerns the balance, in terms of both fact and desirability, of privateness and publicness, whether mixed within institutions or separated into clearly distinguishable private and public institutions.

Principal private sources of higher-education income include student payments (through tuition and fees) and donations by foundations and individuals. Public support comes mostly through either government subsidies to institutions or student grants, but also through low-interest loans and tax exemptions. (I concentrate, except where stated, on recurrent expenditures for undergraduate education.)

Private-public blends, which involve policy choices, involve a number of important questions:

1. Is a given system composed of just one sector or dual private-public sectors?
2. If it is dual, what is the size of each sector?
3. What is the contribution of private funds to each sector?
4. What is the contribution of public funds to each sector?

Questions one and two are dealt with only in passing here. The first question is a structural one. I refer to dual sectors if there are "universities," not just "technical institutions," in both sectors. Obviously, it is possible to develop a more complicated structural schema in order to cover higher education more fully. The second question is a rather straightforward quantitative one. My analysis focuses on questions three and four.

The most extreme possibilities would deal with one sector, financed fully

Table 8.1   Terminology and Variables Used to Define Policy Patterns

---

"SECTORS"

Single or Dual?

Refers simply to the structural question (independent of the mode of financing) of whether the system has one sector (generally considered public) or two sectors.

If single sector:
"Statist" or "Public-Autonomous"?

Refers primarily to whether public funds are distributed by the state ("Statist"), specifically by its ministries, or more by university and buffer organizations ("Public-Autonomous").

If dual sectors:
"Homogenized" or "Distinctive"?

Refers to whether private and public sectors are financed very similarly ("Homogenized") or very differently ("Distinctive").

If Distinctive:
"Minority is Private" or "Majority is Private"?

Refers to whether less than half ("Minority is Private") or more than half ("Majority is Private") of the total enrollment are in the private sector.

NOTE: Criteria elaborated in text at beginning of sections on each pattern.

by either public or private funds. Many nations come close to the public extreme, none to the private extreme. As elaborated in my other chapter on higher education, however, there is no single continuum running between two extremes. A system with a large private sector that receives substantial public funding is not necessarily more private than one with a small but privately funded private sector. International analysis discloses various combinations. In an effort to achieve inclusiveness with parsimony, I consecutively consider five dominant patterns. This does not deny the possibility of creating other, equally valid combinations. Nor does this schema assume that funding alone determines privateness and publicness. Nevertheless, for purposes of this chapter, the schema analyzes only how sectors are financed, not the degree to which they are privately or publicly governed or functionally oriented. In other words, this essay tries to carve out only a very narrow area for investigation. It identifies "private" and "public" universities by legal nomenclature alone and then proceeds to explore how private and public these institutions really are on but one dimension—finance—among several possible dimensions. As one last word of terminological introduction, I add that the private universities under consideration, unless otherwise specified, are legally nonprofit private institutions; the extent to which they are behaviorally nonprofit is touched on in this essay but requires further examination.

Boundaries among the five categories prove a bit arbitrary. Although the center of gravity in Pattern I is far removed from the center in Pattern II, there is ambiguity on the border; the same applies to Patterns II and III. Especially as some systems evolve over time, questions may arise over which

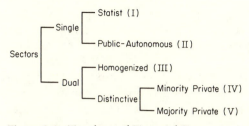

Figure 8.1: Typology of Financial Patterns.

category is most appropriate. I am admittedly trying to order, even force, complex and far-flung data into simplifying categories. In any case, the main purpose is to provide the reader with an orienting guide to the major international policies and rationales, not to pinpoint every case within a finely tuned schema.

Table 8.1 provides a brief guide to the terminology and variables used in developing the five policy patterns that follow. Figure 8.1 adds a tandem graphic overview.

PATTERN I: STATIST (SINGLE SECTOR: PUBLIC FUNDING CONTROLLED BY MINISTRY)

Probably most nations rely on a single university sector, overwhelmingly financed by the state. We might think of a 90%-90% operational guideline: at least 90% public enrollments and state financing. The "Statist" orientation of many of these systems stems from both the 90%-90% factor and from a strong ministerial role in distributing funds. Education or higher-education ministries generally allocate funds directly to given universities and even to units within the universities. There is little freedom of choice, or institutional autonomy, in distribution, although nations such as Sweden and France have recently tried to encourage some. Nor, obviously, is there much administrative choice at the institutional level in structuring income profiles.

Communist systems offer the most obvious and extreme cases, allowing for the expected Yugoslav deviations. So it is interesting to note that even here some private components enter. Soviet economists have acknowledged that higher education depends on private funds insofar as parents sustain their children's student livelihood.[3] There are some individual and foundation contributions in various nations, though figures are scarce. China has exhorted its institutions to "do it themselves" by raising some funds through production. And then there are exceptional cases, such as Poland's Catholic University of Lublin. Mostly, however, the state dominates. There are no tuition fees, and state support for student expenses is even greater than the generous support common in Western Europe.[4] Students are often considered to be as worthy of financial support as workers are of their wages. Obviously, the degree of direct government control over financial allocation is much greater in most Communist systems than in most other Statist systems.

Less obvious is that most Western European nations have chosen to rely so heavily on one sector, publicly funded. Belgium and the Netherlands are two national exceptions, considered later. Among scattered institutional exceptions within Statist systems are Sweden's Stockholm School of Economics and religiously affiliated institutions in Italy and France. Commercial schools, such as those in Greece, may or may not be considered part of "higher education." But most Statist systems lack important private higher-education institutions. Depending on how figures are calculated, university income may come nearly or fully 100% from the state, though sometimes not exclusively from the education ministry. Figures drop substantially lower only when one considers university budgets without professors' salaries—since professors are usually civil servants paid directly by the government. Student fees may appear to cover 20% when they really cover only a few percent of total recurrent costs. There may also be some very limited income from landholdings and endowments, and a few private or special institutions get donations from religious organizations, chambers of commerce, and business firms. Possibly the most important exception to public funding occurs where business firms contribute to particular research endeavors, not computed within the annual recurrent subsidies.

Most nations in Pattern I have chosen to require no fees or almost no fees.[5] Furthermore, widespread government aid covers some student living expenses, often including room, board, and books; loans are also common, usually based largely on parental income. France provides some family tax relief and even some "preemployment contracts" to students pledging to enter government employment. What has varied among the Western European nations has been the extent of student aid and also the balance among different aid mechanisms, not the basic choice to make higher education truly freer than even the absence of tuition would alone suggest.

There is a private-public policy debate, but it is centered very near the public pole. Students have frequently asked for more aid, so that they could cover opportunity costs and achieve the security and quasi-worker status more characteristic of their Eastern European counterparts. But a number of governments now prefer increased tuition (albeit through repayable loans). In fact, recent information indicates that some may choose to risk the political opposition of students by actively and openly considering tuition plans, a radical policy departure.

Many of the less-developed countries also fit the Statist funding pattern. This is generally true, for example, of those tied to France through colonial experience. Many French-African universities are still linked with French universities that underwrite their degrees. Algeria, Benin, Chad, Gabon, the Ivory Coast, Mali, and Niger finance their public universities usually without student fees, by relying on government funds, including French government funds. Similar patterns hold for Belgian-African universities. Statist examples from elsewhere would include Afghanistan (even before the Soviet takeover), Burma, Malaysia, and Sri Lanka.[6] A central rationale for Statism in these less-developed nations, just as it was in Latin America in the twentieth century and Italy in the 1870s, is that fully public and centrally directed systems are necessary to bolster government authority, shape development, and build nations. More latitude for disparate individual and group choices, it is argued, could undermine public policy and national unity. One could find several parallels to the U.S. push, long ago, toward public "common" schools, a push with little parallel at the U.S. higher-education level.

PATTERN II: PUBLIC-AUTONOMOUS (SINGLE SECTOR: PUBLIC FUNDING WITH AUTONOMY)

With certain variations, a number of Public-Autonomous systems could fit the Statist pattern. Again, there is only one university sector. Again, funding for all but the very few privately funded institutions comes overwhelmingly, if not fully, from the state. Yet there are important policy differences between Patterns I and II. While no one questions that universities in Pattern I are public, public-private ambiguity has often surrounded legal and popular usage in Pattern II. Of course, we want to avoid both goverance and complex definitional questions here, but even in finance alone, the term *public* must be qualified in Pattern II. Nations in Pattern I have long traditions of full public funding. By contrast, nations in Pattern II have traditions of mixed public and private funding. Private actors, from foundations to students, have played important roles. Only recently have Pattern II nations turned overwhelmingly to public finance, and private finance is still significant in some of these cases. More importantly, traditionally mixed private-public funding reflects the traditionally non-Statist norms of financial allocation that have characterized—and continue to characterize—Public-Autonomous systems.

Great Britain's universities were historically referred to as "private." They were created by private groups and operated under their own charters. They have generally not been "under" government ministries nearly so directly as have Statist universities. This certainly applied to finance. While most Pattern I nations regarded higher education as basically a state responsibility, nineteenth-century British authorities still saw the proper state role as limited, a greater role as interference. As Halsey and Trow have written: "Higher education in Britain was largely a matter of private enterprise."[7] Until recently, student fees accounted for a considerable portion of university income, much more than in the Statist pattern. But steadily declining fees and rising public subsidies have changed this. In 1920, the government accounted directly for only 34% of the universities' income, with a like share coming from student fees, while a half century later the government figure soared over 80% and the fee figure declined to under 10%. Further-more, the government figure would be higher if we included indirect sub-sidies, for example, payments to students to cover their fees. By 1970 the British universities' income profile came to resemble those of many U.S. *state* universities (less than 10% from fees, more than 70% from govern-ment), except that British finance comes predominantly from the *national* government. By contrast, prior British financial policy had more closely approximated U.S. policies for its *private* universities.[8] As the trend to-ward government finance has continued, however, covering most tuition costs, British university funding has become more and more decidedly pub-lic. No longer does the pattern, increasingly public, so closely resemble that of even the U.S. state universities, especially if we were to exclude Oxford and Cambridge from the comparison.

Even as Great Britain's financial profile became more public, however, public policy allowed the allocation process to remain comparatively au-tonomous. Government funds were neither targeted to specific intrauniv-ersity destinations nor even given directly to the universities. Instead, a much heralded buffer organization—the University Grants Committee (UGC)—played a key role. The UGC was created in 1919 to channel increasing government funds. In theory and usually in practice as well, universities directed their requests to the UGC and the UGC reviewed these and then itself requested a total sum from the government, which in turn funded the UGC; the UGC gave block grants to each university, which then distrib-uted the funds with a degree of autonomy often envied outside Great Brit-ain. Administrative choice at the institutional level would not be crippled along the lines of the Statist pattern. Moreover, the UGC itself has been composed principally of representatives from the academic community. At least until the 1970s, a typical characterization has been that the UGC is an organization that appears on paper "illogical, unworkable and theoret-ically indefensible but which in real life—like so many British institutions deserving the same adjectives—works."[9]

A number of nations historically linked to Great Britain have chosen a similar Public-Autonomous orientation. There are no private universities in Australia (only specialized institutions, such as seminaries); fees, dimin-ishing in importance over time (13%, 1965), were abolished in 1974. But there is significant variation within Pattern II. New Zealand, Ireland, and Israel have Public-Autonomous universities that do derive much of their income from tuition. On the other hand, the government share typically has grown even in these nations. In its early years of nationhood Israel re-garded defense and primary and secondary education as policy priorities and did not publicly fund its universities. As recently as 1965 the govern-ment still covered only half the financial costs, though by 1975 the figure reached roughly 80%, with 10% coming from tuition.[10] Furthermore, all these countries have some sort of UGC replica (e.g., a "Planning and Grants Committee" in Israel), underscoring a degree of institutional choice in fi-nancial allocations.

Policy debate in Public-Autonomous systems centers around the role of UGCs and around fees. Many argue that UGCs, as they have increasingly become funnels for national government monopoly finance, have become mere covers for ministerial direction. In Great Britain itself, inflation, educational retrenchment, and political conservatism have hurt the UGC image among many academics witnessing the UGC's role in imposing the Thatcher administration's severe cutbacks. As Graeme Moodie has summarized the disillusionment: "What good is the UGC if it can't save us?" However, Moodie proceeds to answer by restating "the value of having a known and friendly intermediary. . . . The UGC assures the maximum degree of self-rule possible in a given time period. More cannot reasonably be expected."[11] Not all observers would agree with Moodie, but if there is a prevalent contemporary view it is that a tougher UGC became inevitable as government funding increased notably, small-group understandings between university and UGC officials gave way to bureaucratic guidelines, and gentlemen's agreements could no longer forge public policy. Nonetheless, according to this view, UGCs still offer the universities a degree of protection from the effects of direct and directed Statist allocations.

Some believe that the only solution to increased government control would be decreased government finance. Part of Britain's Conservative party has challenged the basic principles of state funding. Fees have recently been greatly increased, although this basically affects overseas students. And a rather private institution has been founded at Buckingham to break the public monopoly. But, again, as in the Statist systems, the emerging policy debate seems most likely to turn on proposals to impose tuition. Unlike the Statist pattern, the Public-Autonomous pattern has historical precedent for such private funding.

As with Pattern I, there are Pattern II examples in less-developed nations, tracing back to colonial influences. British Africa has generally developed more Public-Autonomous universities (some beginning under direct British tutelage) than has French Africa. Many former British colonies even have their own versions of a UGC, for example, Nigeria's National Universities Commission. But here one must remember that similar structures need not carry out similar functions. UGCs certainly do not guarantee autonomous institutional choice under authoritarian regimes or amid conditions of economic hardship, though they may ameliorate otherwise harsher results. And another factor that assumes increased importance in the less-developed nations is foreign finance. Some of this comes from private foundations, such as the Ford and Rockefeller foundations, while some comes from government-funded agencies such as the U.S. Agency for International Development and the Inter-American Development Bank. On the other hand, policies on student fees show significant parallels with policies in the more-developed nations. In fact, fees have been more common in the former British colonies than in Great Britain itself, though they are often paid indirectly by government. So, for example, Nigeria's University of Ilosho (1968) drew 12% of its income from fees, along with 20% from outside grants (mostly from the Ford and Rockefeller foundations), and two-thirds from the federal government. Restrictively white South African universities follow the tendency in which tuition, still important, has become less important. Before World War II fees provided roughly two-thirds of these universities' income; they now provide under one-third.[12] A non-African Public-Autonomous example from the less-developed world might be Pakistan, but, as with Nigeria and other former British colonies, this depends on the degree to which structure and heritage provide for more than just the mere facade of autonomy.

PATTERN III: HOMOGENIZED (DUAL SECTORS: SIMILAR FUNDING FOR EACH SECTOR)

Some systems that have two university sectors have chosen to finance each pretty much the same way—principally through public funds. Generally the two sectors were once financed very differently, but the private sector could no longer sustain itself on private funds, or it undertook purposes considered sufficiently public to claim public subsidies. The basic rationale for this policy pattern is clear: Existing institutions, that happen to be private, are performing useful functions, and it would be at best pointless, at worst wasteful, to see them perish due to insufficient funds. Increased public finance thus evolves in somewhat the same ways as in Pattern II, except that it now affects two sectors. While some intersectoral financial differences often remain, in the source or in the allocation process, similarities are much more salient. If governance continues to be distinct between private and public institutions, then we may have interesting cases of public subsidy without concomitant control. Although public subsidy frequently means strong public regulation, sufficient private-public distinctiveness has remained in some systems (e.g., the Belgian) to allow a type of choice for various actors, including students, professors, administrators, and donors, that is not easily associated with the single-sector systems, especially the Statist ones.

Pattern III holds for fewer cases than any other. Yet *some* degree of homogenization occurs over time in many dual-sector systems, private institutions relying increasingly on public funds even though not to the same degree that public institutions do. And, significantly, the Homogenized policy pattern at least partly characterizes funding at the primary and secondary levels in many nations.

A nominally private sector holds about one-third of Chile's enrollments. By the 1960s it achieved roughly equal financial footing with its public counterpart, as both sectors derived over 90% of their income from public funds. This development accompanied declining private-public differences in both institutional control and mission. With a dramatic regime change to military rule (1973) and free-market economics, there has been a strong move to make all universities more self-financing. This would make the whole system more private, but would not by itself reintroduce private-public differences intersectorally. Such differences could emerge only *if*, as does not appear likely, the junta imposes the startling plans it announced in the early 1980s; these would continue to limit the size of all existing universities, still funded mostly by the government, forcing other enrollments into new institutions that must be fully financed by private sources.

Education Acts of 1961 and 1970 put the Netherlands' private institutions (holding roughly one-fourth of the enrollments) on equal financial footing with its public institutions. Tuition is minimal, and there are loans and subsidies. The state therefore assumes nearly the full financial burden, though it has tried, thus far thwarted by political opposition, to push a tuition-loan plan. In Belgium too, especially since the University Finance and Control Law of 1971, the substantial private sector (holding roughly two-thirds of the enrollments) has come to be publicly financed.[13] Canada might also fit the Homogenized pattern if one identifies many of its privately founded institutions (e.g., McGill and Laval) as private (thereby making for two sectors). The government has assumed most of the financial responsibility for all institutions, though fees may still be on the higher (Ireland, South Africa) than lower side (Great Britain). The Canadian case points up fundamental similarities between Patterns II and III. In both, the public policies of recent decades have pushed toward a situation in which nearly all universities are publicly funded, regardless of previous practices and structures.

PATTERN IV: DISTINCTIVE, MINORITY IS PRIVATE (DUAL SECTORS: SMALLER SECTOR FUNDED PRIVATELY, LARGER SECTOR FUNDED PUBLICLY)

Next we come to nations that have chosen distinctive dualism: public sectors basically supported by public funds, private sectors by private funds. Pattern IV has private sectors with usually around 10% to 20% (but up to 50%) of total enrollments, drawing their funds fully or predominantly from nongovernment sources. At least some of what are now Pattern III cases were once Pattern IV cases—until the private sector began to rely overwhelmingly on public funds. Thus time emerges as a key factor. Experience seems to indicate that it is difficult, though far from impossible, for private universities to sustain themselves fully over long periods on private funds.

Pattern IV characterizes every Latin American nation save Chile, Brazil, Cuba, and Uruguay. (Colombia is a borderline case between Patterns IV and V.) Most private institutions have been created fairly recently, only a few existing before this century, only a few more by mid-century. By 1980, however, roughly 20% of enrollments in Latin America's Pattern IV cases (roughly 34% for all Latin America) were in the private sector.[14]

This surge of private growth effectively broke the single-sector, public finance tradition, often constitutionally consecrated (e.g., Argentina). The public sector remains as publicly financed as ever, usually charging only token tuitions and drawing at least 95% of its income from government. New private institutions, however, typically draw almost all their income from private sources. Tuition is the largest component, often covering costs completely. It is especially dominant at the lower-quality institutions, though only in rare cases does it cover less than two-thirds of the ongoing costs even at the more elite institutions. In fact, the elite institutions charge the highest tuitions, but they also draw on other private sources. No longer is it true that private giving and corporate donations are uniquely U.S. (or Anglo-American) characteristics. Some institutions, such as Mexico's 15,500-student (1981) Autonomous University of Guadalajara, run strong alumni fund-raising campaigns. Others, such as Venezuela's Metropolitan University (with nearly 3000 students in 1981), rely heavily on business support. Such support is especially important, in much of Latin America, in building campuses and plant facilities, but it sometimes accounts for up to a third of ongoing annual expenses. International finance has also helped with capital expenditures. In return for these domestic and international contributions, elite private institutions are expected to be free from radical political activism, offer high-quality education, and orient themselves toward commercial or industrial fields of study. Some, but not all, Catholic universities similarly attract business contributions, though not as much as the secular elite universities do. Naturally, however, most Catholic universities also count on direct and indirect church financing. In sum, several private organizations, some for-profit and others nonprofit, finance alternatives to the public universities. Private choice therefore shapes public policy where once governments held more to the Pattern I doctrine that public policy be made by the state.

A 1971 study estimated that Latin America's private institutions rely 28% on government sources (versus 87% for public institutions).[15] Even this shows considerable private-public distinction, but it greatly overestimates the public contribution to private institutions by including (1) Latin American nations not included in Pattern IV and (2) a disproportionate sample of older and more prestigious private institutions—both types much more likely than other private institutions to get some public aid. The fact that older (generally Catholic) universities more frequently get such aid supports the hypothesis that over time private institutions may become less privately financed.

Major policy debates about private-public financing often emerge in Pattern IV; three of these are touched on here. One concerns the very growth of private institutions. Many critics regard the private sector as detrimental to public control and coordination of a vital sociopolitical enterprise; most troublesome, they argue, is the private sector's inegalitarian role, as only the privileged can afford the "choice" to attend. High-quality private education allegedly robs the public sector of many of its best personnel and reinforces privilege for the privileged. One response is that dual sectors are more equitable; nearly all university students are privileged, but at least if they choose the private university, they pay their own way. Of course, private universities rarely grow in order to promote equity. More explicit reasons for private sector growth have included changes in the socioeconomic composition of the student body, declining quality, growing numbers, and growing politicization within the public sector. Well-to-do families have been willing to pay private tuitions, and some businesses help fund "responsible" institutions that, therefore, need not depend on public subsidization. We therefore see higher-education parallels here to accounts (provided in previous articles in this volume) dealing with the choice of private schools, despite private financial burdens. These are choices made by elite and other groups when they are dissatisfied with public schools.

A second policy debate is whether these new private sectors should receive any public funds. The private sector itself may be split, some emphasizing the need, others the dangerous strings. The public sector is also split, though more opposed, some emphasizing the high educational benefits-to-costs ratio, most the inequity and the losses for the public sector. A third policy debate concerns tuition in the public sector. Most governments and many economists of education favor it, but fierce student opposition still prevails in almost all cases.

Whatever the future of these debates, private and public finance have been, to date, more intersectorally distinct in Pattern IV than in any other pattern. Pattern IV offers policymakers and other actors the clearest choices between sectoral alternatives.

PATTERN V: DISTINCTIVE, MAJORITY IS PRIVATE (DUAL SECTORS: LARGER SECTOR FUNDED PRIVATELY, SMALLER SECTOR FUNDED PUBLICLY)

Our last pattern characterizes systems where the majority of enrollments are found in the private sector. Again, public institutions are funded almost exclusively by the government. Some, like the Japanese, follow the Statist pattern; others, like the Indian, may incline toward Public-Autonomous pattern. By contrast, private institutions are funded mostly by private funds, but usually not to the (nearly full) extent found in Pattern IV.

Pattern V systems typically evolve where the state either cannot or chooses not to expand the public sector, even in the face of rapidly growing demand for higher education. India offers a clear case. British rulers were not inclined toward massive expenditures in order to educate their colonial subjects. Instead, they gladly aided privately run institutions. Independent India thus found itself with a huge private sector, which it was not about to disestablish. Furthermore, it explicitly made the primary and secondary levels its first two public education priorities, leaving public higher education third. One result is that government has provided almost half of the private colleges' income, mostly through grants-in-aid, and an even higher proportion for the private universities. Significantly, the private colleges hold nearly three-fourths of Indian enrollments. Still, as of 1965, although the government met more than half the cost of Indian higher education, fees covered 35% and endowments and "other sources" the rest.[16] As in Pattern IV, but differently, private actors play a major role in financial policy.

Brazil offers another good example. Economic growth unleashed unprecedented demand for higher education in the 1960s, but the conservative military government would not let public institutions expand as freely as they did in most of Latin America. It kept entrance exams relatively stiff at the public universities, while permitting private institutions to absorb excess demand. The private sector jumped from 42% of the enrollments in 1955 to 63% in 1980. The private sector, particularly the Catholic university subsector, has petitioned for public subsidies, so far unsuccessfully. But Catholic universities do receive substantial public funds for graduate studies and research on the same basis that public universities do.

The internationally best-known case in which the private sector holds the majority of enrollments—roughly 80%—is Japan. The bulk of Japan's enrollment boom was pushed into the private sector by strict entrance examinations at the public universities. Yet the private sector was constitutionally barred from receiving public subsidies. Then, concerned over low quality and especially over potentially serious protests by families with students in the private sector, the government saw fit to change its policy by granting low-interest loans and financing part of the professors' salaries. By the mid-1970s, new legislation authorized the government to finance up to 50% of the private sector's ongoing costs. No longer does Japan have a dichotomous system with private funds for the private sector and public funds for the public sector. Still, a substantial gap remains, and tuition is perhaps five times higher in the private sector.[17]

In much of Pattern V, therefore, private enrollments capture nearly three-quarters or even more of total enrollments. The extreme may be found in the Philippines, with 93% private enrollments, basically financed through private sources, mostly tuition.[18] But similar reasons for private growth, that is, absorbing excess demand, may operate even where the private sector does not capture the majority of higher-education enrollments. This is the case within most Latin American nations, even though they are widely characterized by large public sectors and smaller elite private sectors, and in Turkey, which has no elite private sector but 25% of its (1970) enrollments in the private sector nonetheless. Compared to the nations which truly fit Pattern V (with majority private enrollments), however, these cases generate less pressure for public funding of private sectors.

Let us look briefly at why Pattern V maintains a substantial financial distinction between sectors, but also why that distinction generally does not approach the dichotomous extent found in Pattern IV. It is easy to understand why private-public financial distinctions are found in Pattern V. The public budget is comparatively less strained than in other patterns be-

cause it supports a public sector with a relatively small share of the nation's students. The government can afford to finance this sector. That the
government is not inclined to finance the private sector was suggested by
its disinclination to accept the brunt of enrollment expansion into the public sector in the first place. Furthermore, private sector tuition is feasible
because private actors have such a great demand for higher education, and
because new institutions do not face entrenched student interests defending
age-old expectations of free education.

In fact, demand is so great that it presents special opportunities for profit-
making institutions in Pattern V. The Philippines, with overwhelmingly
private enrollments, is an excellent example. India is another. And, though
Turkey's private sector captures only a minority of total enrollments, it does
accommodate excess demand and therefore can operate on a for-profit basis. Turkish for-profits began in the early 1960s and did so well economically that many others quickly emerged. "The best advice one could offer
an investor interested in high profits over short-term periods would be to
go into the college business."[19] Similar dynamics have in practice operated
in Brazil, even though all its private institutions are legally nonprofits.

Powerful factors may push the state toward policies to subsidize private
sectors, however. The biggest obstacle is sectoral size. To finance the private sector is to undertake financial responsibility for most of the higher-
education system. Yet size itself may invite subsidization. By meeting demand, the private sector is fulfilling rather public functions. Considerable
political pressure for public subsidization may come from students at the
private institutions. The government cannot afford to see those institutions
fold, turning angry students to the streets—or, ultimately, into the public
universities. Nor can it always stand idly by as these students, frustrated
on the job market, claim that low-quality private institutions must be improved through public regulation *and* subsidization. Low quality is often
reflected in the underrepresentation of private institutions among "universities," as opposed to "colleges" or single-subject "schools," as in India,
Turkey, Brazil, and the Philippines. Of these four examples the least private-
public difference is found in the Philippines, and even there 81% of the
universities are private, while 95% of all Philippine "institutions of higher
education" are private.[20]

Socioeconomic factors intensify the pressure for public assistance. Whereas
private sector students in Pattern IV tend to be more privileged than their
public counterparts, in Pattern V the opposite holds and private sector students are less able to afford tuition. And so there is special difficulty in the
equity questions. In Pattern IV, the privileged students pay for their private
higher education; in Pattern V, they go into the public sector and it is the
relatively less privileged students who must settle for and pay for the private sector! In any case, it is doubtful that equity or even political pressures are as important as cost factors in stimulating public funding of private sectors; paying part of the cost of education in a private institution is
far cheaper than paying the full cost if all students must be educated in the

public sector. Both private individual choices and public policy are affected by whether the private sector is small and high quality or large and low quality.

On balance, factors favoring some public funding of Pattern V private institutions have generally outweighed unfavorable factors. At least we have seen that the government has become a major financier in our three most important Pattern V cases, traditionally in India, recently in Japan, and still limitedly in Brazil. But in none of our Pattern V cases does public funding of the private sector approach the scale of public funding for the public sector. Financial policies differ significantly for the two sectors.

CONCLUSION

To summarize the five policy patterns, Table 8.2 compresses the preceding discussion into a one-page sketch. Elsewhere, I have tried to show how U.S. policies can be understood in terms of these patterns; more specifically, policies for different parts of the U.S. higher-education system can be fruitfully analyzed in relation to one or another of the patterns.[21] International perspectives should therefore help sensitize us to the reality, possibly even helping us to analyze it, of how private-public financing questions in U.S. higher education are in fact multitudes of questions, with different patterns and problems dominating in different state systems.

We have seen that there are widely varied public policy options in higher-education finance, each associated with complex webs of advantages and disadvantages; among these advantages and disadvantages are different ramifications for the private choices available to many nongovernment actors. Even many single-sector systems are therefore debating the issues related to different private-public financial policies.[22] Perhaps we can learn something from those debates. And the experience of many dual-sector systems illustrates some major dilemmas in working with different financial blends in different sectors.

But, predictably, if also lamentably, international analysis does not offer clear and attractive alternatives that could be neatly copied in U.S. higher education. On the contrary, other nations (even where they share many of our values, which themselves are obviously in conflict) are also groping for better policies. Each pattern appears to have inherent problems and tensions. Each has been subject to changes and faces at least some possibility of far greater changes. Moreover, this brief analysis, rather than identifying clearly attractive alternatives, may well increase skepticism about a given pattern best promoting some broadly desired value. For example, those who associate government and publicness with equity—and equity has been a major rationale for the Statist pattern and for the growing publicness of the Public-Autonomous and Homogenized patterns—must confront not only possible trade-offs between equity and choice or autonomy but also the reality that public monopolies have often been limited in access and that

Table 8.2 Summary of Five Patterns

	I. STATIST	II. PUBLIC-AUTONOMOUS
SINGLE SECTOR	• Almost no privately funded universities • Funds traditionally received from the state • Strong role of ministries in distributing funds among and within universities *Examples:* Communist nations, most of Western Europe, much of formerly French Africa	• Almost no privately funded universities • Traditionally mixed private-public funding, but now predominantly public funding • Important role of university, or "buffer organization" between university and state, in distributing funds among universities, allowing for choice within universities *Examples:* Australia, Great Britain, Israel, New Zealand, Nigeria

	III. HOMOGENIZED	IV. DISTINCTIVE, MINORITY IS PRIVATE	V. DISTINCTIVE, MAJORITY IS PRIVATE
DUAL SECTORS	• Traditionally two sectors, funded differently • Evolution toward mostly public funding for private as well as public sectors • Sectoral dualism and distinctiveness now depend less on finance than on tradition and possibly governance and function *Examples:* Belgium, Canada, Chile, Netherlands	• Private sector has more than 10% but less than 50% of total enrollments • Private sector relies mostly on private finance • Public sector relies mostly on public finance *Examples:* most of Latin America	• Private sector has more than 50% but less than 100% of total enrollments • Private sector relies mostly on private finance • Public sector relies mostly on public finance *Examples:* Brazil, India, Japan, Philippines

NOTES: 1. Empirically empty cells are omitted. No nation has a single sector that is financed principally through private funds. And no nation had dual sectors that are both financed principally through private funds.

2. As discussed in the text, there are two forms of overlap. One is boundary overlap, where a case lies only a little more comfortably in one category than another. The second form of overlap concerns public sectors within III, IV, V that, by themselves, would be Statist or Public-Autonomous.

public as well as private sectors generally draw off and subsidize only a relatively privileged segment of society; furthermore, Pattern V shows that access is sometimes more open in private than public sectors. The point is not to surrender the hope that concrete guidelines can emerge from analyses of alternative patterns, but to recognize that they will not emerge easily, or clearly—and therefore probably to welcome even modest improvements in our understanding.

NOTES

1. This piece, therefore, does not pretend to be policy relevant in the sense of providing solutions that U.S. or other policymakers will adopt. Instead, it strives for a less dramatic policy relevance based on sketching alternatives and providing orientations and guidelines that some policymakers could find useful.

2. Milton Friedman, *Capitalism and Freedom* (Chicago: University of Chicago Press, 1962), p. 85.

3. Harold J. Noah, *Financing Soviet Schools* (New York: Columbia University, Teachers College Press, 1966), p. 74.

4. Frederic Pryor, *Public Expenditures in Communist and Capitalist Nations* (Homewood, Ill.: Richard D. Irwin, 1968), p. 202.

5. Data on Pattern I come largely from Mark Blaug and Maureen Woodhall, "Patterns of Subsidies to Higher Education in Europe," *Higher Education* 7, 3 (1978), pp. 331–361; Maureen Woodhall, *Student Loans* (London: George Harrap, 1970); Lyman Glenny, ed., *Funding Higher Education: A Six-Nation Analysis* (New York: Praeger, 1979); Barbara Burn, with chapters by Philip G. Altbach, Clark Kerr, and James A. Perkins, *Higher Education in Nine Countries* (New York: McGraw-Hill, 1971). Most comparative analyses of higher-education finance are limited to the more-developed world. Among the useful exceptions are Jean-Pierre Jallade, "Financing Higher Education: The Equity Aspects," *Comparative Education Review* 22, 2 (1978), pp. 309–325; and Douglas Windham, "Social Benefits and the Subsidization of Higher Education," *Higher Education* 5, 3 (1976), pp. 237–252. *The International Encyclopedia of Higher Education*, ed. Asa Knowles (San Francisco: Jossey Bass, 1977), was consulted on all five patterns.

6. The Middle East presents a varied picture. Some nations, such as Iran, Iraq, and Syria, probably come closest to Pattern I. But others have more autonomous public institutions and some have important private institutions.

7. A. H. Halsey and M. A. Trow, *The British Academics* (Cambridge, Mass.: Harvard University Press, 1971), p. 60.

8. The data on Great Britain come from Halsey and Trow, p. 63; Eric Hutchinson, "The Origins of the University Grants Committee," *Minerva* 13, 4 (1975), pp. 612–613; Blaug and Woodhall, pp. 343–347.

9. Sir John Wolfenden, "The Economic and Academic Freedom of Universities," *Royal Society of Medicine* 63 (August 1970), p. 844.

10. Shmuel Bendor, "Israel," in *The International Encyclopedia*, pp. 2335–2336. On Australia, Burn, p. 147; on Ireland's "relatively high fees," OECD, *Reviews of National Policies for Education: Ireland* (Paris: OECD, 1969), p. 25.

11. Graeme C. Moodie, "Los académicos y el gobierno universitario: algunas reflexiones sobre la experiencia británica," in Iván Lavados, ed., *Universidad contemporánea: antecedentes y experiencias internacionales* (Santiago, Chile: Corporación Promoción Universitaria, 1980), pp. 235–258. The classic book-length study dealing with the UGC is Robert O. Berdahl's *British Universities and the State* (Berkeley: University of California, 1959), and Berdahl is now preparing an updated analysis.

12. On Nigeria, Pierre L. van den Berghe, *Power and Privilege at an African University* (Cambridge, Mass.: Schenkman, 1973), p. 62; and A. Callaway and A. Musone, *Financing*

of Education in Nigeria (Paris: UNESCO, 1968). On South Africa, O. P. F. Horwood, "The Financing of Higher Education in South Africa, with Special Reference to the Universities," *The South African Journal of Economics* 32, 3 (September 1964) p. 166. On the British influence in Africa, Eric Ashby, *Universities: British, Indian, African* (Cambridge, Mass.: Harvard University Press, 1966). There are, however, some exceptions to the British Africa–French Africa generalizations. Tanzania, for example, has a quite Statist profile. One possibly important area that I ignore in Africa (e.g., Kenya), as well as elsewhere, concerns commercial schools, offering subjects such as hotel management. These schools are often not included in definitions or data on "higher education," but may be "postsecondary."

13. On Europe's Pattern III, see Blaug and Woodhall, p. 338, and Roger Geiger's forthcoming manuscript, *Private Sectors in Higher Education: Structure, Function and Change in Eight Countries* (Ann Arbor: University of Michigan), chapter on Belgium and the Netherlands. Also see Thomas Schuller, "Higher Education in the Netherlands: Pluralism Old and New," working paper published by the Higher Education Research Group, Institution for Social and Policy Studies, Yale University, 1978.

14. Except where otherwise stated, all information on Latin America is drawn from my forthcoming manuscript, *Higher Education and the State in Latin America: Private Challenges to Public Dominance* (Chicago: University of Chicago Press, 1986). While some of the public institutions enjoy little autonomy, others, not totally unlike counterparts in Pattern II (Public-Autonomous), manage to combine comparatively substantial autonomy (e.g., in distributing funds within the university) with a near government monopoly in finance. I try to show how and why in *University and Government in Mexico: Autonomy in an Authoritarian System* (New York: Praeger, 1980), pp. 100–137. Another English-language source on Latin American financing is Edgardo Boeninger Kausel, "Alternative Policies for Financing Higher Education," in *The Financing of Education in Latin America* (Washington, D.C.: Inter-American Development Bank, n.d.). pp. 321–357.

15. Juan F. Castellanos, *Examen de una década* (Mexico City: UDUAL, 1976), p. 216.

16. On India, Susanne Hoeber Rudolph and Lloyd I. Rudolph, "The Political System and the Education System," in Rudolph and Rudolph, eds., *Education and Politics in India* (Cambridge, Mass.: Harvard University Press, 1972), p. 29; D. M. Desai, *Some Critical Issues of Higher Education in India* (Bombay: A. R. Sheth, 1970), pp. 376–377; Burn, pp. 321, 335; J. L. Azad, "Financing Institutions of Higher Education in India," *Higher Education* 5, 1 (1976), pp. 1–7; G. D. Parikh, "Some Aspects of University Finance" *Quest* (Bombay) 64 (1970), pp. 34–40.

17. On Japan, William Cummings, Iku Amano, and Kazuyuk Kitamura, eds., *Changes in the Japanese University* (New York: Praeger, 1979); William Cummings, "The Japanese Private University," *Minerva* 11, 3 (1973), pp. 348–371.

18. Edith Danskin, "Quantity and Quality in Higher Education in Thailand and Philippines," *Comparative Education Review* 15, 3 (1979), pp. 316–321. Also see Geiger, *Private Sectors*, on the Philippines.

19. Ayse Oncu, "Higher Education as a Business: Growth of a Private Sector in Turkey" (unpublished Ph.D. dissertation, Yale University, 1971), pp. 85–87, 75. Oncu shows that these profits are achieved even though tuitions are low by U.S. standards. In much of the Third World "low" by U.S. standards may be medium to high by local standards.

20. Narcisco Albarracin, "The Private University and National Purpose," *Far Eastern University Journal* (Manila) 14, 3 (1970), p. 282.

21. See the earlier version of this paper, cited in the acknowledgment. This understanding of the U.S. system in international perspective obviously should draw heavily on discriminating analyses of the component parts of each sector; Geiger's chapter in this volume provides such information.

22. For a further analysis of the ramifications of different sources and patterns of funding, a major concern for economists of higher education, among others, see Gareth Williams, "The Economic Approach," in Burton R. Clark, ed., *Perspectives on Higher Education: Eight Disciplinary and Comparative Views* (Berkeley: University of California Press, 1984), pp. 79–105.

9

Finance and Function:
Voluntary Support and Diversity in
American Private Higher Education*

ROGER L. GEIGER

THE FUNCTIONS OF PRIVATE HIGHER EDUCATION IN
COMPARATIVE PERSPECTIVE

A revolution has taken place in the past generation in American assumptions about higher education: It has virtually become a universally accepted responsibility of government to make it possible for all qualified students to attend college. This shift in opinion has been translated quite tangibly into the bricks and mortar of greatly expanded state and municipal university systems, as well as an extensive network of local community colleges. As a result, the 50% of student enrollments that the public sector claimed in 1950 has grown to nearly 78% in 1985. By the somewhat artificial measure of "market share," the private sector would seem to have lost more than half of its clientele. In the more meaningful measure of actual students, however, private colleges and universities have more than doubled their enrollments during this period. In fact, during the latter part of the 1970s the private sector added more students than did its much larger public counterpart.[1] The private sector clearly still plays a vital role in our system of higher education. But just what might that be?

This simple question admits of no simple answer. More than 1500 private colleges and universities cater to students of widely differing ages, aspirations, and abilities. They offer some 300 bachelor's degrees, not to mention additional programs on the graduate-professional level. From another angle, one might note that public higher education is a responsibility of the states. Thus, there are actually fifty public sectors in this country,

---

*An earlier version of this chapter was Working Paper No. 39 of the Program on Non-Profit Organizations at Yale University.

each of which (save that of Wyoming) is complemented by an array of private institutions. Not all of these state private sectors are terribly different from those of neighboring states; but regional contrasts are nevertheless stark between, for example, states where private higher education has evolved alongside large and prestigious state universities and those eastern states where private schools have long been predominant.

The functions of private higher education in the United States are obviously complex. In dealing with such questions, it is sometimes useful to turn to the experience of other countries for comparative insights that might bring order to a complicated situation. Although private higher education is undoubtedly far more studied here than elsewhere, foreign perspectives are of value in this case for at least one compelling reason: Most countries have nationally organized systems of higher education, and these tend to give rise to private sectors possessing a single overriding function. This obviously can simplify the task of identifying the principal role of private sectors.

Japan, for example, with more than three-fourths of its college students in private institutions, is an archetype of a "mass private sector."[2] Throughout its modern development, the number and the size of publicly controlled universities has been kept relatively low. The consistently growing social demand for advanced schooling has consequently been accommodated through the proliferation and growth of private colleges. The breakdown of enrollments in the public and private sectors of Japan today presents almost a mirror image to that of the United States. Clearly, in Japan it has been the private sector that has been responsible for satisfying the rising demand for higher education: Its chief function has thus been to provide *more* higher education than the state was willing or able to offer.

Belgium and the Netherlands are the only two European countries where private universities (they would say "free") exist on an equal footing with those run by the state. Both independence and equality are the key elements of these "parallel public and private sectors." Private institutions in these societies reflect deep-seated cultural preferences of religious communities that have insisted upon their institutions being independent from the state. In the Netherlands, both Calvinists and Catholics have struggled to develop educational systems under their own control (see James's first article in this volume); while in Belgium independent Catholic higher education has a counterpart in the rationalist Free Universities (French- and Flemish-speaking) of Brussels. For these cultural communities, private higher education would have little worth if it were not fully equivalent to that offered by the state. For that reason, the government in recent years has been pressured into assuming virtually the entire cost of operating these independent universities in both countries. Although this has necessarily meant some sacrifice of financial autonomy, it has assured the overriding function of providing culturally *different* higher education in these private sectors.

A third discernible function of private higher education outside the United

States is somewhat more elusive and controversial: providing *better* education than that which is available under state auspices. This can occur under several sets of circumstances. In Latin America, private sectors have been growing in recent decades in apparent response to conditions in the public sector universities. In Mexico and Venezuela, for example, unprecedented growth and politicization in the public sector have led middle-class students to seek private, politically safe schools, which are often avowedly dedicated to preparing for careers in private industry.[3] These private colleges can thus claim qualitative superiority in terms of the academic preparation and social backgrounds of their students. Their quality is thus strongly linked to the process of selection, a process similar to that discussed in Murnane's first contribution to this volume.

A different sort of quality is commonly sought through private instruction in situations where students face severe competitive hurdles. Leaving aside short-term cram courses, which are probably ubiquitous in such situations, private schools for this purpose have become institutional fixtures in France and especially Japan. Although the top *classes préparatoires aux grands écoles* are offered within the leading state *lycées*, some private schools have specialized quite successfully in this task. In Japan, as many as 25% of male college students may have spent a year or more at private *yobikos* to improve their performance on college entrance examinations. When immediate results are all that count, students will pay for quality. This situation has provided an unfailing opportunity for private initiatives.

These brief examples, then, point to aspirations for *more, different,* or *better* higher education as three rationales for the existence of private alternatives to state higher education. In a general way, this finding is quite consistent with the view of the entire nonprofit sector of the economy offered by Burton Weisbrod. In essence, he postulates that a democratic government will tend to provide the kind and amount of services desired by the majority of the population. Those with strong minority preferences for collective goods such as education will thus seek to fulfill them through the voluntary, or not-for-profit sector of the economy.[4] Certainly, *more, different,* and *better* constitute valid minority aspirations with regard to higher education. Moreover, one can discern a rough correspondence with types of institutions in the American private sector.

The private universities that were founded in many American cities were originally intended to serve the educational needs of their immediate area, where public institutions were usually lacking. Even with the recent buildup of the public sector in every major city, many of these institutions have retained a strong service orientation. Thus, they bear some resemblance to the private universities of Japan by virtue of the fact that they have absorbed demand that the public institutions could not or would not accommodate.

The contemporary liberal arts college is in many ways a distinctive American institution, but it fulfills the purpose of providing different approaches to undergraduate education. The original proliferation of these

institutions was partly stimulated by rivalries between Protestant denominations. Many of the surviving colleges still retain their church ties. Often
these *different* religious orientations are their principal raison d'être. A
number of liberal arts colleges have become prestigious and highly selective. They, in fact, largely prepare their students for further, occupationally
determinative schooling at the graduate-professional level. In this respect
they offer the choice of attaining different styles of undergraduate education. In general, then, the American liberal arts colleges today justify their
existence by the differences they offer.

Probably all private colleges and universities feel that they are better than
their rivals at something. American private research universities, however,
are distinctive in their reputations for faculty research and graduate education. What makes this so unusual is that research and scholarship constitute an exceedingly costly form of overhead expenditure for institutions
of higher education. The private American research universities have achieved
their stature by mobilizing substantial private resources toward these qualitative ends.[5] There can be no question about the outstanding quality of
the top private research universities (see below), which results from the excellence of their faculties, the high abilities of their students, and the sheer
concentration of scholarly resources on limited numbers of students. As will
be seen below, there is an inherent connection between private control and
the excellence they have attained.

Without being comprehensive, the rationales of providing *more, different,* and *better* educational alternatives would seem to encompass a good
deal of the American private sector. Nevertheless, while this brief comparative excursus has brought some answers to the original question, these
impressionistic categories cannot yet bear the weight of serious analysis.
After all, to judge from the claims that private colleges and universities make
about themselves, they all could be characterized by "service," "distinctiveness," and "excellence" (to use more elevated diction). This potential
muddle can be clarified, however, if, instead of focusing on what these institutions say they do, one examines what, in effect, they are paid to do.
When sources of revenue are systematically compared, it turns out that these
three rough categories actually reflect important functional differences in
the private sector.

SOURCES OF INCOME FOR PRIVATE COLLEGES AND UNIVERSITIES

Table 9.1 gives the revenue sources for public and private higher education
in a somewhat simplified form that roughly corresponds with actual
education-related expenditures.[6] Compared to the public sector, private
colleges and universities show a higher level of per student income (and
hence expenditure). More important, though, 80% of public sector revenues is derived from public sources, while 80% of private sector income
(ignoring student aid for the moment) is generated privately. Clearly, the

Table 9.1   Selected Per-Student Revenues for Public and Private Institutions of
Higher Education, U.S., 1978–79

	Public Institutions		Private Institutions	
	$	%	$	%
Tuition and Fees from Students	698	17	3056	57
Private Gifts	133	3	799	15
Endowment Income	24	1	402	8
Federal Restricted Grants & Contracts (research)	487	12	856	16
State & Local Governments	2784	67	221	4
	$4126	100%	$5334	100%

SOURCE: Adapted from National Center for Educational Statistics, *Digest of Education Statistics, 1981*
(Washington, D.C.: GPO, 1981), p. 149.

key to the welfare of the American private sector lies in its capacity to tap
private resources. The federal government nevertheless also has a role to
play. The differential impact of each of these sources of revenue is in fact
the key to analyzing the divisions within the private sector. (See the five-
part typology developed in Levy's chapter on international financial patterns.)

Tuition is the largest source of revenue for private schools, and it is also
the source of the greatest disparity between public and private institutions.
In 1983–84, for example, a year's tuition was more than $3500 more at
a private university than at a public one.[7] This pricing "gap" between the
two sectors has long been perceived as a threat to the continued existence
of a vigorous private sector. In fact, the potential harm of this differential
has been softened during the past two decades by federal programs of student financial aid. The general effect of these programs has been to make
the cost of higher education vary somewhat according to a student's ability
to afford it. In 1981 60% of undergraduates in the private sector were receiving some form of federal financial aid.[8] The crucial importance of these
programs provides a common element in the financial equations of the different types of private institution. It is certainly more constant than the
role of tuition itself.

As a broad generalization, it would undoubtedly be safe to say that the
higher the tuition a private college or university charges, the less tuition
dependent the institution is likely to be; and, conversely, the lower the tuition, the greater the probable dependence on tuition revenue. The reason
for this apparent paradox will become evident shortly when the discussion
turns to the subject of voluntary support. Basically, the highest tuition is
charged by research universities and highly selective liberal arts colleges,
both of which have other substantial sources of income. Their students
consequently receive a subsidy for their education from endowment in-

come, alumni support, and other private gifts. The less selective private colleges and universities more often than not have little such supplemental income. Not only are they dependent on tuition revenues, but they are also constrained in what they charge by the capacity of their clientele, even with student aid, to pay. The profile of private-sector revenues given in Table 9.1, then, can be rather misleading, because a considerable number of private institutions do not have appreciable revenues outside of tuition. For that reason, nontuition income is most revealing of the different roles fulfilled by different types of private colleges and universities.

The amount of federal support for academic science a university receives is the single best indicator of its involvement in research in the natural sciences, and hence the degree of institutional commitment to advancing knowledge. The distribution of these funds is powerfully skewed toward the leading research universities. The 20 largest recipients of these funds take in almost as much (42%) of the total as the next 80 (43%), which leaves little for the remaining more than 1800 four-year colleges and universities.[9] Although there is some fluctuation from year to year, public and private institutions are about evenly represented in the top twenty places of this hierarchy, but large state universities outnumber privates by about three to one in the next eighty places.

The private universities that are large recipients of federal research funds also benefit from significant amounts of voluntary support. These private universities seem to use their wealth in ways that guarantee the continuing flow of research grants. But not all affluent institutions follow this course. The relative importance of tuition, federal research funds, and voluntary support in fact differs for private research universities, liberal arts colleges, and urban universities. These different patterns are depicted in Figure 9.1.[10]

Each axis of the triangle in Figure 9.1 represents the percentage of income coming from one of three sources, so that the three coordinates of any given point thus add up to 100%. As one moves perpendicularly away from the left-hand side of the triangle, the percentage of voluntary support in the total of general and educational expenditures increases; distance from the right-hand side indicates increasing percentages of federal support for academic science. The vertical axis of the triangle is thus a residual, which for most institutions is largely covered by tuition. The closer to the peak an institution is located, then, the more completely it depends on student tuition to meet its expenditures.

Area C, representing large urban universities, extends from this point of full tuition dependence down the right side to the level of about 10% voluntary support. The area then extends leftward toward the research side of triangle. This lower part of area C in fact represents the locus of those urban universities having medical schools, all of which derived 10% or more of their budgets from federal research funds. The liberal arts colleges in this sample (area B) all lie along the right-hand side of the triangle, indicating a variable amount of voluntary support, but very little or no research money. Even among the elite of the liberal arts 1, less than 2% of

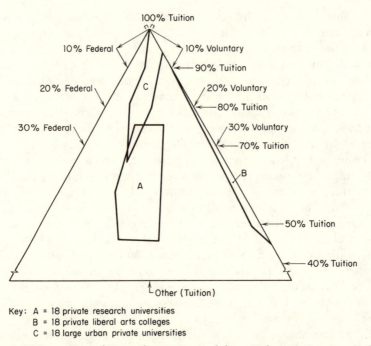

Key: A = 18 private research universities
      B = 18 private liberal arts colleges
      C = 18 large urban private universities

Figure 9.1: Percentage of Expenditures Derived from Voluntary Support, Federal Support for Science, and Other (Mostly Tuition), by Type of Institution.

SOURCE: *Voluntary Support of Education, 1979–80* (N.Y.: Council for Financial Aid to Education, 1981); *Federal Support to Universities and Colleges, Fiscal Year 1979* (Washington, D.C.: National Science Foundation, 1981); representative institutions selected from sample described in note 10.

their budget would be so covered; and the liberal arts 2 colleges receive no funds at all from this source. The research universities in area A occupy the center of the triangle, which means that they combine significant amounts of both research funding and voluntary support. Together these sources account for at least a quarter of the budget, and in several cases more than twice that. Figure 9.1 provides a first cut into the American private sector. There are, however, fairly wide differences among institutions within each of these areas. To break down these three basic types into more meaningful subdivisions requires delving more deeply into the matter of voluntary support.

In 1979–80 private four-year colleges and universities received almost $2 billion in voluntary support, most of which can be attributed to four types of donors. Alumni supplied the largest component of private sector gifts (27%), followed by nonalumni individuals (25%), foundations (23%), and business corporations (16%).[11] The last three of these categories represent rather heterogeneous kinds of giving, while alumni support plays an especially important role for certain kinds of institutions.

The continued devotion of graduates to the colleges they attended is certainly one of the distinctive features of American higher education. It is also the reason that alumni gifts are the single largest source of voluntary support for the private sector. This did not come about by accident. Almost all colleges and universities maintain alumni offices for the purpose of staying in communication with and soliciting contributions from former students. But not all alumni feel the same degree of obligation to their alma mater. Alumni support is related rather closely to the undergraduate, residential college experience. Few commuter students develop deep attachments to the institution whose classes they attend. For graduate or professional students, loyalties tend to be with particular professors, with departments, and ultimately with the disciplines or professions they join. Undergraduates living on campus develop ties, above all, to classmates and college, and these are the sentiments that evoke subsequent gifts.

Colleges that depend on their alumni go to considerable effort to make the collegiate experience an intense and pleasant one. Great care is placed on accommodations and other physical facilities, and the social life of the college is regarded as an integral part of the educational experience. An explicit effort is then made through class reunions and regular alumni communications to establish a student's entering class as a perpetual reference group. Only certain kinds of colleges and universities succeed in inspiring a high degree of alumni loyalty. For that reason, the extent to which a school depends on its alumni for voluntary support turns out to be a significant institutional characteristic. In Figure 9.2, the locations of seventy-four private colleges and universities have been plotted on a graph according to per student amount of voluntary support and the percentage of current giving received from alumni. This procedure differentiates the three basic kinds of private institutions into more meaningful subgroups.

Each of the eleven areas of Figure 9.2 (A1 to C5) represents the loci of three or more institutions of the type indicated in the key. The amount of voluntary support each received in 1979–80 has been converted to a hypothetical "tuition value" as follows:

$$\text{Tuition Value} = \frac{\text{Voluntary support used for current operations} + 5\% \text{ of endowment}}{\text{Full-time students} + 1/2 \text{ part-time students}}$$

Thus, tuition value represents the additional sum each full-time student would have to pay in order to equal the annual per capita subsidy from past and present voluntary support. Discrepancies in tuition value are enormous: Many of the urban service universities have less than $30, while the wealthiest of the Ivy League universities can count on nearly $7000. The horizontal axis measures the proportion of alumni support to total current voluntary support. This ratio turns out to discriminate quite well between different types of both research universities and liberal arts colleges. For urban universities, the interaction between tuition value and this

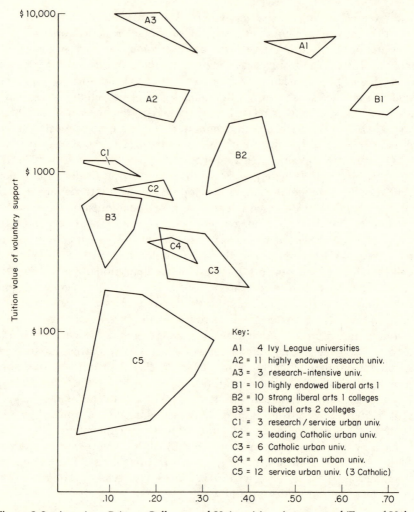

Figure 9.2: American Private Colleges and Universities: Amount and Type of Voluntary Support.

SOURCE: *Voluntary Support of Education, 1979–80* (New York: Council for Financial Aid to Education, 1981). Institutions from sample described in note 10. See following text.

ratio is somewhat more complex. The institutions within the groupings that have been produced here by plotting the amount and nature of voluntary support often resemble each other in numerous other ways as well, including historical origins, participation in research, and student body characteristics. In the sections that follow, the groupings created by Figure 9.2 will be analyzed in order to characterize the roles and functions of these three principal types of private institutions.

THE PRIVATE RESEARCH UNIVERSITIES: PROVIDING BETTER HIGHER EDUCATION

The American private research university has been described as a unique phenomenon in the world of higher education due to the combined effects of "sovereignty, affluence and tradition."[12] Sovereignty has allowed these universities to have their centers of initiative within themselves; their great wealth has given them the wherewithal to pursue their chosen goals; and their traditions have guided each institution in its own fashion toward its vision of academic excellence. The criteria used in the Carnegie Classification identified thirty-six private research 1 and 2 universities.[13] The data employed here have indicated a total of twenty-four such institutions for present purposes. Each of these private universities had voluntary support tuition values in excess of $2000, and voluntary support plus federal research grants were equivalent to at least 25% of their expenditures for current operations. With a few exceptions, the median composite Scholastic Aptitude Test scores of their incoming students exceed 1200 and their graduate enrollment consisted of more than 20% of the total student body. In general, their most distinguishing feature is the combination of considerable wealth and willing restriction of size.

One of the most remarkable features of these universities has been their capacity to meet the rising costs of higher education largely through private resources. Since World War II the expense of higher education in a research environment has escalated far more rapidly than that of higher education in general. This has been due in part to the proliferation of new specialities, the increase in graduate study, and advances in the technology of research. Everywhere this trend has resulted in an overwhelming reliance on national governments to meet these soaring costs. This has, of course, occurred in the United States as well. The American private research universities, however, were in a position to become beneficiaries of the growing postwar federal support for science because of their past use of their own resources. They have gradually restricted their enrollments to students with higher and higher academic abilities. At the same time, the implicit qualitative competition between these institutions has caused them to seek out top scholars and to nurture an environment conducive to scholarship.[14] Thus, when ever greater federal support for research became available and was allocated through the peer review process to the most capable scholars, a considerable portion of these funds was won by private research universities. But what distinguishes these twenty-four institutions from other large recipients, public and private, is the large volume of research funding relative to the number of students.

Only four of these twenty-four universities exceed 15,000 students, and even this size, which is well under the average public university enrollment of about 22,000, is here the cumulative result of numerous units that themselves tend to be of moderate size. Another four institutions have fewer than 5000 students, including Cal Tech, the nation's most selective institution, and Rice, which was wealthy enough to charge no tuition until the 1960s. For all twenty-four the median value of federal research funds per student was about $4500, well above the level of the leading state universities.

Above all, the private research universities are characterized by an overwhelmingly dominant commitment to the academic values underlying the pursuit of knowlege. These values are, of course, no different in the leading public universities. They are in fact common to the communities engaged in disciplinary research. But the independence of the private research universities has allowed them to concentrate single-mindedly on expanding the frontiers of knowledge while also producing superior bachelors and Ph.D.'s. Regarding undergraduates, it can scarcely be an accident that the ten schools with the highest tuition value of voluntary support also had the most select student bodies in terms of SATs.[15] The nation's most academically able students, it would seem, gravitate toward the most highly subsidized undergraduate programs. Concerning graduate study, the success of private research universities has also been evident in the rankings of university graduate departments. In the most recent reputational rankings of graduate programs, ten of the leading fifteen institutions in terms of overall strength were private. When all the major reputational surveys going back to 1925 are combined, eight of the top twelve universities are private.[16] Even with the ascendancy of academic values, though, there is considerable latitude in the manner in which each university pursues its own style of excellence.

In Figure 9.2 eighteen of the twenty-four research universities are located within three distinct clusters of institutions.[17] The area A1 is defined by those Ivy League schools with the greatest per student wealth—Harvard, Yale, Princeton, and, partly by virtue of its small enrollment, Dartmouth. These institutions were among the first systematically to exploit their alumni for support and still depend on them for something like half their voluntary support. Brown and Cornell also share this latter trait, but with less than half as much voluntary support tuition value. The A1 universities, in particular, have been blessed with a large number of alumni who are not only devoted, but quite affluent as well. Their graduates are now located throughout the country, and indeed the world, and their recruitment of current students fully reflects this dispersion. These universities are consequently national institutions, despite historic ties in some cases with cities or regions. Their alumni dependence has a powerful influence on their priorities. Above all, they take great care to cultivate the residential undergraduate college within the research-university setting. Their research commitments must therefore be kept in balance with this overriding goal. The two most urban representatives of the Ivy League would share most of these same values, but in their pattern of voluntary support they fall with the universities of A2.

The universities located in A2 either owe their affluence to one principal source of philanthropy or else have derived it over time from numerous sources within the cities or regions where they are located. Carnegie-Mellon, Tulane, Duke, and Case Western Reserve all bear the name of their chief benefactors; while Chicago, Rochester, and Emory owe their present status to, respectively, John D. Rockefeller, George Eastman and the company he founded, and the fortunes spawned by Coca-Cola.[18] In each case the location of the university has been a crucial factor in this philanthropy. In the cases of Northwestern, Washington University, Columbia, and Penn, the special relationship with their cities has been the chief rationale for sustained voluntary support. The intended roles of these universities, then, has been to provide local centers of culture and intellectual excellence. Their fund-raising consequently tends to be focused on their locale, where it encompasses indigenous alumni, corporations, and certain prominent nonalumni—the latter two sources being particularly important for this type of university. Graduate and professional training has been an important function, with such students comprising more than 40% of enrollments in most of these universities. Chicago is an extreme in this regard, with more than three-fourths of its students in graduate and professional schools. Collegiate traditions, including big-time athletics, are sustained to varying degrees at Tulane, Northwestern, and Duke, which are somewhat less urban than the rest. All these institutions are in some sense national universities, but, in addition, their special relationships with their regional communities are significant components in their identities and sense of insitutional purpose.

The three schools located in A3—Cal Tech, M.I.T., and Johns Hopkins—belong in a class by themselves that might be called research-intensive universities. Their research efforts are so massive as to dwarf the resources directed toward their distinguished undergraduate programs. The per student value of federal research grants ranged from $13,500 at M.I.T. to $21,900 at Johns Hopkins. These schools are also rich in voluntary support, in part because corporations and foundations participate in the funding of scientific research. M.I.T. possesses one of the largest private endowments, and the tuition value of voluntary support in the two other schools exceeds $10,000. Above all, they represent an extreme in the orientation toward research that is the common denominator of all private research universities.

These twenty-four universities thus vary in the emphasis given research in the matrix of institutional purpose. The research-intensive schools stand at one pole, while Dartmouth, which resembles the leading liberal arts colleges in many respects, defines the other. However, the overriding commitment to the values of academic inquiry of each institution is its most valuable asset, on which is predicated the continued flow of both research grants and voluntary support. Alumni dependence, and hence the weight of alumni interests in institutional decision making, also varies considerably across these universities. For the half which are alumni dependent (alumni support is greater than $800 per student) this principally means maintaining a particular emphasis on undergraduate teaching and the residential college. The half of the universities that are not alumni dependent (alumni support is less than $600 per student) tend to rely on external support generated from their roles as regional research centers. This is the case with all but one of the A2 universities, including even Chicago, which plays an indisputably national role in graduate training.[19]

The one mission not emphasized among private research universities is that of service, whether it be construed as meeting the educational needs of a local population of students or fulfilling the training requirements of local employers. By recruiting widely in order to fill their limited places with the best available students, these schools seek to optimize rather than maximize their educational outputs. In doing so, they fulfill functions for which they are best suited—setting high standards for the academic community as a whole, and providing superior educational opportunities for their carefully selected students.

LIBERAL ARTS COLLEGES: HIGHER EDUCATION WITH A DIFFERENCE

Liberal arts (LA) colleges were the original organizational form for higher education in the United States, and the ideal that they represent continues to exert a powerful influence in the age of the university. The LA colleges themselves contribute irreplaceable elements of pedagogic excellence and cultural diversity to the system as a whole. The Carnegie Council in 1970 identified 572 LA colleges, which comprised more than three-quarters of all private degree-granting institutions and enrolled 26% of private sector students. In the decade since, these schools have expanded moderately at about the same pace as the private sector as a whole.[20] The occasional shuttering of one of the weaker colleges has tended to divert attention from the robust health of many others. Apparently, to paraphrase Daniel Webster's famous words, there are still those who love these little colleges.[21] Just who they might be is an important factor in the life of each.

The distinguishing feature of LA colleges is their dominant emphasis on undergraduate education. They have few or no graduate students and, except for sporadic small grants, do not participate in the federal funding of academic science (see Figure 9.1). After this short list of common characteristics, however, a chasm develops between the schools that were designated LA1 and LA2 in the Carnegie Classification. That division was made chiefly on the basis of student body quality as reflected in each college's selectivity. It can also be observed in Figure 9.2 that there are significant differences in wealth between the two categories. These objective factors indicate pervasive differences in atmosphere and orientation.

LA1 colleges have basically adapted to the age of the university by becoming "university colleges," designed to prepare a high proportion of their students for postgraduate training in university graduate or professional schools.[22] For this reason they share the same commitment to academic values that is found in research universities, but without the heavy emphasis on faculty scholarship. Although these values are seldom entirely absent in LA2 schools, they tend to be diluted by an admixture of nonintellectual values emanating from the sponsoring organization, the local community, or the vocational concerns of parents and students. With this dichotomy goes a corresponding difference in the kind of people who love these little schools sufficiently to contribute to them. Those colleges that best exemplify the university college ideal are overwhelmingly supported by their alumni, and this gives the LA1 colleges higher levels of voluntary support and higher per student expenditures. Since they are by definition more selective, this creates a general correlation between selectivity and alumni giving: The higher the median composite SAT scores for a college, the higher per student alumni contributions are likely to be. LA2 colleges typically depend on voluntary support for a nonnegligible portion of their revenue, but the amount derived from their alumni tends to fall well below the average for all colleges of 26%.

In general, LA1 and LA2 colleges share little common ground.[23] The former constitute a major tributary to the academic mainstream of American higher education. They please their alumni by recruiting able students and giving them the kind of close personal instruction that will provide the basis for further, postgraduate academic success. Their alumni respond by providing the margin of support that is necessary to maintain the quality of their programs, and often by sending their sons and daughters there as well. LA2 schools, regardless of their attraction or aversion to the academic mainstream, are perforce oriented toward external constituencies. Not only do these groups provide a needed financial cushion, but they are also likely to be their chief source of students.

There are a dozen LA1 colleges that epitomize this type in terms of affluence, the powerful loyalties of alumni, and high levels of selectivity. Ten of these LA1+ schools are rather closely bunched in the B1 area of Figure 9.2; two others—Swarthmore and Wellesley—differ from these others only in being even wealthier. Five of the twelve are women's colleges (Wellesley, Smith, Mount Holyoke, Wells, and Agnes Scott), and another four only became coeducational in recent years (Vassar, and formerly all-male Amherst, Williams, and Bowdoin). Thus, it would seem that single-sex institutions have had a special capacity for instilling a deep and lasting sense of community among classmates.[24] The three longtime coeducational colleges (Swarthmore, Oberlin, and Grinnell) seem to depend on distinctive traditions of excellence to elicit a comparable degree of loyalty.

The section of Figure 9.2 designated B2 is intended to represent the remaining LA1 colleges, but must be taken more as an ideal type than an average. Some limited generalizations can be made about this group, if accompanied by the blanked qualification that exceptions are rather numerous. Although schools like Carlton and Reed have national reputations, these LA1 colleges are far more likely to have statewide or regional recognition and drawing power. Almost all of the LA1 colleges were founded with a religious affiliation, but their commitment to keep pace with the academic mainstream produced an overwhelming trend toward secularization in the twentieth century. This has occurred even where church ties have been retained, as has been common across the Bible Belt, and also among the comparatively few Roman Catholic LA1 colleges. Perhaps ten LA1 colleges might be identified in which religious commitment plays a central and inescapable part in the educational process, but these exceptions, such as Earlham and Berea, depend heavily on nonalumni support. The voluntary support that the typical LA1 college receives is vital for its existence but does not allow the level of opulence prevailing at the LA1+ schools. The dozen schools in the latter group had per student expenditures averaging $9150, with 38% of that supplied by voluntary support. The eleven schools in B2, however, spent $6250 for each student, 22% of which came from voluntary support.

The LA2 colleges are undoubtedly the most difficult to generalize about, partly because they are the residual category for small institutions in the Carnegie Classification, and partly because there are so many of them (about 450). They might be divided into 100 Roman Catholic colleges, probably four-fifths of which are for women; a large number of Protestant colleges, running the gamut from nominally church related through Christian committed to evangelical fundamentalist;[25] 25 traditionally black four-year colleges; a few dozen struggling urban institutions; and a remainder of independent liberal arts colleges with educational aspirations more or less similar to LA1 colleges. If all these schools are, by definition, small and unselective, they are nearly all rather poor as well. But, as their representation on Figure 9.2 indicates, their poverty is generally assuaged by what is for them a significant amount of voluntary support. For this sample of schools the average per student expenditure was about $3500, and 16% of that came from voluntary support. When the individual types of LA2 colleges are considered, the different sources of this support are evident. The traditionally black colleges have long been dependent on external gifts. An unusual feature of this has been their reliance on national fund-raising sources, despite being extremely localized in terms of recruitment. Most colleges sponsored by Catholic teaching orders exist on remarkable scant resources; but they, of course, are undaunted by poverty, and also benefit from a nonmonetary subsidy from the work of the religious. Church-related colleges, and especially those that can be describes as Christian committed, often rely on existing denominational networks to contact sympathetic donors. And, evangelical Protestants have no lack of flair for fund-raising—or else Oral Roberts University would not be one of the growth industries of Tulsa. The support of the faithful for these schools has allowed them to keep tuition low, and in some cases to begin building a significant endowment.

A number of LA2 colleges could be found in the borderline territory between B2 and B3 of Figure 9.2, but few of them are pure liberal arts colleges, and the odds are greatly against any of them rising to LA1 status. To do so would require simultaneously becoming more affluent and more selective, a difficult feat for tuition-dependent institutions. Movement in recent years has tended to be away from the ideal of a liberal arts college. LA2 colleges wishing to sustain or enhance their drawing power have had little choice but to pursue a greater vocational or service orientation. Many of them now might better be described, somewhat illogically, as small comprehensive colleges.[26]

The broad spectrum of liberal arts colleges offers a bewildering variety of alternatives for undergraduate education. The LA1 colleges, above all, offer a different way to navigate the academic mainstream. They provide a more intimate and supportive instructional environment than do large universities, as well as the choice of myriad cultural overtones. Cultural pluralism is even more important in the case of LA2 colleges with religious commitments. They more or less reconcile higher education with the great diversity of religious conviction across American society. Only among those institutions that have become, in effect, small comprehensive colleges is it difficult to perceive a distinctive role. But despite this partial exception, there can be little doubt that the private liberal arts colleges do more than any other type of institution to provide students with a choice of different styles of undergraduate education.

SERVING THE MULTITUDES: THE LARGE URBAN PRIVATE UNIVERSITIES

Urban private universities are not readily recognized as a distinct category in the United States, but elsewhere this has been a recurrent institutional type. In those European countries where major universities had not been located in urban centers the initiative of local civic boosters made higher education available. The English civic universities are probably the best-known example of this phenomenon, but the same process occurred in Amsterdam, Stockholm, and Gothenburg. In the United States before 1960 state legislators had a decided bucolic bias in the placement of colleges. Only two of the flagship state universities, Minnesota and Washington, were placed in the principal population center of their state. Thus, the original development of urban higher education largely took place under private auspices. In some cases small, originally sectarian colleges grew large with their cities; in others, universities were started from scratch to meet the needs of the population, even though those needs were rather limited until the postwar era. The universities that were fortunate enough to accumulate large endowments, it was seen above, became research universities; but the rest quite naturally assumed a service orientation. This meant the ready incorporation of vocational programs and a tendency to be inclusive rather than exclusive in student admissions. This makes the mission of these universities closer to that of the public sector than any of the types previously discussed.

For the European counterparts of these urban universities, this "publicness" of function ultimately spelled the end of private control. The English civic universities, although still juridically independent, are funded and effectively controlled by the state; and other city universities were simply transformed into state institutions. This same process occurred in the United States as well, but in a rather selective manner. Private universities in Houston, Kansas City, Buffalo, Pittsburgh, and Philadelphia (Temple) went from private to state control during the 1960s. Given the absence of any compelling rationale for independence in these cases, joining the public sector promised rapid growth, improved facilities, higher salaries across the board, and an end (at least, so it seemed then) to chronic financial difficulties.[27] Where there was a viable rationale for independence stemming from either religious ties or a strong research tradition, no such transitions occurred. The rather late development of the state system of higher education in Ohio exemplifies this crucial distinction. Where it was feasible, municiple (Cincinnati, Akron, Toledo) or private (Youngstown) universities were incorporated into the state system, but in those cities with strong private institutions (Dayton, Cleveland) new state universities were founded. The momentum of conversions in the 1960s made it appear to Christopher Jencks and David Riesman that this would be the fate of most large urban privates in the United States.[28] This has not happened, however, even though there are still some willing to trade independence for greater financial security. How have these institutions been able to survive the vast expansion of the public sector within their domains? It has not been easy, but by utilizing every advantage available to them all have survived, and a few have even prospered, through the decade of the 1970s.

The distribution of urban privates in Figure 9.2 lies in an unusual semicircle, which looks like a curved horn because of the logarithmic scale. The wealthiest institutions (C1 and C2: tuition values = $700–$1200) derive relatively little from their alumni; the middle groups (C3 and C4: tuition value = $200–$500) have in the aggregate an average alumni dependency; and the poorest (C5) have little voluntary support from any source. The difference in alumni dependence between the first and second groups turns out in most cases to correspond with emphases on graduate versus undergraduate programs. Some of the Catholic universities were depicted separately (C2 and C3) because they are such a large and important component of urban higher education, and because they have the most clearly defined target population. Yet, on the basis of this data, they differed between themselves and tended to cluster with corresponding types of nonsectarian universities. This in itself may be corroboration that Catholic universities merged with the broader stream of American higher education during the 1960s.[29]

The universities in C1 and C2 are to varying degrees what might be called graduate service universities. Their undergraduate colleges are fairly large, but the overall size is limited by a moderate degree of selectivity. Median composite SAT scores are typically in the 1000–1100 range, and about two of three applicants are admitted. Their graduate enrollments, however, tend to be disproportionately large and concentrated in professional schools. Besides the elite professional schools of medicine and law, they have a proliferation of additional professional schools like business, public administration, education, and social work. The prototype of the graduate service university would have to be New York University. Its graduate enrollment of 21,000 is not only the largest in the country, but is double the number of full-time undergraduates. The undergraduate colleges of these universities draw some students from beyond the metropolitan area, but the nonelite professional schools predominantly serve the local population, many of whom are part-time and evening students. Graduate service courses have been an important area of growth for all types of urban universities during the past decade. The graduate service universities have been quick to perceive and respond to these types of needs. Perhaps the prestige of their elite professional schools has enhanced the attractiveness of their other offerings, and thus given them an edge over less costly public sector competitors. Students of professional schools, of course, are unlikely to become alumni contributors, but the services these universities perform for the surrounding community are usually recognized financially by local philanthropists and area corporations.

There are considerable similarities between the graduate service universities and those located in C3 and C4.[30] Both the level of selectivity and the absolute amount of per student alumni support is approximaetly the same. This suggests that there is considerable similarity among the undergraduate colleges of all these institutions. Most likely these middle-range service universities have reputations for having some qualitative advantage over their more inclusive public competitors. These universities emphasize graduate service programs to varying degrees. Both the University of Detroit and Fordham have more than 30% graduate students, but without the level of research funding of Boston University and George Washington. The chief difference, then, between these universities and the graduate service type would seem to be the latter's greater involvement in research and ability to attract considerably more external support.

The dozen institutions located in C5 represent the extreme of tuition dependence in the private sector and a corresponding emphasis on fulfilling unmet consumer demand for higher education within their localities.[31] They consequently tend to be characterized by a broad range of vocational programs and a relatively large proportion of part-time undergraduates. Since the margin of quality between these pure service universities and their public counterparts is small or nonexistent, they have to be both pragmatic and flexible to maintain a numerous clientele. This results in some novel programs, unorthodox scheduling, heavy advertising, and in some cases the proliferation of campuses or extension centers in order to remain close to the customers. This profile fits some of these institutions better than others. The three Catholic universities, Hofstra, and American University have undergraduate colleges much like the other urban universities; however, the remaining nonselective institutions (median composite SAT is less than 900) are almost all heavily part-time. These tuition-dependent universities are in many respects the antipode of the American collegiate ideal embodied in the alumni-dependent institutions. The very precariousness of their finances makes them responsive to a broad range of semiacademic public demands, to which they can often react more quickly than public institutions. In doing so, they extend access to higher education to many who are uninterested in or unsuited for the academic mainstream, or whose circumstances preclude regular attendance. Thus, they are also a fecund source of innovation—not the type, to be sure, likely to please academic purists, but innovations which will succeed or fail by the test of the marketplace. The twelve institutions of C5 by themselves constitute almost 9% of enrollments in the private sector. There can be little doubt that even these, the most unloved of private schools in terms of voluntary support, make an important contribution toward fulfilling unmet educational needs in our urban areas.

DIVERSITY AND PRIVATE HIGHER EDUCATION

The three basic types and eleven subgroups of private colleges and universities that have been defined here still do not provide a comprehensive account of the many forms and purposes of private higher education. Further analysis might consider, for example, the roles of midsize comprehensive universities in the 3000–6000 enrollment range; of the private engineering "techs"; or of the junior colleges in the private sector. There is no reason to doubt, however, that the same techniques would serve to discern the constituencies to which these institutions are most responsive. The particular groupings of institutions examined here were meant, above all, to establish some fixed types within the continuum of private higher education. Knowing the functions and orientations of these schools creates an implicit framework into which any other private institution may be integrated. Beyond this taxonomic end, however, the deeper importance of this form of analysis lies in the connection it establishes through patterns of voluntary support, between the purposes of private higher education and underlying causes for the existence or persistence of private control.

There are a great many fundamental similarities running across American colleges and universities, public and private. Much of the curriculum is virtually identical; most schools have adopted the convention of recording student progress in terms of credit hours; and it would be difficult to discern significant differences between the twenty private basketball teams competing in the 1984 NCAA Tournament and their thirty-three public counterparts. Nevertheless, the single most crucial difference between public and private schools is that the latter must raise a substantially larger portion of their income from private sources. Three archetypical strategies have been identified for doing this.

Research universities are oriented, above all, to the advancement of knowledge, and this commitment is reflected in the voluntary support that sustains their position. Gifts from philanthropists, foundations, and corporations tend to be related primarily to their research roles, and appeals to alumni are often also couched in these terms. Tuition-dependent institutions are forced to make a continuous effort in the educational marketplace to maintain enrollments. The quid pro quo relationship between tuition and instruction is best examplified by their numerous part-time clientele. What little voluntary support these schools receive is usually designed to buttress instructional programs. The liberal arts colleges, at least in their pure form, operate in a different sort of market—one involving a four-year commitment to the formative influence of a distinctive cultural milieu. Success in this endeavor requires more than attracting the requisite number of students; it requires creating the loyalties that will result in continuing moral and financial support for the ends of the school.

Probably most institutions in the private sector simultaneously pursue more than one of these strategies in order to attain an optimal level and mix of resources (student enrollments, research funds, voluntary support) for their particular circumstances. As they do so, each school is encouraged in those area where it meets success and discouraged where it fails. In this manner the continual search for private resources shapes the existence of private colleges and universities. The unique relationship that each independently acting institution develops with student clienteles and donor constituencies ultimately determines its distinctive character. The perpetual quest for resources, then, is the true wellspring of diversity in American higher education.

The public sector, by the same token, contains far less diversity despite its greater size. This would be due to its essential charter to fulfill majoritarian needs and, more specifically, because its financial sustenance is largely assured by its public support. Pointing this out should in no way belittle the many accomplishments of public higher education, but rather simply indicate its relative shortcomings on this single dimension. However, even if the roots of diversity are traced to private sources of support, this issue can by no means be separated from the realm of public policy.

The existence of the private sector today is critically dependent on the actions of government. The research of the research universities is largely supported by federal funds; the tuition bill for the private sector could not be paid without public student financial aid; and even the generosity of the sector's numerous benefactors is powerfully affected by the federal tax code. While these important issues lie beyond the scope of this chapter, it is worth pointing out that the diversity of the American private sector has been sustained by the manner in which each of these policies has evolved. The pattern of federal science funding that emerged after World War II relied on investigator-initiated project grants evaluated through the process of peer review. This placed every institution on an equal basis in the competition for research funds, while at the same time putting the judging of projects outside of government in the academic disciplines. Federal subsidization of higher education was ultimately handled in an analagous way: Aid was diverted through the students, thereby preserving the existing competitive structure of the higher-education market. And federal tax policies have been quite lenient in protecting donor choice. These are public policies that cannot be taken for granted, but rather must periodically be defended anew. Moreover, there are sound reasons for seeking to preserve the diversity that currently exists in the private sector.

In *Maintaining Diversity in Higher Education,* Robert Birnbaum has approached his topic from the perspective of population ecology, where the advantages of diversity are readily apparent.[32] In the continual competition for resources, institutions will find secure niches that best reflect their own capacities and the demands of those they serve. The likely outcomes of these competitive pressures cannot be easily summarized. Environmental conditions might encourage some institutions to specialize their roles, while others might be drawn toward more general missions. Some institutions will feel the need to innovate continually in response to the needs of their clientele, while others will emphasize stability of purpose that suits the ongoing preferences of their traditional constituencies. Whichever is the case, diversity possesses important benefits for the higher-education system and for the society it serves. A broad variety of institutional types will hold the "solution" to a great many potential problems. As new needs arise or, more likely, increase in magnitude, those institutions, that already possess the capacity for meeting them will provide models for other willing innovators. Diversity in this way enhances the adaptability of the system as a whole, and ipso facto the responsiveness of the system to society's needs.

This chapter has argued that of all the resources required to sustain an institution of higher education, the pattern of private philanthropy provides a signature that is generally indicative of who an institution serves and how. Furthermore, the importance of this support at the margin far outweighs its actual proportion of private sector income. Voluntary support not only plays a vital role in sustaining diversity in American higher education, but also functions as an active force creating that diversity. This giving may originate with a relatively small and atypical portion of society, but in fact there is subtle interaction between idiosyncratic gifts and social needs: Unless these giving choices are validated and endorsed by the choices of students and faculty, they can have little impact. Clearly the impact of voluntary support on American higher education *is* substantial. In particular it has assisted the fulfillment of minority aspirations for *more, different,*or *better* education than that made available by state and local government. By thus enhancing the diversity of American higher education, the voluntary support of private colleges and universities has served, and continues to serve, a much larger public purpose of enhancing individual choice within a pluralist society.

NOTES

1. National Center for Education Statistics, *Digest of Education Statistics, 1981* (Washington, D.C.: GPO, 1981), p. 89.

2. The following examples, except where indicated, are elaborated more thoroughly in Roger L. Geiger, *Private Sectors in Higher Education: Structure, Function and Change in Eight Countries* (Ann Arbor: University of Michigan, 1986).

3. Daniel C. Levy, *Higher Education and the State in Latin America: Private Challenges to Public Dominance* (Chicago: University of Chicago Press, 1986).

4. Burton Weisbrod, "Toward a Theory of Voluntary Nonprofit Sectors in a Three-Sector Economy," in E. Phelps, ed., *Altruism, Morality and Economic Theory* (New York: Russell Sage Foundation, 1975).

5. See, Roger L. Geiger, *To Advance Knowledge: The Growth of American Research Universities in the Twentieth Century, 1900–1940* (New York: Oxford University Press, 1986).

6. Educational and general expenditures for the public and private sectors were, respectively, $4378 versus $5965, compared with total expenditures including hospitals and independend and auxiliary operations of $5372 versus $8210: *Digest of Ed. Stat., 1981,* p. 149.

7. A year's tuition at a four-year institution averaged for 1983–84 $4627 at a private school versus $1105 at a public one: *Chronicle of Higher Education* 26, 23 (Aug. 3, 1983), p. 5.

8. National Institute of Independent Colleges and Universities, "The Impact of the President's Budget Proposals upon Students Attending Independent Colleges and Universities," (March 1982). On the importance of federal student aid, see Geiger, *Private Sectors;* Chester Finn, "Federal Patronage of Universities in the United States: A Rose by Many Other Names?" *Minerva* 14, 4 (Winter 1976–77), pp. 496–529; Michael S. McPherson, "The Demand for Higher Education," in David W. Breneman and Chester E. Finn, Jr., eds., *Public Policy and Private Higher Education* (Washington, D.C.: The Brookings Institution, 1978), pp. 143–196.

9. National Science Foundation, *Federal Funds for Research and Development, 1980* (Washington, D.C.: GPO, 1981), pp. 24–25.

10. See Carnegie Council on Policy Studies in Higher Education, *A Classification of Institutions of Higher Education,* rev. ed., (Berkeley: Carnegie Foundation for the Advancement of Teaching, 1976). The material which follows is based on an analysis of financial and enrollment data for selected representative research universities, liberal arts colleges, and urban universities. Because of the marked asymmetry of these three categories, different methods of selection were employed for each. For private research universities, only 24 institutions met the criteria, and all were examined. Among liberal arts 1 colleges (Carnegie Classification), the wealthiest dozen according to per student voluntary support were analyzed, and nine others which in some way approach this dozen have also been mentioned. A group of eleven other LA1 colleges was selected to represent the remainder. Eight colleges were selected to represent the hundreds of LA2 colleges. Since *large* and *urban* are relative concepts, the 28 large urban private universities examined represent the largest urban or urban-Catholic institutions for which data was available. All 102 institutions analyzed have been identified in the text or notes, but not all of them were incorporated into Figures 9.1 and 9.2.

11. Council for Financial aid to Education, *Voluntary Support of Education, 1979–80* (New York: CFAE, 1981). All further data on voluntary support will be from this source.

12. Edward Shils, "The American Private University," *Minerva* 11, 1 (Jan. 1973), pp. 6–29.

13. The Carnegie Classification (see note 12) identifies ninety-eight research 1 and 2 universities, including Rockefeller University, an independent medical school not included in this study.

14. Jencks and Riesman, *Academic Revolution,* pp. 12–27.

15. These ten are the four Ivies of A1, the three research-intensive universities of A3, and Rice, Stanford, and Swarthmore (the most affluent of the LA1 +). Bryn Mawr and Haverford have a similar level of selectivity with considerably lower tuition value.

16. David S. Webster, "America' Highest Ranked Graduate Schools, 1925–1982," *Change* (May–June 1983), pp. 14–24.

17. The outlying six—Brown, Cornell, Brandeis, Rice, Stanford, and Vanderbilt—show distinctive combinations of the variables producing these three clusters. See Geiger, *Private Sectors*.

18. See especially Merle Curti and Roderick Nash, *Philanthropy in the Shaping of American Higher Education* (New Brunswick, N.J.: Rutgers University Press, 1965).

19. Of the A2 universities, only Case Western Reserve received more than $600 per student in alumni contributions.

20. W. John Minter and Howard R. Bowen, *Independent Higher Education, 1980* (Washington, D.C.: National Institute of Independent Colleges and Universities, 1980).

21. In arguing the Dartmouth College Case in 1818, Webster is reputed to have brought tears to the judge's eyes by saying, "It is, sir, as I have said, a small college, and yet there are those who love it."

22. Jencks and Riesman, *Academic Revolution*, pp. 20–27.

23. The same conclusion reached by Alexander Astin and Calvin Lee in their comparison of "invisible colleges" with a sample of elite liberal arts colleges: *The Invisible Colleges: a Profile of Small, Private Colleges with Limited Resources* (New York: McGraw-Hill, 1972).

24. Alexander Astin found that "Single-sex colleges show a pattern of effects on *both* sexes that is almost uniformly positive": *Four Critical Years* (San Francisco: Jossey-Bass, 1977), p. 246.

25. Jencks and Riesman, *Academic Revolution*, pp. 312–333; David Riesman, "The Evangelical Colleges: Untouched by the Academic Revolution," *Change* (Jan.–Feb. 1981), pp. 13–20; and C. Robert Pace, *Education and Evangelism* (New York: McGraw-Hill, 1972).

26. Allen O. Pfnister, "Survival and Revival: the Transformation of the American Arts College," University of Denver, Occasional Papers in Higher Education, No. 15 (Sept. 1981); and Larry Leslie, Arthur Grant, and Kenneth Brown, "Patterns of Enrollment in Higher Education, 1965–77: Liberal Arts Colleges," University of Arizona Center for the Study of Higher Education, Topical Paper No. 19 (Jan. 1981).

27. See the case of the University of Buffalo: Harold L Hodgkinson, *Institutions in Transition* (New York: McGraw-Hill, 1971), pp. 160–171.

28. Jencks and Riesman, *Academic Revolution*, p. 289.

29. Andrew M. Greeley, *From Backwater to Mainstream: A Profile of Catholic Higher Education* (New York: McGraw-Hill, 1969), pp. 15–17; Jencks and Riesman, *Academic Revolution*, pp. 398–405.

30. C3 consists of, Boston University, George Washington, Drexell, and Syracuse; C4 is Boston College, Villanova, Marquette, Fordham, and the universities of Detroit and San Francisco.

31. In C5 are Adelphi, American University, Bridgeport, Fairleigh Dickinson, Hofstra, Long Island University, Pace, Seton Hall, Northeastern, and the Catholic Dayton, DePaul, and St. John's University.

32. Robert Birnbaum, *Maintaining Diversity in Higher Education* (San Francisco: Jossey-Bass, 1983), pp. 1–37.

10

Cross-Subsidization in Higher Education: Does it Pervert Private Choice and Public Policy?*

ESTELLE JAMES

During the 1950s and 1960s American higher education underwent a major change in size and structure, with a vast expansion in enrollments and increased emphasis on graduate training and research, relative to undergraduate teaching. This chapter explores the implications of this changing product mix for our understanding of costs, subsidies, financing methods, and decision-making structures in higher education. We ask the following questions:

1. How did universities finance their production of graduate training and research (G and R), which usually do not bring in enough revenues to cover their costs?
2. What differences, if any, were there in the behavior of public and private universities regarding the shift toward G and R?
3. How did this change in product mix affect relative costs in universities versus two- and four-year colleges, which still specialize in undergraduate teaching?
4. What are the implications of this analysis for our understanding of the costs and benefits of education and for future public policy? For example, to what degree do state legislators and private donors control the product mix in higher education and who ultimately gains from the resources they provide?

*This chapter is adapted, but very substantially revised, from an earlier paper, "Product Mix and Cost Disaggregation: A Reinterpretation of the Economics of Higher Education," *Journal of Human Resources* XIII (Spring 1978), pp. 157–186. More details about the empirical work may be found in that study. Related issues are discussed in E. James, "How Nonprofits Grow: A Model," *Journal of Policy Analysis and Management* 2 (1983), pp. 350–366; and Estelle James and Egon Neuberger, "The University Department as a Non-Profit Labor Cooperative," *Public Choice*, 36 (1981), pp. 585–612. The original paper on cost disaggregation grew out of a project supported by the National Science Foundation. Subsequent parts of this project were supported by the Program on Non-profit Organizations, Yale University; the Exxon Education Foundation; and the National Endowment for the Humanities.

Specifically, I characterize universities as multiproduct nonprofit organizations (NPOs) engaging in the teaching of undergraduates as a profitable activity, in order to subsidize graduate training and research, which are loss-making but yield direct utility to them. Cross-subsidization by NPOs, then, is an alternative to direct government funding of socially beneficial goods such as research, under certain circumstances. With certain differences that we shall note, this characterization applies to public and private institutions, and the term *NPO* is used for both in this chapter. At private universities, during the 1950s and 1960s, profits were generated mainly by huge tuition increases, made possible by rapidly rising demand, as we shall see below. State universities, too, engaged in cross-subsidization to finance G and R. However, since state universities often do not control or retain tuition revenue, their main device was a decrease in teaching cost per student. Thus, subsidy per (undergraduate) student fell more in the private sector, cost per student fell more in the public sector, but G and R rose disproportionately in both.

This paper argues that when we take account of product mix changes and disaggregate resource use accordingly, we obtain a different picture of relative costs, productivity, and redistribution effects of higher education, with undergraduate costs lower, productivity rising faster, and subsidies far less than has hitherto been depicted. Moreover, we are reminded that external actors, such as state legislators and private donors, have only limited influence over the behavior of universities, because of the substantial opportunities for reallocation and cross-subsidization by internal actors in these educational institutions. In these important respects, public and private universities have more in common with each other than with pure undergraduate institutions (two- and four-year colleges) in their own sectors.

THE MODEL

Before presenting my empirical analysis of product mix, costs, and subsidies, I set forth a behavioral model of the multiproduct NPO. The organization has a utility function, which it wishes to maximize, into which its various activities enter as arguments. Technology is not fixed, in the cost function, as in most economic models. Instead, it enters into the utility function as a choice variable; this may be particularly true of educational and cultural NPOs. The organization also faces a constraint, which says that overall expenditures must equal revenue. However, this constraint need not apply to each product taken separately. Indeed, it turns out that such organizations may be expected to carry out profitable "production" activities that do not yield utility per se, in order to derive revenue they can then spend on the "consumption" of loss-making, utility-maximizing activities; the former in effect subsidize the latter. A mathematical formulation of this model is presented in the Appendix.

Suppose, now, we assume that research and graduate training are viewed as "preferred" activities by the (faculty) decision makers at universities, and expensive small classes are either required or strongly preferred for G. Undergraduate teaching (U) may also enter into the objective function (with a positive or negative sign), but the faculty are assumed to care less about the teaching technology used—that is, professors are prepared to tolerate large undergraduate courses. Then we would expect (and the data confirm) that subsidies (i.e., real cost minus tuition revenue) per student will be higher for G than for U and will be greater for U at colleges than at universities. Moreover, if the demand for graduate training increases and R becomes more prestigious, then (other things remaining equal) we would expect the subsidy for U to decline, indeed, to become negative, as G and R rise. Thus, through the 1950s and 1960s undergraduate teaching was increasingly viewed as a profitable "production" activity by universities; G and R as loss-making "consumption" activities made financially feasible by the cross-subsidy from U; and the disparity between colleges and universities with respect to their costs of and subsidies to U rose dramatically.

The analysis which follows also helps to explain why technologies differ across institution types, why colleges have survived very well without G while graduate institutions are rarely found without U, and why institutions of higher education have been so impervious to labor-saving technological change. Significantly, all these generalizations apply both to private and state institutions. To simplify our model, we assume that the faculty decision makers in both sectors are drawn from the same background and groups, have similar objective functions, and, therefore, behave in very similar ways regarding their preferred product mix and their willingness to use cross-subsidization to achieve it.

MEASUREMENT OF INPUTS AND OUTPUTS

In order to investigate empirically resource allocations within colleges and universities, we need first to define and measure inputs and outputs. For reasons given below, this task turns out to be far from simple.

As for outputs, we are concerned here with three products: research (adding to the stock of knowledge), undergraduate teaching (adding value to the student raw material by embodying in them the results of previous research), and graduate research (teaching others how to do research). Ideally, we would like some index of quality as well as quantity of these outputs (e.g., the increased learning or earning potential imparted by different instructional techniques), but these data are generally not available. As a result, teaching output is measured here (and in most other studies cited in this chapter) simply in terms of student credit hours (SCH) and full-time equivalent students at various levels (FTEU or FTEG), abstracting from the quality dimension. The situation is even worse with respect to research, where we do not even have a crude quantity index. Therefore, quantification of research or research productivity directly has not been attempted here and we simply assume that output is some positive but unknown function of inputs.

Similarly, in our measurement of inputs and their allocation, difficult problems quickly appear: the practical cost-accounting problem and the conceptual joint supply problem. When joint supply prevails, the cost of producing one good depends on whether we are producing the other good and, if so, in what quantity; the production functions are nonseparable. In other words, if one argues that teaching and research can be produced more cheaply together than separately, this implies that (within limits) it is conceptually invalid to speak of allocating resources between them. Separate costs and profits cannot be calculated and cross-subsidization cannot be discussed.[1] I abstract from this problem by assuming that undergraduate teaching is, indeed, separable from G and R. For expositional convenience I also treat research and graduate training as separable; however, this assumption is not crucial to the conclusions presented below. Since good graduate education is rarely found without research and we do not offer an alternative explanation for this fact, the reader may prefer to think of research plus graduate education as joint products with combined benefits and costs.

The cost-accounting problem arises because of budgeting procedures at colleges and universities. The largest budget category, "instruction and departmental research" (I and DR), which covers most faculty and other allocations to academic departments, is used for a combination of teaching and research purposes. While breakdowns by discipline are known, their allocation among U, G, and R are usually not given ex ante nor recorded ex post. Even less is known about the division among U, G, and R of other major budget categories such as general administration, libraries, plant maintenance, or the flow of services from capital resources. I solve this problem by drawing on a variety of studies of the allocations of faculty time, and arguing that this may be viewed a proxy for other higher-educational resources. Strictly speaking, this can be done if and only if the ratio of faculty to other (nonearmarked) factors of production is the same for research and teaching—obviously a strong assumption. I make it, largely for pragmatic reasons, in the absence of better information, but it is worth noting that biases appear to be working in both directions, at least partially offsetting each other.[2]

ALLOCATION OF FACULTY TIME TO RESEARCH AND TEACHING

Usually the assumption has been made that faculty time and other higher-educational resources are primarily an instructional expense. However, this chapter argues that a large and growing share of these resources, particularly at universities, are in fact used for research. As evidence pointing in this direction, Table 10.1 presents a variety of data, from different institutions and time periods, on the allocation of faculty time.

Table 10.1 Percent Allocation of Faculty Time

	LU	AU	U=LU+AU	G	T=U+G	R	G+R	A+O	T/R	(G+R)/U
1953–54										
Berkeley	23.9	25.8	49.7	19.1	68.8	18.7	37.8	12.5	3.5/1	.8/1
UCLA	27.8	28.8	56.6	14.0	70.6	14.0	28.0	15.4	5/1	.5/1
Cal. State Coll.	46.0	44.2	90.2	4.2	94.4	—	4.2	5.6	—	—
Cal. Jr. Coll.	96.0	—	96.0	—	96.0	—	—	4.0	—	—
Avg. 11 Western & Midwestern univ.	29.9	23.2	53.1	11.9	65.0	12.0	21.9	23.0	5.5/1	.4/1
1964–65										
Butter—12 univ.	—	—	20.0	26.0	46.0	33.0	59.0	21.0	1.4/1	3.0/1
Cartter—106 univ.	—	—	23.0	24.0	47.0	24.0	48.0	29.0	2/1	2.1/1
Parsons and Platt—3 res.-oriented univ.			29.0	18.0	47.0	32.0	50.0	29.0	1.5/1	1.7/1
1968–69										
UCLA	5.4	12.7	18.1	25.4	43.5	27.5	52.9	29.0	1.6/1	3.0/1
1975										
Eastern state univ.	—	—	—	—	48.0	29.0	—	23.0	1.6/1	—

KEY: LU=lower-division undergraduate; AU=upper-division undergraduate; U=LU+AU; G=graduate; T=teaching; R=research; A=administration; 0=other.

SOURCES: Rows 1–4: California State Department of Education, *A Restudy of the Needs of California in Higher Education* (Sacramento: 1955), p. 438. Rows 3 & 4: average of data for 3 largest colleges and jr. colleges. Row 5: *California and Western Conference Cost and Statistical Study for 1954–55* (Berkeley: University of California Printing Department, 1960), pp. 26–29. Row 6: Irene Butter, *Economics of Graduate Education: An Exploratory Study* (Washington, D.C.: U.S. Department of Health, Education and Welfare, 1966), average of 12 universities in four disciplines (physics, zoology, sociology, English). Row 7: Allan Cartter, *An Assessment of Quality in Graduate Eduation* (Washington, D.C.: American Council on Education, 1966), average of 106 universities. I have selected the same disciplines that Butter uses. Cartter's sample gave heavy weight to dept. chairmen and, therefore, to A rather than R. Row 8: Talcott Parsons and Gerald Platt. "Considerations on the American Academic System," *Minerva* 6 (Summer 1968), p. 519. Row 9: Colin Bell, Helen Brownlee, and Alexander Mood, "Allocation of a University's Resources to Instruction," in *Papers on Efficiency in the Management of Higher Education* (New York: Carnegie Commission on Higher Education, 1972), pp. 64, 70. Row 10: unpublished data for an eastern state university obtained by the author.

Professors typically resent inquiries about how they spend their time and may (deliberately or accidentally) distort their views. Nevertheless, certain obvious generalizations about the use of faculty time emerge from Table 10.1:

1. By no means can we consider the university as exclusively, or even primarily, a teaching institution: In recent years barely half of its faculty resources have been devoted to undergraduate and graduate teaching. In contrast, two- and four-year colleges use their faculty almost exclusively for undergraduate education. Obviously, the social choice between supporting universities and colleges is a choice about desired product mix, particularly undergraduate education versus graduate education and research.
2. The allocation of faculty resources among higher-education products has not been invariant to time. On the one hand, two-year colleges (overwhelmingly public) have been the most rapidly growing institution type, thereby raising the undergraduate/graduate and teaching/research input mix overall. On the other hand, within universities we have seen a resource shift away from undergraduate education and toward graduate education and research, a shift toward institutional specialization with which we are particularly concerned in this chapter. Specifically, in 1953–54, the teaching/research mix at major western and midwestern universities was 5/1, but by the late 1960s it had dropped to 2/1, or even less. Whereas undergraduate instruction accounted for over half of all faculty time in 1953, its share was only 20–25% by 1967, in many cases surpassed by graduate instruction, which was moving rapidly in the opposite direction.[3] As a result, graduate education and research now dominate the university.
3. We may use the weekly teaching load as a proxy for the teaching/research mix, since a high teaching load leaves little time for research and, conversely, a low teaching load implies substantial opportunity and pressure for research. The teaching load has consistently been higher at colleges than at universities. In 1954 major universities reported an average teaching load of more than sixteen hours per week; by 1963 this figure had dropped to eight. While both sets of numbers may be overstated, the direction and magnitude of change is consistent with and helps to confirm the rising research/teaching mix at universities, noted above.[4] The large increase in numbers of academic journals and article submissions over the past two decades is further evidence of this phenomenon.

Thus, if we use faculty time allocations as an index of total resource allocation from I & DR and other budget categories, and we think of research and teaching as the only two final products of colleges and universities toward which all faculty time and other inputs (including administration) are ultimately directed, it is probably not unreasonable to estimate that in 1953–54 approximately 20% of nonearmarked university resources were spent on research, and this ratio had grown to 40% by 1966–67. Recognizing that these figures are not as firmly based as I would like, I have also done a similar analysis, using 15% and 30%, and find that the cost configurations and policy conclusions are not very different from those presented below.

UNDERGRADUATE COSTS AND PRODUCTIVITY

The falling teaching/research mix at universities and the increased specialization by institution type has immediate implications for evaluation of undergraduate costs, productivity, and rates of return, which I now proceed to explore. I concentrate on the years 1953–67, for three reasons: Major changes were taking place in the structure and activities of American higher education, which is exactly what we want to examine; faculty time allocation surveys are available, as already noted; and a good study of aggregate costs has already been carried out, upon which we can draw.[5]

Between 1953–54 and 1966–67, undergraduate enrollments at universities rose 235%, while graduate enrollments trebled. At the same time, current plus capital costs at universities rose 250% in real terms. Thus, overall resources were rising approximately as fast as enrollments but, as we know from the faculty time surveys, their allocation, and the resulting configuration of relative costs, altered radically over this period. The results are discussed in this and the following section.[6]

Table 10.2 presents figures from a major large-scale intertemporal analysis of higher-educational costs by June O'Neill, which includes I & DR as well as other current and capital inputs. While O'Neill does not disaggregate resources by level of instruction, she draws on other studies to infer a 3/1 graduate/undergraduate cost ratio and 1.5/1 upper-division/lower-division (AU/LU) cost ratio, and she weights student credit hours at each level accordingly to derive an "adjusted" cost per lower-division student credit hour.[7] This appears to be a conservative estimate of the relative cost of graduate teaching; a higher and rising ratio, which some evidence supports, would strengthen the points made in the present chapter.

O'Neill treats almost all nonearmarked expenses as instructional, thereby failing to take account of research funded through the academic departments and, I would argue, overestimating the teaching input. I have adjusted her data under the presumption developed above, that 20% of these resources were used for noninstructional purposes, primarily research, in 1953–54, and 40% were so used in 1966–67 at universities. A 5% adjustment is made for four-year colleges, while two-year colleges are viewed as pure teaching institutions. Our question then is, if these presumptions about resource allocation are (approximately) correct, how does that affect our picture of costs, productivity, and rates of return in higher education?

First of all we obviously obtain a lower social cost for undergraduate education that has hitherto been depicted. In 1966–67, these combined adjustments reduce the cost per LU to less than half the unadjusted values at both public and private universities. Consequently, the social rate of return to undergraduate education has been underestimated, particularly for the more recent years, and that to graduate education has been overestimated, in studies which have simply divided total IHL expenditures by total numbers of students to derive an average cost figure.

Second, in contrast to the "conventional wisdom," it appears that un-

Table 10.2 Average Cost Per FTELU

Year	Public			Private		
	University	Four-Year College	Two-Year College	University	Four-Year College	Two-Year College
Unadjusted for G and AU						
1953–54	991			1042		
1966–67	1481			1691		
Net Change	+490			+649		
Adjusted for G and AU						
1953–54	672	652	554	655	650	700
1966–67	972	902	874	1235	1137	1126
Net Change	+300	+250	+320	+580	+487	+426
Adjusted for G, AU, and R (Current $s)						
1953–54	538	620	555	524	617	700
1966–67	583	857	874	741	1080	1126
Net Change	+45	+237	+319	+217	+463	+426
Adjusted for G, AU, and R (Constant $)						
1953–54	629	724	647	611	721	818
1966–67	425	623	636	539	787	821
Net Change	−204	−101	−11	−72	+66	+3

SOURCE: First two panels are from June O'Neill, *Resource Use in Higher Education* (New York: Carnegie Commission on Higher Education, 1971), pp. 99–101. Instructional costs per full-time student are obtained by multiplying her costs per SCH by 28, the student credit hours taken by an average full-time student per year. To obtain "adjusted" AU & G costs, multiply LU costs by 1.5 and 3.75, respectively, as O'Neill did, based on relative cost estimates. Last two panels are my own calculations, based on the assumption that research allocations were 20% in 1953–54, 40% in 1966–67 at universities, 5% in both periods at four-year colleges, and 0 at two-year colleges.

dergraduate education does not cost society more at the university than at the community college. On the contrary, introductory instruction is much less faculty intensive at the university, where large lecture classes with cheaper supporting staff (e.g., graduate assistants) predominate, yielding lower costs per full-time student. This finding has important implications for the subsidy analysis presented in the next section. Moreover, if average costs are taken as an approximation of marginal costs, a shift of undergraduate teaching from universities to community colleges, holding graduate teaching and research constant, would not reduce total costs in the higher-educational sector.

Finally, a failure to adjust for research understates the "gain" in educational "productivity" between 1953–54 and 1966–67. Education is frequently cited as a labor-intensive industry whose productivity is bound to lag behind that of the economy as a whole.[8] However, when these adjustments for product mix are made, it turns out that real costs have declined substantially in universities over this period. That is, resources were increasingly diverted from teaching to research, thereby producing lower real undergraduate instructional costs and higher instructional productivity. In two- and four-year colleges, on the other hand, productivity is unaffected by these calculations and remains lower than at the university, by an ever increasing amount.

The results, of course, raise serious questions about the meaning and measurement of "productivity" in higher education. What is the social value of the new product mix? If society places a relatively high value on graduate education and research, the new aggregate output/input ratio will be correspondingly high—and vice versa. Does a rising student/faculty ratio, that is, a larger class size, imply higher productivity or lower quality? While students seem to prefer smaller classes, there is no convincing evidence that more is learned in them, despite many experimental attempts to verify this common belief, and I shall continue to abstract from this vexing issue in this chapter.[9]

SUBSIDIES AND CROSS-SUBSIDIZATION IN HIGHER EDUCATION: PUBLIC POLICY IMPLICATIONS

The most important implications, however, concern the issues of educational subsidies and cross-subsidization, the questions raised at the beginning of this chapter. These pictures are grossly distorted if we fail to adjust for product mix. To analyze this question, Table 10.3 presents the annual tuition rate at public and private colleges and universities, as well as the subsidy (cost minus tuition) implied by our adjusted cost figures for lower-division and upper-division undergraduates and graduate students, respectively. As noted above, my behavioral model of NPOs, taken together with a simple academic objective function, would lead me to expect lower (even negative) subsidies for undergraduates than for graduates, lower for undergraduates at universities than at colleges, and, within universities, decreasing subsidies through time as graduate education and research have been increasingly important loss-making activities that need to be subsidized. The pattern presented in Table 10.3 is consistent with these hypotheses, for both the public and private sectors. Some policy implications of these results are discussed below.

Subsidy Variations Across Institutions: The University vs. the College

We previously found that universities have lower undergraduate costs than do colleges. Now we add that tuition is higher at four-year rather than two-year institutions. Hence, the subsidy to undergraduates is much greater, in both absolute and relative terms, if they attend a college, particularly a community college, and, as we shall see, this disparity has increased through time.

While this finding applies both to the public and private sectors, it has particularly important implications within the former. Hansen and Weisbrod, in a controversial monograph, have argued that the prestigious California system of public higher education is regressive because wealthier people are more likely to attend the university, which appears to have higher costs per student than the college of community college. State and local taxes, they hold, are not sufficiently progressive to cover these higher costs accruing to the more affluent families. In deriving these conclusions, Hansen and Weisbrod differentiate costs by level, but they do not adjust for departmental resources devoted to research at the university. If we estimate the required adjustment to be 40%, as described above, we find that the remaining cost differential is more than offset by the tuition differential, with the net subsidies per lower-division student roughly equalized in these institution types in the California system.[10]

Moreover, Table 10.3 indicates that, in the aggregate nationally, community college students cost more, pay less, and hence receive a greater annual financial subsidy than do lower-division university students. Indeed, the subsidy received for two years of study at a community college is almost as high as that received for four years at a public university. The highest subsidy is received by those who do their lower-division work at the former and their upper-division at the latter. The tendency of low-income students to attend community colleges, therefore, does not lead toward regressivity, and a shift of these students into the university would not be a step toward greater progressivity in the public sector.[11]

Changes in Undergraduate Subsidies Through Time; Profits and Income-Contingent Loans

It is obvious that students at all levels and in all kinds of institutions were heavily subsidized in 1953–54. This subsidy, however, has fallen steadily through time for undergraduates. The picture appears in the unadjusted

Table 10.3 Tuition and Subsidy per FTE Student

	Public			Private		
Year	University	Four-Year College	Two-Year College	University	Four-Year College	Two-Year College
	Tuition Per Student					
1953–54	149		67	434		124
1966–67	299		110	1273		836
	Annual Subsidy per FTELU					
1953–54	389	471	487	90	183	575
% of Real Cost	72%	76%	88%	17%	30%	82%
1966–67	284	558	764	–532	–193	289
% of Real Cost	49%	65%	88%	–72%	–18%	26%
	Annual Subsidy per FTEAU					
1953–54	658	781	—	352	492	—
% of Real Cost	82%	84%		45%	53%	
1966–67	576	986	—	–161	347	—
% of Real Cost	66%	77%		–14%	21%	
	Annual Subsidy per FTEG					
1953–54	1869	—	—	1531	—	—
% of Real Cost	93%			78%		
1966–67	1887	—	—	1506	—	—
% of Real Cost	86%			54%		

SOURCE: Tuition and fees obtained from K. Simon and M. Fullam, eds., *Projections of Educational Statistics to 1976–7* (Washington, D.C.: U.S. Department of Health, Education, and Welfare, 1967), p. 94. (The distinction in tuition between universities and four-year colleges is not available.) Subsidies were calculated by taking adjusted cost figures from Table 10.2 and subtracting from tuition figures.

data, but emerges even more clearly after the correction for graduate and research costs in Table 10.3. There we see that all undergraduates (except those at the public community colleges) were paying a much larger proportion of their total cost in 1966 than in 1953 and, in most cases, the absolute dollar value of the subsidy declined as well, despite a generally rising price level.

By 1966–67, lower-division undergraduates at *public* universities were paying half and upper-division undergraduates one-third of their real costs—$299 out of $583 and $875, respectively, per year. Since the remainder will be more than offset by the incremental $5000 in (discounted) income taxes paid by college graduates in future years, it may be thought of as a nonoptional high-interest, income-contingent loan from society to university students rather than as a permanent subsidy. However, the same may not be true of community college students, whose initial subsidy is higher and future taxes lower.[12]

The picture had changed even more dramatically in *private* universities. By 1966–67, lower-division undergraudates had long been paying their own way, and upper-division students had just passed the break-even point—paying $1273 out of $741 and $1112, respectively, per year. Their profitability, as a group, is even greater when one takes into account the fact that many undergraduates make substantial donations after graduation and (the present value of) these contributions appropriately enter into the calculation of average payment per student. Contrary to the popular belief that all students are being subsidized to an ever increasing degree—a belief that is based on cost data unadjusted for product mix—it turns out that the teaching of undergraduates is currently a highly profitable production activity at private universities.

Subsidy from Undergraduates to Graduates: "Consumption" of Graduates and "Production" of Undergraduates

The explanation for these phenomena may be found by comparing the subsidies to undergraduate and graduate students and by reviewing our earlier data on research time. We have seen that graduate costs are at least three times as great as undergraduate costs, and the ratio doubles if research is treated as an input into graduate education. Yet tuition charges are almost identical across levels, and graduate students are frequently given waivers of the nominal amount. Clearly, they are the recipients of huge social subsidies—from governmental and philanthropic sources and, in private universities, from undergraduates as well.

The total subsidy to graduate education has grown through time, as graduate enrollments have increased sharply. Moreover, research expenditures rose much faster than graduate enrollments during the 1950s and 1960s. If research is indeed an input into graduate education, this implies a rising cost and subsidy per graduate student. With subsidy per graduate student growing, with the graduate/undergraduate ratio rising at universities, and without a commensurately large increase in flexible nontuition sources of funds, these graduate training costs require a larger profit (or smaller deficit) per undergraduate. As we have seen, that is exactly what has happened at universities. In community colleges and some liberal arts colleges, on the other hand, any available nontuition income can still be spent on undergraduates, who continue to be generously subsidized.

It has sometimes been argued that the rationale for combining undergraduate and graduate training at one institution is to use the large supplies of cheap graduate students to teach undergraduates, and that the lower cost of undergraduate education thereby attained is evidence of joint supply. The underlying presumption is that graduate "teaching assistants" are paid less than the price of equivalent part-time teaching resources who could be hired in the marketplace. If so, this would partially offset the instructional subsidy they receive. Actually, at least one institutional study suggests that the opposite is true; that is, graduate students serving as teaching assistants receive a transfer payment as well as a wage for their services and can hardly be regarded as "slave labor."[13] Instead, it appears that the causation for combining undergraduate and graduate education may run the other way: The technology chosen for advanced courses is an expensive one, and the heavy resource burden thereby incurred by the "consumption" of graduate education can only be met by earning an implicit profit from the low-cost "production" of undergraduate education. Universities, therefore, find it necessary to employ a cheap (large class) technology for teaching undergraduates, while colleges can and do continue to use a more costly (small class, faculty-intensive) factor mix. It follows that, consistent with empirical observation, undergraduate institutions can survive very well without graduate students, while graduate institutions cannot exist without a large undergraduate base.

The above analysis also helps explain why higher education is so resistent to capital-intensive technologies. Currently, the supply of people who want to be faculty members is more abundant than it would be if graduate students paid for their own training, the faculty wage understates its real cost, and the use of physical capital by colleges and universities has been discouraged in favor of (seemingly) cheap human capital.

PUBLIC AND PRIVATE SECTOR BEHAVIOR COMPARED

The existence of an "implicit profit" from undergraduate education at private universities, used to subsidize graduate training and research, has just been demonstrated. Public universities, too, perceive themselves to be earning a profit on undergraduate education, even though tuition does not cover cost; this profit is paid for by taxpayers at large rather than the students directly involved. My reasoning is that public universities receive most of their funding on a per student basis, an amount which far exceeds the tuition rate. This payment is, typically, much more than the average cost per undergraduate and much less than the average cost per graduate student. Thus, state legislatures think they are paying for the teaching of students, primarily undergraduates, but actually they are paying considerable amounts for graduate training and research, due to the cross-subsidization in which such universities engage. Moreover, the amount of such cross-subsidization has increased through time, together with G and R. In this sense, public and private universities behave in very similar ways.

Private universities can achieve this result by manipulating both tuition and cost; and, as we have seen, most of the increased subsidy to G and R (decreased subsidy to U) was achieved by huge tuition increases during the 1950s and 1960s. Public universities, however, often do not directly control or retain tuition revenues. Therefore, they are more constrained in their ability to cross-subsidize and can do so only by manipulating costs. This explains why the subsidies to undergraduates fell less, but cost per student fell more, in the public than the private sector, and hence the cost (quality?) disparity between the sectors increased during this period (see Table 10.2). While the public university undergraduate subsidizes his fellow graduate student less than his private counterpart does, he also gets less faculty attention. This also explains why public research universities tend to have a larger undergraduate base and a higher U/G ratio than private research universities.

Relatedly, suppose the state legislature (in the case of a public university) or a donor (in the case of a private university) wishes to induce more attention to undergraduates and therefore give the institution an additional contribution per student to spend for this purpose. At colleges, this will indeed be the effect. However, universities may simply choose to increase their profit on undergraduate education, diverting much of it to finance their graduate training and research activities. In multiproduct NPOs, external actors have limited power over the ultimate use of the resources they provide, and the effect of state funding or private donations may be very different from the intent.

CONCLUSION

In summary, this chapter argues that the university must be viewed as a multiproduct nonprofit institution which engages in substantial cross-subsidization among its various activities in order to maximize the utility of its faculty decision makers. Some activities, notably undergraduate education, are carried out to generate a profit which, in turn, is used to subsidize loss-making activities, such as graduate training and research. These profits are maintained in the long run through entry barriers such as accreditation procedures, reputational advantage, and difficulties in raising venture capital for new NPOs. In this way, a greater provision of research is possible than would be the case without cross-subsidization, and the need to fund this "collective good" through direct tax revenues is reduced.

The failure in previous studies to adjust correctly for product mix and cross-subsidization has meant that undergraduate costs have been overstated, the social rate of return to undergraduate education has been understated, estimates of productivity growth have been biased downward, and the distribution of burdens and benefits, subsidies and surplus, has been obscured. The reinterpretation presented here suggests that, currently, the two extremes of community college and graduate students receive a large social subsidy at both public and private institutions. While undergraduates, too, received a subsidy in both the public and private sectors in the early 1950s, by the late 1960s this had eroded away as cross-subsidization increased and graduate training and research took increasing shares of university resources. By 1967, undergraduates at public universities were merely receiving high-interest income-contingent loans from society, and undergraduates at private universities were generating a profit. In private universities, this change was largely brought about by tuition increases as demand rose; in public universities, which often do not control or retain tuition, decreases in real inputs per undergraduate student were the main device used. Nevertheless, public and private universities had more in common with each other than with two- or four-year colleges in their own sector, in these important respects.

How can we evaluate the cross-subsidization in which both public and private universities engage? The efficiency problem is that, since undergraduates pay more and graduate students pay less than their marginal cost, their enrollment decisions may not take real costs into account. On the other hand, one might argue that the research and graduate study at universities create the prestige and variety which attract undergraduates there despite their less preferred teaching technology; in that sense, G and R are properly seen as inputs into university-type undergraduate education and it is appropriate for undergraduates to finance them. In other words, while U is generally separable from G and R, the particular constellation of characteristics one purchases as a university undergraduate may not be separable from G and R, so that the division of costs between them is indeterminate.

Moreover, given that today's graduate students are tomorrow's faculty, it may well be necessary for undergraduates to pay for their training, one way or another. Suppose that cross-subsidization were not permitted and the subsidy to graduate students were eliminated by raising their tuition. This would bring about a drastic reduction in present graduate enrollments and a reduced supply of future faculty, raising their wages and, hence, the cost of teaching undergraduates. While in the short run undergraduate tuition might fall at universities, it would rise again in the long run in order to cover these higher costs. The price increase for undergraduate education and the incentive to economize on faculty teaching time would be even greater in the two- and four-year colleges which are not cross-subsidizing graduate training now but would, under the new system, have to pay for the graduate training costs of their faculty. Thus, a major consequence of the elimination of cross-subsidization would be a convergence of technology, costs, and price between colleges and universities, eliminating many of the former and offering less choice of institutional types to students.

As for research, if we believe that its benefits are substantial and that neither individuals nor state legislatures will voluntarily finance an optimal amount, society at large gains when universities divert resources to research activities. Cross-subsidization can then be seen as a "second best" solution, an alternative funding mechanism to national government lower taxes, avoiding many of the disincentive and informational problems inherent in taxes and central planning. Welfare may be improved by turning decision making about resource allocation over to NPO managers with the "right" objective functions, who, by their choice of product mix and costs, are simply "protecting the public interest." Of course, there is no guarantee that their objective functions are, in fact, "right." In addition, on equity or procedural grounds, many may believe in a more explicit public choice mechanism in which democratically elected representatives, rather than autonomous university managers, determine the allocation of resources to collective goods. Questions occur, particularly, where tax revenues are involved, as in budgetary allocations to state universities. To a lesser extent, the same question arises with respect to tax privileges to private universities.

Our objective here is not to make this value judgment but simply to understand better what is going on. This chapter has tried to throw some light on the real cost differentials and subsidies received by different groups in higher education, the role that cross-subsidization plays in getting collective goods produced, and some ways in which public-private differences in institution type matter or do not matter at all.

APPENDIX[14]

This appendix derives the utility-maximizing product mix for a multiproduct IHL, engaged in undergraduate teaching, graduate training, and research. The institution is assumed to be managed by its faculty members, all of whom have the same utility function, which is assumed to be the "team" objective function of the group.

Let us postulate a simple linear objective function:

$$W = \alpha U + gG + aQUALU + bQUALG + cR(F,TL) + \frac{k(AU+G)}{AUC+GC}$$

The university wishes to maximize this subject to the constraint that:

$$UC + GC = TL \cdot F = TL(U \cdot PU + G \cdot PG)$$

where:

U = no. of undergraduate students = LU (lower division) + AU (upper division)

$LU = AU$; that is, every lower-division student eventually becomes an upper-division student (0 attrition and transfers assumed)

G = no. of graduate students

$QUALU$ = quality of undergraduates; $\delta QUALU/\delta LU < 0$

$QUALG$ = quality of graduate students; $\delta QUALG/\delta G < 0$

$R(F,\ TL)$ = research, a function of F and TL; $\dfrac{\partial R}{\partial F} > 0,\ \dfrac{\partial R}{\partial TL} < 0$

F = faculty

TL = average teaching load = $(UC + GC)/F$

UC and GC = no. of U and G classes, respectively

$\dfrac{AU+G}{AUC+GC} = ACZ$ = average class size at advanced levels

PU = additional revenue (in terms of fraction of a faculty line) that the university gets for each LU student = $PLU + PAU$, since each additional LU implies an additional AU as well

PG = price for each additional G student

$\alpha,g,a,b,c > 0,\ k < 0$

In other words, the university's utility depends positively on the quantity of its students. Faculty welfare depends on student quality as well as quantity, and there is a trade-off between the two. The student-quality argument means that after a point additional students diminish utility, that is:

$$\left(\frac{\partial W}{\partial U} + \frac{\partial W}{\partial QUALU}\frac{\partial QUALU}{\partial U}\right) \equiv \left(\alpha + a\frac{\partial QUALU}{\partial U}\right) < 0$$

The same argument holds for G.

We assume that the collective research of the entire group of faculty enters into the university's utility function. Finally, technology, in the form of average class size, is not given as a technological constraint but as a choice variable that enters into the objective function—with respect to AU and G but not LU. This disparity may stem partly from the faculty's self-serving interest in teaching small advanced classes and partly from an altruistic belief that the educational production function requires this technology at lower but not at higher levels. The decision about class size may also be viewed as a choice about product quality. The existence of this technological (or quality) preference has a major impact on optimal quantities and subsidies at different instructional levels and also influences the desired teaching load *(TL)* and teaching/research mix, as we shall see below.

What must the university decide? It must choose its optimal numbers of LU and G, which in turn determines AU, $QUALU$, and $QUALG$. It must choose its optimal *TL*, which, together with the above, determines *R* and the *T/R* mix. Finally, it must decide how to divide up *TL·F* between *UC* and *GC*.

We shall deal with the latter first. Recall that *LUC* and *LU/LUC* do not enter directly into the utility function nor into the incentive system (i.e., the "price" per *U* is independent of *LU/LUC*). Therefore, we would expect *LU/LUC* to grow very large and *LUC* very small—in the limit, 1. To simplify, then, I assume that $AUC + GC = (TL·F - LUC \sim TL·F$ for large *F*, so that $\frac{\partial(AUC + GC)}{\partial TL} = F$ and $\frac{\partial(AUC + GC)}{\partial F} = TL$, two relationships that will be used below. Then we obtain the following conditions for optimizing *LU, G, TL* (and hence *R/T*):

$$2\alpha + a(\delta QUALU/\delta LU) + c(\delta R/\delta F)PU + k[F - (AU + G)PU]/TL·F^2 = 0 \quad (1)$$

$$g + b(\delta QUALG/\delta G) + c(\delta R/\delta F)PG + k[F - (AU + G)PG/TL·F^2 = 0 \quad (2)$$

$$c(\delta R/\delta TL) - k(AU + G)/F·TL^2 = 0 \quad (3)$$

Note that, because of the low-cost technology used, *LU* is a profitable activity. Then *LU* enrollments expand so long as the direct utility (the first term in equation 1) plus the indirect utility via faculty resources for *R* and *(AUC + GC)* (the third and fourth terms) are greater than the disutility from declining student quality (the second term). The fact that each *LU* eventually turns into an *AU*, raising average class size there, is a further inhibiting factor. At the margin *U* yields disutility and is enrolled only because of the profit it provides for research and small advanced classes.

As for *G*, its expansion is directly retarded by the technological preference. Since the additional faculty generated by incremental *G* is less than the average used for them, enrollment increases necessitate either an increase in class size or a decrease in *R* once *U* is given. This technological preference obviously keeps class size relatively small and limits the willingness of the university to enroll *G*.

Finally, the university must choose its optimum *TL*, realizing that a reduction will increase *R* but will also increase average class size. According to the above equation, *TL* is optimized where $c(\delta R/\delta TL) - k(AU + G)/F·TL^2 = 0$. The second term, $-k(AU + G)/F·TL^2$, is positive and leads *TL* to increase at first, since a higher *TL* implies smaller classes, hence greater utility. However, this term diminishes as *TL* increases, so it eventually equals (in absolute value) the first term, which is negative and constant (a higher *TL* leads to less *R*, hence less utility). At that point, the increases in *TL* come to a halt. Rearranging, we find that equilibrium occurs where $TL = \sqrt{k(AU + G)/Fc(\delta R/\delta TL)}$. (Note that the division of *TL·F* between *AUC* and *GC*, hence the difference in average class size between these two levels, is indeterminate in this simple model. Empirical data suggest that, roughly, a fifty-fifty division may prevail.)

In this model, faculty resources are "produced" by *T* and "consumed" by R. Relatedly, the faculty resource is viewed as a benefit rather than a cost and lower-division undergraduates are viewed as inputs used to produce faculty, rather than vice versa. A profit is generated by LU and used up for G and R. In this sense, undergraduate students are subsidizing all the other teaching and research activities at the university. If G and R were excluded as feasible products, U would be carried out in a more costly way, in order to meet the zero-profit constraint. This corresponds to the fact that U instruction is more faculty intensive at colleges than at universities and LU is most faculty intensive at two-year colleges. Conversely, if the supply of high-quality G students goes up, or the "value" of research increases, U enrollments will increase and average U costs decline, in order to help cover the costs of additional G and R. This corresponds to the increased profitability of U we observed during the 1950s and 1960s.

NOTES

1. Joint supply may exist at the university because of externalities and direct interaction (e.g., between research and teaching), lumpiness and nonlinearity in inputs (such as books and equipment), diminishing returns to specialization (e.g., to the faculty), and market imperfections and transaction costs (involving, e.g., graduate assistants). Of course, if we look at the quantity-quality index of undergraduate education over time, clearly this depends on the availability of faculty and the accumulation of knowledge through prior graduate teaching and research, just as current graduate teaching and research will influence future undergraduate education. Since yesterday's research results are taught by today's graduate students to tomorrow's undergraduates (some of whom will eventually become teachers and researchers), there is clearly a dynamic jointness in the supply of research and teaching for the entire economy—although not necessarily for a particular institution. When Verry and Layard tried multiple regression analysis for Great Britain, they found little evidence of joint supply. See D. W. Verry and P. R. G. Layard, "Cost Functions for University Teaching and Research," *Economic Journal* 85 (March 1975), pp. 55–74.

2. These biases are discussed in detail in Estelle James, "Product Mix and Cost Disaggregation: A Reinterpretation of the Economics of Higher Education," *Journal of Human Resources* 13 (Spring 1978), pp. 157–186. Verry and Davies also discuss these methodological difficulties at length but, pragmatically, end up using faculty time allocations as a proxy for total cost allocations. See D. W. Verry and B. Davies, *University Costs and Outputs* (Amsterdam: Elsevier, 1976).

3. The ratios given here are similar to those reported for Great Britian by Verry and Layard, op. cit.: 48% teaching, 24% research, 28% administration and other. The British fall in teaching and rise in research through time was also noted in Maureen Woodhall and Mark Blaug, "Productivity Trends in British University Education, 1938–62," *Minerva* (September 1965), pp. 483–498.

4. See *California and Western Conference Cost and Statistical Study for 1954–55* (Berkeley: University of California Printing Department, 1960) (referred to as *Western Conference Study*), p. 19; June O'Neill, *Resource Use in Higher Education* (New York: Carnegie Commission on Higher Education, 1971), p. 80. Since professors control their own research time and face a trade-off between research and leisure, as teaching load declines both research and leisure may rise. Hence, the fall in teaching load may reflect in part the general decrease in the average workweek. Particularly, some faculty who secured tenure as "teachers" in the 1940s and 1950s had little research interest or productivity and received a windfall rent in the form of increased leisure when their teaching loads dropped in the 1960s. The rise in research output was therefore probably not commensurate with the fall in teaching time and

teaching loads, especially in the short run. The heavy current emphasis on research in decisions about remuneration and promotions is documented in John J. Siegfried and Kenneth J. White, "Financial Rewards to Research and Teaching: A Case Study of Academic Economists," *American Economic Review* 63 (May 1973), pp. 309–315; David A. Katz, "Faculty Salaries, Rates of Promotion, and Productivity at a Large University," *American Economic Review* 63 (June 1973), pp. 469–477; and Howard P. Tuckman and Jack Leahey, "What Is an Article Worth?" *Journal of Political Economy* 83 (October 1975), pp. 951–967.

5. See June O'Neill, *Resource Use in Higher Education* (New York: Carnegie Commission on Higher Education, 1971), pp. 73, 94.

6. Ibid.

7. O'Neill, op. cit., p. 14, cites, in particular, a University of Michigan cost study. Upper-division/lower-division undergraduate cost ratios ranging between 1.4/1 and 2/1 were also found in California State Department of Education, *A Restudy of the Needs of California in Higher Education* (Sacramento: 1955) (referred to as *California Restudy*); *Western Conference Study;* and Colin Bell, Helen Brownlee, and Alexander Mood, "Allocation of a University's Resources to Instruction," in A. Mood et al, eds., *Papers on Efficiency in the Management of Higher Education,* (New York: Carnegie Commission on Higher Education, 1972), pp. 61–73). Graduate/undergraduate ratios varied more widely, from 2.15/1 to 6/1 in these studies, as well as in others reported in William Bowen, *The Economics of the Major Private Universities* (New York: Carnegie Commission on Higher Education, 1968), and Dexter Keezer, ed., *Financing Higher Education* (New York: Carnegie Commission on Higher Education, 1971), with most of them somewhat higher than 3/1. Moreover, there is some evidence that the relative cost per graduate student has been rising through time.

8. For an example of this point of view, see William Bowen, op. cit.

9. For a discussion of some of these studies, see Eric Hanushek, "Throwing Money at Schools," *Journal of Policy Analysis and Management* 1 (Fall 1981), pp. 19–41.

10. See W. Lee Hansen and Burton Weisbrod, "The Distribution of Costs and Direct Benefits of Public Higher Education," *Journal of Human Resources* 4 (Spring 1969), pp. 176–191. For the discussion stimulated by this work, see "Comments," in *Journal of Human Resources* 5 (Spring 1970), pp. 222–236; 5 (Fall 1970), pp. 519–523; 6 (Summer 1971), pp. 363–374; 10 (Winter 1975), pp. 116–124. Also see W. Lee Hansen, "Income Distribution Effects of Higher Education," *American Economic Review* 60 (May 1970), pp. 335–341, for comparisons of the California system with the Wisconsin and Florida systems. Although organized and sponsored research are excluded from the Hansen and Weisbrod calculations, there is no indication that departmental research was also subtracted. In the 1953 *California Restudy*, which did deduct expenditures on departmental research, UCLA and Berkeley cost less for lower-division instruction than did most four-year and two-year colleges.

11. This analysis of cost-based subsidy yields different conclusions from a measurement of benefit-based subsidy. The latter would be measured by the differences between benefits received and costs privately paid, where benefits might be construed as future earnings streams, which are higher for university students, partly because of the selectivity and prestige of the institutions involved. To measure benefits correctly, one wants value added, and this requires knowing what future earnings would have been in the absence of higher education, a figure which might be different for the university and community college student groups. For a more detailed discussion of the different ways of viewing subsidy, see Estelle James, "Cost, Benefit and Envy: Alternative Measures of the Redistributive Effects of Higher Education," in Howard Tuckman and Edward Whalen, ed., *Subsidies to Higher Education: The Issues* (New York: Praeger, 1980), pp. 121–142.

12. That is, part of the cost of attending college *now* is the increased tax paid *later,* when incomes rise due to higher education. Present taxpayers are charged to make these loans possible, and future taxpayers benefit (from lower tax rates or higher government services) when the educational loans are repaid. (It follows that current taxpayers are similarly benefiting from the educational "loans" that were made in the past.)

As with all income-contingent loans, the repayment is unevenly distributed within a given cohort. Unlike other loan programs, the problems of opting out and adverse selection are avoided; we all must pay higher taxes when income rises due to college education. Because universities are state financed and most income taxes are paid nationally, the net effect is the payment of a deferred subsidy from the state to the federal government, that is, an intergenerational transfer from residents of states with high enrollments in public universities to residents of states with low enrollments. This is a powerful argument for federal subsidies to higher education.

The present value of the additional tax flow from a male college graduate (taking into account the expected lifetime earnings with and without a college degree) was estimated at $4800 by Hansen and Weisbrod, op. cit., for 1965, using a 5% discount rate, and at $5000 by Richard Freeman, "Overinvestment in College Training?" *Journal of Human Resources* 10 (Summer 1975), pp. 287–312, for 1969, using a 10% discount rate. An adjustment for ability, which was not included in these calculations, would reduce the income and tax gain substantially. Nevertheless, since these figures exceed the subsidies to public university students by a factor of three, even if they were cut in half we would have to conclude that the subsidies are being repaid, on the average, with a very high rate of interest.

We do not have reliable data on the incremental taxes paid by community college graduates. However, according to Hansen and Weisbrod, $900 in increased lifetime taxes is paid by a male with less than four years of post–high school education, a group that includes university dropouts as well as community college students. This figure does not quite cover the educational subsidy received by community college graduates, a finding that reinforces the nonregressivity conclusions derived above.

13. At a large eastern university studied by the author, in 1976 the "market rate" for hiring part-timers to teach a single course was $1500, while teaching assistants were paid $1600 plus tuition remission for teaching part of a course. In the same year, graduate students from the university were hired by a nearby community college on a part-time basis for $750 per course.

14. An expanded version of this model is found in Estelle James and Egon Neuberger, "The University Department as a Non-Profit Labor Cooperative," *Public Choice* 36 (1981), pp. 585–612.

Select Bibliography

Alexander, Karl and Aaron M. Pallas. 1983. "Private Schools and Public Policy: New Evidence on Cognitive Achievement in Public and Private Schools." *Sociology of Education* 56.

Antos, Joseph R. and Sherwin Rosen. 1975. "Discrimination in the Market for Public School Teachers." *Journal of Econometrics* 3.

Archer, Margaret, ed. 1982. *The Sociology of Educational Expansion: Take-Off, Growth, and Inflation in Educational Systems.* London: Sage Publications.

Areen, Judith and Christopher Jencks. 1972. "Education Vouchers: A Proposal for Diversity and Change." In LaNoue.

Arons, Stephen. 1976. "The Separation of School and State: Pierce Reconsidered." *Harvard Educational Review* 46.

Ashby, Eric. 1966. *Universities: British, Indian, African.* Cambridge, Mass.: Harvard University Press.

Astin, Alexander. 1977. *Four Critical Years.* San Francisco: Jossey-Bass.

Astin, Alexander and Calvin Lee. 1972. *The Invisible Colleges: A Profile of Small, Private Colleges with Limited Resources.* New York: McGraw-Hill.

Berdahl, Robert O. 1959. *British Universities and the State.* Berkeley: University of California.

———. 1978. "The Politics of State Aid." In Breneman and Finn.

Bidwell, Charles E. 1972. "Schooling and Socialization for Moral Commitment." *Interchange* 3.

Birnbaum, Robert. 1983. *Maintaining Diversity in Higher Education.* San Francisco: Jossey-Bass.

Blaug, Mark and Maureen Woodhall. 1978. "Patterns of Subsidies to Higher Education in Europe." *Higher Education* 7.

———. 1965. "Productivity Trends in British University Education, 1938–62." *Minerva* September.

Boeninger Kausel, Edgardo. n.d. "Alternative Policies for Financing Higher Education." In *The Financing of Higher Education in Latin America.* Washington, D.C.: Inter-American Development Bank.

Bowen, Howard and John Minter. 1978. *Private Higher Education.* Washington, D.C.: Association of American Colleges.

Bowen, William. 1968. *The Economics of the Major Private Universities.* New York: Carnegie Commission on Higher Education.

Breneman, David W. and Chester E. Finn, Jr., eds. 1978. *Public Policy and Private Higher Education.* Washington, D.C.: The Brookings Institution.

Bridge, R. Gay and Julie Blackman. 1978. *A Study of Alternatives in American Education: Family Choice in Schooling*. Santa Monica, Calif.: The Rand Corporation.

Buckley, William F., Jr. 1951. *God and Man at Yale*. South Bend, Ind.: Gateway Edition. Introduction 1977.

Buetow, Harold A. 1970. *Of Singular Benefit: The Story of Catholic Education in the United States*. New York: Macmillan.

Burn, Barbara, with chapters by Philip G. Altbach, Clark Kerr, and James A. Perkins. 1971. *Higher Education in Nine Countries*. New York: McGraw Hill.

Burns, J. A. and B. J. Kohlbrenner. 1937. *A History of Catholic Education in the United States*. New York: Bensinger Brothers.

California State Department of Education. 1955. *A Restudy of the Needs of California in Higher Education*. Sacramento.

Campbell, Roald F., Luvern L. Cunningham, Raphael O. Nystrand, and Michael D. Usdan. 1980. *The Organization and Control of American Schools,* 4th ed. Columbus, Ohio: Charles E. Merrill.

Carnegie Council on Policy Studies in Higher Education. 1976. *A Classification of Institutions of Higher Education*. Berkeley, Calif.: Carnegie Foundation for the Advancement of Teaching.

———. 1977. *The States and Higher Education*. San Francisco: Jossey-Bass.

———. 1979. *The States and Private Higher Education*. San Francisco: Jossey-Bass.

Carnegie Foundation for the Advancement of Teaching. 1984. *Corporate Classrooms: The Learning Business*. Princeton, N.J.

Carper, James C. and Thomas C. Hunt, eds. 1986. *Religious Schooling in America*. Birmingham, Ala.: Religious Education Press.

Center for the Study of Public Policy. 1970. *Education Vouchers: A Report on Financing Education by Grants to Parents*. Cambridge, Mass.: CSSP.

Cibulka, James G., Timothy J. O'Brien, and Donald Zewe. 1982. *Inner-City Private Elementary Schools: A Study*. Milwaukee, Wisc.: Marquette University Press.

Clark, Burton R., ed. Forthcoming. *The School and the University: An International Perspective*. Berkeley: University of California Press.

Cohen, David and Eleanor Farrar. 1977. "Power to the Parents?—The Study of Education Vouchers." *The Public Interest* 48.

Cohen, David and Janet A. Weiss. 1977. "Social Science and Social Policy: Schools and Race." In Carol Weiss.

Coleman, James S., et al. 1977. *Parents, Teachers & Children: Prospects for Choice in American Education*. San Francisco: Institute for Contemporary Studies.

Coleman, James S., Ernest Q. Campbell, Carol J. Holson, James McPartland, Alexander Mood, Frederic D. Weinfield, and Robert L. York. 1966. *Equality of Educational Opportunity*. Washington, D.C.: U.S. Government Printing Office.

Coleman, James S., Thomas Hoffer, and Sally Kilgore. 1982. *High School Achievement: Public, Catholic and Private Schools Compared*. New York: Basic Books.

Coons, John E. and Stephen D. Sugarman. 1978. *Education by Choice; The Case for Family Control*. Berkeley: University of California Press.

Cooper, Bruce S. 1984. "The Changing Demography of Private Schools: Trends and Implications." *Education and Urban Society* 16.

———. 1975. *Free School Survival*. Sarasota, Fla.: Omni-print.

Cooper, Bruce S., Donald H. McLaughlin, and Bruno V. Manno. 1983. "The Latest Word on Private School Growth." *Teachers College Record 85.*

Council for Financial Aid to Education. 1981. *Voluntary Support of Education, 1979–80.* New York: CFAE.

Cremin, Lawrence A. 1961. *The Transformation of the School: Progressivism in American Education: 1876–1957.* New York: Random House.

Cummings, William. 1973. "The Japanese Private University." *Minerva 11.*

Currence, Cindy. 1984. "Corporations Considering Creation of For-Profit Schools." *Education Week* April 11.

———. 1984. "Private Lower Schools Face Deluge of Determined Applicants." *Education Week* March 21.

Curti, Merle and Roderick Nash. 1965. *Philanthropy in the Shaping of American Higher Education.* New Brunswick, N.J.: Rutgers University Press.

Davies, B. and D. W. Verry. 1976. *University Costs and Outputs.* Amsterdam: Elsevier.

Department of Education, School Finance Project. 1983. *Private Elementary and Secondary Education.* Vol. 2. Washington, D.C.

Douglas, James. 1986. "Political Theories of Nonprofit Organization." In Powell.

Doyle, Denis P. 1977. "The Politics of Choice: A View from the Bridge." In Coleman.

Edel, Matthew and Elliott Sklar. 1974. "Taxes, Spending and Property Values: Supply Adjustment in a Tiebout-Oates Model." *Journal of Political Economy 82.*

Eldridge, M. D. 1980. "America's Nonpublic Schools: A Quantification of Their Contribution to American Education." *Private School Quarterly* Fall.

El-Khawas, Elaine H. 1976. "Public and Private Higher Education: Differences in Role, Character, and Clientele." Washington, D.C.: American Council on Education.

Elson, John. 1969. "State Regulation of Nonpublic Schools: The Legal Framework." In Erickson.

Erickson, Donald A. 1971. "The Devil and Catholic Education." *America* April 10.

———. 1962. "Differential Effects of Public and Sectarian Schooling on the Religiousness of the Child." Ph.D. dissertation, Department of Education, University of Chicago.

———. 1969. "Freedom's Two Educational Imperatives." In Erickson.

———, ed. 1969. *Public Controls for Nonpublic Schools.* Chicago: The University of Chicago Press.

———. 1984. *Victoria's Secret: The Effects of British Columbia's Aid to Independent Schools.* Los Angeles: Institute for the Study of Private Schools.

Erickson, Donald A. and George F. Madaus. 1971. *Issues of Aid to Nonpublic Schools.* Report to the President's Commission on School Finance. Chestnut Hill, Mass.: Boston College.

Fetters, William, F. Owings, S. Peng, and Ricky Takai. 1981. "Review of NORC Report, Public and Private Schools." Memorandum, June 26. National Center for Education Statistics.

Finn, Chester. 1976–77. "Federal Patronage of Universities in the United States: A Rose by Many Other Names?" *Minerva 14.*

Friedman, Milton. 1962. *Capitalism and Freedom.* Chicago: University of Chicago Press.

———. 1965. "The Role of Government in Education." In Robert Solo, ed. *Eco-*

nomics and the Public Interest. New Brunswick, N.J.: Rutgers University Press.

Fuerst, J. S. 1981. "Report Card: Chicago's All-Black Schools." *Public Interest* 64.

Gabel, Richard J. 1937. *Public Funds for Church and Private Schools.* Toledo, Ohio: Times and News Publishing.

Gaffney, Edward McGlynn, Jr., ed. 1981. *Private Schools and the Public Good.* Notre Dame, Ind.: University of Notre Dame Press.

Gallup, George. 1982. "The 14th Annual Gallup Poll of the Public's Attitudes Toward Public Schools." *Phi Delta Kappan* September.

Geiger, Roger L. 1986. *To Advance Knowledge: The Growth of American Research Universities in the Twentieth Century, 1900–1940.* New York: Oxford University Press.

———. 1986. *Private Sectors in Higher Education: Structure, Function and Change in Eight Countries.* Ann Arbor: The University of Michigan Press.

Gemello, John M. and Jack Osman. 1981. *Analysis of the Choice of Public and Private Education.* Paper prepared for the Tuition Tax Credit Seminar sponsored by Institute for Research on Educational Finance and Governance, Washington, D.C. October.

Glenny, Lyman, ed. 1979. *Funding Higher Education: A Six-Nation Analysis.* New York: Praeger.

Goffman, Erving, 1964. "The Characteristics of Total Institutions." In Amitai Etzioni, ed. *Complex Organizations.* New York: Holt, Rinehart, and Winston.

Goldberger, Arthur S. and Glen G. Cain. 1982. "The Causal Analysis of Cognitive Outcomes in the Coleman, Hoffer and Kilgore Report." *Sociology of Education* 55.

Goldstein, Stephen R. 1974. *Law and Public Education.* Indianapolis: Bobbs-Merrill.

Graubard, Alan. 1972. *Free the Children: Radical Reform and the Free School Movement.* New York: Pantheon Books.

Greeley, Andrew M. 1982. *Catholic High Schools and Minority Students.* New Brunswick, N.J.: Transaction Books.

———. 1969. *From Backwater to Mainstream: A Profile of Catholic Higher Education.* New York: McGraw-Hill.

Greeley, Andrew, William McCready, and Katherine McCourt. 1976. *Catholic Schools in a Declining Church.* Kansas City, Mo.: Sheed and Ward.

Grether, David and Peter Mieszkowski. 1974. "Determinants of Real Estate Values." *Journal of Urban Economics* April.

Gruson, Edward S. 1977. "The National Politics of Higher Education." *Mimeo* November.

Hannan, Michael T. and John Freeman. 1977. "The Population Ecology of Organizations." *American Journal of Sociology* 82.

Hansen, W. Lee. 1970. "Income Distribution Effects of Higher Education." *American Economic Review* 60.

Hansen, W. Lee and Burton Weisbrod. 1969. "The Distribution of Costs and Direct Benefits of Public Higher Education." *Journal of Human Resources* 4.

Hanushek, Eric A. 1972. Education and Race. Lexington, Mass.: D.C. Heath.

———. 1981. "Throwing Money at Schools." *Journal of Policy Analysis and Management* 1.

Hartle, Terry. 1976. *Recent Research on Private Higher Education.* Washington, D.C.: American Council on Education.

Hendersen, Vernon, Peter Mieszkowski, and Yvon Sauvageau. 1978. "Peer Group Effects and Educational Production Functions." *Journal of Public Economics* 10.

Hirschman, Albert O. 1970. *Exit, Voice, and Loyalty: Responses to Decline in Firms, Organizations, and States*. Cambridge, Mass.: Harvard University Press.

Hirschoff, Mary-Michelle Upson. 1977. "Parents and the Public School Curriculum: Is There a Right to Have One's Child Excused from Objectionable Instruction?" *S. Cal. L. Rev. 50*.

———. 1977. "Runyon V. McCrary and Regulation of Private Schools." *Ind. Law Journal 52*.

Hostetler, John A. and Gertrude E. Huntington. 1971. *Children in Amish Society: Socialization and Community Education*. New York: Rinehart and Winston.

Hunt, Thomas C. and Norlene M. Kunkel. 1984. "Catholic Schools: The Nation's Largest Alternative School System." In James C. Carper and Thomas C. Hunt, eds. *Religious Schooling in America*. Birmingham, Ala.: Religious Education Press.

Hutchinson, Eric. 1975. "The Origins of the University Grants Committee." *Minerva* 13.

Jallade, Jean-Pierre. 1978. "Financing Higher Education: The Equity Aspects." *Comparative Education Review* 22.

James, Estelle. 1986. "Non-Profit Organizations in Developing Countries." In Powell.

———. 1978. "Product Mix and Cost Disaggregation: A Reinterpretation of the Economics of Higher Education." *Journal of Human Resources* 13.

James, Estelle and Egon Neuberger. 1981. "The University Department as a Non-Profit Labor Cooperative." *Public Choice* 36.

James, Thomas. 1983. "Questions About Educational Choice: An Argument from History." In James and Levin.

James, Thomas and Henry M. Levin, eds. Forthcoming. *Comparing Public and Private Schools*. London: Falmer Press.

———. 1983. *Public Dollars for Private Schools: The Case of Tuition Tax Credits*. Philadelphia: Temple University Press.

Jellama, William W. 1973. *From Red to Black?* San Francisco: Jossey-Bass.

Jencks, Christopher and David Riesman. 1968. *The Academic Revolution*. Garden City, N.Y.: Doubleday.

Jung, Richard. 1982. *Nonpublic School Students in Title I ESEA Programs: A Question of "Equal" Services*. McLean, Va.: Advanced Technology.

Keezer, Dexter. 1971. *Financing Higher Education*. New York: Carnegie Commission on Higher Education.

Keisling, Phil. 1982. "Lessons for the Public Schools." *New Republic* November 1.

———. 1983. "How to Save Our Public Schools." *Readers Digest* February.

Knowles, Asa, ed. 1977. *The International Encyclopedia of Higher Education*. San Francisco: Jossey Bass.

Kramer, Ralph. 1981. *Voluntary Agencies in the Welfare State*. Berkeley: University of California Press.

Kraushaar, Otto F. 1972. *American Nonpublic Schools: Patterns of Diversity*. Baltimore: Johns Hopkins University Press.

LaNoue, George R. ed. 1972. *Education Vouchers: Concepts and Controversies*. New York: Teachers College Press.

Layard, P. R. G. and D. W. Verry. 1975. "Cost Functions for University Teaching and Research." *Economic Journal* 85.

Levin, Henry M. 1983. "Educational Choice and the Pains of Democracy." In James and Levin.

———. 1979. *Educational Vouchers and Social Policy.* Palo Alto, Calif.: Stanford University, Institute for Research on Educational Finance and Governance.

Levy, Daniel C. 1986. "A Comparison of Private and Public Educational Organizations." In Powell.

———. 1986. *Higher Education and the State in Latin America: Private Challenges to Public Dominance.* Chicago: The University of Chicago Press.

———. 1982. "The Rise of Private Universities in Latin America and the United States." In Archer.

Lindblom, Charles E. 1980. *The Policy-Making Process.* Englewood Cliffs, N.J.: Prentice-Hall.

———. 1977. *Politics and Markets.* New York: Basic Books.

Lindblom, Charles E. and David K. Cohen. 1979. *Usable Knowledge: Social Science and Social Problem Solving.* New Haven: Yale University Press.

Lowi, Theodore I. 1979. *The End of Liberalism: The Second Republic of the United States,* 2nd ed. New York: W. W. Norton.

Macias, Cathleen J. 1982. "Reactions to Coleman.'" *Private School Monitor* 4.

Maeroff, Gene I. 1984. "Public-Private College Rivalry Heats Up." *New York Times* August 19.

Manley, M. and S. Casimir, eds. 1982. *Family Choice in Schooling: Issues and Dilemmas.* Lexington, Mass.: Lexington Books.

Mason, Peter. 1983. *Private Education in the EEC.* London: National Independent Schools Information Service.

McCluskey, Neil G. 1970. *The Catholic University: A Modern Appraisal.* Notre Dame, Ind.: University of Notre Dame Press.

McDonnell, Lorraine M. and Milbrey W. McLaughlin. 1980. *Program Consolidation and the State Role in ESEA Title IV.* Santa Monica, Calif.: The Rand Corporation.

McGuire, Kent. 1981. *Choice in Elementary and Secondary Education.* Working Paper No. 34. Denver, Col.: Education Commission of the States.

McLaughlin, D. H. and L. L. Wise. 1980. *Nonpublic Education of the Nation's Children.* Palo Alto, Calif.: American Institutes For Research.

McPherson, Michael S. 1978. "The Demand for Higher Education." In Breneman and Finn.

McQuilkin, J. R. 1977. "Public Schools: Equal Time for Evangelicals." *Christianity Today* 22.

Minter, W. John and Howard R. Bowen. 1980. *Independent Higher Education, 1980.* Washington, D.C.: National Institute of Independent Colleges and Universities.

Murnane, Richard J. 1981. "Evidence, Analysis, and Unanswered Questions." *Harvard Educational Review* 51.

Murnane, Richard J., Stuart Newstead, and Randall J. Olsen. 1985. "Comparing Public and Private Schools: The Puzzling Role of Selectivity Bias." *Journal of Business and Economic Statistics* 3.

National Center for Education Statistics. 1984. "Characteristics of Households with Children Enrolled in Elementary and Secondary Schools." *Bulletin* September.

National Commission on Excellence in Education. 1983. *A Nation at Risk: The Imperative for Educational Reform.* Washington, D.C.: Government Printing Office.

National Education Association. 1983. *Estimates of School Statistics 1982–83.* Washington, D.C.

National Science Foundation. 1981. *Federal Funds for Research and Development, 1980.* Washington, D.C.: Government Printing Office.

Nault, Richard and Susan Uchitell. 1982. "School Choice in the Public Sector: A Case Study of Parental Decision Making." In Manley and Casimir.

Neave, Guy. 1983. "The Non State Sector in the Education Provision of Member States of the European Community." Brussels: Report to the Educational Services of the Commission of European Communities.

Nelson, Susan C. 1978. "Financial Trends and Issues." In Breneman and Finn.

Noah, Harold J. 1966. *Financing Soviet Schools.* New York: Columbia University, Teachers College Press.

Noell, Jay. 1982. "Public and Catholic Schools: A Reanalysis of Public and Private Schools." *Sociology of Education 55.*

Nordin, Virginia D. and William L. Turner. 1980. "More than Segregation Academies: The Growing Protestant Fundamentalist Schools." *Phi Delta Kappan 61.*

Oates, Wallace. 1969. "The Effects of Property Taxes and Local Public Spending on Property Values: An Empirical Study of Tax Capitalization and the Tiebout Hypothesis." *Journal of Political Economy 77.*

O'Malley, Charles J. 1981. *Survey of State Regulation of Private Schools.* Unpublished. Florida State Department of Education.

O'Neil, Robert M. 1974. "Law and Higher Education in California." In Neil J. Smelser and Gabriel Almond, eds. *Public Higher Education in California.* Berkeley: University of California.

O'Neill, June. 1971. *Resource Use in Higher Education.* New York: Carnegie Commission on Higher Education.

Pace, Robert C. 1972. *Education and Evangelism.* New York: McGraw-Hill.

Page, Ellis B. and Timothy Z. Keith. 1981. "Effects of U.S. Private Schools: A Technical Analysis of Two Recent Claims." *Educational Researcher 10.*

Peshkin, Alan. 1986. *God's Choice: The Total World of a Fundamentalist Christian School.* Chicago: University of Chicago Press.

Pfnister, Allen O. 1981. "Survival and Revival: The Transformation of the American Arts College." Occasional Papers in Higher Education no. 15, University of Denver.

Powell, Walter W., ed. 1986. *Between the Public and the Private: The Nonprofit Sector.* New Haven: Yale University Press.

Pryor, Frederic. 1968. *Public Expenditures in Communist and Capitalist Nations.* Homewood, Ill.: Richard D. Irwin.

Rauch, Eduardo. 1984. "The Jewish Day School in America: A Critical History and Contemporary Dilemmas." In Carper and Hunt.

Ravitch, Diane. 1984. "The Schools and Uncle Sam." *The New Republic* December 3.

Rebell, Michael A. 1982. "Educational Voucher Reform: Empirical Insights from the Experience of New York's Schools for the Handicapped." *The Urban Lawyer 14.*

Reinhardt, Raymond M. 1981. "Estimating Property Tax Capitalization: A Further Comment." *Journal of Political Economy 89.*

Robinson, Gordon. 1971. *Private Schools and Public Policy.* Loughborough, England: Loughborough University of Technology.

Rudney, Gabriel. 1986. "The Scope of the Nonprofit Sector." In Powell.

Rudney, Gabriel and Murray Weitzman. 1983. "Significance of Employment and Earnings in the Philanthropic Sector, 1972–1982." PONPO working paper no. 77. New Haven, Conn., November.

Rudolph, Susanne Hoeber and Lloyd I. Rudolph, eds. 1972. *Education and Politics in India*. Cambridge, Mass.: Harvard University Press.

Rust, Val D. 1982. "Public Funding of Private Schooling: European Perspectives." *Private School Quarterly* Winter.

Ryan, Mary Perkins. 1963. *Are Parochial Schools the Answer? Catholic Education in the Light of the Council*. Chicago: Holt, Rinehardt & Winston.

Sanders, James W. 1981. *The Education of an Urban Minority: Catholics in Chicago, 1833–1965*. New York: Oxford University Press.

Savas, E. S. 1982. *How to Shrink Government: Privatizing the Public Sector*. Chatham, N.J.: Chatham House.

Schiff, Alvin Irwin. 1966. *The Jewish Day School in America*. New York: Jewish Education Committee.

Schneider, Barbara L., Diane T. Slaughter, and Robyn Kramer. 1983. "Blacks in Private Schools." Paper presented at Annual Meeting of the American Educational Research Association, Montreal, Canada, April.

Schneider, William. 1984. "The Public Schools: A Consumer Report." *American Educator* Spring.

School Finance Project. 1984. *Federal Education Policies and Programs: Intergovernmental Issues in Their Design, Operation and Effects*. Washington, D.C.: U.S. Department of Education.

————. 1983. *Private Elementary and Secondary Education*. Washington, D.C.: U.S. Department of Education.

Sherman, Joel D. 1982. "Government Finance of Private Education in Australia." *Comparative Education Review* 26.

Shils, Edward. 1973. "The American Private University." *Minerva* 11.

Silber, John. 1975. "Paying the Bill for College: The Private Sector and the Public Interest." *Atlantic Monthly* 235.

Skerry, Peter. 1980. "Christian Schools Versus the IRS." *The Public Interest* 61.

Stolee, Michael J. 1964. "Nonpublic Schools: What Must They Teach?" *Schools & Society* 92.

Summers, Anita A. and Barbara L. Wolfe. 1977. "Do Schools Make a Difference?" *American Economic Review* 67.

Trivett, David A. 1974. *Proprietary Schools and Postsecondary Education*. Washington, D.C.: ERIC Clearinghouse on Higher Education Resarch Report no. 2.

Tyack, David B. 1968. "The Perils of Pluralism: The Background of the Pierce Case." *American Historical Review* 74.

U.S. Department of Health, Education and Welfare/Education Division, National Center for Education Statistics. *Selected Public and Private Elementary and Secondary Education Statistics, School Years 1976–77 through 1978–79*. Bulletin NCES 80–B01. Washington, D.C.

Van Geel, Tyll. 1976. *Authority to Control the School Program*. Lexington, Mass.: Lexington Books.

Van Gendt, Rein. 1979. "Netherlands." In *Educational Financing and Policy Goals for Primary Schools*. Vol. 3. Paris: OECD, CERI.

Vontress, Clemmont E. 1965. "The Black Muslim Schools." *Phil Delta Kappan* 47.

Wasdyke, Raymond G., George W. Elford, and Terry W. Hartle. 1980. *Providing*

Students in Nonprofit Private Schools with Access to Publicly Supported Vocational Education Programs. Princeton, N.J.: Educational Testing Service.

Weisbrod, Burton. 1975. "Toward a Theory of Voluntary Nonprofit Sectors in a Three-Sector Economy." In E. Phelps, ed. *Altruism, Morality and Economic Theory.* New York: Russell Sage Foundation.

Weiss, Carol H., ed. 1977. *Using Social Research in Public Policy Making.* Lexington, Mass.: D.C. Heath.

West, E G. 1975. "An Economic Analysis of the Law and Politics of Nonpublic School Aid." In E. G. West, ed. *Nonpublic School Aid.* Lexington, Mass.: Lexington Books.

Whitehead, John S. 1973. *The Separation of College and State.* New Haven: Yale University Press.

Williams, Gareth. 1984. "The Economic Approach." In Burton R. Clark, ed. *Perspectives on Higher Education: Eight Disciplinary and Comparative Views.* Berkeley: University of California Press.

Williams, Mary F., Kimberly Small Hancher, and Amy Hunter. 1983. *Parents and School Choice: A Household Survey.* Washington, D.C.: School Finance Project, U.S. Department of Education.

Windham, Douglas. 1976. "Social Benefits and the Subsidization of Higher Education." *Higher Education 5.*

Wine, Mary B. 1980. *Bibliography on Proprietary Postsecondary Education.* Washington, D.C.: Association of Independent Colleges and Schools.

Winkler, Donald R. 1975. "Educational Achievement and School Peer Group Composition." *Journal of Human Resources 10.*

Woodhall, Maureen. 1970. *Student Loans.* London: George Harrap.

Woodhall, Maureen and Mark Blaug. 1978. "Patterns of Subsidies to Higher Education in Europe." *Higher Education 7.*

———. 1965. "Productivity Trends in British University Education, 1938–62." *Minerva* September.

Young, Dennis and Stephen Finch. 1977. *Foster Care and Nonprofit Agencies.* Lexington, Mass.: Lexington Books.

Yudof, Mark G., David L. Kirp, Tyll Van Geel, and Betsy Levin. 1982. *Kipp & Yudof's Educational Policy and the Law,* 2nd ed. Berkeley, Calif.: McCutchan.

Index